THE EDUCATIONAL INNOVATORS

Volume II: Progressive Schools 1881–1967

By W. A. C. Stewart and W. P. McCann

The Educational Innovators 1750–1880

THE EDUCATIONAL INNOVATORS

Volume II : Progressive Schools 1881–1967

W. A. C. STEWART

MACMILLAN
London · Melbourne · Toronto
ST MARTIN'S PRESS
New York
1968

Published by
MACMILLAN & CO LTD
Little Essex Street London W C 2
and also at Bombay Calcutta and Madras
Macmillan South Africa (Publishers) Pty Ltd Johannesburg
The Macmillan Company of Australia Pty Ltd Melbourne
The Macmillan Company of Canada Ltd Toronto
St Martin's Press Inc New York

Library of Congress catalog card no. 67-25981

Printed in Great Britain by
R. & R. CLARK, LTD.
Edinburgh

TO E.E.S.

Contents

PART TWO: *Three Headmasters*

PART THREE: *Some Facts, Figures and Interpretations*   305

PART FOUR: *Conclusion*   343

List of Plates

A. S. Neill
Sun

Margaret McMillan
Margaret McMillan Memorial College of Education

Deptford street scene
Margaret McMillan Memorial College of Education

The author and publishers wish to thank the Headmasters of the following schools for kindly providing those photographs which are not specifically acknowledged to other sources : Abbotsholme, Bedales, Bryanston, Dartington, Gordonstoun.

Preface and Acknowledgements

THIS is the second volume on unorthodoxy in English education. The first, written in collaboration with Dr. W. P. McCann, appeared in 1967 and covered the period 1750–1880. The present volume takes up the account again in 1889 at the foundation of Abbotsholme, and brings it up to the present day.

I wish in this, as in the Preface to the earlier book, to record my gratitude to the Leverhulme Trust whose financial support made it possible for me to complete the whole range of this inquiry in the span of the two volumes. I should also like to acknowledge my debt to the University of Manchester where for a year I was a Simon Visiting Professor. I particularly remember the help and consideration offered to me by Professor Richard Oliver and Professor Stephen Wiseman. This year of study enabled me to undertake much of the basic research on which this second volume is based.

I have leant heavily on the schools for material for this book. I visited nearly all of them and spent some time at each. I know what a mixed blessing an interested, inquisitive visitor can be to busy heads, their assistants and pupils. I found in every place an open welcome and ready help to find and examine source material. In addition I have followed up many points by correspondence and here again I have been offered every facility. I have made a number of acknowledgements in the text, and in connection with the illustrations, but I would like here to record my thanks to the heads, staffs and pupils of more than twenty schools where I spent time and took up many hours of other people's. I also met many who had to do with educational innovation in this country and abroad, with the international movements in progressive education and with their manifestations in many countries. To them, too, I owe a debt of gratitude.

Libraries and librarians in many places have helped me, and I particularly mention the Libraries of the University of Keele and of the Institute of Education in that University, where the skill and energy of my late colleague John Lea guided me wisely. Like many another, I found the resources of the Curzon Street Library of the Department of Education and Science of the greatest assistance.

Many friends have read drafts and offered valued criticisms and corrections and Mrs. Doreen Brookes and Mrs. Beryl Deane have prepared the typescript.   The index was compiled by Mr. Oliver Stallybrass.   To all of them I am grateful.

Keele   W. A. C. S.

Introduction

SOME people who have had ideas and theories about dealing with children have started schools to practise what they preach, and most of the book that follows is about such teacher-innovators. Others have interested themselves in unorthodox education by writing about it, often as part of a larger social or philosophical analysis, men like Whitehead or Russell or Rudolf Steiner or Karl Mannheim. These were not principally teachers of children, but their ideas had important consequences in educational theory and practice, and they served a function similar to that discharged by Locke, Rousseau, Owen, or Mill, who were considered in the first volume.[1] A man like Percy Nunn was both teacher and theorist and shed light on both activities. There are also those who, as sympathizers, backed new schools with money or ideas while not themselves taking an active part in the day-to-day conduct of affairs, people like Leonard and Dorothy Elmhirst at Dartington or Noel Wills at Rendcomb or Geoffrey Pyke at the Malting House School which Susan Isaacs conducted in Cambridge in the 1920s.

Between them such people brought into existence a number of schools which were in varying degrees unorthodox, and it is these which came to be called the progressive schools. The orthodoxy against which they made their protest was the public schools, the only established body of secondary schools at the turn of the century. The progressive schools were similarly independent and supported by fees, and found themselves after 1902 in opposition not only to the public schools but also to the maintained grammar schools which used the public schools as a model as far as they could.

I could discuss here the semantic problems raised by the epithet 'progressive', but I prefer to examine schools which were considered radical at the time of their foundation and since. In this way the differential features of these schools should reveal themselves and we can arrive at an operational clarification. What was regarded as startlingly different in 1900 or 1930 would not appear so strange now. Bedales became co-educational in 1898, and Summerhill moved to

[1] W. A. C. Stewart and W. P. McCann, *The Educational Innovators 1750–1880* (London, 1967).

Leiston in Suffolk, its present location, in 1927. While Bedales and orthodox schools in England in the 1960s have moved closer together, Summerhill is still poles apart from most secondary schools, although it is probably better understood now than it was in 1930. In other words, the term 'progressive' may be applied to a range of schools which themselves span wide differences in theory and practice as we shall see. At one end is the derogatory connotation 'of unwashed children running wild and swearing horribly'[2] and at the other is a school which is permissive in its human relationships, but has a framework of academic requirements and a recognized discipline.

Where, then, will educational innovation be seen sufficiently clearly ? Obviously in the area of knowledge, and this means predominantly in the curriculum, both in the range and content of subject matter and in the consideration given to children's individual differences, and the methods of learning encouraged. Another area of innovation is the territory of personal relationships, especially those between teachers and pupils and the forms of authority, discipline and punishment. Yet another index of unorthodoxy is experimental approaches to teaching methods. Not all the schools which are considered score equally under these headings, and probably the judgement may appear arbitrary here and there, but I believe that all the schools mentioned have been sufficiently different from the norms of maintained and public schools as to be identifiable in a progressive group.

Education and schools are, admittedly, part of a wider and deeper panorama of ideas and institutions, but the focus in this book is on the practical working out of unorthodox educational ideas in schools which declared their interest and showed their hand. From this descriptive background the special features can be discerned and from these the linking social and economic themes can be developed. It is not my intention to list every progressive school that has existed since 1890, with much argument at the border lines as to which is in and which out. I have examined the principles, practice, and history of more schools than I shall name, but my chief concern is to make sure that I show how the main threads were spun and then how they may or may not have entwined with one another. To suggest that they made a pattern would be to mislead by metaphor and to inject a sense of shared purpose and a kind of teleology which certainly did not exist in the earlier years.

[2] H. A. T. Child (ed.), *The Independent Progressive School* (London, 1962), p. 8.

Part One

Data

Chapter One

THE GROWTH OF SCHOOLS
1889-1898

BY definition the innovating schools were in protest, were asserting their differences, with theory and practice to support their claims. By definition they were enthusiasts who not only protested against something but also urged a positive alternative with conviction. But these schools urged different alternatives — some were for boys or girls only, others were co-educational : some were boarding schools, some day : some were based on religious convictions, some were firmly rationalist, some were neutral : some accepted a hierarchy of authority in the school, others rendered it minimal. I wish to describe the growth of schools to give historical context to this study of unorthodoxy in education. When we know which schools we have to consider we can see the principles and practices which distinguish them one from the other within the broad progressive category.

I

With Dr. McCann I have already examined the achievement of educational radicals in England from 1750-1880 in a period before compulsory schooling became general.[1] Events moved apparently slowly from 1870, when Mr. Forster's Education Act established once and for all the concern of the State for the supply of schools, to 1899 when the Board of Education was formed to rationalize the multiple Whitehall educational organizations, and then to 1902 when Balfour's Education Act established the constitution of Local Education Authorities to

---

[1] W. A. C. Stewart and W. P. McCann, *The Educational Innovators.*

replace the chaos of local School Board organization. ' The Revised Code or 'payment by results' had fixed upon schools supported by public money from 1862 a minutely detailed schedule of work in the basic subjects laid down for each 'standard', or age-group by the Code of the Education Department. The children were examined on this by Her Majesty's Inspectors on a given date each year and grants paid on the standard of achievement reached by the pupils. The long history of oppression, hostility, and organized deception which resulted from the Code continued until 1902, although the system began to break up in 1895. Its reverberations in the attitudes of teachers in elementary schools lasted until well into the twentieth century and the thought of any experimentation in State-supported schools during the period from 1862 was quite killed.[2]

While compulsory general education was becoming a reality in the last quarter of the century the public schools developed a national importance which they had not previously had. Throughout the nineteenth century there had been trenchant criticisms of the public schools which continued despite the reforms of Russell at Charterhouse, Butler at Shrewsbury, and Arnold at Rugby in the first half of the century. In 1860 there were three letters in the *Cornhill Magazine* by 'Paterfamilias', who turned out to be an Etonian named Matthew James Higgins, denouncing the public schools comprehensively and in detail for the profiteering of the masters and Fellows, for the incompetence of teachers who were failing to prepare boys for the examinations which had become necessary for the Civil Service and the army and for corruption and intellectual inbreeding. Higgins went on to recommend a Parliamentary Commission to examine the public schools.[3] Within a month or two many supporters wrote in other magazines of the time like *Macmillan's*, the *Edinburgh Review*, and the *Westminster Magazine*.[4]

[2] For two accounts of this period of more than forty years see G. A. N. Lowndes, *The Silent Social Revolution* (Oxford, 1937), pp. 3–20, and Edmond Holmes, *What Is and What Might Be* (London, 1911). Holmes was Chief Inspector at the Board and the first part of his book written just after retirement was a condemnation of the Revised Code on moral, educational, and psychological grounds. See also C. Duke, 'Robert Lowe — A Reappraisal' in *British Journal of Educational Studies*, vol. xiv, no. i (Nov. 1965), pp. 19–35.

[3] *Cornhill Magazine*: May 1860 pp. 660 ff.; Dec. 1860 pp. 646 ff.; Mar. 1861 pp. 261 ff.

[4] For detailed references see E. C. Mack, *Public Schools and British Opinion since 1860* (New York, 1941), pp. 11, 12, 14.

This was a period for educational Commissions. In 1856 a Royal Commission under the Duke of Newcastle had been instructed to survey the elementary educational system which had grown up since 1833 when the first national grant of £20,000 was shared between the two voluntary bodies which had provided schools in England and Wales, the National Society, an Anglican organization, and its nonconformist co-adjutor the British and Foreign School Society. The Newcastle Commission recommended in 1861 that in future government grants should be paid only to those schools which were reported by Her Majesty's Inspectors as efficient in the teaching of the basic subjects — the 'payment by results' to which we have already referred introduced by Robert Lowe in 1862.

In 1861 the Clarendon Commission began its inquiries into the affairs of the public schools and took three years in which to prepare its Report. Their proposals aimed to redress the vested interests of heads and Fellows by transforming governing bodies into trustees without pecuniary advantages. While continuing to support the classics the Report recommended a widening of the curriculum with modern subjects and natural sciences and a general stiffening of entry standard and broad intellectual requirements in the schools.

There were fierce controversies after the Report appeared in 1864 and the Public Schools Act was passed in 1868. It related to the seven boarding schools among the nine schools nominated as public schools — Eton, Harrow, Rugby, Winchester, Westminster, Shrewsbury, and Charterhouse : the two public day schools were St. Paul's and Merchant Taylors'. Parliament appointed a Commission to ensure that the new governing bodies were set up under the revised terms, and new statutes formulated and by 1874 this had been done. It is worth recalling that many of the schools now thought of as public schools have become so only in the last hundred years either as new foundations or as public schools developing out of existing older grammar schools. Examples of the former are Cheltenham (1841), Marlborough (1843), Rossall (1844), Radley (1847), Clifton (1862), Malvern (1862): and of the latter Repton (1557), Felsted (1564), Uppingham (1584), Aldenham (1597).

The aftermath of the Clarendon Commission in the 1860s and 70s was unsettlement and change in many of the public schools. Dean Farrar's *Essays on a Liberal Education* was a symposium which appeared in 1867. In 1867–70 Ridding, the headmaster of Winchester, introduced English literature, history and science into the hitherto heavily classical curriculum, and Temple at Rugby did much the same. In 1869 Harrow started a 'modern' side to balance its classical side in what would nowadays be called the sixth form. In 1853 Thring began his life's work at Uppingham which lasted for thirty-four years and during that time he introduced art, manual training, gardening, music, and many other innovations. It was he who proposed in 1869, at a specially-convened meeting of headmasters of public schools to discuss the impact of the Endowed Schools Bill then before Parliament, that the assembly should become an annual event; and this was the beginning of the Headmasters' Conference.

These instances of awakening reforms in the public schools could be multiplied, showing the new spirit that was slowly stirring. But the changes were by no means radical — Thring was more or less alone both within his own school and in the others when he said :

> I want to separate my lot entirely from the fashionable schools and to cast it in ... with the earnest working man and smaller schools which one may hope to see doing honest work.[5]

In any case new rich entrepreneurs were established by the 1870s who were using the public schools for their children. Mack sees it in this way :

> The rise to social leadership of a plutocracy without traditions meant, when helped by the growth of science, a breakdown in the strict moral codes of the '50's and '60's. A society arose, which, having erased the social line between aristocrat and plutocrat was rapidly destroying the cherished citadel of Victorian religious and ethical austerity.[6]

There is one other Commission which should be mentioned, the Schools Inquiry Commission under the chairmanship of Lord Taunton which began its investigations in 1864. The Clarendon Commission reporting in 1864 had dealt only with nine public schools and there were very many other grammar and secondary schools existing either on fee income or in a large number of cases on endowment funds as well, and there was also an even greater number of private schools. The Taunton Commission in its 1867 Report found the standards of work in the grammar schools generally low and revealed a consider-

---

[5] G. R. Parkin, *Edward Thring* (London, 1900), p. 146.
[6] Mack, *Public Schools and British Opinion since 1860*, p. 110.

able amount of misappropriation of endowments by trustees and masters who were appointed to teach pupils whom they did not encourage to attend the schools. Equally the Commission found very many private schools which they thought, in general, 'lamentably unsatisfactory' and after their Report in 1867 an Endowed Schools Commission was appointed to be the executive body to carry out the recommendations of the Endowed Schools Act of 1869, the parliamentary outcome of the Taunton inquiry.

At this point we should sum up the points made on educational development in the second half of the nineteenth century. The elementary schooling of the mass of the people became an increasingly obvious necessity: economic competition in agriculture and industry from Europe and America made it obvious, Christian and rationalist conscience made it obvious, political and social expediency underlined it, working-class political solidarity made it inevitable and the Royal Commissions of the 1850s and 60s and the 1880s and 90s provided the data for action. There were three large-scale issues : should everyone be compulsorily educated within an agreed age-range; what should be taught to the masses to ensure that national money was being responsibly spent ; should the national system be centralized or decentralized in organization. The first question was virtually answered by Forster's Act of 1870 which set up the School Board organization throughout the country for augmenting the provision of voluntary schools already in existence and so by a momentum of demand leading on to compulsory general attendance up to ten (1876), eleven (1893), twelve (1899), fourteen (1918). The answer to the second question on a suitable curriculum for the masses was settled by the Newcastle Commission and Lowe in 1862 with the Revised Code which set up and perpetuated for forty years two nations in education, the elementary and the secondary, which it took us another forty years, until 1944, to begin to dismantle. The answer to the third question about centralization or decentralization was to work towards a system in 1902 which represented both and neither. The Board of Education represents centralization, but in its forty-two years of existence it never met. The Local Education Authorities and their elected representatives signify decentralization, but the hazy powers of the President of the Board and of H.M. Inspectors and approved Treasury grants are reminders of the power at the centre. Since 1944 the potentiality of centralization is greater still, but this is another matter.

In the secondary sector the same three questions appear in a different context.   Should everyone be compulsorily educated within an agreed age-range ?   For pupils in the boys' public schools the answer was unequivocally yes and, as the century wore on, in the leading girls' schools too.   In the endowed grammar school the answer before 1870 was too often that parents of poor children of ability could not afford the years at school usually spent on an irrelevant academic curriculum. While the grammar schools were given the chance by the Grammar School Act of 1840 to teach subjects other than the learned languages and many of them took it, the Schools Inquiry Commission Report of 1867 showed how meagre was their response.   Here lies the answer to the second question : what is a suitable curriculum for the secondary schools ?   For all the innovations mentioned above at Winchester, Rugby, Harrow, and Uppingham the evidence is still overwhelmingly that in the 1870s, 80s and 90s at least, classics, 'the grand old fortifying curriculum', took up most of the time-table time for everyone — as Reddie at Fettes in Edinburgh in the 70s and Badley at Rugby in the 80s both detail in their autobiographies.

Finally, did the secondary schools support centralization or decentralization in the government of schools ?   The public schools had no doubts about this at all — they wanted complete independence of state money for reasons of academic and social freedom.   Endowments were one thing, for they left the schools to administer funds which were theirs by historic right.   State money was quite another for it constituted a threat to freedom to choose and to act as the public schools and grammar schools thought fit.   It is a valid generalization to say that most of the grammar schools felt themselves to be the poor relations of the public schools and modelled themselves as far as possible on what the public schools did between 1870 and 1920 while retaining a realistic fellow-feeling for the higher grade schools.

II

Cecil Reddie was the first headmaster of Abbotsholme in Derbyshire, founded in 1889, and he was the first of the educational radicals of the new wave in the nineteenth and twentieth centuries.   A fuller treatment of him and Abbotsholme is to be found later[7] and for the present we wish to show how this radical school began and developed.

[7] See Part II, Chapter 1.

Reddie was born in London in 1858, but was orphaned by the age of twelve and had the rest of his education in Scotland and Germany. He went to Fettes College in Edinburgh, a public school based on the English pattern, for more than seven years and then to the University of Edinburgh where, although he had taken the classical training at school, he ultimately read natural sciences, having started on medicine but withdrawn from it. On graduating he won a scholarship which enabled him to study in Germany for over two years and there he took a distinguished doctorate in chemistry. On his return to Scotland in 1884 he worked as a university demonstrator and then for a year or so returned to Fettes to teach chemistry, whence he transferred to Clifton, a public school near Bristol, to teach science for nearly two years. Clifton, founded in 1862, while giving pride of place to the classics, specialized in systematic scientific teaching. However, despite this novelty which no doubt had attracted Reddie in the first place, he came to feel 'that reform within the old type of school would be difficult if not impossible' and at the age of twenty-nine he applied for the headship of a new day school in London with the support of Dr. Wilson his Clifton headmaster. Reddie did not get the post but he says that Wilson's cordial recommendation put the idea into his head that he might 'open a school in which our dreams and aspirations might, perchance, find fulfilment'.[8]

During the 1880s Reddie was an active Socialist, influenced by the writings of Carlyle and Ruskin, of Hyndman and William Morris, of Edward Carpenter and Walt Whitman. In 1883–4 in Göttingen as a doctoral student he heard a number of lectures on Marxism and when he returned to Edinburgh he joined the Fellowship of the New Life, a movement devoted to purifying cupidity in society by the labours of reformed and redeemed individuals who, through a self-supporting life based on manual work in communities, through education and religious communion and steadfast attention to social change, could reconstruct society. The Fellowship was started in 1883 and one of its leaders, J. C. Kenworthy, wrote later in the Fellowship's journal: 'In economics we are Socialists; in our ideal we are Communists; in politics we are, some of us, Anarchists of Peace.'[9]

The Fellowship was seeking the ideal society and church combined,

[8] Dr. Wilson on retirement became a Canon of Worcester and later lived close to Bedales School and had some influence on Badley.
[9] *Seed Time*, Apr. 1895.

and although its communitarian methods were supposed to apply to the town as well as the country, the communities which actually came into existence were mainly in the country or on the outskirts of towns like Nottingham and Sheffield. The Garden City movement was a later application of the Fellowship principle.[10] It is interesting to note that Cecil Reddie, a member of the Fellowship of the New Life in the 1880s, moved to Welwyn Garden City on his retirement from Abbotsholme in 1927 and lived there till his death in 1932.

Abbotsholme, the school in which Reddie's dreams and aspirations 'might, perchance, find fulfilment' was called in the preliminary announcements 'The New School' and named 'A Fellowship School' in the journal of the Fellowship of the New Life, *The Sower*, of July 1889 — this became later *Seed Time*:

> Some time ago (actually 1886) the New Fellowship issued a proposal for the establishment of a school on lines consistent with the principles which it advocates. Up to the present, circumstances have not admitted of the practical realization of this scheme under the direct auspices of the Fellowship, but the members hail with great satisfaction a separate effort which some friends and associates are about to make to establish just such a school as was contemplated in the circular which the Fellowship issued. An attempt will be made to develop harmoniously all the faculties of the boy — to train him how to *live*, in fact, and become a rational member of society. . . . Negotiations are almost completed for the lease of a commodious house called Abbotsholme, with adjoining land, on the banks of the Dove, near Rocester, Derbyshire, a picturesque yet accessible region. The school will be opened in October next (1889).

A preliminary announcement appeared in the summer of 1889 informing the public that the school was going to open and naming Edward Carpenter, R. F. Muirhead, and William Cassels as partners with Cecil Reddie in the venture. The document admitted the importance of the public schools because they aimed to cultivate not only intellectual powers, but the physical, social, and moral nature of boys as well, and said that these features were appreciated abroad as well as in England: 'Any improvements therefore in education should be based on the ground-idea of the "Public School" system.'[11] Having

---

[10] See W. H. G. Armytage, *Heavens Below* (London, 1961), pp. 370–84.
[11] *A New School*, pamphlet published Apr. 1889.

made these polite preliminaries and shown the company in which Abbotsholme should be considered, the attack is then developed. The public schools are out of touch with contemporary needs, boys spend far too much time on the classics for which in any case the majority of them are quite unsuited. A modern curriculum in history, languages, and science is neglected and no time is given to mental and physical hygiene or to the study of society outside the school. The games fetish is denounced, together with the desperate waste of time spent in compulsory spectating by the mass of boys so that few interests can be developed other than athletic 'shop': 'The want simply of more ideas is one of the chief sources of the corrupt imagination and conversation found in schools.'[12] Reddie considers the university hold on the public schools is damaging and proposes to start a school on the lines suggested by 'the modern Science and Art of Education'. There is to be a carefully worked out programme of general education caring for physical and manual skills, for artistic and imaginative development, for literary and intellectual growth, and for moral and religious training. At present we do not need to consider these in detail but there are some unusual features which should be underlined. Manual labour in the house, the garden, and the field was to be as important in physical training as games and would familiarize the boys of affluent parents with work which was commonly done for them by servants. The boys were to be taught tailoring, boot making, and cookery — we can here detect the influence of Ruskin and Edward Carpenter but as a matter of fact Reddie did not get the tailoring, boot making, and cookery going.

Boys were to learn the rudiments of agriculture and gardening and the care of animals, which besides anything else would be 'a sound preparation for colonial life'. Their school was to be made to look beautiful and as far as possible, by the boys themselves: 'In this we shall follow Ruskin and Thring.' Carpentry, carving, metalwork, and other crafts would be taught to make it possible to achieve such aims.

English, not classics, was to be the foundation of the curriculum and French or German was to be the first foreign language. Latin was also to be taught to everyone without being given any special prominence. The country and industry in towns near at hand were to be explored in excursions, expeditions, and visits, the sciences were to be attended to and music was to be given a high place. Religion would

[12] Ibid.

be undogmatic and nonsectarian and services beautiful, simple, and not according to any particular communion.

While boys were to be prepared for entry to 'the Universities of Britain and Germany' and for other careers of all kinds, Abbotsholme did not intend to 'cram' boys for prizes and scholarships and would use only the mornings for classroom subjects. This was to be a school which would be aware of the British Empire and was aimed at national regeneration and Reddie, for whom the faintest symbol had the lure of Circe, chose for a few years red, white, and blue as the school colours.

Abbotsholme was a school for English boys aged eleven to eighteen 'belonging to the directing classes' and it was laid down as a principle that cordial trust was to be developed between boys and masters and all members of the school. The teaching of hygiene involved systematic courses in sex instruction, and necessitated carefully designed buildings and specially made clothes for the boys, introducing patterns which later became common in other schools — a knickerbocker suit, either no hat or a beret.[13]   This was all very different from Eton suits, stiff collars, and tophats or bowlers, the usual uniform at other schools and was part of the dress reform movement of the time.

Reddie produced the most minutely detailed plans for every part of Abbotsholme life. He was building the prototype school from which he hoped others would follow as Abbotsholme 'colonies'. He was strongly opposed to co-education and his ideal was a boarding school for about one hundred boys aged eleven to eighteen. He quickly quarrelled with his partners and one term after Abbotsholme opened Reddie was the sole owner and remained so until he retired in 1927. In the first decade the school prospered but from 1900 onwards its progress was erratic and after a temporary revival in the post-war boom things went from bad to worse until in 1927 there were only two boys in the school. The main reason for this failure was Reddie himself. He wished to direct everything and quarrelled with almost everybody — colleagues, parents, boys, Old Abbotsholmians, other educationalists, tradesmen, women, the plutocracy, the aristocracy, the working classes. Few things in England were done well, most things in

---

[13] Hely Hutchinson Almond, headmaster 1862-1903 of Loretto, a boys' public school for 150 near Edinburgh, encouraged fitness and toughness in his boys by introducing in the 1860s open windows, flannel shirts, tweed shorts, morning cold baths, no caps, no 'tuck' between meals. Fettes and Loretto have always been great rivals.

Germany were, with the exception of the period of the First World War, which deeply disturbed Reddie's convictions though it did not prevent him explaining why Britain did not deserve to rule its Empire.

The Fellowship of the New Life came to an end in 1898 and by that time Reddie was no longer a Socialist, but he remained a radical, this time of the Right, with political views as extreme and idiosyncratic in the other direction. Even though he nearly ruined Abbotsholme others more stable than he were excited by what he started in Derbyshire and carried forward and developed his ideas both in England and more widely in Germany, in Switzerland, in France, and elsewhere. In 1927 when a council of Old Abbotsholmians was re-establishing the school after Reddie's retirement a pamphlet was published in which it was stated that nearly one hundred schools in various parts of the world had sprung directly or indirectly from 'the New School'. Abbotsholme must be undoubtedly the first school as Reddie must be the first man to come into our reckoning.

Colin Sharp took over from Reddie in 1927 and the school was saved and built up its numbers beyond anything Reddie achieved. Where Reddie centralized Sharp delegated, where Reddie dominated Sharp suggested. We can examine the changes in detail later as they took place under Sharp and his successors.

III

One of Reddie's first appointments in 1889 was John Haden Badley, a man of twenty-four whose affiliations and thinking appeared very similar to Reddie's but whose background was very different. Badley and his three elder sisters were born into the family of a quietly affluent Midlands doctor at Dudley, near Birmingham. His childhood was secure and affectionate in a restrained and disciplined style. His parents were enlightened in many things although not demonstrative, and close affection and regard bound Badley and his sisters through their long lives. He went to Rugby from which he got the top classics exhibition to Trinity College, Cambridge, where he took a First in the Classics Tripos. He did not want to enter academic life, was dissatisfied with the thought of teaching classics at Rugby or any other public school, and at this moment of uncertainty in 1889 was told of Abbotsholme, about to open.[14]

14 For further treatment of Badley and Bedales see Part II, Chapter 2.

Badley had read and admired Edward Carpenter's writings and was and remained generally sympathetic to the Left in politics. Abbotsholme seemed to embody his own social thinking and at last gave an unequivocal lead on his future career. Almost all the distinguishing features of Abbotsholme outlined above chimed exactly with Badley's thinking and he threw himself with immense satisfaction into the life of the school. There were three main problems for him: the first was Reddie himself with his dominating energy, the second was Reddie's antipathy to girls and women (with one or two exceptions, including the accomplished and beautiful Duchess of Sutherland), and the third was Badley's wish to marry.

It is clear from the accounts of life at Abbotsholme in those first three years that Badley was a mainstay of the school and that he learned a vast amount from Reddie. Badley thought that Reddie, a life-long bachelor, would not accept his wife at Abbotsholme and in any case Badley knew his wife, herself a teacher of music, would want to interest herself in the school and that Reddie was 'averse from giving to women's influence the scope and weight in the school that we felt it should have'.[15] So Badley decided to start a school of his own with his wife's help, although as he says, after more than two years at Abbotsholme 'I could not contemplate continuing school-work except under similar conditions'.

When he told Reddie of his intention he had hoped that proposed imitation would flatter, but Reddie saw it all in terms of disloyalty, intellectual theft, and institutional rivalry. According to Badley, Reddie proposed that the young couple should open what amounted to a preparatory school to Abbotsholme on lines laid down by Reddie and this Badley refused as he wanted freedom to work with older children too, so he resigned in the hope that Reddie would come to think that his influence was really being extended by new and clearly indebted foundations.

On the other hand a revolutionary new school owing the originality of its ideas entirely to one man was in the third year of its life and one of its most promising masters, not yet twenty-seven and with only two and a half years of experience wanted to take the public notice given to Abbotsholme as a support to his own new venture. Although Reddie may have been domineering and in any case was powerless to prevent Badley from carrying out his intention, his exasperation was not

[15] J. H. Badley, *Memories and Reflections* (London, 1955), p. 119.

altogether surprising. However, Reddie for many years was publicly hostile to Bedales and Badley appears to have made no reply, although many members of his staff, some of them refugees from Abbotsholme and Reddie, said some very uninhibited things about the monarch of Abbotsholme.[16]

Badley set out his aims and intentions in a pamphlet published in 1892 before his school was opened.[17] He had found a suitable house and grounds called Bedales near Haywards Heath in Sussex and here he and his wife began in January 1893 his school for boys aged nine to fifteen with due acknowledgement and deep obligation to the New School, Abbotsholme. Like Reddie, Badley began with polite deference to the public schools as one who loved in boyhood 'the place of *Tom Brown's School-Days* . . . and later trod the proudest court in Cambridge . . . and who respected and admired the many admirable points in these and the like grand ancient institutions'. Then he shows how faulty they are by the narrowness and intensity of the competition, their early specialization and the limits of their concept of character training. One new idea appears in the Bedales prospectus, befitting a man married a few months before the school opened — the presence and direct influence of women. For the rest, the ideas are almost identical with those of Cecil Reddie, sometimes differently ordered; co-operation is stressed instead of competition and the older boy is to be trusted with a measure of direction. There must be nothing of luxury about the school, but something of comfort and beauty. However, not a word about 'the sons of the directing classes'. And no mention of the German example.

Three boys came in January 1893 and by 1894 there were thirty with seven academic and domestic staff and the school grew slowly. A school song was written which had the chorus:

Hold fast, hand grasp! the grip of the Bedales bond!
Work with Play in the English way we link and Future with Past.
Home with School by the Bedales rule we link them here and beyond
Hold fast, Bedales! Bedales, hold fast!

In 1898 the best known feature of Bedales appeared. By now the children were aged nine to eighteen and four girls joined the school

[16] See C. Reddie, 'The Relation of Abbotsholme to Bedales', in *The Abbotsholmian*, vol. ii, no. 3, July 1908, pp. 13–16.

[17] *Bedales (Haywards Heath, Sussex) A School for Boys: Outline of its Aims and System*, 16 pages.

for lessons and other activities, living in a house near at hand. This is not foreshadowed in the early prospectuses and Badley maintains that co-education grew as the principle of natural development in the school suggested this change — the mother of a Bedalian boy, widow of an Oxford don, suggested that her daughter and three other girls should join the school and that she would look after the house in which they at first lived. Badley said that he and his wife had the education of girls in mind from the first, but it was impracticable, and in this somewhat haphazard way the education of the four girls became co-education.[18]

The Bedales curriculum and organization were very like Abbotsholme's, even including the earth-closet sanitation in which both Reddie and Badley believed, giving back to the earth what it needed and preserving the natural cycle. Physical and manual skills, artistic and imaginative development, literary and intellectual growth, and moral and religious training had the same kind of nurture as at Abbotsholme and Bedales was at first known as an offshoot of Abbotsholme.[19]

Reddie and Badley were unorthodox in their religious belief, though not in the same way. Reddie had developed a liturgy at Abbotsholme where there was and is a special chapel. Bedales, although possessing in 1901 a school Psalm and Hymn Book, uses its Assembly Hall for services and Badley's position was somewhat that of a Unitarian moralist not much interested in religious symbolism.

There was probably more freedom in school government at Bedales than at Abbotsholme in the sense that Badley directed less from the centre than Reddie. Each school was opposed to 'cram' and it was not until 1913 that Bedales took the General Schools Certificate, thinking the London Matriculation too cramping for the school's general education programmes.

Bedales grew up in its own way and developed an identity very different from Abbotsholme's. When it became co-educational in 1898 and moved to its present site near Petersfield in 1900 it became better known than Abbotsholme. Badley was far more successful in building up his school than Reddie and a measure of his success is that a scholar like E. C. Mack can nominate Bedales as the parent of

---

[18] One account of this development appears in J. H. Badley, *Bedales : A Pioneer School* (London, 1923), p. 69. Another account is in *Memories and Reflections*, p. 136.

[19] See *Pall Mall Gazette*, 22 Aug. 1892 and 5 Oct. 1892 ; *Review of Reviews*, 15 Nov. 1893.

the progressive movement in England and make no mention of Abbotsholme.[20]   Bedales may have owed its origins to Abbotsholme but within ten years of its beginning it was a very different place, more unorthodox than Abbotsholme in many ways, less doctrinaire, more democratic.   Reddie and Abbotsholme represent one shade in the spectrum of educational radicalism and Badley and Bedales another.

IV

Alexander Devine was born in 1865, the same year as John Haden Badley.   Devine was the son of a flamboyant Manchester merchant whose ancestors were Irish, and a mother whose ancestors were Greek. Devine *père* had begun life as a Roman Catholic but moved to Congregationalism as time passed and Alexander (who was nearly always known as 'Lex' later on, and 'Mr. Lex' to his pupils) thus grew up in a religious background of unusual fluidity.   Devine senior was a remarkably temperamental business man whose inspirations led almost as often to bankruptcy as success and his son as a result had a limited schooling in Manchester day schools, leaving early to serve an apprenticeship to a printer and later becoming a journalist on Manchester papers.   Like many young reporters he had to work in the police courts of the city and his warm and energetic temperament responded to the needs of young offenders often only a year or two junior to himself.   He became familiar with the appalling living conditions of many of these lads and their friends and the complete lack of leisure amenities.   When he was twenty years of age he was the prime mover in starting the Working Lads Association in Chorlton-cum-Medlock and became secretary to three clubs.   Like his father, Lex proved quite unable to balance his budget and his committee asked him to leave. In 1888 he began the Gordon Boys' Home in Manchester having engaged local support which became much greater when, to the chagrin of many, Lex had engineered a visit to the Home by Prince Albert

[20] Mack, *The Public Schools and British Opinion since 1860*, p. 255.   There are various other small errors in the sections of this important book concerned with progressive education.   J. H. Simpson was headmaster of Rendcomb College not of Churnside, the pseudonym he gave to the school in his account of it in *Sane Schooling* (Mack, p. 382).   A printing error calls Bembridge School Bunbridge (p. 376). Mack speaks of the foundation of a number of schools in the between-wars period quite correctly but includes Friends' School, Saffron Walden (founded 1702), Sidcot (founded 1808), and Sibford (1842) (p. 376).

B

Victor of Wales in October 1888 during a short scheduled stay of the Prince in Manchester. This Home was part of what amounted to a personal probation service which Lex had started for boy first offenders in the Manchester area. He lived with them and he worked for them, trying to place them in jobs, to guide and befriend them, and to steer them clear of criminal careers. But again Lex could not work with his supporters in that as he saw it he could not get the expansion he wanted and as they saw it he was reckless about financial practicalities.

Devine migrated to London in the early 1890s and for a few years tried a number of different jobs including what he called 'a reformatory for bad boys of the Public Schools', his Gordon House venture transposed to a different social key. Creditors still wanted to be paid and Devine had to move more than once either to meet or to evade them. All through his life he displayed his father's irresponsibility about money, professing in a euphoric way that the importance of his projects mattered more than balancing accounts. On this his friends would say he had a blind spot and his enemies would say he was dishonest. Each would admit that he appears to have had unquenchable confidence. J. H. Badley said of him:

> [He never could control money and was] quite unable to keep check on his expenditure, or to think of loans as anything but gifts. In each fresh crisis he would turn to anyone, friend or stranger, for help with which to extricate himself. . . .[21]

By 1896 he had decided not to continue dealing with delinquents and problem children from the public schools because he had come to realize that there was much at fault with the schools themselves. So he founded a school to be 'a liberal, democratic state, not a reactionary dictatorship' and it opened at Enfield in Essex in February 1896. The estate which Devine took on a lease was called Clayesmore and the school kept this name when it moved to Pangbourne in Berkshire in 1902, to Northwood Park near Winchester in 1914, and finally to its present location at Iwerne Minster in Dorset in 1933.

Devine had made a number of connections with public school headmasters by 1896 and they continued to recommend boys to him who had a difficult background, therefore his plan to promote 'a reformed school rather than a reformatory' took time to realize — indeed some of the first boys at Clayesmore transferred there from the earlier

[21] *Memories and Reflections*, p. 202.

'reformatory' Glebelands. After very few years Devine refused to accept any boy who had been expelled from another school and decided to act on recommendations only, although his self-generated idea of himself as Puck (his biographer suggests that it co-existed dangerously with a picture of himself as Napoleon) sometimes permitted him to stretch a point for a particularly stimulating malefactor.[22]

Devine visited Badley and Bedales quite frequently during term time and vacation and they speak of one another with considerable regard. Badley had a number of reservations about Devine, as will be seen, but still he says : 'he remains in my memory as a man of powers as remarkable and of charm as great, as I have known in anyone.'[23] Devine also knew Reddie, but with him he had little in common as a man, with which Reddie pungently agreed. But Devine knew Abbotsholme's educational principles and the connection with Bedales and writing in 1903 to Edward Lyttleton, then headmaster of Haileybury, he said with characteristic aplomb :

> Clayesmore is the third and latest of the 'new' schools ; and though I have not had the advantage or disadvantage of discipleship to either Reddie or Badley, I am quite prepared to admit that there is something in the aim of the three schools which is identical.

By 1900 Devine had a school of fifty boys at Enfield and he began a typical and unusual venture early in the school's history. Bearing in mind his Manchester work for under-privileged and poor people and his concern to share his advantages, Devine decided to invite 'ordinary working men' to visit the 'New School' at Clayesmore. He advertised in a generalized form by letters in the papers and soon had a stream of visitors at the weekends, some coming regularly. There was seldom any formal business but always the opportunity for talk and tea and the chance for boys, masters, and headmaster to make this kind of contact with men whose daily life was very different from their own. In inviting the visitors Devine had asked them to come 'to relieve him from the small world of miniature folk over which he reigned supreme' and over a period of five years at Enfield, for which the arrangement lasted, it is estimated that three thousand visits were paid by these guests. It was not possible to continue similar contacts at Pangbourne or

[22] F. Whitbourn, *Lex : Alexander Devine Founder of Clayesmore School* (London, 1937), p. 221.
[23] *Memories and Reflections*, p. 202.

Northwood Park by reason of distance and, in any case, perhaps Devine's outlook was somewhat changed by then.

Like Reddie, Devine remained a life long bachelor and like him he did not approve of co-education. He had declared in his early prospectus :

> The School makes no pretence to the possession of any elaborate new system ; we are in need of no educational fads. . . . The School makes a practical protest against the neglect of the average boy.[24]

He did not attack the public schools with the sustained criticism that Reddie and Badley brought to bear and in the letter to Lyttleton already mentioned he criticized Reddie because :

> he has apparently shut his eyes deliberately to the virtues and values of our good old schools, has resolutely ignored the useful and splendid work of individual headmasters and takes his stand on the platform of 'There is but one Education, the new Education and Reddie is its prophet !'

Devine had had no direct experience of public schools either as a boy or as a master and as a teacher of misfits he really wanted to reform what he knew of them. But he was fond of men of title, fame, and money, was a great name-dropper, and knew on which side his bread was buttered. Nevertheless, he admitted to Lyttleton that he found Reddie's ideas 'sound at the root, and . . . great because they are scientific ideas'. But his characteristic complaint was that Reddie was carrying them out in a small way. Devine was an impresario who wore a cap and gown, lived at Claridge's, became in 1919 the Minister Plenipotentiary for Montenegro in London enjoying his status and decorations, and inviting as many men of distinction to lend their names to Clayesmore as possible. He offered the suggestion to Reddie and Badley that the three schools should form the ABC of educational reform which amused Badley and infuriated Reddie. At the same time Devine kept some of the practices of the public schools — classical and modern sides in the sixth with the tutor-system ; Eton jackets and top hats on Sundays in winter and spring terms, straw hats with bands in the summer; 'fagging' on a hierarchical basis ; ritual caning for certain types of offender in the Library by the headmaster — often at 10 p.m.

[24] Pp. 10–11.

There were, nevertheless, many ideas from Abbotsholme and Bedales at Clayesmore. The morning run and shower, manual labour and digging and building, the shorts and Norfolk suit for everyday wear. General education was maintained at least until the boy was fifteen with much the same range of options for everyone. Specialization came after that and so the classical grind was avoided. Devine disapproved of the games fetish and the dominance of 'colours' and first of all provided a variety of games and secondly offered estate work as a required alternative on one or two afternoons in the week. He insisted on time being allowed in the programme of each boy for art, craft, and music. No public examinations were taken below the age of fifteen and at a later age only when necessary. In any case Devine wanted to reform the usual type of informational check and to produce tests of understanding and real comprehension. Although not well-equipped technically in psychology he wanted teaching at Clayesmore to be based on a proper understanding of the importance of interest as mental discipline rather than compulsion. Equally he wanted his pupils to be challenged by the genuine reasoning required in experimental inquiry and the initiative expected for research or project work. Like Reddie he was critical of the lack of preparation in the craft of teaching for public-school masters. Devine wanted schools to accept responsibility for the apprenticeship of beginners although he had no formal training himself.

He was a difficult man to work with and few masters stayed with him for long. Payment of salaries was several times delayed over the years and in his open letter to new staff he said blandly: 'the married or about-to-be married Master is a difficulty, I admit. During term-time you have the boys and your wife. Which are you going to neglect?' He commanded and expected loyalty from masters and boys but seemed to be jealous of marked popularity in a colleague and, more than once his biographer tells of Devine's tendency to side with boys in scoring off colleagues as when he took boys off on swims late at night unknown to and against the orders of the housemaster; or when he took part in the boys' practical jokes or joined in their scrapping on the strict understanding that either side could call 'Enough!' When masters came to restore order they would find Devine often in the middle of it all. One of his beliefs was that the boy is always more or less of a statesman, balancing masters' and parental interference to a nicety and creating a policy to meet each situation.

In the early prospectuses there are references to 'self-regulated independence', to 'a system of self-government', and to 'greater liberty than is common' but details are lacking on the working out of these things. There is one gnomic and unwittingly ambiguous sentence in connection with discipline : 'The School does not legislate either for the mature man or for the incorrigible offender.' Devine himself was too much of a virtuoso to develop the settled regime with colleagues necessary for the school to grow steadily as a democracy.

In 1904, two years after moving to Pangbourne, the bailiffs came in at the end of a term and took off the furniture while Devine photographed the scene for his album as 'An incident in the history of the school' and took a bet with the removers that the furniture would have to be brought back. His friends founded a limited company and Devine was able to win his bet at the cost of becoming a salaried headmaster with a bursar appointed to care for the school's finances, and for ten years (which Devine called 'his years of slavery') the school prospered. In 1914 the ownership of the school reverted to Devine and he moved it with about one hundred boys from Pangbourne to Northwood Park. During the ten years when the general control of business matters was in the hands of a governing body there was an improved chance of stability for young staff and the historians of the school record that despite the difficult and possessive attitudes of Devine some wise masters gave a steadiness to the school which enabled it to grow at that time.

The war provided as many hardships for Clayesmore as for other schools of its kind and this put burdens on Devine. The school had further difficulties when Devine himself went to Montenegro in 1915 and again in 1917 at the invitation of the Red Cross to inquire into the fate of Montenegrin refugees — he had been a war correspondent there as a young reporter in the Balkan wars of the 1880s. Despite his absences for some months on each occasion the school continued and after the war began with a boom which subsided somewhat in the years of depression which followed. Devine fell ill in 1927 and was never really fit again before his death at Clayesmore in 1930.

The vice-master, who had been Devine's deputy for nine years, succeeded him and the school moved to its present location in Dorset three years after Devine's death. In 1935 numbers had fallen to about fifty and bankruptcy threatened the school again and a limited company of friends and Old Boys was formed to rescue Clayesmore once more. Within a year under a new head the numbers had risen to one hundred and twenty and have continued to rise — this recovery being financially strengthened by the Desmond Coke bequest in the mid-1930s. In the 1960s we read:

> Clayesmore is a Public School which is deliberately kept to a moderate size with the object of enabling the Master and every member of the staff to know each boy as an individual. The strength of 210–218 is nevertheless large enough for a full corporate life with a complete range of activities.[25]

The *Book* claims that from its earliest days Clayesmore has been a pioneer school in education and that many of its ideas which were regarded as revolutionary when first adopted, are now accepted as sound educational practice. The *Book* quotes Devine's words incorporating the importance of the interest of the learner and the psychological understanding of the teacher and reaffirms them as the educational aim and faith of Clayesmore today claiming that they blend with the great character-founding traditions of the English Public School. Manual work in the open air (which the *Book* claims perhaps misleadingly that Clayesmore pioneered) continues and so do creativeness in the arts and crafts together with the enjoyment of the country, and all of these 'without any sacrifice of learning'. Another account of the school's work puts it like this:

> . . . while adapting itself to the growing need for success in examinations, the School still holds by its first vision. Every boy is encouraged to make something or do something for the common services . . . and far from over-working the boy who is preparing for examinations, it refreshes him. . . . Verses are produced, printed and bound into books, trees are felled, land is tilled and music made, pictures are painted, loud speakers installed for out-of-door occasions, walls built, concrete laid, trenches dug, the School cinema operated, costumes and scenery devised for plays, lighting effects produced, animals cared for. . . . Through many of these avenues boys are led to careers at least as happily as through the examination room.[26]

---

[25] *The Book of Clayesmore School*, p. 1. There is in addition a Preparatory School for about one hundred boys aged eight to thirteen years, eight miles from the main school.

[26] *The Public and Preparatory Schools Yearbook* (London, 1964, p. 115).

The Memorial Chapel opened in 1956 offers a very different setting for the Anglican order of service from the evening services in the school of Devine's day (though he enjoyed Northwood Park partly because it had its own Chapel). He preached often to the school and later in the evening held in his own study an informal gathering of boys which was characteristically called a Levee where reading, story telling, singing, and piano music were mingled with conversation and yarn-spinning.

Clayesmore had and has many of the features of the 'New School' movement while being nearer to the traditional public school than either Abbotsholme or Bedales (the school has been for some years a member of the Headmasters' Conference). Like the two earlier schools it had a remarkable person as its founder-headmaster with whom it is easy to be exasperated. To be sure he became a poseur, a snob, an adventurer, but he inspired shrewd men to enable him despite many crises to run a fairly radical school for thirty-four years and clearly his personal magnetism attracted boys. His biographer may have laid the colour on rather thickly, but the likeness is there:

> Lex's boys worshipped him, but they were not blind to his weaknesses. They were ready to laugh at him among themselves; but never would they betray him to any outsider. . . . He may not have paid his bills . . . he may have broken his promises . . . but his boys loved him.[27]

He did not attract Reddie at all, who wrote, when two masters dismissed from Abbotsholme after the 'great row' of 1900 went to Clayesmore and two others to Bedales:

> If you please, a great effort has been made to get me to enter into a sort of federation . . . with these two schools for the sake of pressing the claims of the New School Movement upon the public attention. Carefully worded articles . . . talk of the three schools as if like love-birds on one perch they were all billing and cooing together in the most fraternal manner. . . . By what we know of these two places we can only say that the heroes [the four masters] have gone to their own Valhalla.[28]

We have already quoted somewhat from Badley's comments on Devine and Clayesmore and we finish this section on the school with Badley's shrewd and sympathetic assessment of its founder:

[27] Whitbourn, *Alexander Devine*, p. 138.
[28] From typed record dictated by Cecil Reddie in Abbotsholme archives.

It was in the early years [of Bedales] that I first met one of the most remarkable men I have known. . . . As Head Master [Devine] was a curious combination of sound educational ideals, great ambitions, boundless self-confidence and an artless egoism. He had — so I thought — little judgment in choosing his staff, and it was only by a process of trial and error that he found some devoted helpers. Of boys, on the other hand, he had a profound understanding . . . and won from them a corresponding loyalty and affection. . . . Puckish humour and an endless fund of amusing stories and his charming manner could carry off the constant self-dramatisation which gave him at times more than a touch of the charlatan.[29]

V

The last school founded before 1900 to be considered is very different in its origins from any of the three schools already mentioned. In July 1897 a preliminary circular was distributed to householders in the North-West London residential suburbs of Hampstead and Golders Green outlining 'A Proposed Rational School' and issued in the name of 'a few parents residing in this neighbourhood'. The circular in its preamble stated that nearly all the high schools and private schools of that decade 'were out of touch with the broader and healthier views of the training of children that science and the scientific study of child nature have roused'. This rational spirit ought to find expression in books and in periodicals but also in institutional form in a school. It was proposed, therefore, 'if sufficient support is accorded to the scheme' to start a school in Hampstead where boys could be educated up to the age of twelve in preparation for entry to the public schools or to sixteen after which they could prepare for their careers. Girls were to be educated so that at sixteen they could prepare themselves to enter one or other of the women's colleges, or at age eighteen they could take up a career which needed no specialist training.

The school was to have a number of distinctive features. As the beginnings might have to be gradual the expected age-range was eight to twelve years and classes would be limited to twelve or fifteen children in each. The aim of the school was to provide an individual training in mental, physical, and moral development, calling upon the help of a medical officer with a special knowledge of children and keeping thorough and cumulative records of each child as he or she

[29] *Memories and Reflections*, p. 202.

moved through the school. As far as the arrangement of studies went, the school was to make every effort to co-ordinate the curricula in order to avoid subject-separation and to enrich the children's under-standing. Learning was to be for its own sake and the increasing maturity which came from it, and as a consequence all prizes or awards were to be eschewed and the pressures of a competitive system avoided. There was to be no homework, at least for the juniors and, while it was hoped that the school would exemplify a religious spirit, no direct teaching of a religious creed would be permitted. Co-education would be a principle of organization on the grounds that this was in line with family living and as supporting argument the pamphlet says that educating boys and girls together 'is the custom in Scotch schools' and that it was well tried in England — not a valid statement in respect of secondary schoolchildren, for whom co-education was (and still is) in England a very small minority practice. The promoters thought that a school based on these rational principles would produce far less strain and 'the need for the present extravagantly long holidays will cease'. They accordingly proposed ten weeks' holiday each year: two weeks at Easter, one at Christmas, and seven in the summer. Finally, they proposed that the school should be controlled by an elected governing body which should, in turn, elect a small executive committee.

As a result of this circular the King Alfred School Society came into being with formal registration under the Companies Act of the Society in June 1898. A number of the matters outlined in the preliminary circular of July 1897 have been modified or extended in the Memo-randum of Association. Among the objects for which the Society is established is 'to carry on Schools to give practical expression to the best theories of Education extant, and particularly to the theories enunciated by Educational reformers, such as Pestalozzi, Froebel, Herbart, Herbert Spencer, Louis Compton Miall, and others working on similar lines'. In addition the Society is committed 'to promote the advancement of Educational Science ... by the diffusion of know-ledge relating thereto' and to establish colleges or departments for students of Education in order to equip them professionally to teach in the Society's schools or similar foundations. In fact the Society has founded only King Alfred School, no training college or department, and its membership has tended to be the parents, staff, and old pupils of the school together with a few well-known educational radicals like

Mrs. Beatrice Ensor and J. H. Badley who have become vice-presidents of the Society. Conferences have been held, but it is true to say that the expansionist plans of the King Alfred School Society of 1898 have not been realized.

The signatories of the Memorandum of Association and the first members of the Society's Council were F. W. Miall, a journalist, Cecil J. Sharp, the well-known collector of folk-music who is called a musician, Alice Mullins, designated the wife of E. Roscoe Mullins, Hans Thornycroft, sculptor, Gerald C. Maberly, barrister-at-law, Isabel White Wallis, wife of E. White Wallis, and J. Godfrey Hickson, solicitor. These are the guarantors, none of them practising educators (although Sharp taught music at King Alfred's in the early days), none of them aiming to be the head of the school or schools to be founded which 'shall be conducted upon curricula based upon the theories hereinbefore mentioned, and not upon the requirements of examining bodies, and the preparation of pupils for examinations, prizes, scholarships, and honours shall be avoided'. However, in addition, pupils over twelve could be prepared for entrance examinations to other institutions, or if over fifteen for scholarships or prizes at some place of further education. Thus competition is avoided in internal organization but pupils able to contend for scholarships or transfer examinations were not to be penalized. Parents of pupils were to have representation on the governing body if they were members of the Society and the school was to be inspected from time to time by a person sympathetic to the Society's aims and chosen by 'some public educational authority wholly independent of the Society'.

The school was opened in Ellerdale Road, Hampstead, in 1898 under its first headmaster, Charles E. Rice, who had been one of the first two masters at Bedales with Badley in 1893. For four years, from 1893 to 1897, he taught mainly science there but he was a man of considerable range of intellectual interest and practical skill. He introduced exploratory and experimental methods in nature study, he taught wood- and metalwork together with some English and mathematics. He had intended to train as a doctor and retained an interest in research and left Bedales in 1897 to go to the Royal College of Science to pursue further studies. It was with this background that he was invited to become the first headmaster of King Alfred School in 1898. Badley remarks : 'He was the first of a dozen members of our staff who have gone from their experience at Bedales to become Heads of schools of their own and thus helped to diffuse more widely the new educational ideal.'[30]

Rice found conducting a school in a number of semi-detached houses in a London suburb very different from Haywards Heath, where Bedales then was. The children lived at home and were not available all the time and although Bedales started to become co-educational in 1898 it had not been so in 1897 when Rice left. Bedales was concerned with country activities, like estate work and farming, impossible to pursue at King Alfred's. Bedales had a liberal Christian basis and King Alfred's was firmly rationalist. Badley was the owner-legislator of Bedales, democratic model though he was: the headmaster at King Alfred's had the Council of the King Alfred Society, usually meeting monthly, as his potential advisers and while the evidence over the years is that the Council on the whole gave the headmaster and his staff a wise freedom, there are instances of friction and some of these occurred in Rice's period of office. In 1901 there was a split on the School Council and it would appear that this was largely due to the desire of some Council members to have considerable control of the day-to-day affairs in the school. Rice was forced to resign and he decided to start another school in Hampstead on King Alfred principles with himself as sole headmaster and independent of the Society's management, but perhaps with a common bond as the Memorandum of Association had suggested in 1897. He was prepared to have routine inspections by an expert nominated by the Society and to continue to support 'the course of rational education'. The Council rejected the proposal and Rice had to sever his connection with the school. A minority on the Council, including Cecil Sharp and the chairman F. W. Miall resigned in support of Rice, who started a school not far away in Ferncroft Avenue, Hampstead, which came to an end just before Rice (who was married to one of Badley's sisters) returned to Bedales in 1908.[31]

King Alfred's would not force children to an examination syllabus, they encouraged the arts and crafts, they wanted small classes, a manageable school community and good relations between staff and children with the maximum of permissiveness and the minimum of coercion, including the abolition of corporal punishment, and all of these features, except the last, were common to Bedales.

[30] *Memories and Reflections*, p. 128.
[31] *The Bedales School Roll 1952*, ed. B. Gimson, p. 358, is in error in stating that Rice was Head of King Alfred's 1898–1908.

The age-range at King Alfred's was, at first, eight to fourteen years with a considerable group of both boys and girls leaving at thirteen to go to public and secondary schools. During the 1920s J. H. Wicksteed, then headmaster, added a nursery and infant school group aged from three to eight years taught on Montessori lines, for he, like many others in the 1920s and earlier, were great admirers of the Dottoressa. This nursery and infant school still exists at King Alfred's.

But to return to Rice. In 1908 he returned to Bedales to teach and remained there until 1911, but then, after nearly twenty years of schoolmastering he decided that it did not offer him the scope that he wanted and so he reverted to his original intention to train as a doctor and followed that career for the rest of his life.

His successor at King Alfred's in 1901, John Russell, was a very different person and he remained headmaster until 1920 and became the father-figure of the school. He was a Foundation Scholar of St. John's College, Cambridge, and a certificated teacher who came to King Alfred's with seventeen years of teaching experience mostly in conventional day schools. He was interested in the work of educational reformers and had edited a work on Pestalozzi and his successors, and had travelled and taught on the Continent. Russell was a strong supporter of the suffragette movement and the campaign for women's rights, and co-education had for him a significance far greater than mere educational wisdom — it was a symbol of achievement by and for women. He was a person with a considerable presence and a fine sense of drama — A. S. Neill, who worked under Russell at King Alfred's from 1918 till 1920, told the present writer that Russell had a voice like Henry Irving and was a born actor. He made the school conventions more formal, introducing blazers and ties and gym-tunics, having the classes stand up on his entry and enjoying the position the children accorded to him. He was a remarkable correspondent and kept in touch with many of his old pupils over the twenty years or so of his tenure of office, which, of course, included the period of the First World War. When he retired in 1920 there were about seventy pupils at the school and he had been able to persuade the Council to consider moving the school to a larger site where both buildings and playing fields were available.

It was Russell who introduced the Children's Council with pupil representation on which the later organization was based. Under him the school was organized, controlled, and led in a way quite different from Rice's regime. Neill, back from the War and fired by his admiration for Homer Lane, writes of the last two years of Russell's headship :

> Old John Russell was Head, dear old J.R., a kindly, humane soul one could not help loving. Alas, under Lane's influence, I began to be a heretical assistant. I kept asking for self-government, stupidly of course, for what self-government can one practise in a day school ? In the end (in 1920) I had to resign.[32]

Russell was highly regarded by the Council of the King Alfred Society and given good support by them in his enterprises, though not always without resistance. He was the stabilizer in the first twenty years of the school's existence. He followed the precepts of co-education, rationalism, co-operation rather than competition, liberal education rather than examination pressure, and participation of parents in the affairs of the school community, as laid down in the first memorandum of the King Alfred School Society.

When Russell retired in 1920 Joseph Wicksteed was appointed as his successor and he came, like Charles Rice, from a few years of service on the staff of Bedales. He was a son of Philip Wicksteed, who had in the last two decades of the nineteenth century taken part in many Utopist schemes, including the Labour Church movement.[33] Joseph had been influenced by the Unitarian wing of the Free Churches and later by the Theosophical Society which through the Theosophical Fraternity in Education, founded in 1915, had provided the effective beginnings of the New Education Fellowship. Wicksteed was a considerable Blake scholar, and so exemplified the combination of Leftist politics, mystical and non-dogmatic religion, and a belief in internationalism which marked a number of educational innovators of the period.

Most of the principles of work at King Alfred's were very similar to those of the Theosophical Educational Trust which had been founded in 1916. Wicksteed followed the Trust in his stress on outdoor life and continued the argument which Russell had begun on moving the school and at last he succeeded. The new site (still the site of the school) was spacious enough to allow the children to camp, to build

---

[32] A. S. Neill, 'My Scholastic Life : 2', in *Id*, Journal of the Summerhill Society, no. 3, Oct. 1960, p. 4.

[33] See Armytage, *Heavens Below*, pp. 321–3.

tree-houses, to garden. Wicksteed, who had been connected with the Garden City movement twenty-five years before, had Barry Parker, one of the Hampstead Garden Suburb architects, to design the main buildings of the new school.

During Wicksteed's period of office the old rationalism was slightly modified. In the original Memorandum it was stated that the education given by the school would be free from any connection with religious organisations or denominations and from political associations and no inquiry was to be made about the religious beliefs of anyone connected with the school. During the 1920s King Alfred's began to teach comparative religion and the study of the Bible was permitted in the context of literature and history.

The school was recognized as efficient by the Board of Education in 1928 having been refused recognition after an inspection in 1921, and had grown from approximately seventy children of all ages at the beginning of Wicksteed's period of office to about one hundred and thirty in 1933 at the end. From the beginning he had Miss V. A. Hyett as his senior mistress and her mark upon the school up to her retirement in 1948 was unmistakable. She came from Wallasey Grammar School with a very different experience from Wicksteed's and she combined practicality in administration with considerable achievement as an historian and teacher of history. She was an ardent feminist, Leftist in her politics, and active in the affairs of the Society for Cultural Relations with the U.S.S.R. and of the Left Book Club. When Wicksteed retired in 1933 Miss Hyett became joint-head with a former senior master, H. de P. Birkett, and it was she who took charge of the school when the children were evacuated during the Second World War.

From 1930 the refusal to admit examinations into the educational practice at King Alfred's was changed and the General Schools Certificate began to be a feasible goal for pupils. Miss Hyett had a great deal to do with this stiffening and rationalizing of procedure and from 1933 children in the fifth form were normally expected to take the Schools Certificate examination with its required grouping of subjects. However, as there is no entry examination of the eleven plus selection type or the thirteen plus Common Entrance type at King Alfred's, there are children representing a wider spectrum of ability than would usually be found in a grammar school. The school is too small to stream the classes so the compromise has been reached, for more than thirty years, of a modified Dalton Plan — a varying minimum of oral class teaching according to age, together with work in what are called supervised Open Rooms where the teacher is available for individual instruction as required. B. H. Montgomery, who was a master at King Alfred's 1932–40, returned as headmaster and later as joint-head from 1944–62, and wrote in a recent account of the school:

> During the past ten years we have found it necessary to modify considerably our attitude to examinations. Competition for university places has become increasingly keen, and many employers now require a good G.C.E. certificate as evidence of a good education. . . . We aim to produce people who are emotionally stable and who are independent and enterprising. . . . At the same time we fully recognize the need for them to gain academic qualifications.[34]

There is a Children's Council which has been in existence in one form or another for nearly fifty years. The school is compact enough for all children over ten (about two hundred) to attend meetings of the Children's Council where their elected representatives discuss school problems each week. The Council is advisory only, with certain defined responsibilities: the heads have a right of veto on decisions if need be though this is apparently scarcely ever necessary. There are also regular staff meetings, often weekly, and from this democratic structure much of the general concern and informality of the school derive. Mr. Montgomery sums up the principles of King Alfred's as follows:

1. We believe in co-education for boys and girls throughout their lives. . . . We have no reservations.
2. We believe in the educational value of personal liberty. . . .
3. There is no formal religious observance or instruction.
4. There is no formal selection of pupils at entry.[35]

Mrs. Paul-Jones, the Joint-Head of King Alfred's, writes in the same article:

> There is still, in my opinion, a great difference between schools like King Alfred's and the majority of grammar and secondary schools. Fundamentally . . . it rests on the attitude we hold to education and the principles on which we base our work. . . . We feel certain that where there are more children in a community than the Head can

---

[34] *The Independent Progressive School*, ed. H. A. T. Child (London, 1962), pp. 90–91.
[35] Ibid., p. 87.

know as individuals, something vital is lost. . . . We believe that children of varying abilities and widely differing interests and capacities (including those who have little or no academic skill) have something to contribute to one another's work and social life.[36]

The King Alfred Society to which one or both parents of each pupil are expected to belong has a Council which constitutes the School Council and as the Heads are *ex officio* members of the Council the parents have a significant liaison with school policy and practice through their representatives. There is no school uniform and a number of the staff are known by their Christian names, features of a modern idiom which was not always there. A town day school, different thereby from Abbotsholme, Bedales, and Clayesmore, King Alfred's was rationalist and co-educational from the start and different from them again. In most of the rest they are all four recognizably similar. In the hoped-for understanding and friendship between teacher and pupil, they all aim for the same things, however different the human context may be. We end these comments on King Alfred's with the obituary by a six-and-a-half-year-old girl writing of Miss Hyett, who died in 1949; the school was evacuated to Royston during the war:

> She is very kind Because she loves flowers She used to take me to her shelter where she slept at Royston we had tea there on the grass.
> She used to teach Anthony and me to throw sticks into the river and watch them come out of the other side of the bridge. I love her and miss her terribly terribly.

VI

These four schools were founded before the Board of Education came into existence in 1899 and the Local Education Authorities in 1902. The four progressive schools have nothing to say about elementary schools and make no attempt to locate themselves in relation to the maintained sector. Each radical school aims to be an educational environment of the highest quality both in theory and in practice for all its members. In addition each school community claims either explicitly or implicitly that it is a model which other schools, and society as a whole, ought to attend to and where possible learn from.

At the risk of tedium, the point must be made early in this study that

[36] Ibid., p. 92.

the educational radicals of the 1890s were, not surprisingly, middle-class intellectuals many of whom had sympathy with the political Left, at least at first, but who ran schools which charged considerable fees and so made any real penetration of working-class life impossible. Yet even this stock economic argument is too simple. The kind of educational reform which Reddie, Badley, and the others had in mind could be based only on an educational sophistication of some refinement which the teachers in the elementary school seldom had. Reddie and Badley were really attacking a culture which was impoverished for the public schoolboy and for the elementary schoolboy in quite different ways, and even if they had wanted to, Reddie and Badley could not have provided a school which would have been sufficiently satisfying for each kind of boy.

Their triangulation point was the public school, the most independent yet the best organized branch, the most individualistic yet the most collectively powerful, free from inspection or control but intellectually almost as constricted by the classical curriculum as the elementary schools were by the Revised Code. Reddie staged a characteristic assault on the public schools: Abbotsholme was for boys of eleven to eighteen years belonging to the directing classes and the New School would win away such boys as at that time were going to the public schools by the simple appeal of a superior commodity. The New School, like Eton or Winchester, would begin at the top.

Reddie knew very little of the English public schools at first hand, although it would not have made much difference to his direct challenge if he had; Badley, on the other hand, knew a great deal about them and was even more fundamental, though less belligerent, in his radical opposition, because he added co-education to his challenges. Devine temporized more and seems a well-intentioned opportunist rather than a proper radical, something of an outsider in both camps. King Alfred's has to be compared with the day public schools like St. Paul's or Merchant Taylors' and the day grammar schools. It is not one man's protest, but an affirmation by members of the intellectual middle class of a London suburb with a liberal reputation.

From 1902 onwards the public schools were also the triangulation point for many of the grammar schools of the new local education authorities, but more for emulation than rejection. The four radical schools of the 1890s found the public schools an extremely powerful educational and social influence, to be strengthened after 1902 by the

grammar schools. The elementary school and the higher grade school
were nothing like so powerful because they were only really beginning
and that from a very inferior position. The Labour movement was
starting to organize itself into a proletariat at the turn of the century
and it is only since 1944 that the phrase 'secondary education for all'
has been used with any real meaning.

In 1900 there were not two, but really three separate systems, public,
grammar, and elementary. In a very real sense the four radical schools
represented a tiny fourth system because of their opposition to one
kind of poverty in the education offered in the public and grammar
school and to another kind of poverty in the Revised Code of the
elementary school.

Chapter Two

MERGING INTO EDUCATIONAL
RADICALISM 1898-1918

THE four schools already described represent the beginning of a new movement. Besides these four, however, there were schools already in existence which had many similar features or which began to adopt quite explicitly many of the principles of the radical schools. Of these we propose to mention the schools of the Society of Friends scattered throughout England, and Badminton, the girls' school near Bristol. These schools merged into the progressive school movement by the time of the outbreak of the First World War. One other group of schools is also to be considered in this period and these are schools tarted by, or associated with, the Theosophical Educational Trusts which came into existence in 1916. They were not individual ventures like those of Reddie, Badley, Devine, or the group of Hampstead parents, but separate expressions of the insights of Theosophy in education.

The educational radicals did not sweep the country before the First World War and there were many reasons for this. First of all, they did not try to do so — it is true that Reddie spoke of helping to create a higher type of human being and of regenerating England but he also spoke of Abbotsholme as a state, a *kosmos* and in fact each of the head-masters gave his energy to getting his own school started. The ABC of educational reform, as Devine suggested it, came to nothing. The King Alfred Society had visions of a number of schools, a training college, and other ventures, but the single school was all that was actually achieved. A second reason for the modest expansion of the progressive school movement was that the national educational system was being planned and enacted in the two decades on either side of the turn of the century and this took up the energies of many men of educational good will. Thirdly, although the New School movement was associated with the beginnings of the Labour movement in the confused days around 1890, by 1900 the outlines of a proletariat with a parliamentary future were becoming clearer and this was going to be a movement of the working class and its sympathizers in society as a whole. The New Schools were by then financially out of reach and intellectually out of touch with the working class. They were for the children of the liberal intelligentsia who are by definition a very small percentage of the population. In any case, after the Balfour Act in 1902 the elementary schools had not the experience or confidence or desire to adopt the principles and practice of what they thought to be the lunatic fringe.

While, therefore, there are mergings into the radical movement in education, there are scarcely any new foundations before 1914. These came after the War for reasons which will appear.

I

The Society of Friends, commonly called the Quakers, is a minority group of about 20,000 which deservedly enjoys a wide respect for its religious integrity and its lively concern in social affairs. Since the foundation of Ackworth in Yorkshire in 1779 there have been schools in England officially associated with the Society and at the present date there are nine English Quaker schools.

In the middle of the seventeenth century, when the Society of Friends first took form, the three main traditions and emphases in the Christian approach to God can be seen. First there was the emphasis on the authority of the Church as Roman Catholics accepted it, 'a visible, hierarchical institution, which is the divinely commissioned vehicle and guarantee of the truth and grace of the Gospel'.[1] Second there were those who emphasized the main authority of the Bible, and historic Protestantism might serve as the type for this; the Anglican, the Calvinist, and the Lutheran had this belief in common. The third main stream of tradition and emphasis may be called rather loosely the mystical and has its sanction for and its source of faith in the spirit of the worshipper, the individual Christian, and of these the Quaker, with his belief in the Inner Light, may be taken as the example. Early

[1] J. S. Whale, *Christian Doctrine* (London, 1942), p. 14.

Friends considered that they were the restored Church of Christ drawing on a unique experience of God speaking to their own hearts. There is a body of belief which is characteristic of Quakerism from a very early period and which we must consider briefly insofar as it influences educational theory and practice.

Friends say that all men have a capacity to listen to, understand, and share spiritual experience. This capacity is often called the Seed or the Inner Light and is, so to say, God's immanence in each human spirit. The belief presents a potential separation of 'natural' and 'spiritual' man which can be seen in Calvinism in different forms at this period. The potential separatism appears sharply for Friends in the relationship between the Inner Light and intellectual learning and much has been written on this in Quaker literature in philosophical, psychological, theological, and metaphysical terms. We will not explore these aspects here, but sketch instead some of the practical outcomes in the Quaker schools.[2]

The response of early Friends to the classical languages was favourable for they, with Hebrew, were biblical languages and had thereby a sanctified utilitarian value. However, the children did not study the language by means of the usually accepted texts, but from books written by Friends like Christopher Taylor and John Matern whose book *Institutiones Pietatis* written in 1676 was full of Quaker precepts and what they called 'savoury and wholesome good matter that may not corrupt children's minds' as the classics would in their estimation if taught as they usually were straight from the heathen authors. So in their schools from an early date Friends tried to make the classics relevant to children's needs as they saw them and in choosing this method they largely discarded the sense of an ancient literature and a linguistic tradition. Besides this break with the classical tradition Friends emphasized that classics was only one subject among many others and English rather than classics was the basis of the curriculum from the start. Some of the schools in the eighteenth century were 'for the poorer sort and quite excluded Latin'.

Perhaps the most noticeable feature of the educational implications of the relationship between the Inner Light and intellectual learning was the interest shown in science. The natural creation was part of God's plan and in it He could be perceived but the expression of this

[2] For fuller treatment see W. A. C. Stewart, *Quakers and Education* (London, 1953), especially chapters i and ii.

point of view in science teaching did not really take shape until early in the nineteenth century.

Friends held clear views on the dignity of labour, believing that no task was degrading, since the Inner Light was available to any man who wished for peace and power. Practical work, therefore, whether it be household duties, the fetching of supplies, the mending of linen and clothes, the care of the land, has always been recommended in one way or another in Quaker schools.

A consequence of the belief in the Inner Light was the particular position Friends took on what may be called the priesthood of believers. If God spoke to each spirit, it was without the need of a teacher or intercessor. No one was to have the special calling of priest because all were called to be priests, so there was no hierarchy in the Quaker church but an assumption of spiritual equality, with women as equal in the priesthood with men.

Friends are well known for their insistence on directness and 'plainness' which has consequences in the Meeting for Worship based on silence and absence of liturgy. Another consequence is the emphasis on ideals of service and probity and a non-violent spirit. One Friend, writing of the Quaker view of children, says:

> The historic Quaker tradition is between the extremes of Calvinism and Progressivism. The child is not naturally good nor is he naturally evil: he is simply innocent. . . . In view of these considerations we find that the Quaker school should be neither authoritarian after the Puritan model nor anarchistic after the ultra-progressive model.[3]

Even from these very brief indications of the point of view of the Society of Friends it is clear that many important educational practices ought to follow, some of them directly in line with the distinctive position of the radical schools. Before looking more closely at this we should learn something of the Quaker schools which are in existence and a little of their history.

Monthly Meetings of the Society of Friends are regular gatherings of representatives of neighbouring local Meetings often for the purposes of conducting business or making decisions and communicating these either to the central organizations of the Society or to the

[3] H. H. Brinton, *Quaker Education in Theory and Practice*, Pendle Hill Pamphlet, no. 9, 1940, pp. 79–83. See also H. Loukes, *Friends and their Children* (London, 1958).

Quarterly Meeting, which is the regional organization. Yearly Meeting in England is the annual gathering of all the Quarterly Meetings and in 1779 Yearly Meeting undertook to be responsible for Ackworth School founded near Pontefract in Yorkshire to which the children of Friends 'not in affluence' were entitled to go. The school taught both boys and girls organized as separate 'sides' and this dual formation continued with cumulative modifications until in 1947 Ackworth became fully co-educational, the last of the six co-educational Friends' schools now in existence to make the change.

The concern of Yearly Meeting to support the foundation of Ackworth in 1779 followed upon a Report presented in 1760 by a special committee which had examined the state of education in Friends' schools. If the period 1695–1725 might be regarded as the high-water mark of the Society's interest in its schools, the state of affairs in the middle of the eighteenth century was serious.⁴ For years after the publication of the Report in 1760 nothing appeared to be happening until John Fothergill, an eminent Quaker physician, David Barclay, a respected financier and banker, and William Tuke, a well-known York merchant, took the matter in hand. Following on the foundation of Ackworth in 1779 the West Country Quarterly Meeting founded Sidcot School near Bristol in 1808 on a plan somewhat similar to that of Ackworth.

There was already in existence in Clerkenwell in London, founded in 1702, a Quaker workhouse for old and infirm people together with a boarding school for some young children. The school was separated in 1786 and moved to Islington where it was reformed in 1811 to approximate to Ackworth. The school moved to Croydon in 1825, and to Saffron Walden in Essex, its present location, in 1879, and Her Majesty's Inspectors say that Saffron Walden in 1879 was for East London, Essex, and the Fen district what Ackworth was for South Yorkshire.

The Quarterly Meeting of Cumberland and Northumberland founded Wigton near Carlisle in 1815 and its general rules are almost verbatim the Ackworth rules drawn up in 1789. All four of these schools were for boys and girls taught separately and from relatively poor Quaker homes. In 1829, however, York Quarterly Meeting gave its official

⁴ See D. G. B. Hubbard, 'Early Quaker Education 1650–1780', an unpublished M.A. thesis of the University of London, 1939, pp. 160–1.

support to a boys' school which had been running for five years as a private venture in the city. This was Bootham School, which was to give, 'a liberal, guarded and religious education, on moderate terms, to the sons of Friends who are not considered the object of Ackworth School.'[5]

In 1831 York Quarterly Meeting founded a girls' school 'similar in its character and general management to the boys' school'.[6] This was the Mount School which was and is the only girls' school under the auspices of an official Quaker committee. These two establishments were for the children of Friends who could afford to pay more and offered a more advanced education. One of the Taunton Commissioners in 1867 said of The Mount: 'The curriculum of instruction is remarkable for the small proportion of effort devoted to accomplishments, and the large share to intellectual culture.'

In the 1830s and 40s four schools were founded by Quarterly Meetings, two of which have survived, for the children of those 'disowned'. These were the children of men or women who had been members of the Society but who for one reason or another had turned away from, or had been turned out of, the Society, mostly for marrying a non-Friend. This strict rule of exclusion affected not only those who 'married out' but members of their family who sympathized with them, and it depleted the Society seriously in the first half of the nineteenth century. By 1860 the rule of exclusion had been rescinded by many Meetings — incidentally W. E. Forster, the architect of the 1870 Act, was a birthright Friend who was disowned for marrying Jane, a daughter of Thomas Arnold. Forster had been educated at two Quaker private schools, Fishponds and Tottenham.

With the rescinding of the practice of disownment the schools set up for those disowned became ordinary Quaker schools, again for those not in affluence. The two existing schools which have this origin are Great Ayton in North-East Yorkshire, which was founded in 1841 as the North of England Agricultural School, and Sibford, founded near Banbury in 1842 by the Berkshire and Oxfordshire Quarterly Meeting.

The only other Friends' school to name is Leighton Park. This was founded in 1890 at Reading by the Friends Public School Company,

---

[5] *History of Bootham School 1823–1923* (London, 1926), p. 22.

[6] H. W. Sturge and T. Clark, *The Mount School, York, 1785–1814, 1831–1931* (London, 1931), p. 36.

a group of concerned Friends who formed a governing body to which Yearly Meeting added representatives. The school was to provide about one hundred boys with preparation for a university or other advanced training. It corresponded in the south to Bootham in the north and it has continued as a Quaker public school, a member, like Bootham, of the Headmasters' Conference. So the Quaker schools are Ackworth (1779), Sidcot (1808), Saffron Walden (1811), Wigton (1815), Bootham (1823), The Mount (1831), Great Ayton (1841), Sibford (1842), and Leighton Park (1890).

During the nineteenth century the integrity and hard work of Quakers had given them an influential position in industrial England, and so too had their active concern for human welfare in prison reform, the abolition of slavery, factory legislation, the care of the sick and the insane, the alleviation of poverty. Their pacifism and plainness tended to isolate them from everyday life as a special group, and while they were committed to the relief of human suffering and to the honest conduct of ordinary affairs they were also aware of their separateness and need for solidarity. Throughout the century one is aware of the conflict between cautious 'guarding' advices and a more expansive, questing outlook. For instance the distinctive Quaker dress had disappeared from Friends' schools in the 1870s and by the end of the century the pupils were dressed like other children. The special forms of Quaker speech, employing 'thee' and 'thou' and other particular idioms, had almost disappeared from the schools by 1879. Non-Friends were admitted to Friends' schools both as pupils and as teachers from about 1870 and the present fluctuating average proportion of Quaker children and teachers in Friends' schools is rather less than half. The crucial decade for these changes was the 1870s, though the roots of change stretch back long before that. In the twentieth century the Society of Friends has ceased to be a separatist group in English society, which in some senses it never really was. As in society, so in education the older 'guarded' concepts have had to be replaced by new modes of perpetuating the Quaker message and beliefs.

In 1864 the Taunton Commission had examined the York schools and given them a favourable report. In the 1860s and 70s most of the Friends' schools began to accept regular inspections by officers of the Cambridge Syndicate or the British and Foreign Schools Society and in 1879 there was an important conference of Friends on education. From this Report we can see how the wind of change was blowing:

> If we want to train good teachers ... we must send them out into the world, to learn from intercourse with the highest minds outside what are the new systems of teaching.[7]

A realistic appraisal of the Friends' schools at that time showed that changes were needed:

> There is not an education offered for all classes in [the Society]. ... We should have a thoroughly well-educated class of men who will be able to take any position in regard to the education of the sons and daughters of any class in our Society.[8]

The Society's schools are clearly seen to be in intellectual competition with other schools and they reflect the social standards of the Society as a whole in late nineteenth-century class structure. Ackworth, founded a century before for the children of those 'not in affluence', was said to have had the effect of raising the families from which the boys and girls came 'rather above the middle class in life' and making rich men of many who would otherwise have been in humble circumstances. Two out of three leavers entered commercial careers and about one in ten went into the professions.

The status of Friends by the 1880s and 90s was such that they became important figures in local government when the Act of 1888 opened the way for local authorities. An American Friend reported in New York in 1881:

> Every person at all familiar with English affairs, knows that a large number of Friends occupy positions of great responsibility and influence. Two are members of the Government, nearly a score are members of Parliament, several are mayors of cities, a considerable number occupy highly important places on school boards. ... The numbers ... are out of all proportion to the Society's membership in the nation ... I can see no significant cause but education, combined with public confidence, and those things difficult to define which are included in the term of 'respectability'. Wealth has a degree of influence, but it does not fit men for such positions, except as it gives them useful information, discipline and culture.[9]

[7] *Report of the Education Conference of the Society of Friends, 1879*, p. 116.
[8] Ibid., p. 135.
[9] J. Wood, 'Education among Friends in England', in *Proceedings of a Conference called by the Committee on Education of New York Yearly Meeting* (1881), pp. 44–45.

Quaker schools had played their part in helping to bring about this shift in social standing. Many Friends were no longer reluctant to seek political power and the Board of Education reported on Friends' schools in 1905 :

> The Schools have been affected by a tendency which is almost universal in England. Schools which have been founded with special regard to the children of the poor have gradually increased their fees and the standard of education, so that they now do a work quite different from that which was originally contemplated. . . . The ambition of a successful school is not to do better the work which it began with, but to pass on to work of a more ambitious character.[10]

By 1900 the nine schools were offering 'a sound education of the secondary school type', the York schools and Leighton Park clearly to a more advanced standard. Much of what they did was parallel to what was being done in the radical schools already mentioned. The classics took a position in the curriculum subordinate to English. The modern languages had their place and the sciences had been taught in the schools since their foundation — Bootham was said to have one of the first laboratories in an English secondary school, opened in 1879, and its Natural History Society, founded in 1834, was an early example of this kind of organization. The arts, including music, had received a general if cautious approval by the 90s of the last century — choral singing in unison was permitted in the 1870s and by the 80s harmonies were allowed. By 1880 class teaching of instruments was widely approved and by the beginning of this century pupils were going to concerts.

By the 1870s and 80s there were craftrooms and workshops in most of the schools in which turning, fretwork, boatbuilding, bookbinding, and metalwork reached a good and sometimes excellent standard according to the Board's Inspectors in the early years of this century. The girls had for many years been engaged in all branches of house-craft and in some of the schools (Ayton, Sibford, and Saffron Walden, for instance) estate work was done in the two middle quarters of the century, but had been dropped in the last quarter although ordinary household work was done by the children in all the schools.

Many Friends' schools had been groping towards co-education in the

[10] *Inspection of Friends' Boarding Schools by the Board of Education* (1905), p. 9.

last two decades of the century. The priesthood of believers was a principle which Friends did not apply to the position of men and women as equal in the Society's councils until 1907 and by that time Sidcot had become fully co-educational and so too had Ayton, Sibford, Wigton. Saffron Walden followed in 1910 but Ackworth did not do so finally until 1947. The Mount remains a girls' school and Leighton Park and Bootham are still for boys only. Sidcot made the change in 1902 under Dr. Bevan Lean and the other three schools had done so by 1904–5, when the Board of Education produced a report on Friends' schools. The Inspectors in their Report said that if co-education in boarding schools could be adopted anywhere with safety and success it would be in schools such as these with their traditional bond of a quiet family life and the restraint of strong religious influence.[11] It is probably this feature of co-education more than any other which brought Friends' schools into the same bracket as progressive schools.

Another feature of Quaker educational practice which linked their schools to the radical group was the growth of Children's Councils in the 1920s and the readiness to give to children a limited sense of responsibility. This is a reasonable application of Friends' belief in the Inner Light, but in the schools no great freedom or power has been given to these Councils — they have been more of a patch on the fabric of the existing hierarchy. Again the non-violent spirit of Friends has made their discipline within the last hundred years relatively humane though it was often surprisingly cruel before that. They discarded corporal punishment about the middle of the last century but some harsh and damaging alternatives like solitary confinement and a generalized ridiculing have not been uncommon.[12]

By 1914 Friends' schools could be located in relationship to the radical schools, having the features we have indicated in common. Friends had merged into the progressive movement quietly but inevitably as they began to apply their own principles to the twentieth-century educational situation. Quakers were, and are, as a body, on the right wing of progressive education. They value order and the sense of continuity and tradition, the need to focus on something beyond the school, the consciousness of religious foundations. They also value, however, the individual spirit and the vision each man or child may have, they respect telling the truth in love and the right to

11 *Ibid.*, p. 36.
12 For fuller treatment see Stewart, *Quakers and Education*, pp. 259–67.

have conscientious objection. Professor Castle writing in 1936 when he was the headmaster of Leighton Park School put it like this: '(Progressive schools) are schools of protest, self-conscious in their efforts, uncertain in their aims, usually non-religious in their foundation ... I do not believe they are the schools our Society can accept as substitutes for our own.'[13] This might be true of some of the foundations of the 1920s, but Friends' schools grew nearer to the first four pre-war radical schools than to any other group.

II

In August 1858 a school for girls began in a small way in Bristol which took the name by which it is now known when it moved to Badminton House, Clifton Park. Mrs. Badock, the founder, said in her first prospectus that 'her aim invariably is first to secure (the girls') affection and confidence and then, by a careful study of the character and mental capacities of each to develop moral and religious principles and impart instruction in the manner best adapted to their individual tastes and dispositions'. Mrs. Badock encouraged her pupils to take the Cambridge Local Examinations from the 1860s onwards, invited teachers from the University College as it then was to lecture to her girls on a range of subjects including botany, natural history, and elementary physics, and the girls supported quite a range of school societies.

Mrs. Badock retired after thirty-five years of enlightened work which would not quite be sufficiently unorthodox to merit including Badminton in the group of radical schools. There were fifty-five girls in the school when Miss Bartlett, aided by two sisters, became headmistress in 1893. Miss Bartlett had been a pupil and a member of staff and by 1904, when a junior section was started, the school had seventy girls aged between thirteen and eighteen, forty of them being boarders. There is an illuminating account of the school at this time in which the writer says that the girls did not work very hard and that not many took public examinations. There was no prefect system and the school centred round Miss Bartlett: 'though we loved her, we all — girls, staff and parents — held her in a very wholesome awe. She was petite, very clever and very charming to look at.'[14] The days were strenuous

---

[13] E. B. Castle, 'The Position of Friends' Schools', in *Friends' Quarterly Examiner*, vol. 70, 1936, pp. 28–29.

[14] *Badminton School 1858–1958* (published by the School), p. 6.

and long walks in all weathers were a regular feature and another writer says of the period 1907–11 :

> It was a good, quiet, old-fashioned school — I mean old-fashioned in its own day — not coveting academic honours but giving a very fair grounding in at least English language and literature. The girls were average, too, in attainment and conduct . . . our goodness was rather negative. Looking back fifty years I feel that on the whole I enjoyed it.[15]

In 1911 Miss B. M. Baker became headmistress with Miss Randall as second mistress. This was their first experience of a boarding school to which they had been attracted by the greater opportunities it offered of developing girls' education than a day school and 'they absolutely shook the school'. The old-fashioned school clothes were replaced by lighter, more hygienic, and more attractive dress, the academic standard was stiffened all round and weakness in particular subjects was answered by flexible 'setting' arrangements. Newspapers had to be read and matters discussed ; meetings and lectures were attended in Bristol ; the school took part in social work and in something like what we would now call youth club activities with children in poor and difficult circumstances in the city ; the seniors went to the theatre not infrequently and saw the *avant-garde* works of Shaw, Galsworthy, and Wilde. The political and social problems of the world were proper matters for Badminton girls. But before going further we should take a glance at girls' secondary education in England in the second half of last century.

The Girls' Public Day School Trust was founded in 1872 and high-level day secondary schools for girls multiplied over the country, giving a chance of work of good academic standard intended as a preparation for professional and university careers which had not been easy for women to come by. There had been a few such boarding and day schools in the first half of the nineteenth century — Godolphin School, Christ's Hospital, and for the daughters of clergy St. Brandon's and St. Elphin's, and The Mount School for Quaker girls. Very active and sustained effort, some of it by university teachers of the new University of London, led to the foundation of Queen's College in Harley Street in 1848 and to Bedford College, which had its beginnings in 1849 and developed to its status as a constituent College of the University of

[15] Ibid., p. 11.

London. Frances Mary Buss, a former pupil of Queen's College, transformed a school run by her mother into the North London Collegiate School in 1850 which was the prototype for the Girls' Public Day School Trust. Dorothea Beale, also formerly of Queen's College, took over in 1858 the Ladies' College at Cheltenham which had been founded as a day school in 1853 with eighty-eight pupils. Twenty years later it was the leading girls' boarding school in the country with over five hundred girls.

The Taunton Commission in 1869 supported the obvious growth of the education of girls and women and said that the education of girls was as much a matter of public concern as that of boys and even ruled that where charitable trusts did not mention girls in their instruments of foundation, funds could be used for their education, unless they were explicitly excluded. In 1869 a Report was issued by a Commission on the Education of Girls under the chairmanship of Miss Beale. In the 1870s Girton and Newnham made their beginnings in Cambridge, the Oxford women's colleges were founded in the late 1870s and after. The University of London opened its degrees and prizes to women as to men in 1878, the University of Manchester did the same in 1880. Oxford and Cambridge at the same time made their grudging admission of women to courses and by courtesy to examinations, but not to official degrees for fifty years and more. After 1902, of course, maintained girls' and co-educational schools were founded to extend the provision at all levels made after the 1870 Act.

These comments are offered as background to the changes at Badminton after 1911. In a sense it was more difficult to transform a conventional girls' school than to give girls a progressive education in an obviously odd organization like Bedales or King Alfred's. For the new girls' boarding schools and many of the day schools the boys' public school was the principal pattern with the result that the curriculum and organization for games assumed the distortions which Reddie, Badley, Devine, Rice, Russell, the Quaker heads, and many others had strongly criticized. At Badminton the new idea in 1911 was to maintain a high academic standard while widening the range of interests to include social responsibility at home and interests in international affairs abroad. Miss Baker was headmistress through two World Wars and retired in 1946 by which time work in the arts, in citizenship, the course in the history of civilization, and a considerable range of responsibility for girls' committees had long been established.

Badminton is and has been an undenominational school. Girls go to their own churches on Sundays and there is a non-sectarian school service in the evening in the Peace Memorial Hall which acts as a combination of assembly room and chapel and was opened in 1928 in an effort to establish 'the defences of peace which must be constructed in the minds of men.'

In the post-war years Badminton took an active interest in the League of Nations, and parties of girls visited Geneva to learn of the League's work and attend sessions of its committees and assemblies; in 1922 a visit was made to Germany and Austria 'to make the acquaintance of our recent enemies'; during and after the War more than one member of the staff took part in the relief work on the Continent organized by the Society of Friends; the school made a point of encouraging girls from overseas to become pupils and they came from many nations in Europe, the Commonwealth, and elsewhere. After the First World War there were refugees from Poland, Russia, and in the middle and late 1930s there were Spanish and Basque children, Germans, Austrians, Czechs. The influx of foreign children in the decade before the Second World War was not just the consequence of a sudden, general wave of sympathy for suffering Europe. Miss Baker and her colleagues had been explicit since 1911 on international sympathy and responsibility. When Miss Sanderson, her successor, writes of the Conference of Internationally-Minded Schools founded under the auspices of UNESCO in 1949 it is natural that Badminton should be a leading member in England.[16]

The curriculum of the four radical schools at the beginning of this century became the curriculum of Badminton after 1911 — no dominance of the classics, but a broad academic course, with an emphasis on English studies. The arts and crafts and music were given a high place in the general education provided. Modern languages, science, and mathematics were important as were informal and friendly relations with the staff. Cramming and specialization, prizes and competitiveness were avoided. Cold baths were the morning rule at Badminton for many years but estate work was not encouraged — partly it was thought to be unsuitable for girls and partly the grounds did not appear to permit it. The traffic of affairs with the city of Bristol could not be emulated at any of the four radical schools except King Alfred's

[16] B. M. Sanderson, 'Badminton', in *The Independent Progressive School*, p. 29. Miss Sanderson has been Chairman of the Executive Committee of C.I.S.

C

and that was a day school. Badminton's insistence on an intelligent interest in history, politics, and current affairs was better organized than in any of the radical schools, as was its social work in the school's own rehabilitation house or at the University Centre. The School Council goes back nearly fifty years and has had a predominantly useful role in an advisory capacity all that time. Badminton is a girls' school but its senior pupils have had contacts for many years with neighbouring boys' schools and taken a full part in co-educational summer meetings of the old League of Nations Union and the modern Conference of Internationally-Minded Schools. Even until 1939 many of these things, now commonplace, were quite unorthodox.

This is a girls' school which aligned itself with the progressive movement in 1911 and had merged with the progressive schools by the end of the First World War as the practices already summarized have indicated. The temper of Badminton has always been liberal and the school may be taken with the Friends' schools as moderately progressive without being radical. In 1931 Badminton became a public school with a Board of Governors of which Professor Gilbert Murray was for a long time the President. Yet it is with the radicals that Badminton is not unwilling to be associated as Miss Baker's contribution to Blewitt's symposium in 1934 and Miss Sanderson's to Child's in 1962, both indicate.[17]

III

Theosophists have made important contributions to educational innovation in England, but it is necessary to set the stage rather carefully so that their work may be seen and understood. Friedrich Max Müller was born at Dessau in the Duchy of Anhalt in 1823 where his father was ducal librarian. The boy proved to be a linguistic scholar of outstanding talent and after studying oriental languages in circumstances of great poverty in Leipzig, Berlin, and Paris, he came to London to work on the rich store of Sanskrit documents in the library of the India Office. He became a Fellow of All Souls and Professor of Comparative Philology at Oxford and for nearly fifty years until his death in 1900 he edited, first the *Rig Veda*, the Hindu hymns which were hitherto unpublished even in India, and then supervised a massive series of translations of the sacred books of the great religions of the

[17] *The Modern Schools Handbook. The Independent Progressive School.*

world in fifty volumes entitled *The Sacred Books of the East.* This monumental scholarly achievement enabled many Englishmen in the second half of the nineteenth century to have some knowledge of Eastern religions and provides an important part of the literary background to Madame Blavatsky, Annie Besant, and the Theosophical movement in this country.

Madame Helena Petrovna Blavatsky was born near Odessa in 1831 and died in her sixtieth year in London. She is supposed to have spent about a third of her life in wanderings during which she discovered in Tibet and the borderlands of the Far East the mysteries of spiritualism and oriental gnostic religions. She wrote many books and with Colonel H. S. Olcott founded the Theosophical Society in New York in 1875. In 1890 Mrs. Annie Besant became a convert to Theosophy largely through reading for review books by A. P. Sinnett and Helena Blavatsky herself, in particular the latter's major work *The Secret Doctrine.* The vision opened up by these writings astounded Mrs. Besant, who had already had a publicly provocative career.

In 1867 Annie Wood married Frank Besant, Vicar of Sibsey in Lincolnshire, when she was 20. Six years later after bearing him two children she left him because she had ceased to be a Christian and later she was legally separated from him. In 1874 she joined the National Secular Society and began to work actively with Charles Bradlaugh with whom she was prosecuted and acquitted in 1877 for the publication of Knowlton's *Fruits of Philosophy* which advocated and defended birth control. In the same year she published her *Gospel of Atheism* and she was deprived of the custody of her children. Her sympathy was with the Left in politics and she joined the Fabian Society in 1885 and it was over this that she broke her association with Bradlaugh who rejected socialism.

Mrs. Besant was militant in her choice of constitutional weapons. In 1888 she helped to organize the girls of Bryant & May who made matches (a firm with Quaker connections) in their strike for better conditions and she remained a firebrand of splendid oratorical power in Fabian causes until she began to adopt a theosophical outlook in 1889. The oratory remained but the loyalties changed. Madame Blavatsky and H. S. Olcott realized what a remarkable acquisition Mrs. Besant was and she came into the movement at the top. When Madame Blavatsky died in 1891 Mrs. Besant was clearly one of the leaders in

England and later of the world movement of which she became President in 1907. In 1893 she visited India and thereafter spent the major part of her life there and in the United States till her death in 1933. India was the sacred land in which Mrs. Besant felt that the full meaning of Theosophy could be understood and it was at Adyar in Madras that the headquarters of the movement was established and still is.

In 1895 William Quan Judge, an American leader in the Theosophical Society, led a secession movement with which many of the American and some European members allied themselves and they formed a new organization, the Universal Brotherhood and Theosophical Society. There were further fragmentations later in the world movement and a major split in 1913 between Mrs. Besant and Rudolf Steiner, who had led the German section of the Theosophical Society since 1902. Steiner and his followers at once set up the Anthroposophical Society which we shall consider separately later, for Anthroposophists have founded a number of progressive schools in England.

The eclectic spirituality of the theosophical movement brought to it many men and women for whom orthodox Christianity, whether Roman Catholic, Anglican, or Dissenting, was too constricting. A generation nurtured on the cosmology and cosmogony of Swedenborg, Blake, Carlyle, and Ruskin, and with Müller's translations available, could quickly savour and taste Theosophy even when it did not swallow it.

Theosophy is based on belief in an immutable, all-pervading principle which pre-exists creation and from which the universe, spirit and matter, growth and decay, all flow. Life and the human mind which is aware of life are ensouled by this principle, this God. What man calls evolution in the world of matter is part of the divine potential which is unfolding itself through the elements, through mineral, vegetable, and animal existence up to the self-conscious phase of humanity. The physical world as men know it is the most dense and obvious, but each man possesses also an astral body which through clairvoyance and telepathy can effect a line of communication forming a second plane of the universe. The third plane of the universe is explored by man's mental body which develops what one may, by metaphor, call the 'senses' appropriate to comprehending the entirely different scope of the spiritual plane. There are four higher planes known only to adepts which we will not here attempt to describe. The physical, astral, and mental bodies represent man's usual working instruments even for an average Theosophist, whose task is, of course, to deepen and extend his spiritual life.

At death man is evolving according to his deeds and understanding of the life just ended, and the unfolding of powers, the evolution of human experience, demands reincarnation as a consequence, by means of which experience can be assimilated and physical, astral, and mental bodies which have been outgrown may be superseded. For this progression to be maintained the principle of *karma* must also operate, which is only the immutable principle, the God, maintaining the growth of the spirit through successive lives. 'As ye sew, so shall ye reap' is a gospel which makes perfection possible seen in the perspective of reincarnation and *karma*. On the other hand these two principles can also help to explain apparent injustices in the world and the mental, moral, and social inequalities which exist. Madame Blavatsky claimed that her special insight into all these matters was based on the esoteric tradition of a Tibetan brotherhood into which she was initiated and whose spiritual discipline and study have produced the evolutionary structure on seven planes which has already been mentioned.

There are many other instances of the theosophical tradition in the Christian world — Plotinus, the Gnostics, Meister Eckhart, St. John of the Cross, Jacob Böhme, C. G. Jung. This eclectic spirituality enabled the Theosophical Society to state that it had no dogmas, no creeds, that it included adherents of all faiths and none, that it represented those schools of religious thought which were seeking insight into the nature of God by mystical or occult experience or from sacred books or esoteric traditions. Doctrines, dogmas, theologies, they said, trapped only part of the meaning and the mystery. However, generalised and vague common agreement developed later into a discovery of difference, a definition leading to schism, as we have seen in the case of W. Q. Judge and of Rudolf Steiner and as was also true of Cecil Reddie's friends Edward Maitland and Anna Kingsford who broke from Theosophy and formed the Hermetic Society. Nevertheless it was Theosophists who made possible an important development in progressive education.

By 1907 there were six hundred and fifty-five branches of the Theosophical Society all over the world and the British section, although it had done nothing collectively in education, had a good number of members engaged in teaching at various levels. Armytage has shown that a number of Theosophists were connected with the Fellowship of the New Life and later with the Garden City movement at the turn of the century.[18]   Mrs. Besant, George Arundale, A. P. Sinnett, and others made Theosophy 'almost fashionable' from 1910 to 1915 according to one of the surviving leaders of the movement at that time.[19] Almost annual visits to England for congresses and other matters enabled Mrs. Besant to publicize her message with what her supporters considered to be wonderful clarity and eloquence and what one of her critics, who arranged meetings for her in Sheffield, considered 'was nothing but the threadbare platitudes I had heard a hundred times over at Socialist meetings'.[20]   The appeal to professional people was considerable and by 1914 the obvious question of education as a piece of public service for Theosophists through schools of their own and through participation in national and local administration was becoming urgent.

The Theosophical Society in 1875 in New York had had one general statement of aim — to form a nucleus of the universal brotherhood of humanity without distinction of race, creed, sex, colour, or caste.   There were two other aims which were more tentative: the first was to encourage the study of comparative religion, philosophy, and science and the second to investigate the unexplained laws of nature and the powers of man.   In 1915 the same kind of spirit appeared in the formation of the Theosophical Fraternity in Education.

For a few years before the outbreak of war an informal group sharing similar liberal views on education had met to discuss a variety of subjects.   In the group was Edmond Holmes, whose books *What Is and What Might Be* and *In Quest of an Ideal*, written after his enforced retirement from the post of Chief Inspector for Elementary Education at the Board of Education, made such an impact.   Miss Belle Rennie, Wyatt Rawson, Beatrice de Normann (later Mrs. Ensor), J. H. Simpson, Miss Alice Woods, and later T. F. Coade, headmaster of Bryanston, were also strong supporters of this group which took the title 'New Ideals in Education' and held its first conference at East Runton in Norfolk in 1914, its main theme on that occasion being the theory and practice of Madame Montessori.   There followed a sequence of annual

---

[18] Armytage, *Heavens Below*, especially Phase IV, pp. 289–384.

[19] In recorded conversation with the author.

[20] A. Freeman, *Who was Rudolf Steiner?*, published privately by Sheffield Educational Settlement, 1944, p. 10.

conferences which lasted till just before the beginning of the Second World War. Reports of these conferences were published separately and the papers appeared in the journal of the group, *New Ideals Quarterly*. The members of the group came from all points of the religious and educational compass but with a certain shared attitude summed up in the Introduction to the Report of the 1923 Oxford conference:

> Having begun as an informal association of friends of education sharing the same views and sympathies, the Conference Committee has now assumed the character of a permanent Council. It does not exist to voice the opinions of any particular pedagogical school or to give exclusive assistance to any sectional propaganda. Its members work together upon the basis of a common conviction that a new spirit, full of hope for the world, is stirring in education. . . . The essentials of the new spirit . . . are reverence for the pupil's individuality and the belief that true individuality . . . grows best in an atmosphere of freedom.[21]

The Theosophical Fraternity in Education was started within the larger organization of the Conference of New Ideals in Education. The moving spirit was Beatrice de Normann, who married in 1919 and whom we shall call by her married name, Mrs. Beatrice Ensor. Mrs. Ensor was a qualified teacher without a degree who in 1910 became the first woman inspector appointed by the Glamorgan County Council. Her duties were to supervise day and evening work for women and girls in the county, and after a few years she was appointed His Majesty's Inspector of Schools mainly concerned with Domestic Science. This appointment she took up in the early days of the War and Mrs. Ensor, beyond her normal duties, found herself reporting on schools for girl delinquents in the south of England and inspecting the working conditions of women in factories. During the years 1910–15 she became sharply critical, by reason of her varied first-hand experience, of the practices in very many schools. The buildings were tasteless and gloomy, the classes dispiritingly large, the discipline was stark regimentation, and when she went to see a Montessori school she found the opportunities for self-development and self-discipline admirable and enviable. As a fellow H.M. Inspector she read Edmond Holmes's writings with eager appreciation, knowing that his model

[21] 'The Discipline of Freedom', *Conference of New Ideals in Education* (1923), Introduction.

school of 'what might be', presided over by 'Egeria', was at Sompting in Sussex. Homer Lane's Little Commonwealth, begun in Dorset just before the beginning of the War, gave her the idea of forming a group of teachers within the Theosophical Society, of which she was a member, to study the changes needed in education, and this became the Theosophical Fraternity in Education of which the keynote was faith in human nature and the spiritual powers latent in every child. The international contacts of the Theosophical Society gave Mrs. Ensor the chance to link together with like-minded persons in many lands. The Fraternity had Sections in France, the U.S.A., India, Australia, and New Zealand.

For five or six years the English Fraternity Group attended the annual conferences of the New Ideals in Education organization, holding sectional meetings of their own during the larger gatherings, until in 1920 with a membership of over five hundred the Theosophical Fraternity was big enough to need to hold its own conference which it did at Letchworth. From this meeting grew the idea and the organization of what we now know as the New Education Fellowship and this we shall examine in detail later. For the moment it is sufficient to say that as the New Education Fellowship grew the Theosophical Fraternity in Education in England withered away. The inclusive and generalized tenets of Theosophy made it possible for many who would not call themselves theists to co-operate with the Fellowship. However, as Mrs. Ensor says : 'It is only fair to record that the first members (of the New Education Fellowship) being mainly Theosophists did give the Fellowship a spiritual impulse which made it a creative and powerful force.'[22]

The Fraternity and the New Education Fellowship represented Theosophy's contribution to theory and practice in education at large.[23] Theosophists also wanted the Society to set up schools of its own to make its point of view more explicit. Mrs. Besant had said at more than one international conference that the Theosophical Society ought to engage through its members in practical affairs and for three or four years before the outbreak of the War Mr. H. Baillie-Weaver, the General Secretary of the British branch, discussed with Mrs. Ensor

---

[22] From an unpublished manuscript sent to the late Dr. William Boyd by Mrs. Ensor and made available for the present author's use. This material has been quoted in W. Boyd and W. Rawson : *The Story of the New Education* (London, 1965), pp. 67–68.

[23] The two Aims of the Fraternity were : 1. To further the Ideal in all branches of Education; 2. To secure conditions which will give freedom for its expression.

and others a proposal for setting up an educational trust. Baillie-Weaver was a Scottish barrister of Labour-humanist sympathies, who had lived in the Paris Latin Quarter for a while earlier in his life and who was a firm supporter of feminist causes:

> Le mouvement féminin est un mouvement pour lequel j'ai beaucoup travaillé, étant convaincu que la responsabilité de la bonne administration de la nation incombe non seulement aux hommes mais également aux femmes qui la composent.[24]

He had great faith in the ability and competence of Mrs. Ensor and, in his turn, was trusted by a group of influential and wealthy Theosophists, among them Miss Dodge, an American heiress, and Mrs. Douglas-Hamilton, whose considerable income came from Wills, the tobacco company. From this group the money for the Theosophical Educational Trust (in Great Britain and Ireland) Ltd. came and Mrs. Ensor was appointed Director when the Trust was formed in the early months of 1916, resigning from the Board of Education in order to give her time to the Theosophical Fraternity of Education, the Conference for New Ideals in Education, the Theosophical Educational Trust, and the tender growth of the New Education Fellowship.

> I was fortunate to be able to give my time to the Fraternity and later to the Fellowship on a voluntary basis and to have a husband who believed in my work and was therefore willing to put up with my absences from home on lecture tours.[25]

In 1915 the Garden City Theosophical School was started in Letchworth, the model community near London with which Theosophists, Quakers, members of the Alpha Union and of the Fellowship of the New Life had had so much to do since the turn of the century. This became the Arundale School named after G. S. Arundale, one of Mrs. Besant's best-known English disciples, when it passed into the hands of the Theosophical Educational Trust as a co-educational boarding school for about eighty pupils. There was a private Theosophical venture in which Mrs. Douglas-Hamilton was specially interested on the outskirts of London at Bromley in Kent where handicapped children or those from broken homes were cared for, at first dealing

---

[24] H. Baillie-Weaver, 'La Co-éducation,' in *The Creative Self Expression of the Child.* Report of the First Summer Conference of the New Education Fellowship in Calais, 1921, p. 44.

[25] Mrs. Ensor's manuscript already mentioned. (Footnote 22.)

with babies, normal children, and crippled or invalid children, but quickly finding this impossible in the limited accommodation and re-organizing to take normal children of three years old and upward from undesirable homes or from none at all, many of the thirty-five pupils being illegitimate. This school, Brackenhill Theosophical Home School passed into the hands of the Theosophical Educational Trust. A co-educational school at Grindelford in Derbyshire and another in Edinburgh, the King Arthur School, together with the Moray School in Glasgow likewise came into the care of the Trust and another was proposed 'in the North of England', the Besant School. Several schools in London and elsewhere run privately by Theosophists were affiliated to the Trust while not belonging to it. Included in these was Leinster House a day school near Hyde Park which aimed 'at preparing girls of good social standing for a definite purpose in life', and had more self-regulation by the girls than any other Theosophical school.

Mrs. Ensor came to think that it would be a notable contribution if the Trust could centre much of its effort on Letchworth which had no secondary school other than Arundale School and a girls' school for forty-six pupils. The Trust took over this establishment, the Modern School, in 1918 and expanded it to accommodate one hundred boys and girls, converting Arundale School into a boarding house for the Modern School, which quickly changed its name to St. Christopher. In the first prospectus we read that this is 'a Day School for the co-education of Boys and Girls up to the age of 19 and the standard of University scholarship'. A report of the Trust's activities in 1920 notes that 'this brings the secondary education of Letchworth largely into the hands of the Trust'. In a very short while the schools at Grindelford and at Brackenhill closed and many of the pupils were transferred from these schools and others to St. Christopher which had a Montessori junior section.

The Theosophical Educational Trust laid out its aims in its Second Annual *Report*:

> to form miniature communities — co-educational and run on demo-cratic lines. The boys and girls are co-citizens, learning self-discipline, first by the Montessori method and then by gradually assuming partial government of the school, with the teachers as elders and guides. The children help so far as is practical in the service needed for the upkeep of the community. On the domestic staff are gentlefolk who have been properly trained in their own

particular line, by whom the children are instructed in cookery, housecraft, gardening and woodwork. . . . A factor in the educational life of all, the practical side is yet not allowed to interfere with the culture side. We are most anxious that the standards of work in all directions shall reach a high level of efficiency, and with a view to obtaining this we have appointed well-known experts in the chief subjects to act as advisers.[26]

Freedom to develop special talents and to grow according to the laws of his being is accorded to each child by means of a well understood discipline based on physical, emotional, and mental self-control. Punishment in this context is really a last resort and corporal punishment is totally rejected. Theosophists have a deep awareness of 'nature' and their schools are often called garden schools because they conduct their work and life as much as possible in the open air. They are aware of the importance of diet in matters of health but also in the understanding of nature and belief in the divinity and unity of all life:

> If this means anything at all, it will not stop at mankind, but embrace the animal creation. . . . Thus, the diet of the whole boarding community is meatless; and the same belief in the oneness of life finds expression in our attitude towards man's treatment of animals and towards the diseases of his own bodily frame.[27]

These last two references relate to the antivivisection principle and to homoeopathic practices in medicine accepted by Theosophists. The Trust in the Report already referred to says that science is taught so that materialistic tendencies are avoided, no dissection of the living animal body is practised and synthetic as well as analytic habits of mind are encouraged. Eurhythmics relating in one direction to games and in another to the aesthetic harmony of music, art, and drama, leads to an acceptance of effort and an absence of tension. Voluntary tests instead of set examinations, a great deal of individual rather than class teaching, the encouragement of co-operation rather than competitiveness — these lead to a proper understanding of learning in which 'the

[26] Nov. 1918, p. 3.
[27] L. B. Pekin, 'The Way of Life at St. Christopher School, Letchworth', in *Progress Today*, vol. xvii, no. 1. 'L. B. Pekin', a well-known writer on progressive education, is the pseudonym of a member of the staff of St. Christopher of many years' standing.

highest reward of attainment is to be appointed a coach to backward or younger children'. Children so educated, the Report comments in passing, should pass matriculation at seventeen without extra preparation. Civics and sociology were considered in 1918 proper studies for St. Christopher provided they were taught practically and the religious teaching was to be based on Christianity presented in a non-sectarian way. While it was not compulsory for any child to attend any religious observances, it was hoped that they all would. Most of these principles still apply to St. Christopher nearly fifty years later. But to return to its beginnings.

In 1919 Mr. and Mrs. Lyn Harris were appointed as joint-heads of the co-educational Junior School at Badminton. He was a Friend, educated at Leighton Park and then at a Hampstead co-educational school and Cambridge and during the war he had been imprisoned as a conscientious objector. In 1923 the senior school in Bristol and the junior school which had hitherto been separately located came together on the present Westbury-on-Trym site on the outskirts of Bristol as Badminton School and Mr. and Mrs. Harris moved to St. Christopher as vice-principals under Miss King, who had become principal in 1920. The school became a focus not only for Theosophists living in Letchworth and elsewhere, it also appealed to a number of individualistically-minded members of the middle-class intelligentsia for whom the refusal of St. Christopher to proselytize for Theosophy and its undogmatic spirituality were persuasive. Such a group, as we have said, was the Alpha Union founded about 1908 which had affinities on the one hand with the Fellowship of the New Life, which had come to an end in 1898, and on the other with the Theosophical Society because the Union aimed to provide through a circulating library and conferences 'an education in the reality of an infinitely beneficent God over all, through all and in all and the reality of the Spiritual nature in (each man) and his fellow-man'. The Union was given a house, 'The Cloisters', by Miss A. J. Lawrence, a sister of the late Lord Pethick-Lawrence, as a centre of education for those who wished to live an open-air life and to train missionaries for 'Social Christianity and Land Reform'. This house was close by Arundale House, to which the whole of St. Christopher School was later transferred and the Alpha Union and its sympathizers are examples of those who discovered in Letchworth and the Theosophical schools there 'a huge experiment where minor experiments can be carried out.'[28]   Armytage has a cartoon of 'a typical Garden citizen':

> Clad in knickerbockers and, of course, sandals, a vegetarian and member of the Theosophical Society, who kept two tortoises 'which he polishes periodically with the best Lucca oil'.   Over his mantelpiece was a large photo of Madame Blavatsky and on his library shelves were *Isis Unveiled* and the works of William Morris, H. G. Wells and Tolstoy.[29]

The Theosophical Educational Trust applied the communitarian principle proper to Letchworth by setting up in the town a number of Guilds which were supposed to be self-supporting examples of co-operative life which at the same time offered to the boys and girls the opportunities they needed for first-hand, meaningful experience of economics, commerce, sociology, and the basic crafts of life   There was a printing guild, a tailoring guild, and guilds for weaving, poultry-rearing, and fruit farming with, in addition, a grocer's shop and a pure food factory.   Ruskin, William Morris, Tolstoy, the Fellowship of the New Life are in the ancestry of such undertakings; so, too, for Theosophists, was Santiniketan, fifty miles north-east of Calcutta, where in 1901 Rabindranath Tagore established his Sanctuary School as an *ashram* where children and adults learned from one another and lived together.

With one exception, these guilds in Letchworth did not really establish themselves.   Complex policy decisions and intricate time-tables and working plans were involved and the guilds had nearly all fallen on difficult days by 1925.   The hope had been that they would teach the children essential skills and that the combination of fabricating cloth, clothes, pure food, and books, combined with caring for poultry and fruit and maintaining a retail shop would cover many of the basic needs of a community as well as enabling the children to see on what it depends and how it operates.   The printing press was the only one to develop and it tried to take some part in the education of the children, but found its role and organization as a commercial under-taking made this increasingly difficult.   When the Theosophical Educational Trust came to an end the press went into the town of

[28] See Armytage, *Heavens Below*, pp. 374–5.   It is worth noting that the Alpha Union and the Theosophical Educational Trust are different organizations and St. Christopher was a T.E.T. school.

[29] Ibid., p. 374.

Letchworth as a full commercial concern continuing to have interest in and association with the school but more for old time's sake than in any organic way.

In 1925 there was a severe premonitory shock to Theosophical education which coincided with disturbances within the Society as a whole. Mrs. Ensor resigned from her directorship of the Theosophical Educational Trust after some major differences on policy and on personal matters and Miss King, the principal of St. Christopher, who was a close friend of Mrs. Ensor's, resigned also. From that date the Trust as a living and active concern began to fade away, disappearing finally in 1930. Mrs. Ensor and Miss King were appealed to by parents to start a school elsewhere on similar lines to St. Christopher and Mrs. Douglas-Hamilton, whose generous support of good causes had brought many needy children to Letchworth, agreed to buy the bulk of the shares in a trust to help a new foundation. In this way Frensham Heights was started in 1925 with Miss King as the teaching head and Mrs. Ensor as the administrative head. The school was (and is) located in a mansion near Farnham in Surrey and was to be almost entirely a boarding school as compared with the combination of day and boarding pupils at Letchworth. The Charrington mansion at Frensham was very different from Arundale House and Farnham was no Garden City. Theosophical principle had to be reinterpreted in a very different setting, for Letchworth had been the community symbol of the new century on which Mrs. Ensor saw that the effort and the physical plant of the Theosophical Educational Trust could best be concentrated.

Mrs. Douglas-Hamilton died suddenly in 1927 and left her major portion of the Douglas-Hamilton Trust to her husband who did not share her concerns for Theosophical causes. In the circumstances Miss King and Mrs. Ensor resigned from Frensham and effectively all connection with Theosophy ends two years after the school started. Mr. Paul Roberts, who had been teaching for some years at St. George's, a co-educational school for boarders and day-pupils started by the Rev. Cecil Grant in 1907 at Harpenden, north of London, was appointed headmaster. Frensham continues to work under the Douglas-Hamilton Educational Trust with many of the Theosophical principles and practices unaltered insofar as they are general progressive principles too. Farnham is close to Petersfield and Bedales and a long way from Letchworth and in the last thirty-five years the connection and the rivalry between Frensham and Bedales have replaced any historical association with St. Christopher, the more particularly since the two headmasters who have succeeded Mr. Roberts, who retired after the end of the Second World War, have come from the Bedales staff.

To return to St. Christopher in 1925. With Mrs. Ensor and Miss King gone, taking a number of the children and one of the main financial supporters of the school with them, St. Christopher and the Theosophical Educational Trust were in severe difficulties. Still further hardships came when Miss Dodge, the American heiress, moved her allegiances from the Theosophical Society to the new group led by Krishnamurti whom Mrs. Besant had proclaimed in 1909, when he was a boy, as a new incarnation of Jesus Christ. Twenty years later Krishnamurti renounced this claim and Mrs. Besant had to accept his denials. He returned all that he could of the money, property, and valuables bequeathed to him and turned humbly and devoutly to teaching. Some Theosophists had found in him a leader with whom they wished to ally themselves and amongst these was Miss Dodge.

St. Christopher and the Theosophical Educational Trust found themselves by 1927 without the secure financial support and the executive leadership which they had had for ten years. Mr. Lyn Harris was appointed principal in 1926 and saw the whole project being gradually dismantled by the Trust under his eyes. In the autumn of 1929 he and his wife, who always worked with him, resigned in protest and this produced an objection from the parents who in many cases were prepared to withdraw their children. An arrangement was reached enabling Mr. and Mrs. Harris to float a company, the St. Christopher School Estate Ltd., which bought the school through a mortgage to the First Garden City Company and to a group of parents and friends and through a second mortgage to the Theosophical Educational Trust which the Trust later renounced in favour of the school. The St. Christopher School Estate Ltd. leased the property to the Harrises for use as a school, which enabled them to acquire large and suitable buildings at a small rental and from 1930 until 1956 the financial responsibility and all capital undertakings were borne by Mr. and Mrs. Harris themselves and the school grew from seven pupils in 1915 to three hundred and sixty in 1955. In 1956 Mr. and Mrs. Harris retired and handed over the responsibility of running the school to their son, Mr. N. K. Harris, and a public non-profit-making company,

St. Christopher School (Letchworth) Ltd. was registered with a board of governors, still essentially a family group.

IV

By 1918 there were at least the fifteen progressive schools we have mentioned. Fourteen of these were religious foundations but of the minority or fringe kind and at King Alfred's the rationalist pulse was strong, but a Theosophist headmaster in 1920 brought comparative religion over the threshold.

The New Education Fellowship was beginning to take shape by 1920 and although its development and influence come later, we must take note that there was already in other countries a radical school movement which arose out of the work of Reddie, Badley, and the rest. It was in existence by 1914 and provided a foundation on which the New Education Fellowship could build after the war. We are accustomed to think that progressive education has its origins in the work of Rousseau, Pestalozzi, de Fellenberg, Froebel, and Dewey and in a sense this is true as the theory of one or another of these outstanding men has been applied in different countries. But the international organization which provided a forum and a fellow-feeling originated in Great Britain and in Geneva in a non-political, idealistic movement with a tiny administrative staff and we must see how this came about.

Chapter Three

NEW SCHOOLS AND EUROPE

1890-1918

I

CECIL REDDIE said that three or four years after opening Abbots-holme in 1889 he needed some advice on developing classroom teaching and J. J. Findlay told him to visit Professor Wilhelm Rein at the University of Jena and this Reddie did at Easter 1893. He visited the Training School, intending to stay in Jena for two nights : 'We saw for the first time what teaching was and for a full fortnight we sat five mortal hours, one after the other, and drank in that which is creating modern Germany.'[1]

He read Rein's *Pädagogik im Grundriss* and saw in Herbartian theory 'a new instructional heaven and earth'. He met Rein and one of his tutors Dr. Hermann Lietz, a man of peasant stock who had studied both theology and pedagogy. Rein paid a short visit to Abbotsholme in 1896 and Reddie was able to arrange for Lietz to spend a year teaching at Abbotsholme as a result of which he published *Emlohstobba* in Berlin in 1897, a detailed account of a flawlessly harmonious Abbotsholme. The book had a considerable vogue in Germany and Switzerland and Reddie translated it into English.[2] The experience of the school had an immense effect on Lietz. One of his German colleagues wrote: 'To think of Lietz without C.R. is impossible. His experiences at Abbotsholme altered both himself and his aims.'[3]

In 1898 Lietz established the first of his *Landerziehungsheime* at

---

[1] C. Reddie, *Abbotsholme* (London, 1900), p. 115.
[2] Ibid., pp. 263-380.
[3] *Fifty Years of Abbotsholme*. Article by Alfred Andressen, who was one of Lietz's successors as Director of the Lietz Country Boarding Schools.

Ilsenburg in the Harz mountains in north mid-Germany, for boys and girls aged six to twelve years in the proportion of one girl to three boys. In 1901 in Thuringia nearly one hundred miles south-west of Ilsenburg he started Haubinda for boys aged thirteen to fifteen years, and in 1904 he completed the range by opening Bieberstein for boys aged sixteen to nineteen in the neighbourhood of Fulda in the Rhon mountains north-east of Frankfurt. Lietz was the Principal of all three schools while being headmaster at Bieberstein and according to Andressen he copied Reddie's work to its smallest detail although in German contexts something different has emerged. At Ilsenburg with the junior boys and girls the routine of rules and orders was kept to a minimum and the custom of a family community in houses of twelve or fifteen was to be the guide. In the curriculum there was as little formal teaching as possible and what we might now call projects or individual work was the method, a kind of guided experience. Religion and morals were presented through the family life, through stories from literature, and Christian teaching free from dogma. With the boys in the middle school at Haubinda, Lietz followed Reddie's lead in the agricultural and craft work and extended it to bring in local workmen and craftsmen or to send the boys to work with them. To Lietz, a farmer and the son of a farmer, this was near to the heart of education and the same actual and symbolic labour was continued at Bieberstein with the older boys whose curriculum also included more work in science and mathematics than was usual. Wilhelm Rein wrote a foreword to *Emlohstobba* in which he spoke of an English school 'which is carrying into practice the high aims so long familiar to us Germans in the works of our great teachers, Pestalozzi, Herbart, Froebel'. Lietz's own admissions and his imitation of Abbotsholme show that, whatever Rein might write of the great German teachers, Lietz thought that no German Abbotsholme existed in fact.

Dr. Erich Meissner had a unique experience of the Lietz schools and their history. He was a pupil at Ilsenburg under Kramer, the first headmaster after Lietz moved on to Haubinda in 1901. He then moved on in the normal sequence to the middle school where Marseille was headmaster and later he completed his schooling at Bieberstein. He studied at the Universities of Berlin and Göttingen and was contemplating an academic career for himself as an historian when he was invited to return to Haubinda as headmaster in 1924 straight from the University and the youngest man on the staff. Lietz had died in 1919 and the post-war confusion and depression had damaged the schools badly. Dr. Meissner remained at Haubinda until 1931, when he left to join Kurt Hahn at the Salem group of schools and with him Dr. Meissner worked for the rest of his career, as we shall later see.[4] Salaries in the Lietz schools were low but the devotion, versatility, and energy which Lietz and his wife displayed were often able to win a corresponding answer from their colleagues. As Dr. Meissner recalled, it was like being in an order, for life was simple and spartan.

Alfred Andressen was the director of the three Lietz schools in 1923 when a further group was founded, all but one relatively close to the existing schools, though nowadays the border of East and West Germany separates those that remain. Gebesee near Jena and Ettersburg near Weimar were founded in 1923, Buchenau near Bieberstein in 1924. Later a girls' school at Hohenwerda was started, also close to Bieberstein. In 1928, after Ilsenburg had closed, a new venture was begun on the Friesian island of Spiekeroog not far off the mainland from Bremerhaven where the rough climate and coastal storms made seamanship a main necessity in the school life of these boys of sixteen and over. An orphanage for boys and girls at Grovesmühle was begun in the Lietz group in the 1920s when after the war so many children without families had to be cared for in Germany.

These eight schools (Ilsenburg, Haubinda, Bieberstein, Ettersburg, Gebesee, Buchenau, Spiekeroog, and Hohenwerda) together with the orphanage at Grovesmühle, are the schools which were founded on Lietz's and so Abbotsholme's principles and they represent in themselves an export from Great Britain which has been too often invisible in discussing progressive education. Of the eight schools Ilsenburg closed after the First World War. Haubinda, Gebesee, and Ettersburg are, after the Second World War, in East Germany, the first two continuing as schools and the third not. Bieberstein, Buchenau, Spiekeroog, and Hohenwerda continue, the headquarters of the administration of the Lietz group being at Bieberstein.

Dr. Minna Specht, who had taught in Lietz schools between the wars and was interned in the Second World War in the Isle of Man, was brought back by the British authorities to Odenwaldschule after the war to regroup the Lietz schools, many of which had compromised with the Nazi party more than some supporters could permit — Frau

[4] Dr. Meissner, who died in 1964, lived in retirement at Hohenfels school near Salem, where he talked with the author.

Lietz herself withdrew from her association with the schools at that time.

Besides these there are several others which are family relations to the schools of Lietz and Reddie, the founders frequently being men who worked under Lietz and who as innovators found that Lietz's novelties were not theirs or else, having the prophet's impatience, they thought that he was changing too slowly. The history of radical change in education as in anything else is often a story of conflict and friction, as we have seen from Reddie, Devine, C. E. Rice, and the Theosophists. So frequently is this the case that it makes the achievement of J. H. Badley all the more remarkable, though even with him Bedales waters were at times distinctly choppy.

Gustav Wyneken and Paul Geheeb worked with Lietz in the earliest days of Ilsenburg and Haubinda but came to disagree with his opposition to co-education for adolescents. They also thought that the adult's responsibility in setting an example to and controlling the children gave the boys too little chance to take a full part in the running of the school. In 1906 Wyneken and Geheeb set up the Free School Community (*Freie Schulgemeinde*) at Wickersdorf, a co-educational school for children aged nine to nineteen with a good deal of freedom and weekly school meetings of teachers and pupils to deal with many matters of school government. In 1910 Paul and Edith Geheeb broke away from Wyneken and founded the New School at Odenwald where they worked for twenty-five years before they left Germany under Hitler for Switzerland. There they set up *L'École de l'Humanité* in which Geheeb worked till within a short while of his death in 1961.

Other schools were started early in the century by Lietz's men. In 1907 Marseille, the head of Haubinda, started his own boys' school at Bischofstein on a pattern very like Abbotsholme's. Lohmann went to Schondorf from Ilsenburg in 1905, Kramer went from Ilsenburg to Holzminden in 1909 to start the Landschulheim am Solling; Luserke from Wickersdorf founded Schule am Meer on the Friesian island of Juist close to Spiekeroog. A leading member of these non-Lietz schools in all their variety says of the present-day situation: 'There are today about twenty *Landerziehungsheime* and *Landschulheime* now. Only six or seven are of more than local importance.'

There were foundations in German Switzerland as well. In 1902 Clarisegg was founded by Werner Zuberbuhler, who had worked at Abbotsholme for a while and in Lietz schools. Herman Tobler founded Hof Oberkirch in 1906 and a French-Swiss Country Boarding School, *L'École Nouvelle de la Suisse Romande* was opened in the same year near Lausanne.

Sufficient has been said to show that Reddie through Lietz had helped to start a movement in Germany. When Reddie visited several of the *Lietz Stiftung* in 1924 at the age of sixty-six he found himself greeted as the *Gross-Vater* of the New School movement and this is no more than the truth although some of his grandchildren were far from the old man's views on religion or discipline or co-education.

One other name might be mentioned here for later reference. Kurt Hahn as a schoolboy about to go to Berlin University in 1902 met three senior Abbotsholme boys and went for a walking tour of the Tirol with them, led by his uncle. Here they told him of Reddie and Abbotsholme with such pride and enthusiasm that Hahn having read *Emlohstobba* thought how different such a school was from his own *Gymnasium* and how preferable. As he said, recalling this incident in 1962 to the present author: 'My fate cried out to me'.[5] Salem and Gordonstoun come later in this story, but Hahn admits that, although he never met Reddie and differed from him in many things, Reddie was nevertheless important to him through those boys long ago and through Lietz, whose schools have much in common with Salem, although Hahn never met Lietz either — he died in 1919 before Hahn had taken up his work at Salem.

The Country Boarding Schools turned from the towns, from the day schools, and sought to regain by labour and living the country ways and natural virtues. This feeling for nature, history, and the good earth was, of course, a romanticized sentiment and in Germany the intensity of passionate folk-lore modulates too easily into mystique. In 1904 Berlin students and intellectuals formed companies of 'wandering birds' (*Wandervögel*) whose purpose was to re-discover the country, the peasantry, the customs, and the lore of the immemorial German land. In 1933 the *Hitlerjugend* had a tighter political organization and a mass compulsion, but the Germanic mists swirled around again.

In the first decade of this century the young people walked the forests and hills at weekends and in the holidays, they camped in the woods, read poems and legends, sang folk songs, met the countrymen,

[5] This incident is also reported in Abbotsholme sources and in Stanley Unwin, *Truth about a Publisher*.

joined in country dancing. The older people often felt this was leading to general unsettlement and moral breakdown and undoubtedly there was a hectic and erotic quality in the movement. There was also an ascetic and high-minded strain — the puritan improvers who shunned alcohol and tobacco and were concerned with hardihood and fitness and the regeneration of the Fatherland. It is easy to see that the *Wandervögel* of 1910 had much in common with the outlook of the Country Boarding School. Gustav Wyneken even proposed a merger of the two movements so that young people of all kinds and in all circumstances could learn from one another, pamphleteering against the domination of adults and the consequent subjection of children in school and in the home. He advocated the extension of his Wickersdorf Free School Community to enable other schools to lead a life of freedom with liberally-minded teachers often taking their pupils away from the circumscribed and authoritarian life of the classroom to live and learn like the outdoor *Wandervögel*. In 1913 the short-lived *Freideutsche Jugend Bewegung* was founded at Hoher Meissner taking as its oath : 'We seek to order our lives with full personal responsibility and in concord with the truth that is within us.'

Distant as the comparison is, the nearest British equivalent would probably be the Boy Scout Movement which started in this country in 1908 and to which Reddie in particular was quick to respond, for the Movement sought to promote good citizenship through woodcraft, camping, nature study, and the outdoor life, a combination of scouting crafts with a code of honour like a medieval knight's. Even the sectional organization by age into Wolf Cubs, Scouts, and Rover Scouts was pleasing to Abbotsholme for in this and most of the earlier features the Scout Movement gave a particular form to principles which the school had proclaimed from its beginnings.

II

When Patrick Geddes was studying in Paris in the early 1870s, at T. H. Huxley's suggestion he met Edmond Demolins the French sociologist and disciple of Frédéric Le Play. Ten years later Geddes was back in Edinburgh and at one of the University summer courses in August 1894 Demolins was present and there also present was Reddie and the two men were introduced by Geddes. Demolins subjected Reddie to a close interrogation and each has a record of the meeting :

We [Reddie] met, for the first time, M. Demolins, little dreaming, as he pertinaciously catechized us about our school, that he meditated incorporating our chance conversation in a book.[6]

Demolins wrote up the conversation at length in *La Science Sociale*[7] and from this it is clear that Reddie and Demolins must together have had a verbal marathon. In 1897 Demolins incorporated the account in his book published in Paris *A Quoi Tient la Supériorité des Anglo-Saxons?* which was translated into English in 1898[8] and in which he tries to demonstrate that the Anglo-Saxons have been far more successful than Frenchmen as colonisers in Canada, America, India; more prosperous as traders; more stable in their governments; more venturesome as explorers. Demolins sees Socialism as limiting both the risks and the opportunities open to a man and considers this kind of collectivism to be the natural enemy of enterprise. Despite the Revolution, Frenchmen are not Socialists, says Demolins, and they rely on their family, their connections, a safe post in the Government, for their security and for this attitude of mind he coins the word 'communitarian'. The third, and for Demolins, the desired classification, he calls particularist, characterized by qualities of independence, resource, and energy. It is in these that the reasons for Anglo-Saxon leadership are to be found and to support the thesis he analyzed deficiencies in French attitudes and competence, showing in each case how the Anglo-Saxons have developed the compensating efficiencies. The Germans come in for even less flattering treatment than the French, and as one reviewer remarked: 'His chapter on education in Germany and the Emperor's views thereon, will more than suffice to cause [the book's] confiscation beyond the frontier.'[9]

Demolins attributes the superiority in part to the habits of family training and the education provided in England. He chooses three schools to illustrate his point, Abbotsholme, Bedales, and the Colonial College, Hollesley Bay, an agricultural college near Felixstowe which a few years later (1904) was converted into a community for the unemployed under the Central Unemployment Committee. Many English reviewers took up this selection and the *Journal of Education* said:

What does astound us is that it never seems to have dawned on

---

[6] *Abbotsholme*, p. 118.　　　　　　　[7] Oct. 1894.

[8] *Anglo-Saxon Superiority: to what is it due?* (London, 1898).

[9] *The Westminster Gazette*, 15 Nov. 1897.

M. Demolins that these schools, so far from being typical of English schools, are almost unique of their kind and that three schools (it would be difficult to name a fourth) are a narrow and unstable basis on which to rest a glorification of Anglo-Saxondom.[10]

Demolins had visited Bedales after his Edinburgh conversations with Reddie and had been so impressed by what he saw there that in 1896 he sent his son Joseph Jules to the school as a pupil and followed this by establishing near Verneuil in Normandy *L'École des Roches* in 1899. Badley remembers him as a stocky man who was a better talker than a listener, sure of himself and his ideas and 'impatient not only of contradiction but of any slowness in acceptance of the principles he laid down'.[11] In France, Demolins and his associates at the school were considered *des bêtes curieuses*.

In 1901 Demolins wrote a second book to explain the provenance of *L'École des Roches* and to outline its programme. This was *L'Éducation Nouvelle*[12] and the book is freely illustrated with pictures principally of Abbotsholme and Bedales. Joseph Jules returned from Bedales in 1899 to finish his schooling at *L'École des Roches* and Demolins recommends to French parents that they continue to send their boys to Abbotsholme and Bedales while also drawing their attention to the French equivalent at Verneuil-sur-Arve complete with *Champ de Foot-Ball et Champ de Cricquet*. His account of the new-style schoolmaster could well have been taken from his son's experience at Bedales[13] and 'La Vie de l'Ècole Nouvelle décrite par les élèves'[14] is taken almost entirely from the *Bedales Record*.

It is to be noted that *L'École des Roches* was a boys' school, which fits the French situation more conveniently, but in this, in 1898 they were also following the Bedales plan, for the English school did not change to co-education until after Joseph Jules left. A few girls were admitted later when Demolins had left the running of the school to the new headmaster, but this was not co-education as it developed at Bedales. The school continues and thrives today.[15]

---

[10] Nov. 1897. The reviewer would have been even more astounded had he known that Demolins never visited Abbotsholme, but rested his account on his talk with Reddie. For similar strictures see *Manchester Guardian*, 11 May 1897; *The Spectator*, 18 Sept. 1897; *Academy*, 24 Sept. 1898; and *The Westminster Gazette*, 30 Sept. 1898.

[11] *Memories and Reflections*, p. 203.   [12] Librairie de Paris, 1901.

[13] See pp. 52–98.   [14] Op. cit., pp. 196–258.

[15] There are accounts of the work of the school in Conference reports, in *The New Era* during the 1920s and in *Pour L'Ère Nouvelle* at the same period.

There were two or three other schools in France, but *L'École des Roches* is the important foundation because it followed upon Demolins's controversial thesis of Anglo-Saxon superiority, and the place of Abbotsholme and Bedales in bringing this about. The book had immense publicity[16] and as a result the two English schools had many visitors from a great range of countries. There were countless foreign press notices and an avalanche of letters from all parts of the world asking for information and applying for admission. Both schools responded as far as they could, but Reddie had no intention of letting Abbotsholme become a 'Cosmopolitan School' and Badley said that if every pupil who came from overseas was counted, whether from the Commonwealth or not, of the first one thousand four hundred former pupils of Bedales just under 20 per cent were 'foreigners', which is significantly high.

At this point we can say that the New Schools, Abbotsholme and Bedales, had international reputations by 1900, especially on the Continent of Europe and served as a pattern for a number of schools in Germany, Switzerland, France, Belgium, and Holland. The Quaker schools and the Theosophical schools had international sympathies by reason of the faith and works of their parent bodies. Badminton from 1911 was an internationally-minded school. The time was ripe to try to bring them all together in some way.

III

A young Swiss, Adolf Ferrière, read *A Quoi Tient la Superiorité des Anglo-Saxons?* in 1898 when he was nineteen years of age. His father, a noted doctor, had been one of the vice-presidents of the International Red Cross, and the young man had similar humanitarian aspirations. He had a comprehensive university training in philosophy, sociology, and zoology and his doctorate was in sociology. Through Demolins, Ferrière first heard of Reddie and Abbotsholme and he resolved that teaching was his vocation with the New School movement as his chosen environment. He went to Germany and started teaching under Hermann Lietz at Ilsenburg in 1900 where he read *Emlohstobba* and he had the opportunity to meet Reddie at Haubinda in 1901, sensing his intellectual daring and magnetism at once.

[16] It ran to ten impressions in the first year.

In 1899 Ferrière started the International Bureau of New Schools in Switzerland at Les Pléiades-sur-Blonay in the canton of Vaud. He had no staff and had to rely mainly on his own money for expenses, but through conducting a massive correspondence and making visits when his teaching duties permitted (he later moved to Clarisegg, the Swiss Country Boarding School) he built up an unrivalled range of contacts and over the years he tried to clarify the definition of a New School, for there were many variations on the Reddie–Lietz theme. At one point Ferrière defined such a school as 'a self-governing country boarding school in which all education is based on personal interest and experience, and intellectual work is combined with manual activities in workshop and fields'.

Ferrière had expansive aims for his International Bureau of New Schools. He hoped to make a list of educational societies throughout the world and to encourage reformers to meet together to exchange ideas and information and to address conferences convened to meet them. He also hoped to establish a multilingual periodical on education and to found research institutes at various centres, all of these undertakings being aimed at facilitating public knowledge and dissemination of progressive ideas in education with a consequential effect on national legislation. Nearly all his large-scale aims had to be shelved with the outbreak of the War, throughout which he was able to keep his records going only to lose them all in a disastrous fire in 1918. The Bureau, however, continued to work alongside the developing New Education Fellowship from its inception in 1921 and Ferrière became in 1922 the editor of *Pour L'Ère Nouvelle*, the French version of *New Era*, the Fellowship's periodical. In 1926 the International Bureau of New Schools merged with the International Bureau of Education which had been founded in Geneva a year before by a grant from the Rockefeller Foundation and placed under the auspices of the *Institut Jean-Jacques Rousseau*. In 1929–30 the *Institut* was officially supported by the authorities of Geneva and the other cantons while retaining its position as an independent organization and thus ceased to have to rely upon voluntary money.

The publications of the International Bureau of Education no longer have a particular interest in the New Schools and Ferrière's work has been carried forward since 1922 largely through the New Education Fellowship, *Pour L'Ère Nouvelle*, *The New Era*, and the German equivalent *Das Werdende Zeitalter*. His expansive aims for the Bureau in 1912 have been realised up to a point in the Fellowship's programme. Ferrière died in 1960 having started and participated in many New School ventures and still maintained a phenomenal literary output including forty books, countless articles, and a correspondence often averaging four thousand letters a year.[17]

In the *New Era* of January 1921 Ferrière summed up the results of an investigation which had taken him a long time to complete.[18] He had built up a kind of questionnaire intended to delineate the characteristics of New Schools and by correspondence or visits had obtained information in answer to each of his thirty points. He awarded a mark for each condition that seemed to be met and in the end worked out what might be considered a Progressiveness Quotient which he states. It is, technically, a very crude investigation for it lays down what a New School ought to incorporate and then, leaving aside the problem of trying to give meaningful answers to some of the conditions, assumes that the 'pass mark' is 50 per cent, so schools which score 15 and above are to be considered in the category New School and those who score less are not. From our point of view the main interest is to see set down what were thought to be the distinctive features of these schools under the general headings of organization, physical life, intellectual life, organization of studies, social education, aesthetic and moral education:

1. The school is a laboratory for experimental pedagogy.
2. It is a boarding school, while it is admitted that family influence, if good, is better for children than any boarding school.
3. It is in the country.
4. There are families of ten or fifteen with a man and woman or at least a woman to act as house-parents.
5. It is co-educational.
6. At least one and a half hours each day are spent in some handicraft.
7. Carpentry is the first of these crafts.
8. There is opportunity for optional work.
9. Physical training is to be done in the open, the children being naked or nearly so. There are to be facilities for games and athletics.
10. Journeys on foot and bicycle, camping out with the preparation of meals, are all encouraged.

[17] See an obituary notice in *The New Era*, Aug. 1960.
[18] There was a second list in *The New Era* of July 1925.

11. In schoolwork reasoning is encouraged rather than memory.
12. Education is at first general with specialization following later, at first through favourite occupations and then through capacities related to a future profession.
13. Teaching is based on facts and the conduct of inquiries encouraging observation.
14. Teaching rests on the personal initiative of the pupil.
15. Teaching takes the instinctive interest of the child into account.
16. Children should undertake research in newspapers, books.
17. There is collective work in well-produced class books which can be an improvement on class text books.
18. Intellectual training is mainly in the morning 8-12 noon. The afternoon is free for individual and independent work.
19. A few subjects are taught in a term.
20. These subjects are taught each day, by activity methods where possible.
21. Children are expected to use their judgment in free moral choice with a mimimum of control.
22. The next best thing to a democracy of children and teachers is a constitutional monarchy. Here the children elect the prefects.
23. Everyone takes part in mutual aid in and for the community.
24. Creative abilities are encouraged.
25. Any punishment or reprimand is related to the offence.
26. Comparison is with the child's own earlier standard, not in competition with the standards of others.
27. The school is a place of beauty.
28. There is music in instruments, singing, orchestra and concerts.
29. Stories are told to younger children to awaken their moral judgment.
30. There is a spiritual ideal and a tolerance of diverse views. Religious attitudes are non-confessional or inter-confessional.

This is a sufficiently daunting list but Dr. Ovide Decroly pointed out that it omitted to state that parents should co-operate in the management of the school. I should also add that, surprisingly, work on the land is not mentioned as such but is presumably included under physical work, optional work, or mutual aid for the community. Under the original thirty headings, Odenwaldschule came first with maximum points, Bedales gained 25, Abbotsholme 22½ narrowly ahead of the Lietz schools, and *L'École des Roches* as only just in the approved list with 17½. Incidentally, only Abbotsholme and Bedales were listed from England, all the others being 'foreign' which indicates how in-complete the coverage of Ferrière's Bureau was at that time, although he says in 1922 in *Pour L'Ère Nouvelle*[19] that sixty-seven schools may be included in the list of New Schools with Abbotsholme as parent and that a complete bibliography on progressive education at that time would contain over three hundred items.[20]

IV

There were New Schools in Canada and the U.S.A. many of which Reddie saw when he crossed the Atlantic in 1906 and in 1919 one of the first *Bulletins* of the newly-formed American Progressive Education Association described the work of the International Bureau of New Schools, calling particular attention to Reddie and Abbotsholme, to Demolins and *L'École des Roches*, to Lietz and the *Landerziehungsheime*.[21] The tentative association of the American Association with the New Education Fellowship developed quickly in the 1920s, but for the moment the point to make is that the impulses from England's New Schools spread principally to Europe from 1890 to 1920. To put it over-simply but not unfairly, Abbotsholme and Reddie and to a lesser extent Bedales and Badley were originators to the Country Boarding School movement in Germany, Switzerland, France, Holland, and Belgium. The schools were started often by sparks of conflict struck between enthusiasts and in any case no new experiment wants for long to dwell in the shadow of the orthodoxy from which it sprang. So Bieberstein was not for long another Abbotsholme, Wickersdorf was not another Haubinda, Odenwald another Ilsenburg. But individua-lists though they might be, there was a family likeness; and the fellow feeling existed that pioneers have for one another over against the cohorts of the conventional.

Reddie admitted a deep debt to Rein and to Herbart and to German initiative, solidarity and organization. But through Lietz, Ferrière and later Hahn he repaid it. Badley's influence was mainly in the first place with Demolins but as Reddie's temperamental waywardness diminished

---

[19] 'Les Écoles Nouvelles à la Campagne,' July 1922. Many articles are to be found, Ferrière says, in the journal *Éducation* published in Paris.

[20] In the 1925 list over thirty English and Scottish schools are listed, together with a number of state-supported schools which have progressive features.

[21] L. A. Cremin, *Transformation of the School* (New York, 1961), p. 248.

his and Abbotsholme's influence, Badley's stability and co-educational daring caused his and Bedales's influence to increase.

The post-war international organization for progressive education becomes more diffuse but there can be no mistake as to the examples by which the European impulses were activated before the First World War.

Chapter Four

PREFACE TO THE POST-WAR

SURGENCE

THE work of Maria Montessori and of Homer Lane made a deep impression on progressive education in this country after the First World War. Each of them claimed to have rediscovered the significance of freedom for children but their practical conclusions were vastly different, so variant that without misprision they may be called the two magnetic poles round which for a time the lines of force in English radical education formed themselves.

I

Maria Montessori was born in Rome in 1870 and spent her early years in the uncertain world of hard-won Italian unity. She was in the mould of European feminists and in 1894 she qualified in the University of Rome as the first woman Doctor of Medicine in Italy. She worked in asylums and psychiatric clinics and became especially interested in feeble-minded children for whom she tried to devise a training which would give them the best opportunity to use the limited capacities they had. She read, and later translated into Italian, the works of Séguin on the treatment of idiots[1] and the earlier classical account by Itard of his attempt to educate the Savage Boy of Aveyron.[2] There were others like J. R. Pereire and Giuseppe Sergi in whose work Dr. Montessori was interested, but it is Séguin whose writing and design of inquiry meant most. Another pioneer in the education of young children,

[1] E. Séguin, *Idiocy and its Treatment by the Physiological Method* (1866); *Traitement Moral, Hygiène et Éducation des Idiots* (1846); *New Facts & Remarks on Idiocy* (1870); *Report on Education* (1876).
[2] J. E. M. G. Itard, *An Historical Account of the Discovery and Education of a Savage Man* (translation, 1802).

Margaret McMillan, also read Séguin but, of course, without Montessori's professional insight. We cannot sketch Séguin's method and assessment here in detail, but two cardinal principles must be mentioned. Instinct, emotion, and the senses provide the materials with which comprehension may be built. But, and importantly, the comprehension is the child's and it is most secure and resilient when he is able to initiate his own experience. With idiots, says Séguin, a teacher will enforce obedience by coercion more often than with normal children :

> *Liberty* and *will* are two words which are permissible only when two preceding words are understood : *obedience* and *authority* words which are too often divorced and which, when divorced have no meaning.[3]

Séguin has a grasp of the growth and cumulative mastery of a child's mental, moral, and social development and he says that the aim of education should be not passivity, but liberty, the first condition of which is the desire to be free. When this desire is combined with confidence in one's own competence within a certain range, then the normal pressure of meaningful activity will indefinitely extend the competence and, in normal people, the range. So, to restate the two key principles in Séguin's work, the first has to do with training and directing or redirecting basic impulses, using the detailed knowledge of each child's neural, muscular, and motor mechanisms to the full and observing these working in his actions while bringing the same precision to bear on his sensory and intellectual training. The second principle gives scope to the child's initiative and curiosity operating within a contrived 'educational' framework, but also accepting the chance, intricate, dense experience gained from the influence of child upon child as well as of child and adult upon one another.

When Montessori was working with feeble-minded children in the Orthophrenic School, which she conducted in Rome from 1898 to 1900, education for her was at first concerned with preventing the ultimate consequences of degeneration and disease and with the removal of obstacles. Her apparatus aimed at improving discrimination of length, size, weight, shape, colour, texture, and, like Séguin, she had to perfect both the apparatus and a precise method of observation, at first leaving little individual scope to the backward child until necessary skills had been mastered as tools. She began with normal children by providing

[3] *Traitement . . . des Idiots*, p. 651.

a physical and educational environment in which things are constructed to make use of each child's physical and sense mechanisms and the regime is ordered so that the children are confronted by but not forced into dealing with these challenges. She found, of course, that normal children could much more quickly see the purpose of the tasks they were set and connect up the knowledge they obtained from the different pieces of apparatus. McCallister goes so far as to say that only then for the first time Montessori envisaged freedom as a means of enabling the pupil to educate himself. She was very successful in improving the standard of reading and writing of her backward children and began to wonder why normal children did not do much better than they did.

In 1907 a philanthropic organization in Rome conceived the idea of having schools attached to tenement buildings in which young children between the ages of three and seven could play and work under the care of a teacher who also lived in the tenement and Dr. Montessori undertook the educational direction of the enterprise. For four years her Children's Houses enabled her to test her methods upon normal children and to perfect her theory of the teacher as background directress rather than pedagogue. She presented the fruits of this experience in the book translated into English as *The Montessori Method*.[4]

Her methods and her apparatus aroused world-wide interest, support and criticism. She was uncompromising in defence of her ideas, taking the line that hers was a scientific approach to child development built without any predisposing theory except loyalty to the truth and a readiness to test the results of experiment and that the same could not be said of the works of most other theorists on child development. But her fiercest denunciation was reserved for conventional class teachers and believers in 'discipline'. In her later writings this became apocalyptic:

> In fact in every educational ideal, in all pedagogy up to our own time, the word education has been almost always synonymous with the word punishment. The end was always to subject the child to the adult. . . . Thus the child repeats the Passion of Christ. . . . The mistress [in the classroom] commands that group of souls, with no witness or control. She will shut the door. . . .

4 The Third Edition is newly translated and entitled *The Discovery of the Child*. It is published from Adyar, Madras, the Indian headquarters of the Theosophical Society.

D

Henceforth those delicate, trembling limbs are held to the wood for more than three hours of anguish, three and three for many days and months and years.

The child's hands and feet are fastened to the desk by stern looks which hold them motionless as the nails of the cross in the feet of Christ. . . . And when into the mind athirst for truth and knowledge the ideas of the teacher are forcibly driven, as he wills, the little head humbled in submission will seem to bleed as by a crown of thorns.[5]

Written when she was sixty-five this is not scientific refutation and it reveals the intensity with which the Dottoressa felt about children, her own work, and conventional parents and teachers. As we shall see, there was also a battle between two armies of freedom which we may call loosely the Montessorians and the other educational radicals. Madame Montessori developed the didactic apparatus and it had to be used complete and not as an incidental aid. She trained her followers personally and as her two staunchest present-day supporters say:

Though her attitude was bitterly resented at the time, Dr. Montessori was probably far-sighted in creating first of all, a body of disciples all trained personally by herself, and in resisting the many facile temptations to go too quickly, for fear of going more slowly in the end.[6]

She designed the furniture, she put the child in the way of teaching himself in his own good time under the discreet control of the directress. The shift of focus was astounding and there were many in England who testified to it. Miss Finlay Johnson, Edmond Holmes's 'Egeria' of the Sussex village, had completed her experiment 'before the name of Montessori had been whispered in this country'[7] but MacMunn says in the Preface to this same book: 'As the doctrines of Rousseau were to the social revolution of yesterday, so, it seems to many of us, the doctrines of Montessori will be to the revolution of tomorrow.'[8]

Edmund Holmes wrote for the Board of Education a warmly favourable report on Montessori's work and in 1912 told the Rev. Cecil Grant, head of the relatively conservative co-educational school St. George's

[5] Maria Montessori, *The Secret of Childhood* (Calcutta, 1936), pp. 274, 279, 281–2.
[6] Mario M. Montessori and C. A. Claremont, 'Montessori and the Deeper Freedom', in *Year Book of Education* (1957), p. 426.
[7] N. MacMunn, *A Path to Freedom in the School* (London, 1914), p. 45.
[8] Op. cit., p. 7.

at Harpenden of the Dottoressa's Roman school which Grant visited in 1913 : 'I knew that I was in the presence of a greater than Pestalozzi and Froebel.'[9]   On his return he roused Harpenden to start a Montessori class adjacent to the senior school and persuaded the originator of the movement to visit Harpenden and speak at a special meeting in 1919.

In the first issue of the journal which a year later became *The New Era* there appears a statement by Mrs. Beatrice Ensor, the Editor : ' In our opinion the Montessori System is a most valuable element in the forward movement in Education, and we propose to devote a few pages to this subject every quarter.'[10]   Mrs. Ensor's Assistant Editor was A. S. Neill and of that more later.   Professor Culverwell of the University of Dublin had published in 1913 as 'a keen enthusiast and careful critic' a book on the new movement.[11]   In 1920 Dr. Percy Nunn wrote of the contrast between the bondage of old methods and the calm, happy, absorbed industry of the Montessori class before which he thought 'the most cautious observer . . . would find it hard to remain a sceptic.'[12]   In 1919 Dr. Montessori conducted a training course in London and about one thousand inquiries were made but only three hundred could be admitted.   A Montessori Committee led to organized support in this country in pre-war days and schools were started in many places for children of nursery school and infant school age. While the Montessori methods were being worked out with older children and for adolescents it is mainly with three to seven year olds that they have gained their position in England.   Mrs. Ensor and the Theosophical Fraternity in Education, and later the Trust, found Madame Montessori's emphasis on the child's freedom to grow, to learn, and to teach himself, in harmony with their views and it is no wonder to find a Montessori nursery school and children's house at St. Christopher, Letchworth.   Mr. and Mrs. Lyn Harris had had a similar school at Badminton before they moved to Letchworth.   From 1917 Bedales had one of the best known Junior Houses in England at Dunhurst run by Mrs. Fish and later Miss Clarke on Montessori lines. King Alfred's has had a Montessori department for fifty years and so has St. George's, Harpenden, although here the junior school is a

9 C. Grant, *St. George's School : A Retrospect* (Address to St. George's Parents' Association, 5 July 1941), p. 20.

10 *Education for the New Era*, vol. i, no. 1, Jan. 1920, p. 11.

11 E. P. Culverwell, *Montessori Principles & Practice* (London, 1913).

12 T. P. Nunn, *Education : Its Data and First Principles* (London, 1920), p. 101.

separate organization. Some of the Friends' Schools have had preparatory departments run mainly on Montessori lines at least for a while.

The radical schools were active in developing Montessori interests in England but the militant Montessori movement cannot really be said to have swept the country. Old battles have led to treaties, truces, modifications, and near-mergers, but for the moment we must look back to the 1920s to understand how severe the conflicts were.

There were four main kinds of objector to Montessorianism. First, the out-and-out opponent of a system which, as was so often said, represented a 'go-as-you-please' regime for the children — teachers and adults generally were resigning the authority they ought to exert. Second, there were those who criticized parts of the system — the apparent discouragement of individual imagination in the child in the interest of precision, the apparent discrediting of class teaching in the interest of auto-didactic apparatus. Third were those who were already committed to another system, like Charlotte Mason who says in a summary of her method as seen in the work of the Parents' National Educational Union:

> When we say that 'education is an atmosphere' we do not mean that a child should be isolated in what may be called a 'child-environment' especially adapted and prepared, but that we should take into account the educational value of the natural home atmosphere both as regards persons and things, and should let him live freely among his proper conditions. It stultifies a child to bring down his world to the 'child's level'.[13]

Cecil Grant, after returning in 1913 from his visit to the Montessori Centre in Rome intended to go to see Miss Mason of Ambleside, 'whose experimental method was our nearest approach to Dr. Montessori's scientific discovery. . . . Before I could do so, an enemy had sown tares in her mind and she became the Dottoressa's most formidable opponent.'[14]

Margaret McMillan, who with her sister Rachel founded an open-air nursery school for poor children in Deptford in 1914, and who was founder and first President of the Nursery Schools Association in 1923,

[13] *A Short Synopsis of the Educational Philosophy Advanced by the Founder of the Parents' National Educational Union* (n.d.).
[14] Grant, *St. George's School*, p. 21.

wrote in 1926 that many people were suggesting that these schools were the product of the Montessori movement. While admitting that Madame Montessori was 'the most successful and popular educational leader of our time' she thought that the nursery school was nearer to the ideas of Froebel than Montessori but that, in any case, it was really a new entity : 'The Nursery School is itself—no part or element of any other thing. For lack of plain speaking we have seen the new birth strangled entirely between the older societies who do not represent it. This must end.'[15]

A former student said of Margaret McMillan that she was convinced that a child's imagination was of primary importance in the growth of his own understanding and education and she was equally convinced that Dr. Montessori had left this out of her reckoning. This conviction was apparently so emotionally charged that she would brook no discussion of the matter. The same writer quotes Margaret McMillan as follows : 'We (Dr. Montessori and Miss McMillan) have nothing in common. My educational system and hers are entirely different. I do not want her name to be used in connection with my work.'[16]

The fourth group of objectors was small but most radical of all, and A. S. Neill is the most obvious example. Where the first group objected because there was too much freedom in Montessori schools, the fourth objected because there was too little. Writing in *The New Era* as Mrs. Ensor's Assistant Editor from the Dalcroze School in Dresden, Neill said in 1921 :

One thing pleases me : among Dalcrozians there does not appear to be that unfortunate Montessorian habit of waiting for guidance from the Fountain-head. I see Montessorianism becoming a dead, apparatus-ridden system. . . . Thank heaven there is no apparatus required for Eurhythmics!'[17]

Neill thought Montessori did not really leave the children free at all but simply disguised her moulding control. McCallister takes a

[15] Margaret McMillan, 'The Nursery School', Child Study Society, London. *Journal of Proceedings*, vol. vi, 1926, p. 47.
[16] 'A Former Student' writing in G. A. N. Lowndes (ed.), *Margaret McMillan* (London, 1960), p. 33. This is a Centenary Volume produced by the Nursery Schools Association a century after Margaret McMillan's birth.
[17] *The New Era*, vol. 2, no. 8, Oct. 1921, p. 221.

similar position on a more theoretical examination of the Montessorian theory and practice:

> ... one looks in vain for any definite recognition of those differentiations of the environment which are necessary for the growth of strongly individual tastes and qualities. There seems no room for any real self-determination of the forms which growth shall take. The pupil of eleven or twelve years usually shows a decided tendency to enter upon a higher form of spiritual integration than the Montessori exercises permit.[18]

Montessori had shifted the focus from the teacher to the child more completely than any other educationalist. The teacher as expositor, as inspirer, as initiator, as example, is at a minimum and the child teaches himself to conquer an ingenious and exciting set of problems with built-in answers. Make-believe and fantasy and anti-social aggressiveness are beyond the customary standard deviation which may be permitted in the group.

Montessori represents a biological individualism in the midst of the group and has produced an excitingly conceived rationalist training for small children. The ferment of ideas and practice which she helped to stir up resulted in some passionate conflicts of dogma, nevertheless the concern for knowledge of child development and enlightened educational procedure has gone furthest and spread most widely in work with pre-adolescents. Pestalozzi, Freud, and Froebel have their place of honour in this outcome and so too has Montessori, though in the 1920s it was mainly the radical schools that gave her recognition in England.

II

In 1912 Mr. George Montagu, later the Earl of Sandwich, visited some of the Junior Republics which had grown up in the United States with a view to seeing if the same kind of community might be set up in England. He was greatly impressed by what he saw, and his uncle, then Earl of Sandwich, offered Flowers Farm, an unoccupied holding in Dorsetshire near Dorchester, as a home for the new venture, the English version of the George Junior Republic. A committee was formed of people interested both in penal reform and in progressive

[18] W. J. McCallister, *The Growth of Freedom in Education* (London, 1931), p. 430.

educational ideas and they asked Mr. Homer Lane, an American who had worked in the Ford Junior Republic with success, to come to England and advise them and the first superintendent, Harold Large, on setting up the Little Commonwealth. He came in 1913 and stayed to replace Large as the leader of the whole enterprise, his wife and family joining him before the end of the year.

W. R. George had been a holiday-time worker with tough and often delinquent youths and later he and his wife set up a permanent residential community at Freeville in New York State for boys over the age of twelve, which he subsequently raised to sixteen, a Junior Republic which was copied in a number of other parts of America.[19]   He was no permissive psychologist and for a considerable time, as he says, he had not sufficient faith in the boys he worked with to delegate to them any real powers of self-government.   His early acts of generosity to individual boys did not produce a good spirit in the Republic or a general respect for other people's property.   George concluded that an economic basis for the life of the community was essential, and work ought to be done for wages both to keep the community going and clean, but even more importantly to enable the boys to acquire and value possessions.   There were, of course, lazy and thieving members of the community, but George found that the boys were far more zealous in seeing that their own laws were applied than they were with any of his devising.   In the end George gave up thrashing and disciplining and passed over the administration of punishment to the community who, through a judge and jury of citizens, maintained order with some rigour.   People who lazed and so were paupers in the Republic on the charge of the taxpayers were shocked by a law passed through the legislature saying that if boys who could work did not do so they could be left to starve to death.

The community was organized like a state with a constitution based on the American Constitution and incorporated a judicature, a legislature, a police force, a civil service (with appropriate examinations for membership), a miniature army with wooden rifles, and a gaol. George was the first President and adults at first took the main senior offices. The gradual relinquishing of these positions in favour of the boys was part of the educational technique of the community and, as George frankly confesses, he proceeded in this and in other ways as his own

[19] See W. R. George, *Citizens Made and Remade* (1913); *The Junior Republic: Its History and Ideals* (1910).

understanding and insight grew. The boys worked from 8.30 a.m. to
12 noon and were paid according to their output in the Republic's own
currency and instruction was offered in school for part of the day.
McCallister has this comment to offer:

> The Junior Republic, then, is the history of a successful attempt to
> take boys at their own level and to lead them gradually to perceive
> the justice and relevancy of communal demands. Its evolution shows
> that community control is a much more influential and efficacious
> force in the adolescent life than the old method of adult domination.
> Control of this kind frees many of the life forces and gives them
> glimpses of reasonable and relevant lines of self-assertion.[20]

George's methods spread elsewhere in the United States and were
tried in schools, clubs and prisons in other countries as well. Homer
Lane claimed that he came to his similar solutions in Detroit about the
same time without any knowledge of George's work.

The story of the Little Commonwealth has been well told by Miss
Bazeley and by Mr. Wills.[21] The community beginning in the autumn
of 1913 was for boys and girls, as distinct from the Ford Republic
which Lane had run in Detroit for boys only, and they were all difficult
and usually delinquent children. From the chaos of noise and aggression the children were supposed to discover the need for some kind of
law and from the readiness of some children to break the law the community was expected to see the need for order and so grew up the
parliament and the court. But the turmoil and disorder that occurred
before these decisions were even remotely accepted are painfully clear
in Miss Bazeley's and Lane's accounts.[22] Through it all Lane says he
preserved outward calm and watched and by 1916 the citizens had
assumed entire responsibility for their government, the reason for this
being that in the Commonwealth the children were encouraged both in
good actions and bad ones. Lane claims that he took no authoritative
role but really left the children to learn how to be citizens and how, as
officials, to deal with brazen defiance. James the destroyer, whose
ferocious resentment encouraged by Lane was vented in breaking cups,
plates, and saucers, was finally tested to a shattering climax by the offer

[20] McCallister, op. cit., pp. 518–19.

[21] E. T. Bazeley, *Homer Lane and the Little Commonwealth* (London, 1928 and 1948).
W. David Wills, *Homer Lane* (London, 1964).

[22] Homer Lane, *Four Lectures on Childhood: The Age of Loyalty* (ed. Rev. H. H.
Symonds).

of Lane's gold watch to smash which he furiously refused to do. In the traumatic catharsis (which loses nothing in the telling on the printed page and must in the original lecture have had the audience by the throat) according to Lane, James worked off his delayed self-assertive tendencies and caught up with his new social responsibilities.[23] This is the justification for encouraging children both in their good and their bad actions, because only so will they discover how to discard futile and false ideals.

Lord Lytton, of the Executive Committee of the Little Commonwealth, writes that there were three principles in the experiment which could be of universal application. The first was the law of love in the sense that Lane was on the side of each child, prepared to approve and champion him in whatever he did, believing that 'badness' was simply misdirected goodness. The second principle was to teach the citizens that there is no such thing as absolute freedom because we can never escape the consequence of our own actions and the main compulsion by which this lesson was learned was economic. The citizens kept the community solvent and viable and were paid for their labour. They all started in debt to the community for their clothes and their food and until and unless they earned they were a charge on the household in which they lived. The freedom of Homer Lane's Commonwealth was the liberty to discover that a community disintegrates if it does not discover how to maintain itself. The 'go-as-you-please' version of the regime arose from the agonizing conflicts and crises which disturbed children produced in one another and which Lane, with a kind of terrible meekness, often persisted in precipitating for obviously generally exhausting psychological reasons.

The third principle was concerned with self-government. The members of the community elected the authority they were prepared to accept and made their own laws. Eighteen boys and girls living in one house normally formed a family, together with the house-mother and one or two adult helpers. The boys had rooms at one end and the girls at the other, with living rooms used in common. The family was the economic and emotional anchorage of the system and the community meeting was the gathering of the families (for most of the Commonwealth's existence there were two main families) for community discussion and decision-making twice a week. The family made the rules

[23] See the three versions of the same story reported in Wills, *Homer Lane*, pp. 140-4.

which governed the life within the cottage and enforced its own discipline:

> The Little Commonwealth was not an inimitable institution, the product of a single genius, but a model reformatory the principles of which could be applied with equal success to other institutions for the reformation of adult criminals as well as in the treatment of delinquent children.[24]

Lane always strenuously denied that as a person he was responsible for any success the Commonwealth may have had, but all commentators make clear the dominant part he played in his role as non-directive counsellor. He claimed that any children's community given real freedom within the demands of economic self-sufficiency could succeed as the Little Commonwealth succeeded but when all the necessary reservations are applied it can be seen, as Lane affirmed, that good qualities do not unfold spontaneously in the free atmosphere, but that results have to be worked for with every resource. Despite five years of careful preparation Lane did not really get the teaching side of the work started. The children were, of course, over fourteen, the age of compulsory schooling, but were often backward and in need of remedial teaching. Nevertheless, while the needs of the war effort made it difficult to extend the basic farm work, the citizens were not really ready to receive instruction, nor were they prepared to think with any constancy about religious issues, no matter how sensitively Lane and his helpers tried to bring these questions forward. Miss Bazeley sums up with characteristic candour:

> During the last two years of the Little Commonwealth Mr. Lane was working for and expecting the development of a final phase in the life of the community and this final phase did not arrive. He had all along expected that the very strong Commonwealth spirit of loyalty to the community would, at any rate at points, be touched into loyalty towards higher ideals and towards the spirit behind ideals. He did expect that we should develop from communal loyalties towards spiritual ones — and this did not happen.[25]

The story of the end of the Commonwealth is well known and

---

[24] Lord Lytton, Introduction in Bazeley, *Homer Lane and the Little Commonwealth*, p. 19.
[25] Bazeley, *Homer Lane and the Little Commonwealth*, p. 146.

pathetic. On 30 December 1917 Florence and Annie, two citizens of the Commonwealth, having robbed the office safe ran away and charged Lane with sexual improprieties toward them. The Home Secretary, Sir George Cave, proposed to withdraw the certificate of recognition which had been given to the Little Commonwealth in March 1917, but the Committee of the Commonwealth persuaded him not to do so at least until they, together with the Chief Inspector of Reformatory and Industrial Schools, had investigated the matter fully. The Committee had already made a preliminary inquiry, and despite the discovery of a history of severe unrest and serious premonitory signs in Florence's case, had given Lane a unanimous vote of confidence. However, before the proposed full investigation was begun the Home Secretary decided to hold a private inquiry into the affairs and government of the Little Commonwealth and appointed Mr. J. F. P. Rawlinson, K.C., M.P., to carry it out. He began on 30 January 1918 and completed his interviews early in April. On 6 June the Home Office wrote to Lord Sandwich, representing the Little Commonwealth Committee, to say that the certificate of recognition would be withdrawn if Lane continued as superintendent but would be continued if another superintendent were appointed and certain modifications of practice were made. In these circumstances and still offering their belief in Lane's innocence, the Committee closed the Commonwealth 'with the greatest reluctance . . . for the duration of the war. They have every intention of reopening it when the war is over and when conditions are more favourable for securing an adequate income and a sufficient staff to deal with all the phases of this educational experiment.'[26]

Lane turned to the practice of psychotherapy with adults in London, hoping to return to work with children. In 1925 he failed to notify a change of address and this offered a technical reason under the Aliens Act for the police to demand his exclusion from Great Britain. A few weeks later in September 1925 he died of heart failure at the American Hospital in Paris.[27]

[The Little Commonwealth] failed only in establishing the general applicability of the principles on which it was conducted. . . . It was the tragedy of [Homer Lane's] life that to the end men never

---

[26] From the *Report of the Committee on the Closing of the Little Commonwealth*, July 1918. Wills, *Homer Lane*, has given the fullest account available of these transactions.

[27] Again Wills, *Homer Lane*, has the fullest available account of this period of Lane's life up to the time of his death.

said of him, 'What admirable principles, let us adopt them', but always 'What a marvellous man, he is inimitable.'[28]

While this is substantially true in the case of work with delinquents in the 1920s it is not true of radical educationalists in general and we choose three examples of men who saw in Lane's work a lead for their own practice with children who had not fallen foul of the law.

Norman MacMunn was a teacher of modern languages who worked for a while in grammar schools before and during the First World War, developing at first a partnership system between pairs of pupils learning French, as a beginning of his practical experiments in freer methods.[29] MacMunn saw in Homer Lane's work what he called a wonderful and inspiring example of which he wrote:

> Surely every logical and progressive teacher should be tempted by such victories of the principle of liberty to remark: 'Either these young criminals are better than my boys, or my boys are not quite so incapable of self-direction as I have been taught to believe.'[30]

MacMunn went on to try to practise at Tiptree Hall in Essex many of Lane's principles with a small number of boys (usually about nine or ten) and although the school did not have a long life, his book *A Child's Path to Freedom* (1926), was written to prove that self-government of the Homer Lane pattern was going to be the basis of the education of the future: 'From the commonwealth colony for young delinquents to the commonwealth school for normal boys is scarcely a step at all.'[31] The only restraints would be imposed on boys (MacMunn was not convinced about co-education) by the collective will of their fellows through courts and school meetings. As an admirer both of Montessori and Lane, MacMunn wanted his pupils to create a new spirit in which their willing partnership blurred and later abolished the border between work and play, where living rooms and classrooms would not be distinguishable. He rejected the desire of teachers to 'appropriate the souls of those whom they teach' on the excuse that Arnold and Thring had set the example, for according to MacMunn few teachers had the equipment and gifts to make this transaction

---

[28] Lord Lytton, Introduction in Bazeley, *Homer Lane and the Little Commonwealth*, p. 13.

[29] N. MacMunn, *Differential Partnership Method of French Conversation* (London); *The MacMunn Differentialism: A New Method of Class Self-Teaching* (London).

[30] N. MacMunn, *A Path to Freedom in the School*, pp. 7–8.

[31] Ibid., p. 149.

anything other than a violation of freedom and an unwarranted presumption.[32] MacMunn thought that in theory and practice Montessori and Lane had most nearly reached the stage to which he aspired: 'The will to guard and to develop the freedom of another can only come when man is entering upon a supremely great stage of racial development.'[33]

The second man who acknowledges a deep debt to Homer Lane is J. H. Simpson and probably more than anyone else in England Simpson carried out Lane's principles for a number of years in different contexts. James Simpson had been a boy at Rugby in the 1890s, of which he wrote a sympathetically critical account in 1954[34] from which we find most of Badley's comments on the school where he was a pupil twenty years before Simpson were still applicable. After graduating at Cambridge and teaching at several schools, including Gresham's at Holt,[35] Simpson returned to Rugby as a master in January 1913 and it was during the autumn of this year when Simpson was visiting Holt that he met Homer Lane, an American 'working at some kind of reformatory' and his talk on that occasion began to effect a radical change in Simpson's whole outlook on education. He visited the Little Commonwealth at Christmas 1913 and on many occasions during the succeeding three years; 'In those years I came to know the Commonwealth pretty well, possibly as well as anyone who had no definite connection with it.'[36]

Simpson regarded Lane well this side idolatry — he thought Lane's denial of personal influence absurd and said his tendency to dramatize incidents went over the brink of self-deception, while his non-directive role in general meetings of adult helpers and disturbed children led in Simpson's opinion as often to public agonizing as to understanding. But Simpson had seen enough of Lane's intentions to want to try out some kind of self-government, and MacMunn's experiments in teaching (themselves inspired by Lane's work) suggested to him that a single form in a school might serve as a beginning. It says much for Simpson and Dr. David his headmaster that he was able to do this original work at Rugby.[37] It should be added that Dr. David was a member of the Managing Committee of the Little Commonwealth.

[32] *The Child's Path to Freedom*, p. 30.   [33] *A Path to Freedom in the School*, p. 7.
[34] *Schoolmaster's Harvest* (London, 1954), ch. 2.
[35] J. H. Simpson, *Howson of Holt* (London, 1925).
[36] *Schoolmaster's Harvest*, p. 138.
[37] See J. H. Simpson, *An Adventure in Education* (1917).

In 1919 Simpson was invited to become the first headmaster of
Rendcomb College and here from 1920 till 1931 he was able to work out
his ideas in much greater detail, as we shall see later. For the present
we want to acknowledge the continuity of Homer Lane's educational
principles.

> I wish to express my gratitude to Mr. Homer Lane, whose work is a
> continual source of inspiration. . . . [The Little Commonwealth] is
> the most inspiring educational establishment in England. [I dare
> not] attempt to express the measure of my personal debt to Mr.
> Lane, which is indeed incalculable.[38]

This young schoolmaster, already impatient with public school
conventions and restrictions, responded to the liberty and responsibility which when given to Lane's young delinquents seemed to call
forth unsuspected qualities and capacities. Yet his was not always an
eager, spontaneous response: 'Occasionally the challenge to my beliefs
and prejudices at a previous visit had been almost unbearable, so that
in my thoughts of the next there was some faint mixture of reluctance.'[39]

The third man to respond to Lane and his work is the best known.
A. S. Neill says that it was a fan-letter from a lady in Hampstead who
had read and enjoyed *A Dominie's Log* and *A Dominie Dismissed*
(Neill never has been dismissed and considers this book a kind of
fictional autobiography) which first brought Homer Lane to his
attention. The lady said that Neill might be interested in Lane's work
and enclosed a copy of one of his lectures. As an officer-cadet in the
artillery in 1916–17 Neill was stationed in Trowbridge in Wiltshire and
wrote to Lane who agreed to his visiting the Little Commonwealth.
The consequence is best told in Neill's own words:

> That weekend was perhaps the most important milestone in my life.
> Lane sat up till the early morning telling me about his cases. I had
> been groping for some philosophy of education but had no know-
> ledge of psychology. Lane introduced me to Freud. I asked Lane
> if I could come to work in the Commonwealth after the war and he
> said he had just been going to ask me to come, but when I was free
> the Little Commonwealth had been closed by the Home Office.
>
> I owe a great debt to Lane. It was from him that I learned that
> unless a teacher could see a child's motives he could not help him to
> be happy or social. He was a genius although his 'education' was

[38] *An Adventure in Education*, pp. ix, 3.
[39] *Schoolmaster's Harvest*, p. 138.

limited. He spoke from his unconscious mostly. He found writing, even writing a letter, difficult. But with delinquent children he was simply wonderful. I consider it appalling that, since he died in 1925, so far as I can see his great experiment has had no visible influence on the State treatment of delinquent children.[40]

Neill had a long psychological analysis from Homer Lane in London in 1919 which he recalls as being 'far from perfect' because he considered Lane's interpretations as clever, satisfying the mind but not the emotions. This reservation notwithstanding, Neill reaffirms in his eighties his primary debt to Lane, and Summerhill has many practices which are recognizably similar to those of the Little Commonwealth.

III

Both Montessori and Lane considered that their methods were based on the freedom and self-determination open to the child. However, in the practice of each of them the teacher's control of environment and the structure of authority in the group are very different. Montessori's directress has furniture, play equipment, teaching material, and a school and classroom organization which are devised to stimulate learning. She knows within limits what she wants the child to discover he wants to learn and her teaching skill and tact consist in presenting the problems and data when the child most wants to confront them. Although the order that exists in a Montessori class seems to reside in and be maintained by the children's group, the background directress is a *dea in machina* who separates the anti-social child from the rest, permitting him to have the things he wants and relying on the magnetism of the group to make him want to join in again on the generally approved terms. Hers is the ultimate but unobtrusive authority.

Homer Lane's self-government was with older children and its framework was the needs of a self-supporting community to live together and pay its way. The children never got as far as academic learning in a school context. 'Daddy', as they called Lane, had no more say in the self-governing councils than the boy or girl chairman allowed him. He did not want his word to be law, he wanted the children to discover the need of law and to legislate as their collective wisdom guided them.

Montessori's teaching arranged the group and the scale of problems

[40] A. S. Neill, 'My Scholastic Life — 2', in *Id.*, Oct. 1960, p. 3.

to stimulate motivation to learn while keeping the disruptive factors within adult control. Lane's teaching prescribed very little ; money had to be earned by work and the will of the school community as expressed by a majority vote had to be the controlling authority — and even this piece of raw politics was hammered out after newcomers had ruined the sleep and peace of mind of their fellows by a tireless racketing.

To what extent do children know what is best for them ? This is the key question which sorts the Montessorians from the Laneites, to which Summerhill gives one answer, Abbotsholme another, and Winchester another.

Chapter Five

THE POST-WAR SURGENCE: THE TWENTIES

1. Beginnings of the New Psychology

DESPERATE elation and exhaustion were part of the post-war reckoning, an emancipated disenchantment discerning an ideal in the League of Nations on the one hand and revealing bitter hostility in the General Strike on the other. The second wave of radical schools in England appeared in this decade and in their beginnings made manifest social, economic, psychological, and religious currents of the time.

I

John Howard Whitehouse was born in Birmingham in June 1873, the son of George Whitehouse, a brass founder and plate-worker and a staunch Gladstonian Liberal. George Whitehouse became, after 1870, a local inspector of schools and his son attended board schools in Birmingham until the age of fourteen when he left to earn his living, first in an accountant's office and then with a saddler. The young lad educated himself in the evenings at the Birmingham Institute and Mason's College which has since become part of the University of Birmingham.

In 1894 at the age of twenty-one Howard Whitehouse went to work at Cadbury's and this experience of enlightened industrial practice and the place of welfare and educational programmes in the life of the work people greatly influenced his whole way of thinking and his career. He moved from office work to take part in the social and educational enterprises of the Quaker policy-makers. He worked mainly with young employees, establishing a library and a youth club whose members often travelled and camped away from Birmingham.

Liberalism and Quakerism were two of the formative principles of Whitehouse's life. A third was his deep respect for Ruskin's politics, social and artistic ideals, and writings. We have already seen how Reddie, Badley, and the communitarian Left had the same deep admiration for the great man's work and how his palpable decline before his death in 1900 had saddened his followers. Whitehouse had from an early age organizational flair of a high order to go with his Liberal, non-conformist convictions. He founded the Ruskin Society of Birmingham and made a great success of its programmes before, at the age of thirty-one, he left Birmingham to spend a short time as first secretary of the Carnegie Trust in Scotland. It was here that he met Patrick Geddes whose work for sociology we have already noted and whose friendship with Reddie brought him into the New School movement. Geddes acted as an Inspector at Abbotsholme in 1904 round about the time when he met Whitehouse. Both Geddes and Whitehouse were active in the affairs of the Guild of St. George, as it came to be called, the society formed to perpetuate the principles and the memory of Ruskin, and Geddes remained for Whitehouse an admired and influential friend.

Whitehouse left the Carnegie Trust and Scotland after only a few months and moved to the Toynbee Hall Settlement in London's East End, founded as a memorial to Arnold Toynbee the economic historian who was one of the pioneers of the Balliol tradition in adult education and social work among poor people. The Settlement was opened in Whitechapel in 1884, a year after Toynbee's death, as a centre of reconciliation between young men from university and privileged backgrounds and the working classes. When Ruskin had been a Professor at Oxford, Toynbee had been one of his disciples and derived much inspiration from the ideas of the master. It is no wonder, then, that the move to Toynbee Hall attracted Whitehouse and that he found kindred spirits there. W. H. Beveridge was a Sub-Warden and a joint editor, with Whitehouse, of *St. George*, the magazine of the Ruskinian Guild. The Warden was a Friend, T. E. Harvey, and another member was E. T. Cook, one of the editors of the massive edition of Ruskin's works.[1] Whitehouse was the secretary of the Settlement and became a school manager and the founder of the National League of Workers with Boys through which he came into contact with Baden-Powell who began the Boy Scout Movement in 1908, the year when Whitehouse moved from Whitechapel to St. George's School, the co-educational school founded in 1907 at Harpenden by the Rev. Cecil Grant who transferred his school to Harpenden from Keswick in Cumberland. Despite its name, St. George's had no connection with Ruskin and after a year as Sub-Warden, Whitehouse moved at the age of thirty-six to be Warden of Manchester University Settlement at Ancoats, the Toynbee Hall of the North.

It appeared as though this might be the ideal post for a man of Whitehouse's experience and social conscience. Reared in industrial Birmingham, nurtured by Quakerism, Gladstone's Liberalism, and the beliefs of Ruskin, versed in social work in a Whitechapel Settlement, eager to encourage youth movements, he had all the opportunity in Ancoats a man could want to promote social improvement. But in 1910, a year after he became Warden of Manchester University Settlement, Whitehouse became a Member of Parliament, elected for the mining constituency of Mid-Lanark which he held until the end of the war. He was in turn Parliamentary Private Secretary at the Home Office for a while, where his concern for the social welfare, especially of children and refugees, had scope. Later he served at the Treasury when Lloyd George was Chancellor of the Exchequer, but Whitehouse broke with him in 1916 when Lloyd George introduced conscription. Ruskin and Gladstone were still important influences in Whitehouse's thinking and between 1916 and 1918 he made a journey to the United States as a member of a minority opposition in the Coalition Government seeking to bring about a negotiated peace. Whitehouse lost his seat in the House of Commons in 1918 and he contested every election between 1922 and 1935 in his efforts to re-enter the House, but his parliamentary days were ended.

In 1919 at the age of forty-five Whitehouse founded Bembridge School in the Isle of Wight of which he remained as Warden until 1954, dying on 29 September 1955 aged eighty-two. Once again we use the public schools of the time as a point of reference by which to trace the differences of belief and practice in this new school. Whitehouse was

[1] E. T. Cook and Alexander Wedderburn, *The Works of John Ruskin* (London, 1905).

a prolific writer and a public lecturer who often gathered his addresses into printed symposia or brochure form, and from these and the school records it is possible to piece together what he hoped to do at Bembridge, 'a school where, without, we hope any weakening of the literary and academic side of education, arts and crafts . . . are regarded as instruments of spiritual and intellectual education'.[2]

This is what one might expect from a devoted Ruskinian. He considered creative education to be that which leads to a child finding out what he can do, what interests him, and for this manual activities, especially in art and craft, were potentially of the greatest importance and should have a place of honour in every school. To this end Bembridge had, almost from the start, a museum and art gallery in which every term there was a special exhibition of paintings or furniture or drawings or scientific exhibits or the like. One term each year was devoted to exhibitions of work by the boys in the school which, for example, on one occasion illustrated the history of the Isle of Wight and on others exhibited boys' paintings, poetry, models, craft-work, and printing. A printing press was an important part of the school's apparatus and such equipment was found at Abbotsholme, St. Christopher, Bedales, and a number of other schools. It was in line with Ruskin's pride in craft and workmanship and with William Morris's Kelmscott Press. Whitehouse maintained that work at the press helped to acquaint boys with good writing while incidentally improving their spelling, it encouraged taste and discrimination in type-face and layout, it opened a small window into the work of an ancient craft and a modern industry, it gave to some boys a real interest and a skill.

The painting, drawing, woodwork, pottery, script writing, and play production characteristic of Bembridge ring familiarly in these days, but in 1919 few of these were encouraged in public schools (White-house called Bembridge a public school, not a progressive school) and were certainly not given a firm place in the school timetable. Natural history and biology were more favoured at Bembridge than chemistry and physics, and history was merged with a real concern for the recent past, the present, and current affairs. Whitehouse was a great admirer of America and introduced a study of American history to Bembridge.[3]

He gave his boys practical responsibility for organizing societies and

[2] J. H. Whitehouse, *Creative Education at an English School* (Cambridge, 1928), p. 2.
[3] See J. H. Whitehouse, *America and Our Schools* (Oxford, 1938).

meetings and like Badley, Reddie, and Devine he thought that games ought to take a part only of a boy's free time: 'We want a richer and nobler range of activities than would be afforded merely by games.'[4] Yet with all this concern for personal development and despite his position as Chairman of the Society for Research in Education (there is no evidence that he took part in what would today be called research) he had no place for the Dalton Plan: 'I am filled with something approaching horror when people tell me that if I dole out a programme to a boy or girl a month or a year ahead that is going to lead to anything satisfactory.'[5]

Whitehouse was sympathetic to and influenced by the Society of Friends and he spoke of religion as the practice of goodness in the spirit of Jesus Christ without the teaching of dogma. Equally, Whitehouse spoke with asperity and vigour against all military training in schools and sought to promote the ideals of kindness and gentleness. He wanted all schools 'dissociated from the War Office', and to his implacable opposition to Officers' Training Corps he added his perpetual hostility to fagging at public schools, which he considered to be a degradation and waste for the younger boy and a lure to cruelty and exploitation for the older.

Reddie, Devine, and Whitehouse were all bachelors who devoted themselves to work with boys. Reddie and Devine were both thirty-one years old when they started Abbotsholme and Clayesmore, and Whitehouse was forty-five at the foundation of Bembridge. Reddie had a very good academic record, Devine had none. Whitehouse used the evening facilities offered by Birmingham and later in his life was made an honorary M.A. of Oxford. His political and social work had given him the acquaintance and friendship of a large circle of liberals. Indeed, his obituary suggests that he had 'too many irons in too many fires'[6] which was also true of Devine, but certainly not of the single-minded monarch of Abbotsholme. Whitehouse's school, while the first of the post-war wave, was one of the least radical of the new schools and by 1919 Ruskin was regarded as being on the right of socialism which now had a militant working class and a Russian revolution as its spearhead.

Bembridge can be thought of as in continuity with Abbotsholme,

---

[4] J. H. Whitehouse, 'Ideals and Methods in Education', in *A Boy's Symposium* (London, 1932), p. 26.

[5] Ibid., p. 27.   [6] *The Times*, 30 Sept. 1955.

Bedales, and Clayesmore, but Whitehouse came thirty years after Reddie and while his school could merge into the 1890's schools in their temporary post-war boom, the new schools of the 1920's were to go much further than Whitehouse was prepared to go.

In his days in Whitechapel and Ancoats the young Whitehouse came across at first hand the elementary schools of the mass of the people and in 1908 in the magazine of Toynbee Hall he wrote an article on reform in the elementary school.[7]   In it he pleaded for an end to the building of schools isolated from each other in crowded districts of cities where sites are desperately difficult to come by and play space is always too little.   He proposed that schools should be built in groups at certain bases which could afford amenities for the children in that section of the city.   The parks would be near and a swimming bath, a gymnasium, kitchens and dining rooms, library, concert rooms, and art rooms could be shared by a group of schools and so more adequate recreation and culture space be found.   In 1908 these were revolutionary ideas and they came to nothing, though the Cambridgeshire Village Colleges of the 1930's are in the same family of ideas.

In 1943, just before the 1944 Act, Whitehouse wrote again on the school base and he says :

> Under this scheme every town would be divided into areas, and each area would have its own School Base in the country.   In many cases it would be within two or three miles of the area. . . .   It would be possible to provide all the educational needs of a big town at one base. . . .   Except in the case of small towns, more than one School Base will be required.[8]

Here, for the whole country, Whitehouse sketches the resources of Bembridge and the Cambridgeshire Colleges writ large.   Some later writers have tangled these ideas up with proposals for the comprehensive school, but the sketch in this booklet of forty-seven pages is far too general for that.   Whitehouse believed that for older children the School Base should be in the country, but he travelled no real distance in facing up to the practical implications of this.   Bembridge was his most complete contribution to progressive education, not a very radical school, a public school for boys with resemblances to Clayesmore and more like it than, say, Bedales and nowadays unwilling to be in the progressive group.   As the *Times* obituary of Whitehouse

[7] *The Toynbee Record 1908.*
[8] J. H. Whitehouse, *The School Base* (Oxford, 1943), p. 11.

puts it: 'No-one could consider Bembridge a "freak school".'
But no one could confuse it with Harrow, either.

II

Bembridge was not the only unorthodox foundation in 1919. Rend-comb near Cirencester in Gloucestershire was started by J. H. Simpson who was appointed in 1919. Simpson was like Badley, a Rugbeian who went on to Cambridge. He taught for a little at Charterhouse and Clifton and for two and a half years at Gresham's School, Holt, in Norfolk, where he developed a strong admiration for G. W. S. Howson, the headmaster, a man of conservative educational ideas and very strong moral principles which he expected the boys to share. Later in life Simpson became more critical of Howson's personal dominance but he admired the honesty and vitality in the school. After Gresham's, Simpson returned to Rugby as a master, but not before he had had two years as a junior inspector of the Board of Education. He found the prevailing attitudes in elementary education coarse and depressing but the conditions in which the teachers worked and the needs of the children he never forgot. He was, like Whitehouse, a manager of elementary schools but he differed from the Bembridge Warden in that he had been academically and professionally trained to teach. He was one of the few heads of progressive schools who up to that time had taken an education qualification as well as his degree.

Simpson was critical of the educational class structure. His year in Bolton as a junior inspector, contact with the deprived and impoverished delinquents of the Little Commonwealth, work on the boards of management of elementary schools — all these things are straws indicating his growing hostility to the public schools which reared him. This is summed up in a pamphlet he produced as late as 1943 in which he wrote:

> I do not feel guilty of the least inconsistency in admiring their past achievements and certain educational virtues which the best of them still retain and believing at the same time that they are not the schools which this country will require in the coming years. . . . It is the specially favourable jumping-off place afforded by the public schools to boys of quite ordinary ability and character which excites the strongest hostility.[9]

9 J. H. Simpson, *The Future of the Public Schools* (Rugby, 1943), p. 6.

Simpson was an assistant master at Rugby from 1913 till 1919 and during that time he had special responsibility for boys of only average ability who, he thought, were given a far less apt and rewarding education at Rugby than the intellectually gifted. He put all the routine of orderliness, punctuality, timing, and delivery of work in the hands of a committee of boys of his form and later he gave the form a much larger say in the arranging and assessing of work-programmes. When Simpson went into the army in September 1917 he had discovered how demanding, exciting, and limited his Rugby experiment in self-government was and knew that he would want to try it out more extensively either with a house or with a school.

F. Noel Hamilton Wills of Misarden Park, Oxford, wrote to Simpson shortly after his demobilisation in January 1919 saying that he had read Simpson's book *An Adventure in Education* with great interest and asking for the opportunity to discuss :

> an educational experiment which has been in my mind for some eighteen months. Briefly, the idea is as follows : A school for 50 boys, selected by scholarship examination from the Primary Schools of [Gloucestershire]. It is hoped that by giving the best possible education at this establishment a proportion of the boys (who would be a very select community, picked out of some 40,000 children) might prove able to take scholarships at Public Schools and some of them later at the Universities. These scholarships would be subsidized under the scheme.[10]

Wills, 'with a good bit of help from my brother', was going to provide the money to found this school which had at first no unusual educational ideas about it. Simpson agreed to becoming the first headmaster and after the school opened in June 1920 quickly persuaded his Governing Body to drop the principle of sending scholars on to the public schools, which would at once have made Rendcomb into a preparatory school. In 1922 the Governors agreed to a suggestion made by Simpson that fee-payers should be admitted. This was a change occasioned in part by Simpson's discovery that the endowment was not sufficient to enable the school to expand beyond forty boys, and he wanted it larger for educational and economic reasons. Part of the

[10] From a letter to J. H. Simpson dated 7 Jan. 1919. Copies of correspondence relating to Rendcomb, biographical information and many other valuable records were made available by Mr. C. H. C. Osborne, a former colleague and close friend of Simpson, and Mr. A. O. H. Quick the present headmaster of Rendcomb College. To these gentlemen I am greatly indebted for their help and kindness.

educational reason was to achieve what Simpson called 'a social mixture'. The fee-payers could come from any part of the country and from many home backgrounds and so the purpose and range of the school were widened. Again, one of the attractions of Rendcomb for Simpson was that it gave him the chance to bring into being what he called a 'self-governing' school. It was based on the Little Common-wealth, but with several differences.[11]

There was a General Meeting to which boys aged thirteen and older belonged. Offices were held for a term and holders were elected by the boys, as were appointments to the many sub-committees, the Games Committee, the Finance Committee, the House Committee, and so on. There were Games Wardens, three Shopkeepers, a Banker, an Auditor, and a Council of seven boys who were elected for the duration of their school life and who acted as a boys' judiciary. There was formality and order in the General Meeting and after various experiments the staff were not included as members and Simpson sat in as a non-voting attender. Minutes of the first General Meeting are dated 30 June 1920, a month after the school opened.

Responsibility was real and money was spent by the officers on behalf of the boys. In 1921 Simpson persuaded the Governing Body not to provide money for equipment directly to the school, but to make the grants as an allowance to each boy with the instruction that they were to provide all necessary games equipment and arrange to keep the grounds in order. Thus the boys were given a task to do involving committee decision, estimating, and some quite considerable budgeting.

> Economics . . . gave a solid basis of reality to the 'self-government' and, above all, made it easier to let the boys learn by making mistakes. . . . They should learn to spend judiciously, and sometimes boldly, and at the same time the results of their efficient, or inefficient, management should be seen immediately in their everyday life.[12]

This is a feature which continued although Simpson left Rendcomb in 1932. With such scope for the participation of boys in the dis-ciplinary and economic life of the school, he coupled active learning in

[11] Full accounts are given in Simpson's books, *Sane Schooling* (London, 1936) and *Schoolmaster's Harvest*, chapter v. In *Sane Schooling* Rendcomb is called Churnside, a flimsy anonymity.

[12] *Schoolmaster's Harvest*, p. 162.

group situations and he took the unusual course of adopting Greek as the main ancient language for study. He thought it a language with a richer literature and mythology than Latin. The teaching was enlightened and experimental, and in a school of forty to fifty pupils it could be personal. But this is not the distinctive pulse of Rendcomb among the radical schools of the 1920s and in trying to discern it we discover again the change of thought patterns in the last fifty years.

Noel Wills as Simpson recalls him was sensitive, versatile, generous alike in thought and action, courageous to think of supporting elementary schoolboys at a boarding school against the encrusted prejudice of county families, convinced of the need to make a new world of understanding after 1918. The proposal was to pay the fees of about fifty of Gloucestershire's most capable eleven-year-olds, to give them 'the advantages of opportunities which have hitherto . . . been restricted to boys of gentle birth'. This was said by Wills in another way in an article he wrote for *The English Review* in June 1924. 'Rendcomb College was founded in the belief that the true aristocracy among men is in reality simply an aristocracy of brains and character.'[13] This was the first progressive school that came to some terms with the maintained system. The Gloucestershire Authority gave the responsibility of selecting pupils to the Governors, who, on their part, gave substantial funds for the fees and equipping of the boys.

Noel Wills had seemingly not greatly enjoyed his own public school days but perceived how they could have been enriched. He was a man of wealth, belonging to the family for which the tobacco concern of W. D. and H. O. Wills and later the Imperial Tobacco Company had built prosperity. The Wills family had a tradition of generous giving and of public service — Noel's brother, Gilbert Alan Hamilton Wills, who became the first Baron Dulverton in 1929, was a Member of Parliament 1912–22, President of Imperial Tobacco Company, and a founder of the Dulverton Trust. An earlier generation had given handsome support to Bristol University and while Noel Wills's concern for Rendcomb was the result of his own thinking it was in keeping with the enlightened philanthropy of his family. It was from the same family that Mrs. Douglas-Hamilton came, whose generous support of the Theosophical Educational Trust during the period 1916 to 1927 we have already seen.

The moulds of conventional schooling, of class and political structure

[13] Op. cit., p. 797.

were beginning to crack after 1918, and Noel Wills, who was only thirty-three when Rendcomb began in 1920, wanted to play his part in the new world. He wrote to Simpson just before the latter's appointment in 1919.

> ... While recognising that I must not tie the hands of a Head and specialist, I repeat that I want to enjoy a position of mutual confidence and co-operation and to be sure in advance that there exists a fundamental conformity in our aims.
>
> The aim is decidedly social, moral and intellectual education, rather than mere scholarship; the latter being only a desirable evidence of the better things.[14]

Simpson had the public school stamp, he had the merit of originality in his teaching career as his writing showed. He might be thought to be the right kind of enlightened liberal. However, by the beginning of 1922 the local resentments and suspicions had produced the scandals and rumours which we have seen at other progressive schools, and Sir Thomas Davies, a Member of Parliament, was invited to visit the school and report to the Governors. He said that charges had been made that the school was irreligious, but he found Scripture on the timetable although church attendance was not enforced. Again it was alleged that the boys were luxuriously fed, lodged and clothed and Davies reported that the Governors provided everyday wearing apparel as part of the boys' equipment while parents provided underclothing. As for the accommodation and food it was such 'as would be found in, say, Circencester Grammar School'. Rumour suggested that the boys could do what they liked in their free time and ordered their own affairs, but Davies stated that games were played and that committees saw to many day-to-day arrangements and routines. There were twenty-nine boys in the school and the timetable was not yet fully developed, two years from the beginning of the foundation and Davies makes one or two tentative criticisms, but concludes 'the various rumours and reports about the conduct of the school and its pupils have no foundation'.[15]

Wills did not have a social and educational manifesto. He wanted as many boys as he could afford to maintain given the 'advantages' of an enlightened boarding school. Simpson wanted an experimental

---

[14] Letter dated 15 Apr. 1919.
[15] From a letter to Sir Francis Hyett, one of the Governors, dated 7 June 1922.

boarding school, an educational corrective to the complacent public school. He had a general sympathy for the underdog, but he was neither an uncritical admirer of the underprivileged, nor a devoted servant of freedom in the Rousseau style. He spoke of the majority of elementary teachers in his Junior Inspector days as timid, unimaginative, hurried, harried and either cowed or falsely aggressive and none too careful of elementary personal hygiene. After he left Rendcomb in 1932 he became the Principal of a Church of England Training College for men, St. Mark and St. John in Chelsea. He said that here he struck something new in collective bad manners, a coarse juvenility that compared ill with all that he had aimed for at Rendcomb. It is true that he went on to say how this changed as time passed, but his analysis of students and colleagues in the early days is direct and astringent.[16]

As to freedom in school, even in a progressive school, Simpson writing in 1954 of his work at Rendcomb thirty years before says that he believed in the limited value of self-government to teach the use of a committee structure. He believed too in the economic scheme and in the general feeling that the rules are 'ours' not 'theirs' which helped boys to shed inferiority, to become tolerant and sanely critical, and far less likely to be the slave of obsessional schoolboy customs. Yet Simpson admits on reflection to being guilty of confused thinking, because he attributed to self-government what was equally due to the ethical tone and spirit of the school as a whole. In his zeal for his *idée fixe* he thought he underplayed direct ethical teaching, and even more, religious education. He considers that like many another post-war left-wing schoolmaster (his own terms) he groped for the meaning of freedom in education at the expense of the virtues of religious education: 'It seemed easier and safer somehow to think of social education solely in terms of human relationships, without asking whether human relationships can be perfect except in the knowledge of a personal God.'[17]

Again, under the influence of 'the new psychology' he assumed that strong personality in a headmaster meant a repressive and dominating leader, and so used self-government as a protection for himself and his pupils against his own potential despotism. However, he considered that the extreme cult of self-effacement could be a rationalization for a

---

[16] See *Schoolmaster's Harvest*, chapter 6.
[17] Ibid., p. 178.

kind of cunning directed at a more pervasive, a subtler kind of manipulation. Equally, he considered the *laissez-faire* principles by which some headmasters tried not to inhibit their pupils represented a failure to face responsibility. Steering, therefore, amid these reefs and shoals of self-deception and lazy thinking, he remarks that his own attitude to self-government entailed patience to permit things to go wrong, and faith in adolescents to detect error and discern how to correct it. Yet this was not to be made an ultimate principle if a word or an action by the headmaster could prevent major damage. Simpson did not abrogate authority and give it finally to his boys. His criticism of Homer Lane was that he said he tried to do just this, and sometimes the anguish for children was too costly; and in any case Lane was too obviously the spiritual leader of the place for anyone else to believe in the reality of his self-effacement. Simpson, however, used his judgement to give a lead, to quell a riot, to drop a hint. After all, he was a schoolmaster and not a psychotherapist.

Noel Wills died in 1927 at the age of forty. His family still plays a leading part in the Governing Body of Rendcomb, but this particular philanthropic impulse did not extend to other families in other parts of this country. That Wills found Simpson was the happy accident that made a social venture into a progressive school. Yet, although its ideas are original its impact has not been great and this is partly a consequence of its small size. Fifty boys in 1926 became one hundred and nine in 1963, with the promise of further expansion to come. More significantly, the egalitarian experiment which suggests a precedent for proposals like those of the Fleming Report, has not produced consequences in other areas, or even elsewhere in Gloucestershire. Philanthropy for forty boys represents a generous if numerically limited opportunity to extend 'privilege' to poorer boys. The desirable feature is the boarding school and a few authorities like the London County Council, Suffolk and Lancashire have lately begun to provide their own.[18] Simpson made Rendcomb not just another small public boarding school, but rather another small public-progressive school which could be placed to the left of Bembridge. There were others who held much more radical ideas of the educational reforms the new schools were waiting for.

[18] Also see R. Lambert, *The State and Boarding Education* (London, 1966).

Chapter Six

THE POST-WAR SURGENCE:
THE TWENTIES

2. *The Wave of the New Psychology*

IN his biography of Sigmund Freud,[1] Ernest Jones places the beginnings of international recognition for the psycho-analytic movement between 1906 and 1909. In April 1908 the first International Psycho-Analytical Congress was held in Salzburg which was attended by forty-two persons from many countries and it was then decided to produce the first periodical to be devoted to psycho-analysis, the *Jahrbuch für psychoanalytische und psychopathologische Forschungen* which lasted till the outbreak of the First World War. It was directed by Eugen Bleuler, a Swiss, and Freud himself and edited by C. G. Jung. Freud had been producing papers for specialized audiences since the last decade of the nineteenth century, but these had not had much circulation outside Austria and Germany except through visiting specialists. He had also in German by 1906 at least three books of major importance, *The Interpretation of Dreams*, *Psychopathology of Everyday Life* and *Three Essays on the Theory of Sexuality*, and the output continued. *Totem and Taboo* appeared in 1912 and the two parts of the *Introductory Lectures on Psycho-Analysis* were written during the war.

An American worker, A. A. Brill, who attended the Salzburg Congress in 1908 obtained Freud's permission to be his English translator and until 1920 he was Freud's imperfect representative in English. In 1909 Freud was invited to Clark University in Worcester, Massachusetts by its President, Stanley Hall, to give a course of lectures

[1] E. Jones, *The Life and Work of Sigmund Freud*, 3 vols. (London, 1953, 1955, 1957).

to celebrate the twentieth anniversary of the foundation of the University, and this Freud felt was the first official international recognition of the Viennese work.

The Second International Psycho-Analytical Congress took place at Nuremberg in March 1910 and there the International Psycho-Analytic Association was set up, after a stormy prelude, with Jung as President and with branch societies in the various countries. There were tiny signs before 1914 of some interest in psycho-analysis in England at the meetings of the British Medical Association.

After the war translations of all Freud's works from a number of hands appeared in England and in the United States. There was a great deal of talk about Freud and his theories in intellectual circles in this country. The British Psycho-Analytical Society was reorganized in February 1919 and psycho-analysis extended into the discussions of at least the new Medical Section of the British Psychological Society. J. C. Flugel, who became one of Freud's leading expositors in this country, and W. H. R. Rivers, the distinguished anthropologist, were, with Ernest Jones, early members and leaders of this movement. William McDougall and Havelock Ellis declined to join.

In 1920 Percy Nunn, Professor of Education in the University of London, brought out a remarkable and influential book *Education: Its Data and First Principles*, in which he tried to chart his way between theories of natural selection and physical inheritance and McDougall's postulation of a varying number of innate tendencies, instincts and capacities; between the 'adjustment' model of Dewey, the *élan vital* of Bergson and the genetic forces of Freud, Jung and Adler. Nunn wrote as a liberal thinker who wished to enable each child to realize his potential more completely and he called upon knowledge of human psychology and educational practice for this purpose. He wrote as a scholar with thirty years of reading and thought to back his analysis. He provides the guide-lines for educational clarification and the prolegomena to practice. While his examples from schools are chosen both from within the maintained system and from the independent sector, including public and progressive schools, there can be no mistake that his prescriptions advise emancipation, the chance to experiment, to play, to create. He acknowledges the place and necessity of routine and ritual, but as a ground and soil for the security from which independence grows. These are principles dear to the heart of the educational radicals.

Far more than Herbert Spencer before him Nunn represents an educational theory based on science (especially the emerging science of psychology) and philosophy and he focused for a decade the thinking of many people concerned with education and teaching. Educational radicals saw in him an ally who gave theoretical depth to their practice, a sympathizer who instanced what was being done by Homer Lane, by J. H. Simpson, by Badley, by Caldwell Cook in Cambridge and put it all into a much larger intellectual framework. But, although he gave space to the work of the dynamic psychologists, Nunn's impact was nothing like as profound on the progressive schools as Freud's, whose concentration of attention on the significance of infantile experience was of the greatest importance to radical thought in English education and we can best illustrate this from individuals and the schools which they started.

I

We shall return to A. S. Neill and his school in fuller detail later and here we need only say enough to put him in his position as the first of the Freudian radicals in education.[2] Neill is an East Coast Scot who was born in 1883 as the son of a Scottish dominie and one of a large family. His school record was bad and he seems to have stumbled into pupil-teaching when his father could not think what his youngest son might do. He reached Edinburgh University as a mature student, read English for his degree and, when he graduated in 1912, went into publishing and contributed many pages to an encyclopaedia of the time. As we have already seen he met Homer Lane in 1916 and would have returned to work at the Little Commonwealth had it still been open when he was demobilised. Instead Neill went to teach at King Alfred School in Hampstead where he stayed for two years, becoming increasingly galled by the limits placed on the children's freedom, as he saw it. In 1920 he resigned and began four years of work in Germany, Austria and Holland, dealing with refugee children and ultimately conducting schools on the outskirts of Dresden and then in Austria.

During these years Neill met Wilhelm Stekel, who had been one of the original group of psycho-analysts in Vienna. In 1911 Stekel had broken away from Freud, but much of his analytical technique was like

[2] See Part II, Chapter 3.

Freud's. Neill had an extensive period of analysis with Stekel which he later said was of little help. Nevertheless Neill saw psycho-analysis as the chart by which he wished to steer and Freud as his pilot. When he returned to England in 1924 he started Summerhill near Lyme Regis and the ideas he had expressed in *The New Era*, when he was joint Editor for two years with Beatrice Ensor, now had the chance of coming to reality. While there have been some changes in his outlook and practice over the last forty years, probably Neill's Summerhill has remained the most consistent and the most extreme of the radical schools :

> Freud showed that every neurosis is founded on sex repression. I said, 'I'll have a school in which there will be no sex repression'. Freud said that the unconscious was infinitely more important and more powerful than the conscious. I said, 'In my school we won't censure, punish, moralize. We will allow every child to live according to his deep impulses'.[3]

This school, first in Dorset and later in Suffolk, was the first of the new wave of the radical schools of the twenties whose main differences from the other groups that we have mentioned so far are directly related to the emphasis on the nature, interpretation and importance of infantile experience to be found in psychoanalytic theory and practice.

II

No one English educationalist, by reason of her teaching, writing and practice has had more influence on the treatment and understanding of young children than Susan Isaacs. She was a student at the Universities of London, Manchester and Cambridge in the first decade of this century, being trained in philosophy and psychology to which later she added a deep understanding of psychoanalysis both as a student of its theory and as a practising analyst concerned particularly with children's problems. In addition to this impressive academic preparation she had trained as a teacher and had taught in schools, a training college and just before the outbreak of the War in the University of Manchester as a Tutor in Logic. In 1924 at the age of thirty-nine she became the first and only Principal of the Malting House School in Cambridge for children mainly aged from three to seven years, attracted to this

---

[3] A. S. Neill, *Summerhill : A Radical Approach to Education* (London, 1962), p. 294.

E

unusual enterprise by the prospect of pioneering teaching and research. However, before we consider the school further, we should turn back to the work for young children of another remarkable woman, whose name we have already mentioned, Margaret McMillan, and who may be regarded as a forerunner of Susan Isaacs in some ways.

Rachel and Margaret McMillan were born in New York State in 1859 and 1860 to Scottish parents who had emigrated to America after the clearances of the Scottish Highlands. Their father and a beloved younger sister died when the girls were five and six years old and Mrs. McMillan took her two young daughters back to her parents in Inverness. Life became austere and subdued for all three of them : 'Hitherto we had been the objects of quiet but intense interest and solicitude. Now we have no claims. . . . Our mother had passed into shadow. It was as if she had done something wrong in becoming a widow.'⁴ The girls were given a 'good Scottish education' at Inverness Academy where, as Margaret wrote, there was little child study but there was scholarship. In a letter written to a friend sixty years later Margaret said that her school life had made her a rebel and reformer.

Rachel stayed in Inverness and nursed her grandmother for eleven years until her death in 1888, and then at the age of twenty-nine Rachel became junior superintendent of a working girls' hostel in London where Margaret, who had trained in Switzerland and worked as a governess, joined her. The sisters became devoted servants of the Socialist cause, hearing the leading speakers, meeting Keir Hardie, Hyndman, William Morris, Shaw, Annie Besant and many others, reading and distributing literature.

In 1887–8 the two sisters tried to befriend Whitechapel working women, to introduce them to poetry and to singing and to show them some simple political facts. These women came to the class for a joke after a long day's work and submitted the earnest, forceful and gifted Margaret to shouts, cat-calls, counter-singing, unprintable parodies, collapsible chairs, jets of water and other liquids, and to a general physical manhandling. Rachel, who accompanied her sister to encourage her, and who was much less of a public personality, grew more and more dubious of the value of these classes. Margaret's confidence

---

⁴ M. McMillan, *The Life of Rachel McMillan* (London, 1927), pp. 15, 16. Yet Margaret McMillan dedicated *Labour and Childhood* (London, 1907) : 'To the memory of my grandfather who was as a father to me and whose gentle and chivalrous character first taught me to have faith in humanity.'

and ebullience were badly shaken : '[The Whitechapel girls] I am bound to say led me a dreadful life ... and my school was a Babel where everyone amused herself as she chose. .... The East End did not want me. It had no use for my feeble powers and vain offerings.'5

Depressed by this experience, but as staunch a Socialist as ever, Margaret took employment with Lady Meux in 1888 as governess to a child she had adopted. In her *Life of Rachel McMillan* Margaret refers to her patron as Lady X and in another memoir she is referred to as Lady Harknett, a 'pseudonym for a name which has brought refreshment to many'.6 Lady Meux's husband was a well known and highly successful brewer.

Margaret was placed in a most favoured position in the Park Lane household. Lady Meux was a quixotic and modish society hostess who regarded this striking and idealistic woman as a rare acquisition. Margaret was given beautiful clothes and trained over many months as an actress by leading producers, experts in voice production and a doctor who taught her to understand the importance of developed breathing to health itself as well as to elocution. By 1892 Margaret had finished two trainings and no longer wished to be either a governess or an actress. She had also come to sense that she had been exploited as a novelty in what she called Lady Meux's 'cynical kind of Bohemia backed by Mammon'.

The stresses in this explosive patronage became dangerous. Margaret wrote an article in 1889 in *The Christian Socialist* which attacked the Church for its failure to examine political and economic conditions. At Lady Meux's invitation she had brought Louise Michel, whom Margaret and Rachel had often visited and heard speak, to dinner in Park Lane with some of the coterie of Lady Meux's friends. *La Vierge Rouge* played her anarchist role with such relish that as the exhibit she disturbed the spectators even beyond their sophisticated expectation.7 One of the party heard Margaret speaking in Hyde Park on May Day 1892, supporting action by the workers against exploitation. The governess had not been tamed and this realization intensified 'the intermittent fever' of Lady Meux's whims and produced the final break in 1892 when, according to Margaret, Lady Meux spoke as her final, histrionic words, 'Go ! You may blot me out of your memory !'

---

5 Ibid., pp. 38, 39, 42.
6 D. Cresswell, *Margaret McMillan : A Memoir* (London, 1948), p. 48.
7 For an account of the meeting see M. McMillan, *Rachel McMillan*, pp. 63–71.

However, they saw one another and wrote from time to time.

We have no reason to look longer at these four years of Margaret's life and the curious, ambivalent affection that existed between the society hostess and the dedicated Socialist to whom she said before she died in 1910 that the budget was killing her and that Margaret was helping to bring this about.

In 1892 we come to the beginning of the known achievements of the McMillan sisters, but even these few brush strokes covering the first thirty years of their lives give some hint of how different their story is from that of Reddie, Badley, and Devine. When Rachel and Margaret went to Bradford to start upon their life's work for child health and nursery schools Susan Isaacs, whose life was also so very different, was eight years old.

The Socialist group in Bradford sent a formal deputation to London in 1892 to invite Margaret to make her home in Bradford and this she did, Rachel going with her. They found themselves members of a Labour Church and of the newly formed Independent Labour Party. Margaret was to be a propagandist and in time was to run as a Labour candidate for election to the School Board. She lectured pretty well all over the country, especially around Bradford, and now 'our Margaret' found she was not at odds with Whitechapel working women, but was at one with the positive Yorkshire working-class movement. The Independent Labour Party was committed to war on capitalism and competition, to promote the creation and distribution of wealth in a new way and to care for the unemployed and the needy. In 1894 Margaret McMillan was elected to the Bradford School Board, scraping in at the bottom of the poll: 'I was elected to fight . . . the battle of the slum child.'[8]

There were four services that Margaret McMillan fought to have provided, school baths, the provision of school meals, medical inspection and treatment and finally, nursery schools. In Bradford she and her colleagues were able to obtain the first school baths and even the first recorded medical inspection of school children. In the campaign for these services which Rachel and Margaret conducted in London ten years later, Sir Robert Morant, then Permanent Secretary at the Board of Education, wrote to Margaret whom he greatly admired: 'There is no Act on the Statute Book that gives any power to a local authority to carry on this kind of work in schools. You did it

[8] M. McMillan, *Rachel McMillan*, p. 86.

in Bradford, you know: you didn't know the law — didn't want to know it, I think.'

Margaret resigned from the Bradford School Board and left Bradford in 1902, the year of the Balfour Education Act, to return to London to be with Rachel who had meanwhile completed a training as a sanitary inspector and was working for the Kent Education Committee mainly teaching mothers and children some elementary hygiene. Margaret lectured for the Ethical Society, for the Workers' Educational Association, founded in 1903, for the Independent Labour Party on whose National Administration Council she sat in 1907 and she was on the Council of the Froebel Society. She was vastly busy and in demand for all Leftist educational causes, and most general inquiries into children's conditions and needs. In 1900 she produced *Early Childhood*, a book which called on her practical experience as a teacher of young children. She wrote of their moral and manual training, of the needs of feeble-minded children and the fatigue of half-timers, youngsters who worked half-time in mills and factories and spent the rest of their time in school. In 1904 she wrote *Education through the Imagination* from which many of her later disagreements with Dr. Montessori may be deduced. She wrote a number of pamphleteering articles about this time, like *The Child and the State* in 1907 attacking the evils of dirt, drink, disease and hunger, and *Citizens of Tomorrow* (1906) in which she placed educational development 'in the radiant light of the forward-swinging torch of medical science'. Other titles which speak for themselves are *Schools of Tomorrow* (1908) and *London Children: how to feed them and how not to feed them* (1907). She crowned this with her book *Labour and Childhood* in 1907. Ten years earlier she had been a frequent contributor to Blatchford's *Clarion*, Campbell's *Christian Socialist* and the *London Echo*. Besides this output in writing and speaking she and Rachel were able to see a seal set on this part of their life's work when in 1906 the Education (Provision of Meals) Act was passed and in 1907 the Education (Administrative Provisions) Act which included as Clause 13 the provision for medical inspection of school children by a local authority.

In 1908 Margaret and Rachel followed on their Bradford venture by opening up a school clinic at Bow in East London. For two years it was not a great success, despite heroic work. In June 1910 they moved over the Thames and a few miles up river towards the City, to Deptford. This time they had about £500 a year from that tireless and wayward philanthropist Joseph Fels and the use of a house and a hall without rent. They were on the right side of the law on this occasion and the clinic was opened by Sir John Gorst, President of the Board of Education and Sir Cyril Jackson, Chairman of the London County Council. About six thousand children a year attended. In 1911 an open-air camp school in the garden of their Deptford house was opened. Seventeen girls aged from six to fourteen slept under canvas each night, taking shower baths beforehand; and soon on nearby waste-ground a similar camp for boys was started. There was suspicion and hostility locally and dire results were prophesied, but Margaret, calling upon her earlier training, had great faith in correct posture, carriage and breathing and found that the open air and cleanliness, even in the slums of Deptford, made the children healthier. A day nursery school was started for children under five and the medical care and educational provision developed all the while, both the sisters working ceaselessly and gaining the respect and grudging admiration of their neighbours. After the outbreak of war in 1914 they ran a night-and-day nursery school in what was a dangerous area and they found their task a killing one as the call for women munition workers became more insistent. Their premises were badly damaged by a bomb. Rachel died in 1917 after herculean labours for which, as Margaret wrote, the training of finely-nurtured English girls did not equip them. Both the sisters, with all their love of children, knew in their heart's core 'the brutishness, the vermin and all the plagues of the pit.'

In 1918 the President of the Board of Education H. A. L. Fisher opened the new Nursery School building, and Margaret of the I.L.P., the Ethical Society and the suffragette movement was made a C.B.E. In 1921 Queen Mary opened the extension to the Nursery School and in 1930 she opened the Rachel McMillan Training College, Margaret's memorial to her sister. Margaret having been awarded a Civil List pension in 1927 was made a Companion of Honour a few months before her death in 1931.

In 1923 Margaret McMillan became Founder-President of the Nursery Schools Association and in an article she wrote in 1926 she summed up the aims of the school for which she and her sister are best known. It was for children of two to five years of age though this could stretch to seven or nine. Its type of education, curriculum and regime should be related to the open air as much as possible with buildings and staff (not all of whom need be teachers) prepared to deal with one hundred and fifty to three hundred small children and their parents, with whom close association ought to be established. The training of the children was to be related to their sense experience, and learning was to develop imaginatively from common objects, animals and experiences and not from the didactic apparatus of Montessori. The Fabian-Socialist, the member of the I.L.P., the political evangelist, appeared in the assertion that such a school would help to break down class and professional prejudice. Lastly, Margaret saw in these schools a wonderful opportunity for research and child study. She had herself done too many things, fought too many political and administrative battles, to have written the works of research for which, in any case, she was not equipped but which she rightly saw as waiting upon investigators with training and insight :

> The open-air nursery-school as envisaged by Margaret McMillan is the starting point of new 'preventative medicine' where the doctor will no longer be needed. She prophesied that the extension of its principles into education, and still further projected into the people's health centres of the future, could effect a revolution as yet undreamt of. Research and experiment on these lines, she said, would lead to startling discoveries.[9]

Which brings us back to Susan Isaacs and the Malting House School. On 22 March 1924 a full-page advertisement appeared in the *New Statesman* seeking

> An Educated Young Woman, with Honours degree — preferably first class — or the equivalent, to conduct the education of a small group of children aged $2\frac{1}{2}$–7, as a piece of scientific work and research ... someone who has considered themself too good for teaching and who has already engaged in another occupation. ... Large salary ... Preference will be given to those who do not hold any form of religious belief, but this is not by itself ... a substitute for other qualifications.

The advertiser was Geoffrey Pyke a man of erratic and eclectic brilliance. In 1921 his son had been born and Pyke, having read some psychoanalytic writings, decided characteristically that the infant must be educated free from neurosis. From the time of the child's birth the father began to read widely in educational literature and he decided on four things. First, that he would have to undergo psychoanalysis in order to equip himself to discharge his duties and responsibilities as a wise father. Second, that his son must go to school early to grow up and learn with other children. Third, no school that he knew in Cambridge could provide the emancipation and challenge that he wanted, so he would have to get one started himself. Fourth, that this school would discover things that would benefit other schools and in time it could affect the education given to young children throughout the country provided that a research function were realized from the beginning.

Other than his own schooling Pyke had had no previous educational experience and his eccentricity had kept him from completing any formal academic training although his ability was known to be great. But we are only concerned here with his extraordinary career for a few years.[10] As part of his strategy for the model school he wanted he devised in the early twenties an ingenious, daring but carefully worked out plan for investment in the purchase and sale of metals, based on meticulous observation of the world's metal supplies and the share-market. He amassed a great deal of money and with this behind him and with his wife's agreement he placed the advertisement already mentioned in the *New Statesman* and rented the Malting House in Cambridge with its spacious garden. Susan Isaacs agreed to become the Principal provided that she was in full charge and was responsible for all the educational decisions. It did not need Susan Isaacs' psychological training to discern the need for clear understandings with so quixotic a personality as Geoffrey Pyke. For his part he signed an agreement, saying that he would act like the monarch under the British Constitution, putting forward ideas which Mrs. Isaacs was under no obligation to accept, and on this understanding the school opened in October 1924.

Susan Isaacs as a scholar of wide experience was interested in the educational ideas of many people and she was particularly influenced by the thinking of Maria Montessori, John Dewey and Sigmund Freud. She saw the importance of sequence, of challenge, of sensory material and of individual learning in the Montessori system. However, Mrs. Isaacs was also interested in the work of John Dewey who had started with his wife the Laboratory School at the University of Chicago in 1896, 'to discover in administration, selection of subject-matter, methods of learning, teaching and discipline, how a school could become a co-operative community while developing in individuals

---

[10] For a fuller account see D. Lampe, *Pyke the Unknown Genius* (London, 1959.)

their own capacities and satisfying their own needs.'[11] In 1899 Dewey published *The School and Society*, three lectures he gave to parents and patrons of the School in which he said:

> [We must] make each one of our schools an embryonic community life, active with types of occupations that reflect the life of the larger society, and permeated throughout with the spirit of art, history and science. When the school introduces and trains each child of society into membership within such a little community, saturating him with the spirit of service, and providing him with the instruments of effective self-direction, we shall have the deepest and best guarantee of a larger society which is worthy, lovely and harmonious.[12]

These ideas are developed in range and complexity in *Moral Principles in Education* (1909), *How We Think* (1910), *Interest and Effort in Education* (1913) and above all in *Democracy and Education* (1916) and in a number of other books and articles, some of them devoted, like *My Pedagogic Creed* (1897) and *The Child and the Curriculum* (1902), to the business of how and what to teach. Mrs. Isaacs knew Dewey's work as an educationalist and a philosopher and accepted the stress placed on the social role of the school both in its internal organization and activity-method, and in its adaptation outward of curriculum, method and aims to the requirements of a society undergoing rapid transformation.

There is a vast literature by and about Dewey and in much of it the social emphasis is so heavily stressed that Dewey's insistence on the ultimate understanding and participation by individuals is often overlooked: '(Education) is that reconstruction or reorganization of experience which adds to the meaning of experience, and which increases the ability to direct the course of subsequent experience.'[13] In other words education is for fullest individual growth. Mrs. Isaacs recognized the significance of this rather heavily self-evident maxim expressed in Dewey's radical and most original practice. She describes the Malting House School in the first volume of what was intended to be a trilogy[14] and acknowledges that what she did may well

---

[11] K. C. Mayhew and A. C. Edwards, *The Dewey School* (New York, 1936), pp. xv–xvi.

[12] J. Dewey, *School and Society* (New York, 1899), pp. 43–44.

[13] Op. cit. pp. 89–90.

[14] *Intellectual Growth in Young Children* (London, 1930), chapter ii, pp. 14–18. The second volume *Social Development in Young Children* appeared in 1933. The third one was to be case studies of children and this did not appear.

have been the first expression in England of Dewey's practice. She says in the later volume:

> I was a trained teacher of young children and a student of Dewey's educational theories. . . . [The school] was an application to the education of very young children of the educational philosophy of John Dewey. This was my active inspiration.[15]

Whereas the Deweys in their Laboratory School started with sixteen pupils in 1896 and reached one hundred and forty in 1902 the Malting House School opened with ten boys in 1924 and ended as far as Mrs. Isaacs was concerned with twenty boys and girls in 1927. This small school, where the age range varied from two years eight months to ten years five months at different times, provided all the data for the two important books. As the location was Cambridge the children were mostly from professional families, many of them university families, and the mental ratio ranged between 114 and 166 with a mean of 131. At first it was a day school only but boarders were taken in the second year and in the end about one third of the children lived in a house attached to the school and in another a little way away. In all cases the children had their own bed-sitting room built to scale, brightly painted and with a lock on the door, the key being in the possession of the occupant.

There was a hall which gave out on to a larger garden where trees, sand pits and water pools and the first 'jungle gym' in England provided chances for adventure and discovery in plenty. At the back of the hall was a gallery where visitors, including parents, could observe this unusual school in action. However, after a while the number of visitors grew too great and a ban was enforced. Under the gallery climbing bars and swings offered undercover agility. The children were encouraged to cook, bake and make drinks, using the gas cooker, utensils and crockery provided. Shelves, tables, chairs and simple beds were all made to scale, and paper, clay, plasticine, crayons, paints (both artist's colours and the housepainter's variety), blackboards and easels were available. A complete kit of tools, including a double-handed saw for cutting up logs, was in constant use together with the miscellaneous materials needed in any informal work with young children — the rope, paste, paper, building bricks and fabrics of all

[15] *Social Development in Young Children*, pp. 18–19.

kinds. These children had also a hand lens, Bunsen burners, flasks, tubing, tripods and the impedimenta of simple science teaching. They had dissecting instruments, specimen-jars, a human skeleton, anatomical diagrams and a small menagerie of pets and animals ranging from rabbits, mice, dogs and cats to snakes, salamanders and silkworms. On the formal side of teaching the Malting House had the entire Montessori equipment and several of the specially constructed sets of books and materials for reading and number not to mention a typewriter and a range of maps.

Mrs. Isaacs believed that many nursery and junior schools in the twenties encouraged art and craft, literature and music, all the arts of self-expression, together with reading and writing. She wanted to make use of children's curiosity about everything, the electric light, drains, water-supply, the gas cooker, the telephone, the policeman. And, of course, after a while, their own bodily development and habits. This factual curiosity was as important to Mrs. Isaacs' view of education as the ideals of self-expression and make-believe and the basics of reading, writing, and computing.

There was no fixed curriculum and no class teaching, but an emphasis on discovery by the child, with a corresponding quick-wittedness in the teacher to take the chance offered by a question like 'Where does the stuff we use in sewing come from?' to begin simple weaving and to visit a shop to see how big the bales of cloth could be when machines were used. Or to start on a dissection when a dead mouse or rabbit had been found and curiosity led that way before the obsequies supervened.

Free discussion was characteristic of the method and little or no restraint was placed on the children — they were co-investigators with their teachers. They were also expected to be precise and responsible about certain things : they had to wash up their own crockery, to clear up apparatus at the end of a lesson, they had to order their meals from a menu with prices, often on a limited budget, and the order had to be lodged with the cook by a certain time or a meal from the menu was not provided. There was no retributive punishment but there was the discipline of a required routine. The older children could prepare itineraries from maps and go on a sight-seeing bus tour having established the cost and the timing of the whole operation. Many of these features arise out of an approach to school that is strikingly like John Dewey's. The connection was strengthened for a short while in

1927 when in answer to another of Pyke's full-page advertisements (in *The Times* on this occasion) for 'a scientist of the first order ... for the beginnings of a research institute into the problems connected with education. ...' Richard Slavson, a thirty-six-year-old Russian-born educator from New York, was engaged from over one hundred and fifty applicants, seven of them university teachers. However, difficulties in the relationship with Pyke were beginning to appear and Slavson was only in Cambridge for a few months.

We have already seen that Mrs. Isaacs was sympathetic to Dr. Montessori's methods, but not a committed disciple. She thought that:

> (Dr. Montessori) has given her genius for devising techniques to the narrow ends of the scholastic subjects. ... To us the direct interests of the child in the concrete processes in the world around him seem far more significant in themselves, and as a medium of education, than knowledge of the traditional 'subjects' of the schoolroom. In other words we see no reason to let the school and its conventions stand between the child and real situations in the world.[16]

The third influence upon Mrs. Isaacs' theory and practice was Freud. If Dewey gave an unusual and permissive informality to the Malting House routine and regimen, while Montessori and other teaching aids gave a certain experimentalism in pedagogic techniques, Freud brought the most shocking of the innovations. Susan Isaacs could say that she had been a student of Dewey's and Montessori's ideas long before she knew anything of Freud, but it was the cross-indexed detailed evidence supporting infantile sexuality in its oral, anal and genital phases which was the most explosive material in *Social Development in Young Children*, and in the articles which preceded it: 'I was just as ready to *record* and *study* the less attractive aspects of [young children's] behaviour as the more pleasing, whatever my aims and preferences as their *educator* might be.'[17]

In her Introduction to *Social Development* Mrs. Isaacs gives a clear account of her difficulties. She knew that the absence of reproof and the freedom of behaviour would lead to an obvious and aggressive interest, either verbal, actual or symbolic in sexual and excremental

---

[16] *Forum of Education*, vol. v, p. 131.
[17] *Social Development in Young Children*, p. 19.

expressions and this shocked a number of parents and helped to spread the *canard* in Cambridge to which we have become accustomed in other progressive schools even when they did not take the scientific, emancipated and psychoanalytic line that Mrs. Isaacs followed. The Malting House was a bedlam of foul-mouthed, unwashed, sexually precocious brats according to this report. Mrs. Isaacs' own account of the pupils' subdued beginning, followed by the discovery of the freedom to run about, to play, to quarrel without adult reprisal and the resultant aggression and hostility, reminds one of the accounts of the behaviour of Homer Lane's adolescents: 'Then gradually, and with occasional resurgences of mere wild disorder, the group began to take a definite social shape . . . until by the end of the year . . . [there was] full give and take of friendly adaptation.'[18]

Miss Evelyn Lawrence who started teaching at the Malting House in 1926 wrote of the expression of crudity and savagery and of sexual interest and curiosity. 'If Malting House children hate a person they tell him so', if they wanted to smoke they did so with the adults present, if they felt like swearing they could, and talk on sexual subjects was not shameful and unmentionable. 'I was not without doubts about the possible effects on the children's future manners and habits of the degree of freedom which they were allowed.'[19] She wondered what would be the outcome in the growth of kindliness, unselfishness and restraint in personal relationships but comes to the conclusion that she need not have worried to judge from her later knowledge of the easy manners and social conscience of her former pupils.

The school received much public attention; journalists visited it and wrote many articles with varying degrees of sympathy and understanding. Miss Mary Field made a film about it. Pyke began to favour a large expansion intending to take in not only the self-selecting children of professional men but to take also a cross-section of all people. While Susan Isaacs was not averse from some growth and expansion, she was anxious not to upset the research function and the continuing precise recording of data. Difference on this and other issues led to some fraying of relationships between the two and without declared hostility Susan Isaacs resigned in 1927. Pyke's

[18] *Social Development*, p. 22.
[19] E. Lawrence, *National Froebel Foundation Bulletin*, Feb. 1949. Miss Lawrence married Nathan Isaacs some years after Susan Isaacs' death in 1948.

success on the metal market fell quickly and steeply and he ended in bankruptcy in 1928. Slavson returned to the United States and for inescapable reasons Pyke closed the school in 1928. Before his death nearly twenty-five years later he had a number of further different careers each of them characterized by a *dégagé* brilliance.

Margaret and Rachel McMillan were political reformers fighting poverty, squalor, dirt and under-nourishment. They pioneered the provision of school baths, school medical inspection, school meals. Public health, hygiene and preventive medicine were their arenas at first and they were campaigning for twenty years for these causes as part of the Socialist strategy before they stumbled upon the need to care for children even before they came to school. Although they were well-read women with educational ideas, the Deptford open-air school had as much to do with hygiene and health as it had to do with teaching.

Susan Isaacs was not dealing with poor children nor with ignorant parents. She could take physical health and cleanliness for granted from the home interest and solicitude. Being an unusually gifted scholar and researcher she directed the favourable conditions with which Geoffrey and Margaret Pyke provided her to furnishing teaching experiences and data based on a school never bigger than twenty children, and on these her seminal books are based. In the course of writing these not only does she refer to Dewey, Montessori and Freud as important to her thinking, but she subjects the hypotheses of Jean Piaget to a most searching scrutiny, providing evidence to suggest that his generalizations might be too dogmatic, especially in relation to particular chronological ages of children. If Edmund Spenser has been called a poet's poet, Susan Isaacs might be called a psychologist's educator and an educator's psychologist. Her synthesis has in it a Freudian element altogether absent from the thinking of Dewey, Montessori, Piaget — and Margaret McMillan.

The radical nursery school for Margaret McMillan was the by-product of poverty, want, ill-health and need, and for Susan Isaacs it was the laboratory of the children of the intelligentsia and the occasion for a unique piece of research. These women revived something which Robert Owen, James Buchanan, and Samuel Wilderspin had explored each in his own way a century before. Although the Malting House School existed for only three years its indirect influence has been out of all proportion to its life-span or size : 'The fact that the nation as a whole is advancing rather rapidly in its ways of handling young children both at home and at school is due to [Susan Isaacs] more than to any other single person.'[20]

20 From an obituary by Evelyn Lawrence, *New Era*, Dec. 1948, p. 223.

Chapter Seven

THE POST-WAR SURGENCE:
THE TWENTIES

3. The New Communities: Dartington and Beacon Hill

I

OF all the schools considered in this book there is only one which is founded as part of a larger social experiment. Dartington Hall Trust began as a rural community enterprise in which the school was a necessary development which did not come right at the beginning. But we must go back before 1925 to see how all this came about.

Leonard Elmhirst is a Yorkshireman whose family have lived in that county for over six centuries. There were eight sons, Leonard being the second, and after going to school at Repton he went up to Cambridge to read history and theology thinking that he might follow his father in taking Holy Orders. He decided not to do this and had not settled on his career when the First World War broke out. He spent the period 1915–18 in service with the army in India and became deeply concerned in the social, political, and agricultural problems of the sub-continent. The objectives he had been seeking for his career became plain and in 1919 when he left the army he decided to undertake a training in agriculture, and finding no course in England to satisfy his needs he chose Cornell University where the programme included a training in science and economics as each is related to practical farming, which was what Mr. Elmhirst saw as the kind of preparation needed. His family was not wealthy and he earned his keep and paid his way through Cornell with the help of a scholarship in a kind of life very different from his Cambridge days. In 1921 he completed his degree at Cornell and in the same year he met Rabindranath Tagore in New York: 'I remember how you came fresh from your university and you were absurdly young, but you were not in the least academic or aridly intellectual'.[1]

Tagore had a sanctuary-school at Santiniketan which preserved and in some sense transformed the Indian style of life in dance, music, drama, and poetry. He saw the need to extend this liberal education for the children of prosperous parents much farther and wanted to help in the reconstruction of the social and economic life of the villages, and he saw in Leonard Elmhirst the man to lead the venture. In February 1922 Mr. Elmhirst, with a tiny staff and ten Indian students, all of whom said they wanted to be farmers, went at Tagore's invitation to the village of Surul about a mile and a half from Santiniketan. The new school was called Sriniketan, 'the abode of grace', which they preferred to the English title, the Institute of Rural Reconstruction. At that time, instead of plenty, Mr. Elmhirst found as he said 'monkeys, malaria and mutual mistrust' and it was his task to conquer hostility and apathy and to present a subsistence programme not at all unlike the later Basic Education programme of Unesco and United Nations. Mr. Elmhirst called upon his experience of Baden-Powell's Scout Movement in England and similar American groups, seeking to find a new type of education for village children which took full account of their natural surroundings. At a later date Tagore and Leonard Elmhirst worked out the details for a boys' boarding school called Siksha-Satra which began in 1925 after Mr. Elmhirst had left India, and which still continues.

Mr. Elmhirst was able to rouse village boys and girls to grow vegetables, to put out fires, give first aid, sing songs, administer quinine and 'see the pill swallowed'. Craftsmen who were starving were subsidized and retrained and some of the elements of orderly marketing were presented. After a period of mistrust village scoutmasters began to come forward and by the time Siksha-Satra was ready to start, many of the features which appeared in its five-day boarding school week had been tried out in the Sriniketan experiment. Duties in the dormitory,

---

[1] From a letter to Mr. Elmhirst from Rabindranath Tagore quoted in a book edited by the former, *Rabindranath Tagore, Pioneer in Education* (London, 1961), p. 28.

the kitchen, the garden, poultry-run and dairy were coupled with weaving, preparing food, washing, ground cleaning and clearing drains. The children were taught to use their hands in woodwork. The closeness to the needs of village life effected many changes in the community for the better, for lessons in rotation of crops were taught, public responsibility was accepted in guarding against fire and against theft and in the constant attack on mosquitoes and bacteria. This became, in the schools where it was practised, an important public service and was intimately concerned with the welfare services that were provided. Mr. Elmhirst thought that by a little practical training 75 per cent of the ill health of rural India could be eliminated in a few months by the children and as an example he chose malaria which affected 90 per cent of any village which it attacked. The children could map out the village, its dwellings, storage tanks, drains; cesspits and water channels could be dug, all of this being an aspect of social geography. Keeping health records, tracking and locating the breeding ground of anopheles and disinfecting brought knowledge of chemistry, bacteriology, zoology, and social welfare. To understand the linkages between cleanliness, water supply, pollution, sanitation, and the need for firm laws with police sanctions in the interests of health was to learn lessons in civics, local politics, morals, and hygiene which showed more than anything else how close-knit the village community is. At the other end of the scale the experiments carried out by the boys in growing vegetables and producing new crops contained lessons in nutrition and agricultural botany that adults might pick up from their children.

Mr. Elmhirst learned to read the barometer of Hindu village life: 'With your instinctive humanity you came into the closest touch with the living being which is the village and which is not a mere intellectual problem that could be solved through the help of arithmetical figures.'[2] His village schools were 'home schools'; even Siksha-Satra was a 'home school' although the boys boarded. The main features of the schools were the spirit of neighbourly service and the sense of being in touch with life in all the school work. Meteorology was found in the relationship between the weather, and the crops. History was the data of local industries, crafts and social enterprise; it was in the religion, the music, the drama, the customs. The motto of the school was 'Freedom for growth':

[2] *Rabindranath Tagore, Pioneer in Education* (London, 1961), p. 29.

Of all the conflicts in the field of education, that between Imagination and Discipline is the most bitter and prolonged. . . . If a child is to have freedom for growth it must have freedom to regulate its own life, freedom from interference and supervision. . . . The minimum of discipline that is necessary for the maximum of liberty. To encourage the children to set their own bounds and to reason out their own discipline needs a real faith in their capacity and a real courage.[3]

Mr. Elmhirst left Sriniketan in 1924 to travel with Tagore as his secretary to China, Japan, Argentina, Italy, and back to the United States. Before we turn to the new chapter in his life that leads to Dartington it would be wise to underline some of the features in this first phase.

Leonard Elmhirst is a countryman with a family history of country associations. He was a young man of undogmatic religious idealism whose war experience put him in the way of seeing for himself what squalor and poverty villagers of another sub-continent either had to endure or made for themselves. America and more particularly Cornell gave him the training to combine tradition and human understanding with modern agricultural and social science. When he returned to India he had to work out an educational programme for, and win the trust of, villagers with traditional working habits, strong caste lines, no mechanization or modern agricultural knowledge, and the spectre of hunger always present. Behind the immediate local problems which faced him he saw the huge issue of India poised between three cultures: the ancient traditional fatalism; the ancient and modern folk-education of Gandhi's village *Nai Talim*; and the inevitable modernism of the machine.

The book on Tagore which has already been mentioned has as its dedication :

To Dorothy Whitney Straight who made Sriniketan possible.

Dorothy Whitney was the daughter of William C. Whitney, a noted American financier who also served his country as a Secretary of the Navy at Cabinet level. He died when Dorothy was seventeen and left her an independent fortune. She took her university education in New York at a time when Dewey, Thorndike, and James Earl Russell were building the international reputation of Teachers' College. In 1911 she married Willard Straight whom she met in Peking while on a world tour. Straight was a graduate of Cornell University who served for some years in China before returning to America where he continued to offer support to Chinese industrial, rail, and cultural enterprises. After volunteering in 1917 he died in France in 1918 leaving his wife with three young children and in his will he asked that something should be done 'to make Cornell a more human place'.[4] In working out a plan for a Students' Union called the Willard Straight Hall, Mrs. Straight called on the help and advice of Leonard Elmhirst who was at Cornell from 1919 to 1921. When he went to India, to Surul, Mrs. Straight gave financial backing to the enterprise and continued to support it until 1947. When Mr. Elmhirst returned to the United States he and Dorothy Whitney Straight were married in April 1925; they came to England and in September 1925 they bought the estate at Dartington near Totnes in Devonshire to which the whole of the rest of their lives has been devoted.

Dartington was an estate in pre-Norman times and maintained continuity through a thousand years. In the second half of the sixteenth century it came into the possession of the Champernowne family from whom, three and a half centuries later the Elmhirsts bought it, then reduced to about 820 acres.[5] They had two principal aims, to develop the natural resources of the estate and rehabilitate it both for itself and as a source of employment and livelihood, and second, to provide the housing, social services, aesthetic activities, education, and personal enrichment necessary for country life to gain and regain a health of its own.

In 1931 the Elmhirsts established a Trust in which are invested all the land, buildings, and services and the shares in commercial enterprises both inside and outside Dartington. The commercial enterprises owned or partly owned by the Trust provide the money which gives backing to other activities that may and usually do not run at a profit. Dartington Hall Ltd. controls farms, a textile mill, and a shop selling products from Dartington and elsewhere; Dartington Woodlands Ltd. manages 2,000 acres of forest as a commercial undertaking; Staverton Contractors Ltd. is a building and civil engineering firm with an extensive joinery and furniture shop attached; the Dartington Sawmills Ltd., partly owned by the Trust, deals in cut timber in all forms of the trade.

---

[4] Quoted from information supplied by Mrs. Elmhirst.
[5] The area of the land now owned is over 4,000 acres.

The non-commercial activities are called the Trustee Departments and include the school, the Arts Centre as it was formerly called,[6] the Adult Education Centre, research projects, grounds and gardens, and the estate department responsible for the maintenance and upkeep of all land and buildings. The progress of the scheme owed nearly everything to the generosity of the Elmhirsts in the early years, but now the Trust has a balanced budget as a considerable enterprise. At first, however, Dartington had more than budgetary problems to face. The Elmhirsts did not hunt or shoot or fish, nor did they pay formal calls; although Leonard Elmhirst was an Englishman, his wife was American and he was thought to have assimilated many transatlantic notions and practices. In a world of rural conservatism the new Dartington community was cosmopolitan and politically far to the left; the interest of foreigners, socialists, and pacifists in the experiment introduced strange and controversial persons to Totnes. The work done in the arts brought painters, sculptors, composers, musicians, actors, and dancers to Dartington. The revitalization of the country crafts had some colour of local success in the first ten years, but the life of the arts centre was too violent a contrast for rural assimilation. Even the new enterprises in forestry, farming, and general agriculture ran into trouble because of their sheer enlightenment. Buildings were erected or remodelled with taste and style, new houses for estate workers were architect-designed. According to Bonham-Carter, in the first five years pay was more generous than was offered by many local farmers, and pensions, sickness benefits, holidays with pay were all disturbingly liberal in a traditional farming county.[7] Some neighbouring employers resented the unfair advantages offered by these inexperienced intruders and were aggrieved at the competition in a time of high unemployment. All kinds of obloquy were levelled at Dartington and Bonham-Carter writes that while some of it was ignorant, prejudiced, even vicious, in other cases Dartington asked for it by its aggressive, *avant-garde* self-sufficiency, by the amateurs, the eccentrics, and the fanatics who took advantage of the generosity of the Elmhirsts and the Trustees. At the centre of the Dartington community was the school, and this too was conceived in the same spirit of radical liberalism as the rest.

[6] This enterprise is now called the College of Arts and is mainly concerned with the training of teachers in the arts, in conjunction with the Institute of Education of the University of Exeter.

[7] See Victor Bonham-Carter, *Dartington Hall* (London, 1958), pp. 25 ff.

Mrs. Elmhirst had three children by her first marriage who had been educated at Lincoln School, New York, founded by Abraham Flexner in September 1917 by arrangement with Teachers' College to which the school was attached and with the General Education Board of the Rockefeller Foundation by which the school was generously financed. Flexner considered that progressive schools in the United States had been too timid and he said: 'Modern education will include nothing simply because tradition recommends it. . . . It proceeds in just the opposite way: *it includes nothing for which an affirmative case cannot now be made out.*'[8]

His curricula were organized around the themes of science, industry, civics, and aesthetics together with a wide range of options. He employed an extended 'centre of interest' method developing many of the lines of theory and practice started by Dewey and his wife over twenty years earlier in Chicago. Flexner regarded Lincoln School as a laboratory which would test and evaluate the bases of its own theory and the results it produced and these are words almost identical with those used thirty years earlier by Reddie about Abbotsholme. The Lincoln School earned the kind of ferocious hostility and barbs of ridicule familiar to the progressive schools in England, not least to Dartington, the school which was plainly and firmly based on American example.[9]

The Elmhirsts had in mind as part of the Dartington idea that a fully-equipped and staffed co-educational boarding school could provide the basis of a common life for pupils, children of teaching and estate staff, and children of work-people, artists, and administrators, helping to dissolve differences and remove barriers. The estate undertakings could be used as part of an education as utilitarian, pragmatic, and un-structured as American experience, amateur enthusiasm, and secure finance could make it. Professor Lindemann of the New York School of Social Work met eleven members of the estate and teaching staff in preliminary discussion for five days in mid-September 1926, a few days after which the school opened with ten pupils. As Mr. and Mrs. Elmhirst said with engaging modesty in 1962 to the present author, after forty years of most remarkable work, they were all in 1926 quite remarkably inexperienced for the task of running a school based on a

[8] A. Flexner, *A Modern College and a Modern School* (New York, 1923), p. 120.

[9] For comments on Lincoln School and a valuable biography see Cremin, *Transformation of the School*, pp. 280–91 and 381–2.

discipline of persuasion in which staff and pupils consulted one another on the diet and the arrangements for safety, first aid, cleanliness, and rest. In the first five years the numbers had grown to fifty and the transience of staff (twenty-two in this five-year period) had produced a somewhat unsettled community. For the first few years, on the principle of equality, no one on the staff was given the authority and responsibility of being the head of the school. Each child had a 'second' or moral tutor whose task was to act as counsellor to the boy or girl and adviser to the parents, to whom personal reports were sent if requested, but not as a termly routine. One of the masters offered rudimentary psychotherapy to the children if needed, part of the technique being dream-interpretation.

After about eighteen months Dr. Williams, the school doctor, reported that the children were being fatigued and burdened by too much discussion and consultation with consequent effect on their schoolwork and that the belief in freedom at the cost of routine and secure order had gone too far. In June 1928 Dr. Bonser of the Teachers' College, Columbia University, was invited to report on the school (the Trustees have a willingness to invite outsiders frequently to scrutinize and assess what is going on) and this American critic from a stronghold of pragmatism and freedom in education said quite roundly that while Dartington relied on advanced psychological theories it had not a sufficiently experienced team of teachers to make the theories effective. The children were unpunctual and undisciplined, the psychotherapy given by a master was unsuccessful and undesirable. If the children's resistance to hard work was overcome by a disciplined approach to learning, their progress would bring its own reward. Bonser was equally severe with the practical work. He said that the Estate Departments were unsuitable agencies for educating the boys and girls. The children needed constructive and well-devised tasks for their own mental growth and the commercial enterprises were presenting them with problems connected with buying, selling, and profit-making. Besides this, the estate managers had neither the time nor the training for teaching and if the link was to be forged between the school and the estate it would have to be striven for by a better planned organization in pottery, gardening, woodwork, and estate work.

This report led to a new disposition of occupational interests between the school and the estate. The commercial enterprises were put under a Management Committee in 1927 and a limited company was founded in 1929. An Education Committee was constituted in a definite form in 1928 and the intimate structure of the early experiment began to disappear. The Bonser Report showed that expert knowledge and teaching skill were needed for a progressive school (perhaps especially for such a school) and that the existing staff were mostly amateurs. What would have suited ten or twenty pupils would not do for a much larger school. This sharp and realistic criticism unsettled many people and the uncertainty spread through the whole Dartington community : 'The school had sunk from the position of being the focus of the whole experiment to that of a poor and rather disreputable relation.'[10]

The Elmhirsts and their advisers decided to extend the schooling available by adding a primary school for children of nursery and infant school age and to provide new accommodation for all the children from the ages of two or three to eighteen. They took note of the need for expert teaching and direction and decided to appoint a head of the school who would also be Director of Education for the Estate as a whole. The nursery and primary schools were to be the nucleus of a department of child study staffed by the Director, the nursery school teachers, a psychologist with part-time help from a doctor, a nurse, and a dietician. The help of a secretary and a household manager with assistants was to provide the ancillary aid on which enlightened teaching and the research function could take place. The Elmhirsts looked for their staff in America where they found Winifred Harley, an Englishwoman working at the Merrill-Palmer School in Detroit. It was she who planned the Dartington nursery school buildings while still in Detroit with Delano and Aldrich, American architects. The Merrill-Palmer tests were to be used to assess the progress of the Dartington children and an English psychologist was sent to the University of London by the Elmhirsts to restandardize the American material for English use.[11] In 1931 the Director was appointed and his responsibility included the oversight of nursery, kindergarten and later the middle and senior schools, together with the Adult Education programme and the School of Dance and Mime.

At this point it should be said that four phases of the school have been combined in different ways at various times according to buildings,

[10] Manuscript source in Dartington Hall records.
[11] See a reference to this work done by Miss Hilda Bristol in H. R. Hamley, 'The Testing of Intelligence', *Year Book of Education* (London, 1935).

numbers, practical problems of accommodation, and educational experience. Without elaborating the detail of change over the years, at present the nursery and junior schools can take between them up to fifty children who are day pupils only, aged three to six in the nursery school and six to between nine and ten in the junior school. In other days there have been boarders, children of two have been in the nursery school, and the ages of moving between sections of the school have varied, as has the accommodation used. The middle school now takes boys and girls aged between nine and ten to between twelve and a half and thirteen and a half and it is at this stage that boarders are admitted. In the senior school the age-range is from about thirteen to eighteen or nineteen. Mention has already been made of the design of Aller Park as a nursery school and child-study centre planned by Miss Harley and American architects and opened in 1932 and extended later. Also in 1932 Foxhole, which now houses the senior school, was designed and opened, the first Director and Headmaster joining with the Trustees and the architects (British this time) in planning the accommodation. The first head was William Burnlee Curry who served the school from 1931 to 1957 and became, with Badley and Neill, one of the best-known names in progressive education.[12]

Curry was a Northumbrian born at the turn of the century. He did well at Alnwick Grammar School, ending as head boy and Senior Scholar of Trinity College, Cambridge, where he read Mathematics in the First Part of his Tripos in 1919 and natural sciences in the Second Part in 1921, gaining a Third in each: results not at all in keeping with his quality of mind. One of his former colleagues writes: 'Many of his staff had Firsts in the early days, and he was unquestionably their intellectual superior. I suppose one can make various deductions, according to inclination!'[13]

Curry says of his own school days that he had been brought up conventionally and had been more than content with his success at an orthodox grammar school. He was not among those who turned to progressive education in bitter revolt — interestingly enough, neither has any other pioneer progressive educationalist whom we have mentioned. Critical of the public school or grammar school teaching they all were, but with the exception of Neill, none of those so far considered smouldered at his own schooling, at any rate while he was

---

[12] Curry died after an accident in the summer of 1962.
[13] In a letter to the author in Dec. 1962.

undergoing it. Curry, like Reddie, Badley, Simpson, and Susan Isaacs said that while he was at school he saw no reason to question the system. In 1919, however, he read Bertrand Russell's *Principles of Social Reconstruction* and found his assurance deeply disturbed. The book was based on a series of lectures that Russell gave in London in 1916 on the conduct of the war (he advised the immediate conclusion of a peace on the best terms available); on a rational approach to marriage as the basis of the family and a form of social contract but not as an indissoluble relationship; on notions of authority, liberty, and intellectual freedom; and, of course, on education. Russell noted that at the beginning of 1914 men and women seemed to have a zest for the War and in an attempt to understand this apparent welcome to death, killing, and wounding he turned to Bernard Hart's *Psychology of Insanity*. Hart was one of the few English neurologists who had read and understood Freud — in 1911 he had written a masterly essay on the psychoanalytic concept of hysteria[14] and *The Psychology of Insanity* was a landmark in the popular recognition of unconscious impulses. Russell saw the positive growth of freedom in infancy as of central importance for future peace and discerned in repressive systems of education a predisposing influence toward aggression and savagery.

In 1916 Russell had been tried before the Lord Mayor at Mansion House for issuing 'statements likely to prejudice the recruiting and discipline of His Majesty's Forces' — as a member of the No Conscription Federation he had written a leaflet objecting to and publicising the sentence of two years hard labour passed upon Ernest Everett, a conscientious objector who had been conscripted and then refused to obey orders. Russell was found guilty and fined £100. The Council of Trinity College, Cambridge, decided unanimously in July 1916 to dismiss him from his lectureship. Three years later Trinity was Curry's College and he found as an undergraduate at Cambridge with the veterans of the post-war generation that Russell and the whole post-1918 world were detonating explosions in his schoolboy assumptions. If Russell was the passionate sceptic, Curry was beginning to become the passionate rationalist and this passage from Russell Curry quotes more than once in his writings as an early inspiration:

Where authority is unavoidable, what is needed is *reverence*. A man

---

[14] B. Hart, 'Freud's Conception of Hysteria', in a symposium on hysteria, *Brain* (1911). The bibliography contains 281 references, mainly to psychoanalytic literature.

who is to educate really well and is to make the young grow and
develop into their full stature must be filled through and through
with reverence. . . . The man who has reverence will not think it his
duty to 'mould' the young . . . [he] can wield the authority of an
educator without infringing the principles of liberty.[15]

Not only at Cambridge, but through nearly all his life thereafter
Curry found in Russell's writing and conversation a stimulus and a
clarification for his own thinking.

Curry's first teaching post was at Gresham's School, Holt, where
Simpson had been ten to fifteen years earlier. Simpson had found
Howson's 'honour' system at the time an astringent and bracing
experience but Curry unequivocally detested it as a form of moral and
emotional blackmail.[16] In 1922 he went to Bedales where he taught
physics until 1926 and where his first experiences of experimental
education began to take shape. Like Russell, Curry thought that the
fundamental questions had to do with the kind and quality of life that
was worth living and the conditions which could make it possible.
Three special questions plagued him all through the years — peace was
a necessity for the quality of life he sought; people were not emotionally and intellectually prepared for the rational alternatives to war and
nationalism; the existing methods of education did not put the pre-
requisites first — the fundamental social attitudes of children growing
up to a world needing understanding and international law. These
preoccupations are best summed up in Curry's own words:

> A modern school is one which recognizes that the social order must
> be radically changed if civilization is to survive at all and which also
> recognizes that education will have perhaps the most difficult and
> the most important part to play in the changes which must come
> about.[17]

Elsewhere in the same book he says that the primary aim of education is the creation of civilized communities; that the school should
provide a model for such communities was possible only when art,
intelligence, and knowledge were acknowledged as good in themselves
and not only as servants to usefulness. In civilized communities
citizens were sociable and responsible without necessarily being

---

[15] V. Bonham-Carter, *Dartington Hall*, p. 196. The passage is from Russell's
Principles of Social Reconstruction.
[16] For a personal account of the system about the time that Curry was at
Gresham's, see W. H. Auden, 'Honour', in *The Old School*, ed. Graham Greene
(London, 1934), pp. 9–20.   [17] W. B. Curry, *The School* (London, 1934), p. xii.

gregarious, they were tolerant and valued liberty while also permitting talent to thrive. Co-operation in such a society would mean more than competition, moral and intellectual autonomy would be prized and understood. More and more it would tend toward becoming a world society. These were the guide-lines for politics and education in his writing and his practice.

Curry had reason to be grateful to Badley and to Bedales for his first real glimpse of co-education and radicalism in education, but he did not think it was radical enough. Badley, for his part, remembers Curry as a good teacher, lucid in discussion and argument and as much concerned with politics as with teaching — a headmaster recalling a polemical assistant thirty-five years his junior.[18]

Curry went from Bedales to Oak Lane County Day School in Philadelphia which had been started in 1916 by a group of local business men wishing to finance and begin a school which would apply John Dewey's educational theories. The sponsors and participating parents then hired the teachers in the usual American pattern. Oak Lane was given solid financial backing and the sponsors went to seek advice in 1916 from Eugene Randolph Smith the first headmaster of Park School, Baltimore, a centre of educational innovation. When Curry arrived in 1926 Oak Lane was well-established, taking the life of the community into its ambit both as providing data and as influencing independent inquiry and investigation. Much of the school government was shared between teachers and pupils and the initiative which the learning projects demanded was matched by an exceptional provision of materials, books, and all manner of teaching aids. In 1927 Curry became head of the school and remained in Philadelphia until his appointment to Dartington in 1931. He brought three main impressions back to England with him. First, a concern for individual children and their way of learning; second, the need for and the predicaments of pupil participation in school government; third, an exasperation with the assumption by uninformed parents in Philadelphia that their views on education and teaching could be pressed upon teachers. Curry felt that the head of a progressive school should work according to his own conscience, listening to criticism but not necessarily accepting it, especially if it came from the more conventional world 'outside'.

The Elmhirsts and their advisers had, as already mentioned, ap-

---

[18] In a recorded conversation with the author in 1962.

pointed Miss Harley, an Englishwoman working in Detroit, as the head of the nursery school and the department of child study. In Philadelphia they found Curry, an Englishman with an unequivocal dedication to progressive education and ten years of experience at Bedales and Oak Lane to back it, and he became the first (indeed, the only) Director of Education for the estate as a whole. He had general control of all kinds of educational work with children and young people aged from two to eighteen (including Miss Harley's sector) and with adults both on and off the estate. Not long after his appointment the Director told the Trustees that he could not manage oversight of all this work and his proposition that he should concentrate on the school, or schools, was accepted and responsibility for the Adult Education programme and the School of Dance and Mime was transferred to others. The concept of the grand strategist in education for Dartington faded away and has never revived.

Curry dedicated *The School* in 1934 to Mr. and Mrs. Elmhirst 'for the opportunity to practise what I preach' and said a year before his retirement that the views he set out in that book 'are still substantially my views in 1956'.[19] While the Trustees had the general planning responsibility for Dartington as a whole there can be no doubt that Curry's was the guiding mind for twenty-six years and the school during that time became one of the best known co-educational schools in England.

The school now houses about two hundred and eighty boys and girls aged from eleven to eighteen, having grown to this size from the thirty-two with which Curry started in 1932. In terms of physical organization Dartington is on principle and in practice the most consistently co-educational of all. While I shall concentrate for the sake of brevity on the secondary age group the same ideas, with only slight modifications, apply to the other age-ranges. Each child has a study-bedroom of his or her own, the school is split into three houses for social and not competitive purposes and boys and girls have their rooms next to one another as they might do in a family. The washing and sanitary arrangements are shared as in a household and Curry and the Trustees planned the buildings in this way with a housemother for each group of about forty boys and girls. There never has been a school uniform and dress is as informal as children may wish to make it.

[19] V. Bonham-Carter, *Dartington Hall*, p. 189.

A large part of the discussion of progressive education is concerned with some aspects of freedom, authority, and discipline: 'No good society is conceivable except in terms of good individuals, and good individuals cannot be produced by educators lacking in respect for personality.'[20]   Curry accepted the need for authority and thought that educators should do all they could to encourage love of truth, vitality, initiative, friendliness.   He was fond of quoting Whitehead's dictum that an education which does not begin by evoking initiative, and end by encouraging it, must be wrong.   For such an education one of the basic requirements was the security consequent upon a right relationship with adults, one in which the adult is seen to be on the child's side.   To this end there was and is at Dartington a considerable degree of self-government.   Curry was opposed to complete self-government for much the same reasons as Dr. Williams and Dr. Bonser who, as we have seen, reported on this and other matters a few years before his arrival.   According to Curry, putting nearly everything in the hands of the pupils would give too heavy a load of responsibility, reduce the sense of security which adult support and competence could afford, and probably lead to harsher rules and punishments than were necessary.   However, to give children the chance to obey and often to make the law and to understand why they do so is to enable them to see the world in terms of the victory of persuasion over force.   At various times Curry had a Headmaster's Advisory Council which later became a Rule Making Body which discussed and amended rules and later still developed into a School Council and to the Moot which was served by an inner cabinet or Agenda Committee.   Curry gives a full account of the changes which took place over the years in the organization of the widely permissive self-government by the pupils.[21]

For a time there was a pupil chairman, changing at regular intervals. Later Curry became the chairman and had the right of veto which he scarcely ever had need to consider using.   Where Neill's School Meeting decides almost everything and is chaired by an elected pupil, Dartington for a time moved away from this although for several years now pupils have acted as chairmen.   The agenda is prepared and displayed after due notice from suggestions submitted, and only these items can be discussed at the meeting of the Moot, which the whole senior school and the staff can attend at will, although other matters

---

[20] Curry, *The School*, p. 25.
[21] See Curry, *Education for Sanity* (London, 1947).

can be raised under 'any other business'. In the summer term of 1961 the Moot gathered together, codified and promulgated twenty-five rules with sub-sections, many of them rules that were already in existence, but not collected in this form. The twenty-five rules covered such things as time limits within which general noise, including the playing of radios and gramophones, was permitted; areas in which ball games might be played; a prohibition on electric heaters in private rooms, on riding pillion on motor cycles at any time, and on airguns or other weapons, including catapults; the inspection of bicycles. According to these rules permission from parents had to be obtained for a number of undertakings such as canoeing or spending a night away from Dartington: smoking was permitted in private rooms and common rooms only; except in cases of illness classes could only be missed with the permission of the tutor; teachers might make any rules of conduct they considered desirable for their own rooms (it may be noted that this does not give to teachers control of the pupils' behaviour in the rest of the school, or in the children's own rooms). Anyone who wanted to go swimming or to climb in a nearby quarry had to have responsible companions with him. Some pupils thought that one rule was the most important of all, maybe the only necessary one: 'Every person should at all times behave with due consideration for the happiness and convenience of others.'

These rules indicate that Dartington is not a school without discipline or without a structure of law. The pupils cannot 'do what they like' as the cliché of critics often puts it. But they have more freedom from convention and expected behaviour than is usual. Curry believed that the nature of the society teaches more effectively than proclaimed rules; for him a school was an actively functioning society, not just a collection of children learning lessons and obeying orders. He accepted such moulding of young lives as took place on the assumption that children were able to manage their own affairs wisely when sympathetic adults gave them the freedom and security to do so. As his prospectus had it: 'Good feeling is more important than good behaviour and will ultimately lead to it.'[22] The authority of the adult was seldom displayed and Curry wanted children to learn to understand and accept law rather than simply to obey superior persons. Children were to be free from all forms of tyranny of the headmaster and really free speech was a necessary prerequisite of the system.

[22] Prospectus for 1954.

School was to be a place in which reason and persuasion were the main ways of influencing behaviour.

Curry saw co-education as a necessary condition for the proper education of the emotions and for the harmonious development of sexuality : 'It is surely best that this problem should first be faced under conditions which are deliberately devised in the light of educational considerations.'[23]   He believed that in the family context of the school the naturalness of affection, of heterosexual feeling and desire could easily find expression and the community could create the necessary controls.   Nude bathing for boys and girls was permitted in Curry's day as part of the family ethos although there have been modifications of the arrangements in more recent years.   When Curry was challenged about this as he often was, not least by His Majesty's Inspectors after an inspection in 1949, he said that children who found it in any way embarrassing or upsetting were free to wear a costume and the rest of the school family would accept this as an understandable preference.

Over the years each pupil at Dartington has had a tutor whom he or she can, within very wide limits, choose and it is the tutor's responsibility to keep general oversight of his charges, usually seeing them once a week to offer general advice and help and to keep their class attendance and work record constantly under review.   In general terms Curry recognized that not all children wanted to work when expected to do so and in 1956 he spoke in the prospectus of some children 'to whom pure scholarship is largely meaningless, and we foresee the possibility therefore that we may have to refuse in special cases to prepare children for examinations'.   However, in 1949 the school had been inspected by six of His Majesty's Inspectors following through from the right of the Minister consequent upon the 1944 Education Act to inspect all schools. The Dartington Trustees invited the visit of the Inspectors, but Curry had resisted inspection as long as possible.   Nevertheless he found the Inspectors thorough, experienced and considerate, with a gift for candour and tact.   Their candour compelled them to indicate serious inadequacies in some of the teaching, as well as high ability elsewhere. As we have seen in some other reports on progressive schools the Inspectors found too little zest both in some pupils and teachers and in a few cases their criticisms were precise and mordant.   Later visits by the Inspectorate have indicated how this has changed and in 1959 the

[23] Article on 'Dartington Hall' by W. B. Curry, in *The Modern Schools Handbook*, ed. T. Blewitt (London, 1934), p. 63.

Abbotsholme—five headmasters :
   Dr. Reddie (1889–1927) in 1930,
      aged 72
   Colin Sharp (1927–1946)
   C. Arthur Humphrey (1946–1955)
   Robin A. Hodgkin (1956–1967)
   David Snell (1967–)

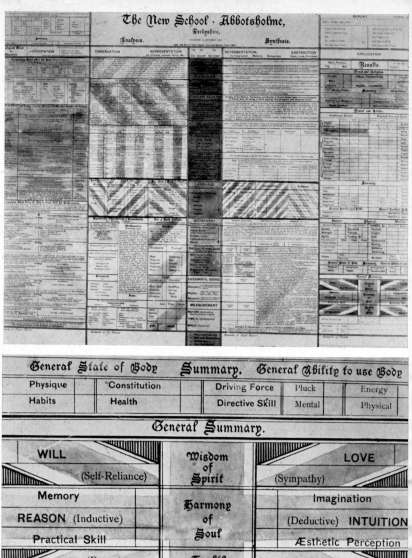

Above: *The fifth revision of a report form at Abbotsholme first used in 1897*

Below: *A detail of the report*

A music lesson under Dr. Reddie's portrait

Dissecting a fish at Abbotsholme

*The Goetheanum designed on
Steiner principles in
Switzerland*

Mr. and Mrs. Badley in their early married life

Three headmasters of Bedales:
H. B. Jacks, J. H. Badley, F. A. Meier

The present Head of Bedales, T. W. Slack, with some former pupils

Work in the laboratory at Bedales

The War Memorial Library at Bedales

T. F. Coade,
Head of Bryanston 1932–1959

F. G. R. Fisher,
Head of Bryanston 1959–

The south façade of Bryanston with gardens and tennis courts

Year: 1967
Term: Spring

BRYANSTON SCHOOL CHART

Name: D. Newman
Tutor: A.B.P.

C SUBJECT Set and Time		Week No. 1	Week No. 2	Week No. 3	Week No 4
ENGLISH ① 2/2	Work			B+	✓
	Time	✓ c.c.	c.c. 1.1 4	c.c. 1.1 4	c.c. 1.1 4
HISTORY ① 2/2	Work				α
	Time	✓ c.c. 1.1 4	c.c. 1 3	c.c. ① 1.1 5	E.E. 1.1 4
GEOG/GK/GER ③ 3/2	Work	α–	R8	B+	R8
	Time	c.c.c. 1.1 5	c.c.c. 1.1 5	c.c.c. 1.1 5	c.c.c 1 4
LATIN ⑤ H/2	Work	β–	β–– 9/20	β+ 16/20	β–– 17/20
	Time	c.c.c.c. 1.1 6	c.c.c.c. 1.1.1 7	c.c.c.c. 1.1 6	c.c.c.c. 1.1 6
FRENCH ⑤ H/2	Work	β	β+	B	β–
	Time	c.c.c.c. 1.1 6	c.c.c.c. 1.1 6	c.c.c.c. 1.1 6	c.c.c.c. 1.1.1 7
MATHEMATICS ③ 4/2	Work	β+	β–	H	β
	Time	c.c.c.c. 1.1 6	c.c.c.c. ① 1.1 7	c.c.c. 1.1.1 6	c.c.c.c. 1.1 6
PHYSICS ③ 2/1	Work	β	① β	α–	β+
	Time	c.c. 1 3	c.c. 1.1 3	c.c. 1 3	c.c. 1 3
CHEMISTRY ③ 2/1	Work	β	β+	α–	γ E W
	Time	c.c. 1 3	c.c. 1 3	c.c. 1 3	c.c. 1 3
BIOLOGY ③ 1/1	Work	α	β H	B+	β H
	Time	c. 1 2	c. 1 2	c. 1 2	c.c. – 2
DIVINITY ① 1/1	Work	β+	αβ	B+	β–
	Time	c. 1 2	c. 1 2	c. 1 2	c. 1 2
ART Pottery ② 2	Work				
	Time	c.c. 2	c.c. 2	c.c. 2	c.c. 2
GYM ① 2	Work				
	Time	c.c. 2	c.c. 2	c.c 2	c.c. 2
MUSIC ① 1	Work				
	Time	c. 1	c. 1	c. 1	c. 1
Violin ○ 2	Work	✓	β+	β++	✓
	Time	c.c. 2	c.c. 2	c.c. 2	c. 1 2
TOTAL	48	48	49	49	48

A Bryanston work chart. The red, blue and black colours in the original gradings do not show in this illustration (see pp. 175–6 for description)

Above: *The Library of Dartington School*
Top left: *J. B. Curry, Head of Dartington 1931–1957*
Bottom left: *Hu Child with a committee of pupils*

Kurt Hahn,
Head of Gordonstoun 1934–1953

F. R. G. Chew,
Head of Gordonstoun 1953–1967

Schule Schloss, Salem, Baden

The Round Square,
an enclosed court at
Gordonstoun

Painting at Gordonstoun

Dr. Maria Montessori

The Dottoressa in a Montessori classroom

Homer Lane and two of the girls at the Little Commonwealth

A. S. Neill

Margaret McMillan

Deptford street scene

school became 'provisionally recognized', a formal step from its full recognition by the Ministry which took place finally in 1965 after another full inspection.

Curry retired in 1957 after twenty-five years at Dartington, and he was succeeded a year later by Hubert and Lois Child: 'When we took up our duties in 1958 it was at our own wish that, both having the appropriate qualifications, we should hold the headship jointly as man and wife.'[24] Mr. Child is a scientist educated originally at Oundle and Cambridge, who saw service in education in Northern Nigeria before returning to England to teach at Bedales where Mrs. Child was at that time also teaching. Mr. Child was able later to follow up his interests in vocational guidance and psychology and after leaving Bedales worked with the National Institute of Industrial Psychology and during the War as a psychologist with the Admiralty. For ten years after the War he was the Senior Educational Psychologist to the London County Council in whose service one of Mr. Child's distinguished predecessors had been the then Dr. Cyril Burt. From the L.C.C. Mr. Child with his wife, who had been working in a training college, moved to Dartington to share the headship so that a man's and a woman's point of view could be available in a co-educational school. In principle many of their views coincide with Curry's, but they have also made their own mark.

Where Curry had spoken in 1956 of possibly refusing to prepare some children for examinations, the Childs expect nearly all children to take Ordinary levels or similar tests and to start the school course with a full range of subjects which can be modified later on tutorial advice — 'the necessity of taking external examinations inevitably makes demands which cannot be ignored'.[25] In 1956 Curry had said that it was part of the tradition of the progressive school movement to give a new emphasis to art and craft right through to the sixth form and this Dartington continues to accept. The school is rightly proud of an art and craft block built in the early 1960s which matches the excellent laboratory and library provision and the proximity to the full facilities of the new College of Arts at Dartington has already been mentioned.

Curry could say that there was no religious instruction in the sense that the school presented any particular religious doctrines, although the children were encouraged to discuss religious questions and to

[24] *The Independent Progressive School*, ed. H. A. T. Child, pp. 42–43. In December 1967 it was announced that Dr. Royston Lambert of King's College, Cambridge, would succeed the Childs as Head in 1968 and would take his Research Unit to Dartington with him. [25] *Prospectus*, p. 8.

F

attend church if they wished. The Childs maintain this position, claiming that the school society teaches good social habits and that freedom of spirit in a child is more important than any dogma or ritual. For the oldest boys and girls a class in comparative religion is provided.

In 1960 two Bedalians visited Dartington for a short while and later wrote some highly critical impressions for the *Bedales Chronicle*.[26] In a later issue of the same journal some Dartington pupils made reply, correcting many factual errors and denying the charges of apathy and mediocrity made by the Bedalians.[27] Round about the same time, however, the Childs themselves said that some pupils were doing the minimum of intellectual work and that improved rapport in teaching technique as well as a change from 'the casual "get-by" attitude' of the pupils was needed. This is a standard criticism of progressive schools by more conventionally minded educators, but these reservations by the Childs themselves at the time lend colour to the view. A number of visitors have written about Dartington more recently and Edward Blishen refers in an article to matters considered at greater length by Jusmani and others.[28] Blishen says that there are three rather large gnats at which controversial educationalists would strain. First, 'the uncompromisingly genuine co-educational quality of the school' which is faced and backed by the Childs' declared opinion that sexual restraint is the price of freedom and that if any individual is unable to exercise it Dartington cannot be the right place for him or her. Second is the problem of academic pace and here Blishen asserts that until the sixth form is reached the rate of work is slower than in conventional schools and this is a comment we have often met in the other progressive schools. Dartington sees this as the virtue that enables children to grow at their own pace but a critic would say the pace is being kept too slow, although the Childs have sharpened it in the last ten years. Blishen offers the opinion that Dartington has opted out of the academic rat-race with perhaps some loss in the intensity of learning, but to the general benefit of the children and at no apparent cost in opportunities for higher education and this is the traditional progressive school argument. The third gnat is the secular humanism that is the prevailing moral and ethical spirit of the place. However, Blishen

[26] Vol. 44, no. 2, Spring 1960.   [27] Vol. 45, no. 1, 1960, pp. 4–5.

[28] E. Blishen, 'The Lessons are Now Compulsory,' in the *Daily Telegraph*, 22 Apr, 1966. A. A. Jusmani, 'The Attitude to the Child in Progressive Educational Theory and Practice in England since 1890' unpublished M.Ed. thesis, University of Leicester, 1961.

and Jusmani agree with Curry and with the Childs in thinking Dartington 'a remarkably law-abiding yet dynamic society'.

In the matter of discipline Dartington stands well to the left of Abbotsholme and rather less to the left of Bedales, but well to the right of Summerhill, though Neill claims that he was nearer to Curry than almost all the other progressive heads. Heckstall-Smith went to Dartington after a period at Gordonstoun with Kurt Hahn and found the change 'like a dressing on a burn'. He says that Curry's 'tireless attempt to tell the truth as he saw it, was for me something wholly new in education'.[29]

Dartington is a progressive school in the setting of a thriving, liberal community which combines rural industries and agricultural craft with high excellence in the dramatic and visual arts and music. The school was conceived in 1926 by the Elmhirsts as an educational experiment and an agency for social equality. While it has remained under Curry and the Childs the first, it has never succeeded in being the second — the style of life and the permissive methods were not really accepted by the estate workers. The financial support of the Trustees has given to the school buildings equipment and financial backing which must be the cause of envy in other radical schools.

II

Bertrand Russell married Alys Pearsall Smith, of American Quaker stock, in 1894 and this marriage was dissolved in 1921 after ten years of separation and before that a long period of estrangement.[30] There were no children. In 1921, aged nearly fifty, he married Dora Black and when Russell wrote *On Education* in 1926 they had two young children whom they were anxious to educate as well as possible. Pyke had started the Malting House School in 1924 for a similar reason. The Elmhirsts had started their school at Dartington in 1926 for the enlightened education of their own and other children and it was this same impulse at about the same time that stirred the Russells.

Bertrand Russell had stood unsuccessfully for Parliament as a Labour candidate in 1922 and 1923 — he had been similarly unsuccessful as a Liberal candidate in 1907. Dora Russell who had also stood as a

[29] H. Heckstall-Smith, *Doubtful Schoolmaster* (London, 1962), p. 141.
[30] A full account of this period of Russell's life is to be found in *The Autobiography of Bertrand Russell 1872-1914* (London, 1967).

candidate earlier took over from him as the Labour candidate for Chelsea in 1924, but she too was not elected. Their parliamentary aspirations were not renewed and their concern for their children's education took on a new insistence. In the Introduction to *On Education* Russell wrote 'The cause of educational reform is forced upon conscientious parents, not only for the good of the community, but also for the good of their own children.'[31]

In September 1927 the Russells rented Telegraph House at Harting near Petersfield in Hampshire from Frank Russell, Bertrand's brother who had succeeded to the earldom over forty years before. Here they tried to work out their educational theories as Pyke and Susan Isaacs, Neill, and the Elmhirsts were all trying to do at about the same time. Where Pyke became a financial impresario to finance the Malting House and the Elmhirsts backed Dartington with a secure and substantial subsidy each year, Russell, as on many other occasions in his life, relied on his tongue and his pen to earn the necessary money. He admitted that he was writing entirely for cash and that he had no pride to prevent him earning from what he called 'pot-boilers'.

Dora Russell was the leading spirit in starting and running the school.[32] Bertrand Russell was there from 1927 to 1932 helping a little in teaching and much more in administering and in planning the programme and the regime. In 1932 at the age of sixty he left Beacon Hill prior to a divorce from Dora Russell in 1935 and marriage in 1936 to Patricia Spence who had been a worker and helper at the school. Dora Russell continued to run Beacon Hill, taking it to various locations, and ending up at her house in Cornwall where with very few children at the school in 1943 she decided to close it down. She had herself a distinguished academic record at a Girls' Public Day School Trust establishment in Sutton and at Cambridge where she was a Scholar of Girton, taking a First in modern languages and later becoming a Fellow for two years before her marriage to Bertrand Russell. In a letter to the present author she said that she had often been tempted to write about education after her sixteen years at Beacon Hill but she had not done so, her work having lain in other directions since the end of the War. If she had written, she considered that what she would have to say would be meaningless to present-day planners and here is the key to

[31] B. Russell, *On Education* (London, 1926), p. 9.
[32] For a recent short account see D. Russell, 'What Beacon Hill Stood For', in *Anarchy*, Jan. 1967, pp. 11–16.

the work which was carried out at Beacon Hill both during the five years of the joint headship of Bertrand and Dora Russell and for the remaining eleven years of Mrs. Russell's control. It was concerned primarily and mainly with growing persons living in as much freedom as possible.

While admitting that they differed in many matters, it would be best from our point of view to consider the educational ideas of Bertrand and Dora Russell as though they were one. They were opposed to war, they were in an intellectual sense committed to the Left in politics, they had both read Freud, Adler, and Jung and had acquaintance with behaviourist psychology, they both tried to find rational bases for the kind of influence they wished children to be exposed to. Russell was by this time what may be called a liberal-socialist whose original liberalism had been transformed by the War which to him was a consequence of capitalism. He had maintained his rational rejection of war as a wildly stupid way to try to solve contentious problems and in 1918 had spent some time in Brixton jail. But he was not a doctrinaire pacifist. His biographer quotes a most significant passage:

> I have longed to feel that oneness with large bodies of human beings that is experienced by the members of enthusiastic crowds. . . . I have imagined myself in turn a Liberal, or a Socialist or a pacifist, but I never have been any of these things in a profound sense. Always the sceptical intellect, when I have most wished it silent, has whispered doubts to me. . . . I would tell Quakers that I thought many wars in history had been justified, and Socialists that I dreaded the tyranny of the State.[33]

The intellectual, the fastidious rationalist, the critical individualist, was stifled by the utilitarianism and indifference to beauty and humane values when he visited Russia in 1920, and *The Practice and Theory of Bolshevism* alienated many of his socialist and pacifist friends. He and Dora Russell did not take easily to the Labour Party in England in the 1920s and after their conspicuous failure at the polls in 1922–4 they decided to start a school in order to make a statement about quality in living which they thought the Labour Party was not exemplifying. Russell's restless and formidable intelligence was too essentially aristocratic in its loneliness and distinction to be in willing submission to the proletariat. If politics is the art of the possible it also rests on a man's skill in playing consensus against conflict. This Russell, the

[33] A. Wood, *Bertrand Russell: the Passionate Sceptic* (London, 1957), p. 115.

individualist champion of the human race, has always found difficult.

The motto which Russell invented for education as for other human affairs was that it should be based on science wielded by love and a living example of this principle was Margaret McMillan who was greatly admired both by Bertrand and Dora Russell, although in detail their programmes were different from hers. They believed that children should grow up in a group which tried to make explicit principles characteristic of a reformed society. Opposed as they were to war and militarist thinking they considered that nationalism was a potent influence towards aggression. Their school would be international and it would welcome children from the age of two because, while the family was the matrix of growth, it could become a divisive and defensive agency, the cause of feud and faction. Children should learn to be members of groups wider than the family as soon as possible so that co-operation and mutual helpfulness should be the counterweight to competition and limited sympathies. The school, like Bedales and Dartington, the Malting House, Summerhill, and Abbotsholme, was to provide a model community in which quality of life, content of curriculum, methods of teaching, and style of human relationships were to be in themselves a way of living and learning the good life. When they became adults the pupils would have had prior knowledge of the kind of community they wanted and how to set about getting it.

There was no direct religious or political teaching at Beacon Hill but the children became aware of religion and politics through their study of the history and economic structure of other societies and their moral education grew out of the daily give and take of the community. The very small children had a regimen of their own in which the contributions of Montessori were given place with those of the McMillans and to some extent of Susan Isaacs, although Mrs. Russell had criticisms of her work as we shall see. Children of three and four used hammers, saws, and scissors as they did at the Malting House School and Dora Russell thought that by four years of age her boys and girls were more independent and developed than children brought up within the average family. Beacon Hill never had more than about thirty children on the roll and the total staff for all purposes was, at its peak, nine or ten which makes a very generous proportion of adults. The school was co-educational from the start although the Russells were prepared to admit that in adolescence the sexes might want to draw apart. This they did not have to decide upon because Beacon Hill did not have a sufficient number of children staying on through adolescence.

The Russells thought that children would signal their readiness to read soon enough and at that point the opportunities of good material would be offered to them. As their parents were often intellectuals, usually of the Left, among them refugees and professional men, frequently the readiness developed quite rapidly. The Russells were believers in oral work and the children produced and later wrote their own plays[34] and they were introduced to French and German from the age of four or even earlier, Dora Russell herself being the main teacher of languages. She would have liked to teach Spanish, Russian, and Chinese because on social, economic, and political grounds she thought these were the languages of the future. In fact they did teach Russian for a time, one of their science masters being of Russian extraction, but French and German, the main Western European languages, proved more immediately relevant in 1927 than the long-term internationalism of the Russells.

As at the Malting House School, so at Beacon Hill science was taught by experimental methods to children of four or five, even before their reading capacity had enabled them to use books. This was not the nature study which was, and still is, found in many infant schools, for the Russells worked on the basis that many things were learned and left in the unconscious knowledge of young children, to emerge later as and when needed. They had a simple laboratory where children learned from elementary experiments about air pressure and the composition of the atmosphere, about the behaviour of water. They grew crystals, they did simple experiments in physiology, they collected fossils and rocks and studied rudimentary geology. The Russells tried to be educationally original while retaining their regard for intellectual standards. History and geography were taught as aspects of 'the science of life' in which astronomy, chemistry, and biology were related to history, geography, and archaeology in order to suggest some concept of the unity of mankind developing from primeval human beings to the diverse competence and organization of modern society.

Beacon Hill had its School Council on which every adult, from the principals to the gardener, and every child of five years old and over,

---

[34] A number of these were collected and published under the title *Thinking in Front of Yourself* (London, 1934).

had a place and a vote. On the Council ordinary community rules were discussed and agreed upon, the adults having the responsibility for seeing they were obeyed, and there is the usual history of changing decisions and methods. At one time attendance at lessons was compulsory but later this was revised provided the absentees did not disturb the workers and kept away from the classrooms. At another the Council gave the matron the right to make the rules for community order, discipline, and cleanliness but later changed to as near to complete freedom in routine as possible, arriving in due time at a framework of necessary rules. Mrs. Russell sums up the attitude as follows: 'The most important thing to our children seems to be the feeling that they are not being compelled, but are doing a thing from their own choice, either because they like to, or because they think the thing reasonable.'[35]

The Russells considered that adults force patterns of behaviour on children too early and that from this resentment builds up. Adult society and national aspirations showed clear signs of the impulse to dominate. The Russells accepted that in the school there was bound to be some assertive and domineering behaviour because children and adults were like that, but their main aim was to release children from adult controls and social directives so that they could win time in which to build a sense of personal values. The free community would be tolerant to stress and would respond with vigour and a dispassionate realism. Children who grew up in a school which had a humanist ideal, a scientific attitude to diet and hygiene, and a respect for developmental psychology, would grow to understand one another and the society they wanted to live in. The Russells had between them faith in democracy and a belief in the usefulness of the liberal democrat; they had a non-technical understanding of post-war psychoanalysis and its near relatives; they had at any rate for a time the conviction that a model community of children would, as the years passed, have an impact on society and on other schools, but they were too sophisticated to prescribe a Beacon Hill type of education as the answer to aggression in all its forms.

Bertrand Russell was not able to devote his energies for long to a school of thirty children and he left Beacon Hill in 1932 after five years, Dora Russell carrying it forward for another eleven years. Russell was a close friend of W. B. Curry, who, as we have seen,

[35] *The Modern Schools Handbook*, p. 38.

returned to England to work at Dartington Hall in 1931, and it is mainly through his interest in the education of his own children at Dartington and Curry's critical admiration of his ideas that Russell continued his association with radical schools after his departure from Beacon Hill.

The Russells were the most consistently intellectual of the heads of radical schools except for Pyke and Mrs. Isaacs at the Malting House, and the differences between them are important and interesting. It will be remembered that Geoffrey Pyke's first advertisement in 1924 was for an educated young woman 'to conduct the education of a small group of children aged 2½–7, as a piece of scientific work and research'. Mrs. Russell's comment on the Malting House enterprise is that it was more of a study of children than a school and that Beacon Hill was too often placed in the same bracket with the Cambridge school.[36] Pyke and Susan Isaacs were working to a psychological model, making discoveries about learning theory, adjustment, motivation, and unconscious influences as the 'research' proceeded, and, of course, making certain internal assumptions about mental health as they went along. Bertrand and Dora Russell were working to a social and political model in which democratic and anti-militaristic ends were to be reached along many of the same paths as those followed by Pyke and Susan Isaacs, and all of them often spoke of emotional maturity and stability.

The Russells began their school as a result of personal political conviction and experience and without previously having taught children, but with the conviction that other unorthodox intellectuals would want to send their children to Beacon Hill. Russell has never been only an academic philosopher and in his attempts at full human engagement his concern for education both in exposition and practice is a sub-heading to the general title that life should be lived on a basis of science wielded by love. Dora Russell was the person who translated this into action, and where the Malting House lasted for three years and has left its mark in Mrs. Isaacs's books, Beacon Hill lasted for sixteen years and is reflected to some extent in the writings of Bertrand Russell on education and in the largely forgotten methods and regime of the school which in the 1930s was nearest to Summerhill and Dartington.

[36] In a letter to the author, Apr. 1964.

Chapter Eight

THE POST-WAR SURGENCE:
THE TWENTIES

4. Rudolf Steiner and Anthroposophy

I

ALL through his writing Steiner proclaims that he could never accept the sense-world as an ultimate. Physical perceptions are real enough and so are sense-data and everyone can agree that thinking and systematic logic represent an analysis of situations and experience which can be more or less verified:

> I wished to turn away from that road to knowledge which looked toward the sense-world, and which would then break through from the sense-world into true reality. I desired to make clear that true reality is to be sought not by such a breaking through *from without*, but by sinking down into the inner life of man.... When from within man sense-free thought comes forth to meet the sense-perception ... the human spirit, living its own life within, meets the spirit of the world which is now no longer concealed from man behind the sense-world, but weaves and breathes within the sense-world.[1]

This finding of the spirit within the sense-world is not a question of logical inferences or progression from sense-data. It is a further phase of man's evolution and so far much of the metaphysics of Steiner's analysis marches with the interpretations of Theosophy. For both an

---

[1] R. Steiner, *The Story of My Life* (London, 1928), p. 116.

all-pervading principle pre-exists, or at any rate co-exists with and through, Creation. Life, and the human mind which is aware of life, are transformed beyond matter by this manifestation of God. Man is able uniquely to test and experience this, according to Steiner, because evolution is not simply a process of natural selection with men as the most developed and adaptable of the animals:

> It was a personal distress to me to hear men say that the material economic forces in human history carried forward man's real evolution and that the spiritual was only an ideal superstructure over this substructure of the 'truly real'. I knew the reality of the spiritual. The assertions of the theorizing socialists meant to me the closing of men's eyes to true reality.[2]

This discovery of the spiritual by Steiner took a long time to form itself. He was born in 1861, the eldest of three children, in Kraljevec on the border between Hungary and Croatia to the wife of a minor official on the Southern Austrian Railway. The parents were Austrian Catholics, though the father went through a period of 'free thinking' in middle life. There is no evidence of an intense religious atmosphere in the Steiner home. When the time came to choose Rudolf's secondary school training, his father decided that he should attend the *Realschule* rather than the *Gymnasium* as he wanted the boy to follow him in a railway career. The *Realschule* emphasized the sciences and Rudolf was grounded in physics, chemistry, and mathematics, especially in geometry. His own interest and ability enabled him later to undertake the classical work of the *Gymnasium* with such success that he acted as a tutor to a boy who was undertaking the full *Gymnasium* course.

In 1879 Steiner entered the Vienna *Technische Hochschule*, ostensibly continuing at the university level the science emphasis of the *Realschule*. By this time he had read and been fascinated by Kant's *Critique of Pure Reason* and had begun on Fichte's *Wissenschaftslehre*. He officially enrolled for mathematics, natural history, and chemistry and carried these studies through with the intention not of entering the railway service but of returning to teach in the *Realschule*. His primary interest was in philosophy and literature and he attended classes both in the *Hochschule* and the University for he felt in duty bound to seek through philosophy for the truth. When he was nineteen he read Goethe's *Faust* for the first time about fifty years after Goethe's final version of the work. Steiner

[2] Ibid., p. 104.

found the unity of Goethe's sensibility such as to attract him to read widely both in his literary and his scientific writings and in 1884 he contributed to a symposium on Goethe. At the age of twenty-seven he was invited to Weimar as a co-editor of the scientific papers for the Standard Edition of Goethe's works published by the Goethe Archives. For the first time he had some limited financial security and his intellectual intensity brought him to the attention of many of the leading philosophers and social theorists of the time. He had been schooled in the thinking of Kant, Fichte, Herbart, and Haeckel, he had read Nietzsche, Marx, and Engels, and he later came to know the work of Breuer and Freud. Steiner had listened to leading German thinkers lecturing on the theories of Hume and Darwin and his scientific training enabled him to assess Einstein's work on relativity. By the time he was forty he had arrived at the basic hypotheses of what later came to be called Anthroposophy, the wisdom of man the spiritual being. It is exceedingly difficult to describe this briefly, because Steiner's output in books, articles, and lectures was phenomenal and covers exposition of his difference from other *Weltanschauungen*, his notion of sensory realities, presentations on fancy and imagination, visual art, literature, drama, and architecture as expressions and symbols of the spirit. He developed a moral theory which he called ethical individualism by which moral life was to proceed by the unfolding of the human spirit and not by way of precepts obeyed. If it is very difficult to describe Anthroposophy briefly, it is equally difficult to describe it clearly because the starting point is personal and unlikely to yield adequately to words : '[About 1900] the germ of Christianity was beginning to unfold within me . . . as an inner phenomenon. . . . The evolution of my soul rested upon the fact that I stood before the mystery of Golgotha in most inward, most earnest joy of knowledge.'[3]

In his major work *The Philosophy of Spiritual Activity* and in other books like *Mysticism* and *Christianity as Mystical Fact* and in lectures Steiner recounts examples of spiritual activity in classical times, before the Christian revelation, and in the Christian centuries in gnostic and other mystical groups from the Rosicrucians to Jacob Böhme. He took the example of Buddha as a precursor to Christ, but at all points he claimed that historical examples were not the evidence that he valued. His understanding was received by hard, sustained thinking to clarify the philosophic issues, and by inner discipline to perceive the existence

[3] R. Steiner, *The Story of My Life*, p. 264.

and reality of the spirit world and to enter into it. From a Germanic training in philosophy and science and a personal vision, Steiner had by 1900 accepted many of the Theosophical principles expounded by Madame Blavatsky, which in her case were based on Eastern occult writings. Most obviously, the spirit-principle is common to both and the belief in reincarnation and *karma*. The physical self, the astral self, and the etheric self are to be found in each, together with a multi-dimensional understanding of life and the universe. There were, however, chasms of difference and perhaps the best way to make these clear is to look at Steiner's career in Theosophy up to 1913.

In 1902 the Theosophical Society decided to set up a German branch and invited Steiner to be its general secretary and he agreed, with a number of reservations. Undoubtedly, Steiner continued to proclaim Anthroposophy to German Theosophists, saying that he had made this position quite clear to Mrs. Besant and the Theosophical Society when first agreeing to the formation of the German section. He disapproved of the Society's impartial support of religions and its generally numinous attitudes. Yoga, Eastern techniques of spirit-composure, the practice of spiritualism and above all the depreciation of the significance of Jesus Christ, made it increasingly difficult for Steiner to continue to give loyalty to the Theosophical Society. In his idiosyncratic way, he had become Christocentric. The life and death of Jesus were not, for Steiner, just unusually powerful manifestations of spirit-centred man which could take their place with the sacrifice of Socrates, the life and serenity of the Buddha, or the confidence and sacrificial courage of Mahomet. The Christ phenomena were the unique statement both of man's hostility to God, and of the permeation of God's spirit. The gathered self-knowledge of Jesus in his acceptance of the spirit-world was a sure guide to men. Again, Theosophists seemed to be too dependent on the past and had too little knowledge of the scientific revolution, whereas Steiner wanted to accept the society of today insofar as these are the conditions in which the self-knowledge necessary in Anthroposophists has to be won.

In 1910 the final rift between Steiner and the Theosophical Society began to appear when Krishnamurti was presented by Mrs. Besant as the boy in whom Christ would live in reincarnation. A group within Theosophy grew up to support 'the Star of the East' and Steiner and his followers refused to have a branch of this movement in the German section and began to found the Anthroposophical Society. In January

1913 Mrs. Besant wrote to Steiner to tell him that he was no longer to be regarded as the leader of the German section of the Theosophical Society which included Austria, Germany, and German-speaking Switzerland. Steiner responded by holding the first General Assembly of the Anthroposophical Society a month later. He was over fifty years of age, an Austrian not very well known outside Germany and with a difficult and unpopular creed to proffer. Eighteen months after the foundation of the new Society, Germany was at war with the rest of the world and therefore the main impact of Anthroposophy on Europe as a whole and on Great Britain in particular was felt only after 1919, and Steiner died on 30 March 1925.

II

Steiner had spent twenty years of his life from his university days onwards as a part-time tutor usually to the children of well-to-do families. He also taught courses in an adult education centre, the Berlin Workers School, and among the countless lectures he gave in his journeys over Europe before 1914 was a series on education on which he later based a published essay *The Education of the Child in the Light of Anthroposophy* which contains the essence of his subsequent writings on the subject. The first practical test of his theories came in 1919 when Herr Emil Molt, the owner of the Waldorf Astoria cigarette factory in Stuttgart decided to initiate improvements in the working conditions of his operatives and to try to transform the spirit of the working relationship. In the discussions which followed some of the reforms were effected but many of the workers felt that educational programmes which Molt proposed were not likely to succeed with them. However, together with Herr Molt they proposed that Steiner should direct a school for their children; and so began the *Freie Waldorfschule*, the prototype of Steiner schools. While Steiner recognized that the division of labour was unavoidable for adults, he wanted the children who went through the school to have a depth and range of experience. For these spiritual resources unusual teaching was required and he gathered his men and women from Germany, Austria, Switzerland, and even Russia. Few of them had trained to teach and Steiner conducted three courses in the fortnight before the beginning of the first term and these have been the skeleton on which later and more elaborate training courses have been constructed elsewhere, as we shall see.

In 1919 there were three hundred boys and girls at the Stuttgart school and within a few years there were one thousand. Numbers rose to one thousand three hundred in 1938 when the Nazis closed the school as a potentially subversive institution. It was reopened six months after the end of the Second World War and another school was started in Stuttgart. At present there are twenty-six Steiner schools in Germany, all receiving support from the state and eighteen of them rebuilt after the destruction of war. In Germany and Switzerland one child in every six thousand goes to a Steiner school, a small enough ratio, but about fourteen times larger than the proportion in Great Britain which is one child in eighty thousand. There are now seventy Steiner schools spread throughout the world in Germany, Holland, Switzerland, France, Norway, Denmark, Sweden, Belgium, Great Britain, Finland, Austria, Italy, United States, South Africa, New Zealand, Australia, Mexico, Brazil, and the Argentine. These do not include the schools and homes for children in need of special care for whom Anthroposophists feel particular concern — there are another one hundred and twenty of these. Neither does it include the Training Colleges for teaching which are run in conjunction with seven of the schools in Germany, Switzerland, Holland, England, and the United States.[4]

In the summer of 1922 Steiner gave a course of lectures in Oxford on education which was published in 1947 under the title *The Spiritual Ground of Education* and in 1923 he gave a second course at Ilkley in Yorkshire. These lectures were published in 1954 as *Education and Modern Spiritual Life* and it was at this conference that Margaret McMillan presided. Each had a great respect and admiration for the other and some of Margaret McMillan's beliefs in the last ten years of her life may well have had more than a tincture of Anthroposophy in them, although she was always unwilling to discuss them. After the Ilkley conference she wrote to a friend of hers, Mrs. Sutcliffe: 'Yes, Steiner is a wonderful, glorious man. . . . [He] came here [to Deptford] and everything seemed new and wonderful when he entered the room. . . . No-one need tell him anything about themselves. He seems to see one. . . . He never condemns or criticizes or has bitter thoughts like me.'

Others felt this inspiration and magnetism and a committee was formed and money promised to start a Steiner school in England. He

[4] *Child and Man*, Summer, 1964, p. 5.

was again invited to England in 1924 and at Torquay he gave the kind of training course to the pioneer teachers that he had given in Stuttgart five years before. It was one of his last public acts, for he died a few months later.

The New School was opened at Streatham in London in 1925, later transferring to Forest Row in Sussex where it now is under its present name, Michael Hall. This school was recognized as efficient by the Ministry of Education in 1950 as was Wynstones School in Gloucestershire in 1952. The other four schools, one in Edinburgh and the others in Worcestershire, Derbyshire, and Hertfordshire, are either not yet ready for or are not seeking this approval at the moment. It is already clear that Anthroposophy is a radical and unorthodox faith and we must now see how the schools, all of them co-educational, reflect it.

The teaching body is a 'college', where the responsibility is shared and no one is, in the conventional sense, head. Ethical individualism and respect for spiritual harmonies in a like-minded community make hierarchy and the bearing of authority seem superfluous. It is not necessary to invoke promotion as reward for spiritual maturity or teaching skill. The teaching body in a Steiner school, of which a high proportion are Anthroposophists, is nearer to a lay order than to the staff of a conventional school.

The same attitudes and beliefs relate to the children:

> Childhood assumes quite another importance for us if we learn to view it as an incarnating process which partly conforms to the laws of physical nature and partly transcends these laws. Indeed the true nature of man lives in his *non-nature*, in the world beyond nature which declares itself in him. Thus each human life is the revelation of an immortal spirit which *was* before birth and which *will* be after death.[5]

The consequence in Steiner education is that all formal instruction is avoided in the 'sleep' of infancy because the child needs all his powers for his bodily, moral, and spiritual growth, and to introduce intellectual forms during this period encourages a precocity which throws the balance of growth askew. Small children need kindness, encouragement, love, and trust and they will not only respond similarly, but these moral and emotional qualities will affect physical growth too, will relax and strengthen breathing, encourage muscle-use, bring general

[5] L. F. Edmunds, *Rudolf Steiner Education* (London, 1962), p. 15.

confidence and somatic harmony. The fullest scope in Steiner schools is given to spontaneity in play, in art and in movement, in drama, in folk- and fairy-tales and in seasonal festivals, the archetypes of experience. Singing in English, French, and German lays the basis for later and wider understanding. Undoubtedly practices in most nursery schools are similar to those in a Steiner Nursery Class, though the structure of the archetypal past, the forms of eurhythmy (not meant to be the same thing as Dalcroze eurhythmics, though obviously related) and the European languages and folk-tales are more theoretically consistent because they are based in Steiner theology and cosmology. The Nursery Class in a Steiner school continues without the introduction of reading or computing until the child is six or seven, a year or two after the child in a maintained school has started more formal work, however informally taught, at the age of five and six in the infants' section.

The second phase of growth for Steiner is the years of childhood from seven to fourteen and he emphasizes that man has time to mature, he has the benison of restraint which no other animal has, and that this is true both physically and mentally. The ego is the aspect of self which co-ordinates thought, speech, action, and acts of will, and through the period of childhood Steiner sees the advantages of what Freud called the latency period. Anthroposophists would say that in these seven or eight years soul-awareness fuses with ego-consciousness and experience becomes far more personal and realized than in childhood. This is the period for education of the feelings, for deepening of response to others before the differentiation of intellect diversifies the self: 'If the heart forces are not educated rightly, the intellect, left to itself, isolates men one from another. . . . Then we have parties but not community . . . . The education we are describing sets out to try to overcome the primary evil, egotism.'[6]

In Steiner schools the chronological age determines entry to a class and there is no streaming. The class teacher remains with the class throughout the eight years of childhood, teaching many if not most of the lessons and making with his or her pupils a secure and sensitive family of learners — or, at least, this is what is postulated and often achieved. Brilliance in a child is deepened by experience of wisdom, patience, tolerance, and compassion and not whetted as an instrument in a competition with other children. Thus the transition from the

6 Ibid., pp. 30–31.

fantasy of the small child to the abstract thinking of the adolescent should be a gentle process, and the intellectually able child should be protected from exploitation by society and by parents.

Anthroposophists believe that children not only recapitulate in their growth the biological history of the human race but its psychological and cultural history too and they base their curriculum on these principles. This means that reading is not taken as a special enterprise but is built up by movement, gesture, painting, and ideograph, into writing and to an outcome in reading itself. The practical consequence of this recapitulation of man's story is that reading is usually delayed in Steiner schools longer than in the conventional school and it is at a late stage that letters are tied to sounds. Thus it is supposed that letters are not seen as conventional symbols only, but the alphabet and written communication are felt to be descended from more rudimentary needs and cruder representations. Hence, to use a common phrase in Steiner terminology, the growing self-identity of the child 'begins to turn earthward'.

The age of nine and ten is the heart of this childhood phase, the time of growing awareness for the child of the aloneness, of the individuality of persons, others as well as himself. Again, Steiner says, the child needs the security of a past which is not only his shallow family childhood, but his deep racial heritage, and in this the boy or girl can begin to bear and understand the polarity of continuity on the one hand and separation on the other. The Old Testament is the source for these personal and cosmic themes — Adam, the son of the Father and the rebellious man, Noah, Abraham, Moses, the Patriarchs, all of them with a sense of mission but with a sense of origin, too.

Other themes are also important at this time, like farming, the soil, the seasons, man the husbandman who knows, respects, and fears nature. Or housebuilding, the perennial statement of the need for shelter from which so many other activities flow, rooms for eating, for preparing food, for talking, for study, for washing, for excreting, for sleeping.

As children move closer to puberty so they become aware of growth, depth, and range, says Rudolf Steiner, and one of the consequences in the school is the study of geology, physics, and mathematics. The children bridge the discomforts of their own lack of co-ordination by the use of tools in carving, and in cultivating the soil. History is given the characteristic Steiner symbolism. The Romans are appropriate for study by the twelve-year-old because they were at once temporally competent and they made actual by law, by rational building, by respect for minorities what the Greeks had begun to do. These achievements form the prerequisite for the speculative thought of Byzantium and Islam and the prelude to the Arthurian legend. Steiner's use of history as a kind of text book of cosmic themes has about it the daring if not the range or precision of Toynbee's vast historical undertaking.

The third phase of growth is adolescence and here again Steiner had some unusual emphases to offer. At this time he sees the beginning of an independent life of thought, a questioning of the experience and opinion of others and of oneself, a search through ideas for some binding truth. This quest can take various forms of expression, nearly all of them restless — ambition, assertiveness, a factitious adulthood, romantic imaginings. Always, for Steiner, these represent a stirring of the spirit startled by the wakening mind and its self-sustained ideas, dismayed by the apparent loneliness and the personal inadequacy. For Anthroposophists there are two special antithetical difficulties in adolescence, egotism in material things and scepticism in spiritual things : 'the first makes too much of the earth, the other too little of heaven.'[7]

To maintain this balance Steiner schools lean heavily on art. From the start children have been encouraged to experience and to experiment with colour and through this to learn a language of moods and modulation. This is, of course, related to Goethe's theory of colour which Steiner studied and knew so well. In Steiner schools clear colours have qualities which can be modified and transformed in line and harmony : yellow is a confident, radiant colour which deepens and matures in gold and amber ; blue has qualities of form and firmness and depth ; red is the colour of energy, of passion. From the first day in the Nursery Class children in Steiner schools have a weekly lesson with simple water-colours and from this, as they mingle the colours and shades, they learn a language of contrast, harmony, modulation, restraint, conflict, with which they can paint their moods, their fears, and their understanding in colour compositions which Steiner considered far more expressive, in the early years of limited control of the medium and restricted grasp, than the formless appearances of so much child art. The colours make a dialogue within a discipline that is

[7] L. F. Edmunds, *Rudolf Steiner Education* (London, 1962), p. 54.

appropriate in art for young children and is the basis of freedom within forms, which Steiner valued.

At puberty children in Steiner schools cease to work in colour for a while and use black and white. Steiner thought this was the appropriate change of medium to comport with a new awareness of contrast, a clarity of definition, a sustaining of the line of argument which develops in adolescence. The austerity required by the black and white medium is thought to aid children of fourteen or fifteen to a greater stability, and when they return to colour around sixteen their compositions are expected to have more balance, often a more direct theme. Anyone familiar with the use of art in diagnosis and therapy as Jung and others have employed it will see resemblances to what Steiner proposed, although the Anthroposophical doctrine may appear too cloudy in its psychological symbolism and too restrictive in its abstract colourwash form when one thinks of the sheer vitality of a great deal of child art.

Music, drama, eurhythmy, and the growing range of subjects like mathematics, geography, science, English give to adolescents an intellectual challenge and the means of maintaining depth in the whole range of activity. Whereas in the years from six to fourteen the class teacher was the continuing parent-figure, in adolescence the teaching is by specialists as in most secondary schools. The child is expected to do more himself to bring together and to co-ordinate the subjects he is being taught, his interests are given every encouragement while the education is still kept wide. One distinctive feature in all Steiner schools is the Main Lesson which is the first lesson of the day and which lasts for two hours and is devoted to either mathematics, English history, geography, or science. This regime starts in Class I at the age of six or seven and goes through the school and into the Upper School. Not only is there this daily concentration, but each subject may be taught each morning for several weeks before a change is made to the next. Anthroposophists maintain that this allows the children time both to receive and to give; they can listen to the teacher's words, they can translate them into movement, recitation, individual work, and discussion and quite often this is undertaken in three-day cycles. Steiner postulates that what is taught on the first day merges into rhythmic functioning of the child during sleep on the first night and on the second night more deeply still into the child's metabolism. Again the spirit symbolism of Steiner unites ideas and mental activity with the working of the body.

Eurhythmy is an art of movement developed by Steiner and it is related to gesture, to rhythm, to harmony of mood or idea, and movement. Ballet, mime, drama, dance are all part of this body-language and in its medium it has a part to play in Steiner education as art does in a different mode. It is intended to have the expressiveness, freedom, discipline, and restraint which many modern schools of movement have built upon and it was conceived to encourage creativeness and personal therapy while being another means of presenting archetypal themes in a stylized form.

In Steiner schools discipline is taken seriously as might be expected when teachers speak of restraint as well as freedom:

> If children are left only to do as they will, what benefit can it be to them? Sooner or later it leads to a kind of exhaustion. . . . One gains the impression at times that with the self-expression enthusiasts anything 'odd' is accounted 'remarkable'. The only way to real freedom is through schooling.[8]

This might have been written by any *status quo* reactionary, but the particular meaning for an Anthroposophist is very different from a traditional 'us' and 'them' kind of view. Physical fear and corporal punishment have no place in a Steiner school, neither have prizes and obvious awards in competition, but correction for wrong doing is regarded as both right and proper. The main initiative in maintaining discipline is with the teacher and there are no precise rules or methods of control or punishment available to him because it is assumed that both pupil and teacher, each from his point of view, are prepared to accept co-operative enterprise as the real purpose of school and classroom — indeed of life as a whole. Bringing order out of disorder is not mainly a matter of organization but rather a therapeutic exercise both for teacher and child, and consequently any punishment to be worth while puts a burden on the teacher because the core of true discipline is willing discipleship. The heart of the matter is a deep sense of peace in heart and mind, in home and school, in these days especially in the school. There is no belief in child self-government: 'Contrary to the methods of self-government practised in other schools, in a Waldorf school authority rests only with adults.'[9]

The schools make no pretence of the fact that their purpose is to

[8] L. F. Edmunds, *Rudolf Steiner Education* (London, 1962), p. 48.
[9] Ibid., p. 84.

hold back a too-rapid intellectual development in the interest of what they call 'greater force of imagination' and this means that they do not shape their courses in the upper school with national examinations in mind. 'The examinations required for entering college or the professional schools . . . invade and compromise the curriculum of our upper classes. . . . To safeguard the Waldorf curriculum the examinations are generally taken later.'[10] The phrase used in the prospectus of the Steiner schools on this matter is that pupils are prepared for the General Certificate of Education or its equivalent 'in as many subjects as are necessary for the career they have chosen'.

Anthroposophists have become widely known for the work they do with and for handicapped children, or as Steiner called them *Seelenpflege-bedürftige*, children in need of special care. He wrote to one of his friends : 'Only the physical body sustains the injury, but the Spiritual Being which lies behind the physical body remains unharmed. This Spiritual Being is a reality for me, just as much a reality as the hydrogen in water is for the chemist.'[11] The problem for the teacher in a Steiner home for such children is to discover in what ways, if any, the etheric body and the astral body are damaged, as the physical body clearly is. The children are not regarded as simply unfortunate, but as human spirits with whom little successful contact through the intellect is going to be possible. The deeper self may be clouded because the physical body and the stunted ego offer little transparency. To Anthroposophists, however, the enigmas of the phases of reincarnation and *karma* exist, of which these abnormalities are clear and saddening expressions and from this affliction the seeds of future growth and correction come. In this the work of the doctor, the nurse, the teacher moves not only, or even mainly, in temporal cycles, It is not our main concern here to write of work with abnormal children, but it would be a serious omission not to mention, even thus briefly, the radical work done by Anthroposophists based on their initial religious positions for handicapped children and, come to that, maladjusted children.

We can sum up the purpose of the Steiner schools thus :

> To take the adolescent through the history and development of art as the revelation of evolving manhood ; to educate him into the meaning and appreciation of poetry as the medium wherein the centre

[10] L. F. Edmunds, *Rudolf Steiner Education* (London, 1962), p. 81.
[11] Quoted in Joan Ruder, 'Curative Education', in *The Faithful Thinker*, ed. A. C. Harwood (London, 1961), p. 207.

in man finds kinship with the heart of all creation; to unfold the nature of love, by way of the great sagas and literatures of the human race, as the search of man for his own kingdom; to show that the ideals man carries are the earnest he has of his true estate, that there is conception in the spirit as well as in the body, that moral imagination is not a chimera of the mind but a power for renewing life; to discover that history follows a mighty plan of promise and fulfilment, that it leads from a state of moral and spiritual dependence towards the goal of self-mastery and self-determination, from community by descent in the past to community by assent: to demonstrate . . . that as man grows in insight so will the ultimate goal of science be attained, the rediscovery of the divine; to come to an understanding of the spiritual heritage of the East and to an appreciation of the spiritual promise of the West . . .; to perceive mankind, with Paul, as many-membered but filled with One Spirit . . . and to see the many deaths that man must die to gain immortality; . . . to pursue all this with enthusiasm and with faith.[12]

The Steiner epistemology, ontology, and teleology are not located fully in time and the sense of the eternal moment is strong, at least in Anthroposophical writings on education. It is not surprising that one writer considering teaching machines in a recent issue of *Child and Man* found them to be the antithesis of what Steiner schools stand for and programmed learning was 'the stillborn offspring of desiccated calculating machines' intended to emasculate the human spirit. A spiritualised theology provides little nourishment for sociological thinking and so Steiner schools are, of all those so far mentioned, the most radical because they are the most comprehensively different. In their way they are as radical as Summerhill in its way, and the report drawn up by members of His Majesty's Inspectorate on Michael Hall when it was first inspected in the 1930s makes the same point:

We have visited many types of school in this country. The ethical colourings in those schools might be different according to whether they were state, public, private, denominational, progressive and the rest, but the actual education offered was essentially the same in all of them. This is the first school we have met in which the philosophy of the school has totally altered the character of the education offered.

Anthroposophists consider their belief to be a way of living and they have no forms of worship. There is, for them, a distinction between

12 Edmunds, *Rudolf Steiner Education*, pp. 57–58.

approaching the spiritual world by means of individual initiative through thinking and approaching it through the common path of a religious liturgy, ritual, or form of worship. When individual understanding has been reached, Anthroposophists consider that there is no longer any need for a communal religious approach. Here is the heart of an apparent paradox — on the one hand the difficult, idiosyncratic life-view of Steiner forming a kind of imprecise orthodoxy, and on the other the truly anarchic principle of ethical individualism. So in education there is an agreed canon of Steiner theory and practice, different in many particulars from orthodox teaching in schools. It is different also from the ethos and practice in any of the radical schools we have so far considered. Whereas they grew out of English life and institutions and took up their stance in relation to the public schools, the liberalism of early political emancipating movements, religious unorthodoxy, and the anglicized transplanting of Freud, Steiner schools are and always have been based on a thought-system and a creed which bears clear marks of its Germanic origin.

The Inspectors were right in saying that the character of the education in Steiner schools is deeply affected by the philosophy of life of Anthroposophy itself. As this is a product of German and Eastern thought it does not graft easily on to an English stem.

Chapter Nine

THE SLACKENING TIDE:

Bryanston

In the first prospectus of Bryanston school, issued before the school opened in January 1928, appears the following statement:

> The Bryanston scheme has been launched to meet the difficulty felt both in this country and in the Dominions of gaining admission to our public schools. . . . Bryanston will therefore be a new English public school in which provision will be made for applicants from throughout the Empire.

The first headmaster was J. Graham Jeffreys, an Australian who graduated in Melbourne before going up to Christ Church, Oxford, and the school opened with twenty-three boys in what had been Lord Portman's fine house on a 400-acre estate near Blandford in Dorset. The building had been designed by Norman Shaw in 1897 and remains the main accommodation, although surrounded now by the additional buildings appropriate to a much larger school.

The explicit alignment to the public schools may be thought to rule Bryanston out of the radical group we are considering and admittedly it is on the borderline, but in its later development it is more clearly like others on the right wing of the progressive group. The first issue of the school magazine in December 1929 contains a contribution from the head which shows the way he was thinking: 'Let [each boy] be a gentleman in the best and widest sense of the word — courteous, kindly, considerate, discreet.' A contribution to a later issue, thinking back to those early days says that Mrs. Jeffreys helped with the cooking and the relationship in the school family was rather that of a club:

'Jeff seemed more like the breezy second officer of a ship.... [He had] tremendous promotional flair.'[1]

Jeffreys claimed that Bryanston had been founded and directed by men who were old boys of great English public schools and who had imbibed their spirit. They started by admitting boys of between thirteen and fourteen and a half on a test of general ability with a view to providing resilient systems of teaching, but in 1931 the more usual Common Entrance Examination for thirteen to fourteen year olds coming from preparatory schools was required. Jeffreys spoke more than once about this time of a public school which gave a realistic working method for average boys who wanted to enter the armed services or the learned professions or who had no pretensions to a professional career. They should all become honest, manly, and Christian citizens of the Empire. In the article in the *Anniversary Saga* already quoted, the author says of the first twenty-three pupils in January 1928 that all had this in common — 'we were either delicate or backward: I was both'.[2]

Corporal punishment was administered by masters only and not by prefects and as an instance one stroke was given for every cigarette smoked in the term. Yet alongside these traditional public school patterns there were other features unusual for 1928. There was no classical side, although Latin and Greek were available for those who wanted them. Modern subjects included a variety of languages, as well as biology and the physical sciences. A seminar and discussion methods in teaching, classes of sixteen or less, and houses of not more than forty are reminiscent of the assumptions and methods of progressive schools in the 1920s. Boys at Bryanston were expected to dispense with personal domestic service to avoid 'undue luxury of living'. In the summer they wore shorts and open-necked shirts as weekday school uniform and their winter outfit was informal by the public school standards of those days. On Sundays the differences were less obvious — for a few years bowler hats or straw hats were worn by all. Although they had to play school games for their first three years, they were free in the last two years in school to choose their own form of exercise. From the beginning there was a system of tutorials and what we would now call 'setting' for the teaching of certain subjects and an organization closely akin to the Dalton Plan, though in a number of

---

[1] *Anniversary Saga, 1928–1949*, article by M. P. Phillips from an early edition of the magazine, p. 12.　　　　[2] Ibid., p. 12.

public statements on the Bryanston scheme round about 1930 the absence of reference to Helen Parkhurst and the Dalton programme suggests that this was not a direct descendant. Here was another unusual feature in what might otherwise have been characterized as a new public school for not-so-bright boys from England and the Empire who were finding entry to the older schools too difficult.

In February 1932, with the numbers having increased in four years from twenty-three to nearly two hundred and fifty, Jeffreys resigned. He reported in the third prospectus, just before his departure, that the maximum number to be aimed at in Bryanston was three hundred. When His Majesty's Inspectors first made a full inspection of the school early in 1933 they reported that there were one hundred and ninety-two boys in the school, only fourteen of whom were doing sixth form work: 'The first Head Master, who was the founder, has left very recently and the new Head Master has scarcely had time to make his influence felt.'[3] The new headmaster was Thorold F. Coade who retired in 1959 and died in 1963 and although he was not the founder he represents for Bryanston what Badley means for Bedales — the sustained leadership for more than a quarter of a century of a remarkable man. In 1957, one of his old boys wrote: 'T.F.C.'s Headmastership may well come to be regarded by those qualified to judge as the most significant in educational development over the first half of this century; there is no doubt that T.F.C. will be looked upon as one of the outstanding headmasters of this age.'[4]

Making allowances for anniversary euphoria, we have here a notable tribute. Coade had been a young master at Harrow and in correspondence[5] gives some indications of how this viewpoint on education developed. Between 1922 and 1932 he was a member of the informal group which took the title 'New Ideals in Education', and to which so many of those we have already mentioned also belonged. The group had its first conference at East Runton in Norfolk in 1914 and later published a journal *New Ideals Quarterly*. From 1922 Coade attended the group conferences and was familiar with the ideas of all the schools we have so far considered. It will be remembered from the account given earlier that the Theosophical Fraternity in Education and later the New Education Fellowship grew out of this group.

---

[3] *Report by H.M. Inspectors on Bryanston School, Blandford*, 1933, p. 2.
[4] *Saga* (Summer 1957), p. 4. This is the school magazine at Bryanston.
[5] Kindly lent to the author by R. A. Wake, H.M.I.

Coade also speaks of the importance of the New Education Fellow-ship in helping to shape his educational thinking.

A number of able young men had returned from their war-service to Harrow, and Coade, an old boy of the school, joined with a number of others in forming a Junior Masters Club to which speakers with interesting ideas were invited. It is from meetings arranged by this Club that the *Harrow Lectures on Education* appeared in 1930 which showed some of the unorthodox thinking going on at the time among the younger men. Coade had been a leading figure in arranging these meetings and edited the publication.

Miss Helen Parkhurst and her Dalton Plan of individual assignments had attracted his attention, mainly through his contacts with the New Education Fellowship. Another whom he said he met through this society was one of its leading French members, Professor Émile Marcault. 'Marcault illuminated my mind on this subject of individual education, "individual" in this sense being the exact opposite of "individualist". He defined leaders as "those who habitually live on a higher level of consciousness".'[6] This emphasis Coade sums up as essentially Christian, exemplifying the principle that the school com-munity, like the Sabbath, is made for man and not *vice versa*. He laid great store by the quality of the life of the school community, which, especially in a boarding school, gave scope and experience for the growth of Christian love which he defined as the steady, determined activity of the mind directed toward fellowship. The writings of Evelyn Underhill gave Coade a clearer idea, as he said, of the nature of God as a Creator and as a lover of His creatures. Coade saw both these aspects merging into one in a good and lively school community and for him the main factor in education was the impact of person on person, hence the paramount importance of the selection of staff and the attitude of responsibility which the older boys were expected to have to the younger. At the time of Coade's retirement in 1959 one of his former pupils wrote of Coade's arrival in 1932: 'A shy, diffident figure sidled down the main corridor. . . . Slowly the school grew round him, alive and sensitive. . . . He who loves God loves his brother also: such a man is Thorold Coade.'[7]

H.M. Inspectors said in 1951 that he delegated authority and avoided any appearance of being a great figurehead, yet his personal influence

[6] In private correspondence.
[7] G. S. Udall, *Saga* (Winter 1959), p. 6.

was pervasive and the success of the school had to be attributed largely to him. He did not meet Reddie, nor did he see his ideas working out at Abbotsholme, though later he knew Sharp and the work of the school. Characteristically Coade gives Reddie all credit for being 'a great man and an innovator', but finds him from report and evidence of practice too much of an egotist. Coade did not meet Badley until his own views had become fairly clear and his Bryanston work was established. However, he came to know Kurt Hahn well from 1929 onwards and in 1932 boys from Bryanston and from Salem exchanged schools for some weeks: 'I learned much from him about the need to get boys to focus on some worthwhile objective which might become for them a *grande passion* shepherding them through the difficult adolescent years; also his stress on physical achievement outside organized games struck me as highly important.'[8]

Coade had another concern, another emphasis. He wanted boys at Bryanston to use their hands, to feel, to know, and to create through the plastic arts, the crafts, and music. Every boy could have in some way his chance of a creative moment, and this really was an article of faith with Coade; again in 1951 the Inspectors show how the school had matured in this since 1933, reporting a fine art and craft tradition, ambitious and successful sculpture, good pottery, woodcarving, typography, and a splendid development in music. Time was set aside for such activities for each boy in the normal run of work and on one or two evenings each week. This programme still exists and the 1961 Inspectors also commend it.

The occasional caning in Jeffreys's time was not repeated under Coade and the relaxed friendliness of relationships continued, punishment runs and 'gatings' being found enough in the way of deterrents. But the most unusual feature was the consistent adherence to the Dalton Plan which began in some form under Jeffreys in 1930, as we have seen. In 1941 the first edition was produced of an account of this scheme as it was then working at Bryanston, and this was revised in 1947.[9] The principles of the system were that a boy should learn to work on his own initiative, discovering how to study and bridging the gap between classroom instruction and university work by making progress at his own pace on assignments which he completed by studying often by himself and sometimes with classes or groups. His teachers were

---

[8] In correspondence.

[9] D. R. Wigram, *The System of Work at Bryanston School* (1947).

available for advice, guidance, and teaching, and the pupil kept a time chart and a mark record.[10] All of this continues in substantially the same form and resembles fairly closely what Miss Parkhurst laid down.

At the age of sixteen Helen Parkhurst found herself in a log-cabin school in Wisconsin responsible for the teaching of forty children in eight grades. She started then to plan individual schemes of work and enabled some children to work by themselves while she taught others. Over the next fifteen years she perfected this programme, visited other innovators and became a co-worker with Maria Montessori. In 1919 she was given charge of a school for crippled boys where she introduced her full 'laboratory plan' which quickly gained a great deal of public attention, made all the more intensive when Mrs. Murray Crane, a philanthropist much interested in education, urged the adoption in 1920 of the laboratory plan in the State High School of Dalton, Massachusetts, Miss Parkhurst's home town. The scheme came to England through Belle Rennie, the tireless secretary of the Conference of New Ideals in Education, who saw the Dalton school in operation right at the start and within three months had written to *The Times Educational Supplement*[11] offering full information to anyone interested. There were four hundred inquiries within a week and in November the paper stated that over six hundred schools were using the plan in Great Britain and by 1926 it was claimed that over two thousand schools were working it. In 1921 a Dalton Association was formed with Miss Rennie as secretary and Miss Parkhurst visited England to give lectures and see the schools. The method was practised in many countries in Europe and Asia and was even proposed as a national system for Poland and Japan. Yet within fifteen years it was dead in England as a real innovation and in general had either been submerged by a return of class teaching or assimilated into an individualized assignment system. The teaching rooms tended to go, the individual assignments were accompanied by an encroaching amount of formal instruction, the working group replaced the private study of an individual.[12]

But Bryanston has kept to the Dalton plan in all main essentials. Before we look more closely at this work it is worth remarking that

[10] D. R. Wigram, *The System of Work at Bryanston School* (1947).

[11] 6 May 1920.

[12] See 'The Dalton Plan', in *The Times Educational Supplement*, 2 Aug. 1963, p. 149. H. Parkhurst, *Education on the Dalton Plan* (London, 1923). E. Dewey, *The Dalton Laboratory Plan* (London, 1924). A. J. Lynch, *Individual Work and the Dalton Plan* (London, 1924). *Adolescent at School*, ed. V. Mallinson (London, 1949), chapter vii.

Miss Parkhurst was one of a group of Americans connected with San Francisco State Normal School who aimed at providing individual rather than collective learning in schools. Perhaps the originator was President Frederik Burk who began this kind of innovation in 1912 and three of his best-known followers and disciples were Carleton Washburne, who as superintendent of schools in Winnetka, a comfortable suburb of Chicago, developed a system which became internationally known: Willard W. Beatty who worked for a while in Winnetka with Washburne and later went to Bronxville as superintendent: and Helen Parkhurst who through the Dalton plan became best known of all in this country.[13]

As reported by Wigram, the Bryanston scheme worked (and in all essentials still works) as follows. Usually the thirteen year old entry is placed in a year-Block D, moving a year later to C, then to B, where General School Certificate Ordinary level examinations are normally taken. For those who want it, two years between the ages of sixteen and eighteen are spent in Block A, the sixth form in other schools, but boys of high ability go into Block C on entry and spend three years in Block A. Each boy has a monthly chart which has to be carefully kept; it records the number of forty-minute periods spent on each subject. The work of all these subjects is split up into topics and references, called assignments, and a space is left on the chart for recording marks given by the teacher on the work done in the assignments. These marks convey not only the quality of the knowledge displayed but, by use of colours, the degree of effort. Thus alpha in red indicates very good work and diligent effort. Blue markings indicate medium effort and black represents a lack of diligence and concentration. It is possible for a boy to get a blue beta for one subject and a black beta for another, showing that the quality of work is similar in each, but in one he scores low on diligence.

Each boy has a tutor who acts as his guide and adviser. The tutor decides with the boy at the beginning of each session what subjects he will take and will have previously consulted the parents. The curriculum offered is the usual grammar school range with divinity, music, current affairs taking a compulsory share of the total programme throughout the whole five years and physical education is also required in varying forms. The Blocks are 'setted', an arrangement by which boys are grouped together and may work with others of their own

[13] L. Cremin, *Transformation of the School*, pp. 295–6.

standard. For instance a boy in Block C may be good in mathematics and so in set C1 for that subject, weak in Latin and in C4 for that, and moderate in French and in C2 for that.

Within this Dalton system there is scope for class or 'set' teaching and there is a good deal more of this in Block D than elsewhere so that new boys may learn gradually to acquire the necessary self-discipline. Some subjects need more of it than others — a modern language needs more than history, similarly mathematics more than English. There are no form rankings, no class prizes, and the story of a boy's performance and progress is to be found in his work-chart which is filled in every day, gradings entered and initialled by the subject-master and the whole record examined regularly by the tutor. This system permits of tests and examinations as required.

The basis of the whole plan is the assignment, a scheme of work set weekly or fortnightly, or over a longer period in Blocks A and B, and provided on a typed sheet for each boy. The assignment has to be completed in a fixed period of time, and here the Bryanston scheme differs from the Dalton Plan, for in the latter children worked through the assignment at their own pace and no group could be expected to be at the same point in the programme at the same time. At Bryanston each set is kept working on basically the same assignment for the same length of time, the faster and abler pupils being expected to produce a deeper and more extensive coverage. The assignment is not only a statement of the work to be done, but covers reading references, requirements of notes, questions for written answer, correlations with cognate assignments in other subjects. By this means it is thought that pupils can see the strategy of the course, teachers have been compelled to chart their programme with long-term foresight and short-term care and the record of a boy's achievement in all his subjects is kept by him on his chart.

The whole system demands discipline and organization, as much from the teaching staff as from the boys, for work has to be marked and returned quickly, a variety of class periods taught and availability for consultation arranged and known both to boys and masters. On the boy's side it is assumed that if he finishes a week's assignment in one subject in less than the total of, say, seven periods allotted for it, he has that time available to spend on a weak subject where he needs more time. The boys work usually but not necessarily always in the subject-rooms where the books and materials for a particular subject are to be found and the master may be consulted. Studies, the library, junior common rooms, the open air may also be chosen as places of work. Or again during these periods a master can go over work with a boy in what is sometimes called a correction time.

None of the other schools mentioned in this volume has organized its teaching on the Dalton Plan for so long or in such detail. Many of them had a programme of the kind for a while—Bedales, Abbotsholme, more than one of the Friends' Schools, St. Christopher, are examples, and vestiges of the organization remain in some cases. H.M. Inspectors in 1951 and again in 1961 speak well of the system at Bryanston and consider that ordinary boys show a cheerful attack on their work. One commentator, with impregnable condescension, considers that at worst the boys are not being bored and at best are developing maturely. As a gauge of the effectiveness of the Bryanston-Dalton Plan for boys going on to higher education, 44 per cent of those leaving the school between 1948 and 1951 went on to university, 'a proportion surpassed by few schools'. Of those leaving between 1958 and 1961, 41 per cent went to universities and if one adds the boys who went to colleges of art, music, drama, or other forms of full-time higher education the percentage is 59, which is conspicuously high by any standards. When we re-call that in 1933, at the beginning of Coade's headship, only fourteen of the one hundred and ninety-two boys were doing Sixth Form work we can see how the school has changed, and it is during this period that the Dalton Plan innovation was systematically organized and applied.

To work the Dalton Plan with any success it is necessary to have a good collection of books, whether in the central library or in the subject-rooms, and the 1951 Inspectors thought that the total number of books was not large and that growth had not been rapid enough. In 1961, when there were about eleven thousand books in all for the school's use the holding was thought to be commendable — the number now, in a school of over four hundred and fifty, is considerably larger.

All boys are expected to belong to the Sea Cadet Corps or to the Pioneers, a school organization which came into existence in 1933. In the early 1930s the mounting crisis of the ineffectiveness of the League of Nations and the rise to power of Hitler were accompanied by a desperate desire for peace and economic recovery after the Great Depression. It was no accident that the year after he became head, Coade brought the Pioneers into existence to provide in a school

G

'where much attention was given to individuality an organization aiming at a sense of corporate unity directed to positive ends through constructive work'. For Coade, who had served in the First World War, the Pioneers were an educational liberal's answer to the O.T.C. The aim was training for citizenship, the membership voluntary, and boys worked (as they still do) usually in groups of about six to ten on community service projects in building, maintenance, conservation, and improvement. Among many projects the Pioneers have built a new boathouse, and a causeway to the river, very necessary for a rowing school; they have put up a new rifle range and an observatory and over a period of seven years have constructed a fine music school; the Greek theatre took two years to complete. There are also Pioneer holidays in which boys either live and work with people whose background or way of life is different, or undertake expeditions requiring enterprise and endurance and providing more than a tincture of adventure. Of the first kind were expeditions to Iceland, Norway, Russia, Finland, and the Pyrenees, to a building project in a South Wales village or decorating a Youth Club in the East End of London. Many of these needed enterprise too, but other examples of the second kind of Pioneer holidays are expeditions with the British Schools Exploring Society to unexplored territories and periods spent at Outward Bound Sea and Mountain Schools, or voyages on trawlers.

Many of these undertakings are now common practice in a number of maintained or independent schools not in the progressive categories, but Bryanston has been run on these lines since 1933 when this whole outlook was very new and compulsory games was the orthodox physical enterprise. Bryanston's schemes were, of course, related to Abbotsholme's and Bedales's estate work, to Leighton Park's venture scholarships and to Kurt Hahn's similar schemes first at Salem and from 1934 in Scotland at Gordonstoun. We have already seen that Hahn had influenced Coade very much and it was natural enough that Coade should want his boys to enter early into the Outward Bound scheme bent on discovering the resources of skill, knowledge, courage, self-reliance, and determination which a boy has and enabling him to face and assess these things for himself.

The Sea Cadets were started at Bryanston in 1946 to provide opportunities for pre-service training and again the influence of Hahn and Gordonstoun can be seen. In the 1930s the Pioneers had been a specifically non-military organization but during the War many of the older boys had been active in pre-service and civil defence units and there was still, in the post-war situation of conscription, a body of opinion among boys and parents supporting some form of preparatory organization. The Sea Cadets offered drill and sea-training, boat-work, courses of various kinds, and visits to naval and Marine establishments as a preliminary to entry to the Royal or the Merchant Navy if boys so wished. Some parents were glad of this more formal and disciplined training and saw it as a valuable contrast to the informality of the school, even where no future career in the service was intended. Others saw this development as an extension of the range of careers for which a Bryanston education might be directly relevant. Some parents thought it a surrender to orthodox practices and the choice of Sea Cadets as the favoured organization shows a nice discrimination in trying to meet all shades of opinion.

This in a particular form is the familiar problem for all the progressive schools — indeed, for any school. What degree of freedom of choice and compulsion will there be ? If physical fitness is a part of education how much compulsion should there be to that end ? Are organized games a compulsory element ? Ought there to be a choice of games played ? Should physical work offer moral, social, and idealistic opportunities beyond the enriching or stunting possibilities in the team spirit ? In sport, is a school committed to individual education as well as to team spirit ? Is there a special virtue in the discipline, willing obedience, and pride in appearance to be found in pre-service training ?

Bryanston's answers were unorthodox in 1932 and have become more generally accepted now. In the liberal-conservative spectrum of the progressive schools Bryanston was and is at the conservative end. The traditional games, with rowing, swimming, athletics, and tennis, are played regularly and to a good standard. The more individual sports like climbing and canoeing are encouraged and it is the school's policy to leave boys free to choose what form of exercise they will take with the proviso that it has to be strenuous and they can choose their games each term only if they undertake to turn out regularly. Summerhill or Dartington or Bedales or the Steiner schools or St. Christopher are more permissive in these and other matters than Bryanston. In the matter of pre-service training amongst the progressive group Bryanston and Gordonstoun are almost alone.

There are about fifty clubs and societies in the school to which boys belong and time is given in the evenings and at other parts of the day for boys to engage in work in the societies of their choice and without doubt this is a remarkable feature in the school. Art, pottery, photography, natural history, archaeology, printing, politics, sailing, gliding, science, sculpture are amongst the interests of the societies. Two of particular importance are music and drama, both abiding interests of Coade. The concerts, operas, and oratorios are notable occasions and there have been more than ten each year since the school was founded, many of them including original compositions by boys. The plays have been strikingly ambitious and consistently successful.

Since 1946 Bryanston has had a sister school, Cranbourne Chase, founded on the same principles and intended to be a partner in many kinds of educational and social activities. None of the other single-sex progressive schools has done this except Bootham and the Mount — Abbotsholme, Clayesmore, Bembridge, Rendcomb, Gordonstoun have no sister schools and Badminton has no brother school. Bryanston and Cranbourne Chase have shared teaching resources as well as offering one another the complementary advantages obvious in drama, music, and social life. The schools were originally rather more than twelve miles apart when Cranbourne Chase was at Crichel but now are eighteen miles from one another as the girls' school has moved to Wardour Castle, and effective contact is difficult to maintain.

At Bryanston there are prefects and monitors who are responsible to the head for the discipline of the school, and a School Council elected by house representatives makes recommendations to the head on matters of daily routine. In 1938 the Council met fortnightly and had certain judiciary powers, boys accused of anti-social behaviour sometimes being handed over to it for judgement, but its powers and the use made of the Council have varied a great deal in the last thirty years. It has never been an integral and central part of the organization of the school as it clearly has been at Dartington or at Summerhill or at King Alfred's. The structure of government at Bryanston is relatively conventional, but based also on a relaxed and informal discipline which gives a quality to the human relationships which minimizes the dominance of masters or prefects and the submission of the rank and file pupil. Coade saw this possibility of friendship and respect as rooted in Christian belief. Soon after he arrived in 1932 he preached in Chapel:

> To acquire Christ's power of effortless radiation is the goal which you should aim for if you are to be educated fully . . . and share that

fullness with others. . . . To attain to the fullness of the stature of
Christ . . . is the aim of Education as I see it.[14]

Elsewhere the school is committed to the Christian revelation of the
nature of God and the Universe:

> Education must, therefore, be *essentially* religious if it is to fulfil its
> purpose. This means not only attendance at services and scripture
> lessons, but the cultivation of the art of looking and listening in
> relation to the activities of the Spirit revealed not only in the Bible
> or in sacred literature generally, but in the works of artists, musicians
> and men of letters, as well as in the works of Nature.[15]

In its curriculum Bryanston covers the usual ground but was early in
the field with the study of economics and sociology, and the sixth-
form humanities course incorporated ethics, philosophy, and the history of science. Spanish, Italian, and Russian were taught at Bryanston
when they were seldom known in other schools and scarcely ever
all together in one. This has required generous staffing and the ratio
from the start in 1928 has been of the order 1 : 11, favourable,
expensive, but probably necessary for the Dalton Plan arrangements
and for the exceptional range of teaching offered in a school now of
about four hundred and fifty boys.

Bryanston started by taking boys not all of whom could pass Common Entrance at thirteen. Its character has changed and it seldom
takes boys who cannot succeed at the Ordinary level and now about
80 per cent stay through for a full sixth-form course and 60 per cent
proceed to some form of higher education.

In 1942, £30,000 was raised to enable boys from what were then
called elementary schools to be educated at Bryanston and the school
strongly supported the recommendations of the Fleming Report which
proposed that at least 25 per cent of the entrants to independent
schools should come into this category. Certain firms paid the fees
of sons of employees to attend the school and at least two Local
Education Authorities also sent boys. After ten years the figure of
boys at the school in what may be called the Fleming group was just
under 10 per cent and it has not climbed higher. The school made
efforts to come to some kind of terms with the conditions of the time

[14] T. F. Coade. From an address on Sunday, 12 June 1932.
[15] The 1962 Prospectus, p. 24.

and was more successful in this than any others who have hitherto been mentioned, except perhaps some of the Quaker schools.

Bryanston is not very unorthodox in its curriculum or in its forms of government, while being liberal enough in both to be considered as just falling in the group of innovators. It is notable for the quality of its work in the arts, the crafts, music, and drama yet it has also a good academic and sporting record. The practical building and maintenance work done by the Pioneers is remarkable by any standards. Perhaps the two most significantly different features of the school are its unequivocally Christian basis and its adherence to the Dalton Plan. Other progressive schools are specific in their Christian claims — the Quaker schools and the Steiner schools, for instance. But Bedales, St. Christopher, Dartington, King Alfred, Summerhill, Frensham Heights are much less explicit on their religious position or are not Christian. Bryanston declares its interests. As for the Dalton Plan, Bryanston is unique in this group of schools in the detail and consistency of its adherence to the Plan as a method of teaching.

In 1934 Coade contributed an article on the school to *The Modern Schools Handbook*, the symposium on radical schools to which reference has been made in earlier pages. There is no article from Bryanston in *The Independent Progressive School*, the 1962 sequel to the earlier book and partly this is because the word 'progressive' has become a less favourable, more presumptuous term, partly because Bryanston would now prefer to see itself on the left of the public schools than on the right of the radical schools. Some people will dismiss such a distinction as arbitrary and misleading, but it can be defended as representing a shift which a number of the schools we have considered have either deliberately made or have found is becoming relevant. In this category might be found some of the Friends' schools, Bembridge, Rendcomb, Clayesmore, and certainly Bryanston.

Chapter Ten

THE SLACKENING TIDE:

The Thirties and Gordonstoun

MOST of the schools we have considered so far have had their origin in the ideas and drive of one person or a small group — Reddie, Badley, Devine, Whitehouse, Neill, Simpson and Wills, the Elmhirsts and Curry, Dora and Bertrand Russell, Susan Isaacs and Geoffrey Pyke, Steiner. Of course, there is the essential backing and day-to-day support of assistant staff, governors, parents. But if anything is true of the radical schools we have named it is that the large majority of them owe their origin not so much to an educational movement as to a person, to an educational individualist. This is also true of Gordonstoun and its predecessor and progenitor, Salem.

I

Kurt Hahn was born in 1886 of Jewish parents with Polish ancestry and he was brought up as a Jew. His middle-class family was prosperous and cultivated, with iron-founders, teachers, musicians, and doctors scattered through the generations. Hahn was educated at the *Wilhelmsgymnasium* in Berlin where much of the teaching was academic and arid but to some of it he responded eagerly and carried lasting influences through life from the work he did then and later at the university in the classics and on Plato in particular. A few months before taking his *Abitur* Hahn says he suffered an attack of sunstroke which was not taken very seriously at the time but which had many and more serious consequences.

In 1904 Hahn's father, who had had some of his own education in England, sent his son to Oxford where, at Christ Church, he studied classical philology and discovered to his dismay that many of his English classmates were well ahead of him in classical scholarship and he returned disheartened to Germany in 1906 for further study at the Universities of Berlin, Heidelberg, Freiburg, and Göttingen. At the age of twenty-four Hahn returned to Oxford where he stayed for nearly four years before returning without taking a degree to Germany in 1914 just before the outbreak of war.

Hahn took a great deal back to Germany from his ten years of pre-war contact with Oxford. He came to know a number of Etonians when he was at Christ Church and he admired the training for leader-ship through membership of the Eton Society, otherwise called 'Pop'. These were the opportunities open to aristocrats, and in Hahn's view Rugby offered, *mutatis mutandis*, a responsible introduction to leader-ship for boys of the middle classes through the prefect system and its development since Thomas Arnold. In 1902 Hahn had met Alan Marcan, Arnold-Brown, and Ben Simpson of Abbotsholme and later followed the progressive tradition in Germany in the schools of Hermann Lietz. In his autobiographical comments Hahn tells how, when he went to Christ Church for the second time in 1910, he saw clearly, in the regime of the university, concern for the body, the mind, and the future career of the undergraduates which he found different from the German assumptions he had been used to. At that time he met J. L. Calder, a bursar at Oxford from the University of Aberdeen. Calder came of farming stock from Morayshire and as the recurrent aftermath of his earlier attack of sunstroke made it necessary for Hahn to spend the summers away from the heat and glare of Germany, he went with Calder to his home in the north-east of Scotland. Hahn rented a house and was visited at his home in the Findhorn valley by many friends as he lived the summer life of a wealthy young Jew. He felt the integrity and the grace of the Calder family and enjoyed the friendship of others in that area, especially Alastair Cumming and his mother Lady Smith-Cumming and the editor of the *Inverness Courier* Evan Barron. At this time Hahn had been giving a great deal of thought to a school which might realize some of his developing ideas and he discussed this with J. A. Stewart, one of his Oxford tutors, Karl Reinhardt, and others, but it came to nothing by the time war broke out. After the end of the War the sketch plan of 1913 became the Salem reality of 1920.

During the War Hahn was attached to the German Foreign Office and at the end of hostilities he was secretary to Prince Max of Baden, the last Imperial Chancellor, who had a major responsibility in the negotiation for the peace treaty and the consequent demand for reparations.

In July 1919 Prince Max took up residence again in Baden at his castle in Salem and Hahn began sifting the mass of material for the memoirs which Prince Max ultimately published in 1927. The Schule Schloss Salem was opened in 1920 in the castle at Salem with which three other satellite schools at Hohenfels, Hermannsberg, and Spetzgart, several miles from one another, were later associated. In the 1960s there were about five hundred children in the schools, about one hundred and twenty of them girls.

The religious history of Baden reveals severe conflicts between the Protestant north and the Catholic south; its political history provides periods of French dominance, of peasant revolt, of alliance with Austria against Prussia, and later alliance with Prussia against France. The proximity to Switzerland, to Austria, to Bavaria has provided Baden with a history of conflict and also a liberal tradition, both of which appear in the political changes of the nineteenth century. The constitutional form of government of the Grand Duchy later became what it now is, a *Land*, roughly like an English county.

The castle at Salem had been a Cistercian monastery for seven hundred years and its broad stone corridors and rooms of plain proportions have been enriched by the baroque decorations and religious furniture characteristic of southern Germany. In Salem the ruling family maintained the continuity from the monastic beginnings and developed further the beautiful estate the monks had built up over centuries and for the last forty-five years the boys and girls in historic surroundings have been working out what were at first new educational ideas based on the thinking of Kurt Hahn more than any other of his German colleagues.

When the school started in 1920 Hahn was put in charge of the boarding side with Miss Marina Ewald who is still at Salem. The Director of Studies was Karl Reinhardt, the founder of the Frankfurt Reform Gymnasium who was over seventy in 1920, but whose experience gave shape to the academic work of Salem. Kurt Hahn was thirty-four when Salem was founded and he had had no sustained experience of schools or of teaching. With Prince Max he was dismayed at the moral anarchy of Germany at the end of the War and they wanted to provide some bulwark against the creeping decay. Salem was their answer. As the principles and the practice of Gordonstoun are in essentials the same as those of Salem, we can examine them in detail later. For the present we can trace the steps which brought Hahn to England in 1933.

Salem started with very few boys and girls and built up its numbers quite quickly. Prince Max's name drew the children of aristocratic families to Salem and rumours spread that it was 'a school for princes'. In the first forty years something under 20 per cent of the old boys and girls were from aristocratic and titled families, both within and outside Germany — which may well be thought a high proportion. Parents who could not afford the fees were encouraged to discuss their situation with the school authorities and were offered some remission. Over the same period about 30 per cent had such financial help.

Hahn has always been concerned with physical fitness and at no time more than in the first years of Salem, when most boys and girls had suffered from malnutrition in the Allied blockade of Germany at the end of the War. By 1930, together with physical fitness, his preoccupation was to train a moral independence devoted to finding 'a moral equivalent to war' (a phrase of William James's which Hahn never tires of quoting). The school by its connections and its twin heredity, on the one hand in the German and English establishment, and on the other in the progressive movement in education, was in an uncommonly strong position even after Prince Max's death in 1929. There were masters and boys and girls from a variety of countries, including England, and Salem had a living quality, according to some a self-sufficiency of purpose, that occasionally strayed over the borders into arrogance. It was and was not of Lietz's *Landerziehungsheimen*, it was and was not a relative of the *Wandervögel* movement, it was and was not an English public school, it was and was not like Abbotsholme or Bedales, it was and was not Plato's Athenian Academy transposed to Baden. Hahn, the moving spirit, was of the Jewish middle-class intelligentsia and not an aristocrat, an Anglophile in devastated postwar Germany, an internationalist and liberal whose spirit and whose school and whose ethnic origins could not have been more at variance with Hitler and the Nazi movement which had begun in Bavaria across the borders from Baden and which by the late 1920s was growing in power.

In the autumn of 1932, in the so-called Potempa incident, five of

Hitler's S.A. men kicked a young communist to death at Beuthen before the eyes of his mother. They were tried and sentenced to death, but Hitler intervened and greeted them as 'comrades' in a telegram and sought for their release. In response to this Hahn sent a letter to all old boys and girls of Salem in the following terms:

> By the telegram of Hitler to the 'comrades' of Beuthen a fight has been initiated which goes far beyond politics. Germany is at stake, its Christian way of life, its reputation, the honour of its soldiers; Salem cannot remain neutral. I call upon the members of the Salem association who are engaged on S.A. or S.S. work to break their allegiance either to Hitler or to Salem.

This is the clearest summary of Hahn's personal convictions: his passionate belief in the need for moral independence and for a school that spoke out through its present and its past pupils for human values. Erich Meissner, who served Salem and Gordonstoun for nearly thirty years, recalled this period in a speech he gave to the Gordonstoun Society in 1942, and said that many friends of Salem, who were reasonable and brave persons, strongly disapproved of Hahn's letter for they saw that when Hitler came to power there would be revenge. In any case they thought it gratuitous and foolhardy to the point of arrogance to pit the strength of a public school with some two hundred boys and girls in it at the time against the ruthless power of the Nazi party. However, Kurt Hahn followed up his letter with two public speeches elaborating his implacable opposition to this degradation of human dignity, the German reputation, and Christian compassion. Of course, Salem was a powerful school at which were the children of some of the leading aristocratic and industrial families in Germany together with a substantial minority of the sons of influential persons from other countries.

On 30 January 1933 Hitler was appointed Chancellor by President Hindenburg after the dismissal of von Schleicher, and charged with forming a national government on a constitutional basis. Hahn knew as well as anyone that his denunciations would not be overlooked and following on the Reichstag fire of 4 March he was amongst those arrested in the mass imprisonments of liberals, socialists, and communists. He was placed in Überlingen gaol on 8 March and at once the Margrave of Baden and other German friends and supporters sought for his release and so too did those in other countries, including Ramsay MacDonald, the British Prime Minister at that time, whose interest in Bedales will be seen. William Temple, the Archbishop of York; Geoffrey Bell, the Bishop of Chichester; and Geoffrey Winthrop Young were friends who supported Hahn both then and later. He was released after five days at Überlingen and in July 1933 he left Germany for England.

Prince Max's son, the Margrave of Baden, declared himself responsible for Salem which almost certainly saved the school from immediate victimization, and a little later Meissner became head for some weeks during a period when the Nazi attack on the school and what it stood for was mounting dangerously. One of the English masters, who later moved to Gordonstoun, took Meissner, who was in some danger, over the border to Switzerland in 1935, but the school continued. A violent press campaign grew up against Salem and as Meissner put it 'the local S.A. formations began to consider Salem as a territory that must be conquered and occupied'. The familiar, vile tactics of intimidation of children and families became more obvious, together with the invitation to serve the Fatherland by informing the police and the party of 'anti-German' behaviour or opinions amongst the pupils or the masters. By stressing loyalty to the party, the Fatherland, and the Fuehrer the main attack was directed against the Salem idea of citizenship and internationalism.

The Salem principle of physical fitness could be distorted to serve Nazi purposes, and undoubtedly later to some extent it was, but it is significant that only in 1944 did the S.S. take the school over. The resistance which Hahn's 1933 letter encouraged appears to have been maintained to some extent even throughout the War. After 1945 Hahn returned to Salem to help to encourage its revival and he lives for part of each year now in his retirement at Hermannsberg.

II

When Hahn came to England in July 1933 he was forty-seven years old, a refugee without money, dejected, and apparently defeated. But he had good and influential friends who knew and admired his work in Germany and 'the Friends of Salem' advised him to start a similar school in this country. William Temple, Lord Tweedsmuir, better known as John Buchan the novelist, G. M. Trevelyan the historian, the Headmaster of Eton, and Geoffrey Winthrop Young were among the Friends of Salem. Hahn has always managed to find powerful allies. He returned to Scotland and two months after his arrival was tutoring boys at Doune of Rothiemurchus in Inverness-shire. He met again the Cumming family and it was from them that the Gordonstoun estate was leased for a very low rental in 1934, the school opening in April of that year. The history of the estate can be traced from the thirteenth century and the history of the area farther back still. The house is a mixture of styles and periods and lies above the Moray Firth with the harbour of Hopeman village a mile or two away in one direction and the small eighteenth-century Michael Kirk a mile in the opposite direction with the Cairngorm Mountains to the south and the north-west highlands across the firth in Sutherland and Caithness.

Like Salem, Gordonstoun opened with a few boys but, as Henry Brereton, later the Warden, points out, the difficulties were far greater in Scotland than in Baden. The devotion and labour of a Cistercian community had developed and maintained Salem as a beautiful, prosperous, and ordered estate which the pride and taste of the Grand Dukes enriched still farther for the school, but at Gordonstoun everything had suffered from years of neglect and the uninhabited buildings and grounds cried out for capital to be spent on them. In 1934 English and Scottish public schools were going through a bleak period and the competition between them for pupils was sharp. The first Gordonstoun boys came from a small group of parents who knew of Hahn and his work or they were boys who were failures or misfits in their previous schools. After the commanding position of Salem which could be exclusive in any way it chose Gordonstoun found itself dealing with a fairly high proportion of frail or difficult or intellectually mediocre boys, which was seen to be a doubtful blessing because success in this field tends to make it more difficult later to recruit boys of good ability. Hahn admitted boys to Gordonstoun on the basis of selection tests and interviews and Gordonstoun did not at first find itself in a position to demand Common Entrance qualifications even if this had seemed desirable. The school was in a precarious financial state from the start, with little capital from which to cover both renovation and expansion. However, Hahn tried to add thirty new boys each year and had been so successful that by 1939, after five years of edging forward in this way, there were one hundred and thirty-five boys in the school. The guardian, or head boy, in 1939 was Prince Philip of Greece who had come with a few German boys and others from

Salem preparatory school in 1934 to be among the first pupils at Gordonstoun.

The reputation of the school was beginning to offer some prospect of stability in 1939 when war finally came. Despite Hahn's anti-Nazi record, his naturalization as a British subject, his repeated condemnation of Hitler's regime, and his known concern for refugees, he was almost inevitably under a cloud in the early days of the War. There were about a dozen German adults at the school at that time and rather more German boys. The German nationals were interned and H. L. Brereton recalls with rueful amusement that British masters, who were not already on the reserve, were at first rejected when they volunteered for service with the Local Defence Volunteers. North-east Scotland was no place for a school at that time and after nine months of confusing and difficult circumstances the school was evacuated in June 1940 to Plas Dinam the Welsh home of Lord Davies who had two sons at Gordonstoun and whose sympathy for and active work in international causes drew him to the ideals for which Hahn strove.

For Gordonstoun, as for all schools, the war years were exceedingly difficult — the school had to divide into two, the numbers dropped by over one-third and there was a financial crisis which very nearly finished the school altogether. Yet there were opportunities which Hahn took during those five years which established him and his educational ideas more firmly by the end of the War than in 1939. The County Badge scheme had started in 1936, but the beginnings of what has become the Outward Bound movement, of which we shall hear more later, are to be found in the war years and Hahn's opinions on leadership and training methods were listened to with respect by the Admiralty and the War Office between 1940 and 1945.

When the school returned to Morayshire in 1945 the problem of re-establishment was huge. Military occupation had badly damaged all the buildings and Gordonstoun House had been gutted by fire, the post-war shortages of money and supplies made it seriously possible that the school could not take proper advantage of its new ascendancy. As with other schools, austerity within and outside munificence brought Gordonstoun through this storm and today it is a school of over four hundred boys with a strong reputation which is no longer dependent on the presence of Hahn, who retired from the headship in 1953. But it is Hahn's ideas that have given the framework of the school.

Hahn summarized his educational principles and practice in a broadcast talk he gave in 1934:

> Nothing was original in Salem. We cribbed and copied from many sources; from Plato, from Dr. Arnold of Rugby; from Eton, from Abbotsholme, from Hermann Lietz, from Fichte and from Wilhelm Meister.... We did not believe in originality in education nor in experiments on human beings.[1]

He considered that there were three characteristic approaches to education: the Ionian; the Spartan; and the Platonic. The Ionian view is called after the reputation for self-indulgence and individualism linked with the Ionians of the fifth century B.C., and the modern equivalent for Hahn leads to the child-centred and self-expression theories from which the child never feels the sting of defeat or the hard challenge of painful effort. This is not the way for Salem or Gordonstoun. The second approach he calls the Spartan where the emphasis is on service to the school and the state, especially through excellence in academic or athletic activities. More ordinary children are rated second best and everything has to be done for the sake of the school, not by the individual choice of persons. This, too, is not the way for Salem or Gordonstoun. The Platonic view is the answer for Hahn and he lists six 'Salem laws' which are intended to do justice both to the community and to the individual child. Hahn does not present these laws as abstractions supporting a particular view of man or of education. Instead, he is quite specific and practical.

1. Put all the children in dress which does not hide their limbs and this will encourage a pride in physical fitness. The school uniform at Gordonstoun for normal day wear as at Abbotsholme, Bryanston and Clayesmore is an open-necked shirt, pullover, shorts and stockings.

2. Build up the physical fitness of every child and this should start from the basic skills of running, jumping and throwing. The formal and more sophisticated skills for specific games can follow later, but a boy should be responsible for his own exercise and it should be part of his routine all the year round four or five times a week and, if he does not take to it at first it will be accepted in time:

   > I should think as little of asking [boys] whether they want to train as I should think of asking them whether they feel in the

1 Reprint from *The Listener*, 28 Nov. 1934, p. 10.

mood to brush their teeth. . . . Self discipline really is the condition of self-expression.[2]

3. Restrict team games to two days a week; they should be compulsory on those two days and should be prohibited on all other days, weekdays and Sundays. In this way Hahn sought to control the games fetish, but to give a place to team competition and skill.

4. Give children genuine opportunity for self-discovery, because in Hahn's view every boy or girl has a *grande passion* (a favourite expression) which too often has not had a chance to express itself. A variety of activities is needed, each a challenge and test of self-reliance and self-expression and each a vital and dignified part of community life, not put into a pocket of time away from the normal flow of the day and called a hobby. Maybe the *grande passion* (Hahn appears to think of one supreme, and not of many equally absorbing competitors) will be found in playing the trumpet or the cello, in writing plays, in a programme of scientific inquiry, in climbing mountains or sailing boats, in sculpting, in building, painting or caring for animals. This is Coade's 'creative movement' and in one way or another all innovating schools seek to provide a variety of valid experiences, as do most other good schools in these days. But the significance attached to non-curricular, individualist work has been greater in the progressive schools from their beginnings than in more orthodox establishments. The importance that Hahn attaches to it is at times almost hectic:

> The wholesome passion once discovered grows to be 'the guardian angel' of the years of adolescence, while the undiscovered and unprotected boy rarely maintains his vitality unbroken and undiluted from eleven to fifteen. We do not hesitate to say: often the spiritual difference in age between a boy of fifteen and a boy of eleven is greater than that between a man of fifty and a boy of fifteen.[3]

For Hahn puberty is a period of 'poisonous passions' and childhood a period of natural reverence, and to these romantic and questionable polarities we shall return.

5. Make the children meet with triumph and defeat, at first building carefully on their gifts and potentialities to ensure success, but later teaching them to overcome defeat in harder enterprises.

6. Provide periods of silence, following the precedent both of the Quakers and the monasteries. To this end, besides rooms for

---

[2] Reprint from *The Listener*, 28 Nov. 1934, p. 11.   [3] Ibid., p. 12.

quiet work and reading, boys at Gordonstoun walk the mile to service at Michael Kirk in silence and are encouraged to make space for contemplation and reflection. As the current Prospectus puts it :

> If aloneness means boredom then the intellectual life has been mismanaged or neglected. Therefore care must be taken to see that the variety of occupations does not engulf the individual.[4]

In 1938 Hahn put the same point this way :

> Neither the love of Man nor the Love of God can take deep root in a child that does not know aloneness.[5]

Gordonstoun is an organized boys' school having little in common with the permissiveness of Summerhill or Dartington. Hahn is not a man with precise medical training, nor was he an outstanding athlete, but he kept the same kind of regime of daily habits as Gordonstoun boys until late in his period as head of the school. The physical self-discipline was formulated into a Training Plan which continues now and it establishes a routine of daily habits for which a boy early becomes responsible. The Plan is a chart relating to house regulations, personal habits, and work preparation. As an example, the following headings are included as daily routines : a morning run on rising, two warm washes in the day (soap all over), two cold showers, before breakfast and after afternoon activities (additional showers if other strenuous exercise is taken at another time of the day), two cleanings of teeth, sixty skips, five press-ups, eating is forbidden between meals except at precisely stated times, set duties are recorded, hair is washed once a fortnight, conditions for study are included in the records — and so on.

For the first two terms boys are supervised in filling in their Training Plans which they have to do daily, recording plus for the tasks completed and minus where they have been left undone. Usually from about his third term at Gordonstoun a boy is left to fill in his Training Plan himself as a daily task and normally no one checks it because it is regarded as a matter of honour for him to complete it. Hahn and his successors have laid great stress on this principle of trust which is approached from several points of view and for which deliberate training is needed, the Training Plan being one clear example. Older boys have modifications of detail, but a boy must tell the truth to

---

4 Op. cit. p. 12.   5 *Education for Leisure.* Lecture given in Oxford, Jan. 1938, p. 8.

himself on his record of daily habits even when it might lead to reporting the need for correction because of an accumulation of faults.
'Walking punishments', a graded series of walks required as punishments of varying severity, have to be completed by boys without
supervision. At Gordonstoun the point is clearly made that the
Training Plan requires no real introspection, for the information is
factual and the right answer clear. The habit of providing a voluntary,
accurate, unflattering record can be salutary self-discipline, and the
need to provide a record at all is a steady reminder of the framework
of necessary routine.

In addition to the Training Plan, boys keep their own records of
school marks on a system borrowed from the Dalton Plan, but whereas
the Training Plan becomes a matter of personal information which
may be inspected by a house master only for some exceptional reason,
the work record is checked by a form supervisor each week and the
progress of boys considered in staff meetings two or three times a term.
Gordonstoun boys are trusted when they have been trained to trust
themselves and there is no suggestion that the pupils know best what
is good for them. The grades of status in the school illustrate the limits
within which this trust applies in the hierarchical system.

When a boy enters the school, usually at thirteen, he is inducted into
the arrangements for a time and normally by the end of his first term
he is given permission to wear the full school uniform (there are two
uniforms, one for the day and the other, the 'school uniform', for the
evening). Usually by the end of his third term he has the responsibility
for marking his Junior Training Plan himself and by the beginning of
his third year the housemaster changes this to the Senior Training Plan.
In the houses certain older boys are recommended for responsible jobs
as is common in any boarding school and at Gordonstoun the housemaster recommends to the headmaster that these boys be given a White
Stripe. Up to this point the transitions from one phase to the next
have been in the hands of the housemaster and the headmaster; White
Stripers can now become eligible, on the basis of responsible work
conscientiously carried through, for promotion to Colour Bearer
Candidates and the proposals for these changes come from the body of
Colour Bearers themselves. This has some affinity with the arrangements for 'Pop' at Eton and it gives to the Colour Bearers, never more
than one tenth of the school, a position of standing without much in the
way of privilege. The headmaster selects from the Colour Bearers a

small group to be Helpers and one of these to be the Guardian or head boy of the school. The Helpers are usually in charge of a house, or bear special organizing responsibility for a sector or department in school affairs like health, practical work, seamanship, expeditions and they have powers of command. Tasks of lesser responsibility are usually in the hands of Colour Bearers who are 'expected to maintain, if necessary to defend, the standard of the School and its written or un-written laws. The emphasis is on additional obligations rather than special privileges.'

This complex dispersal of responsibility resembles what is done at Abbotsholme and Bryanston, but it has more formality at Gordonstoun. Prefectships are not the only distant and legitimate elevations for younger boys. However, the extended hierarchy can have the possible effect of confirming a boy who never becomes a Colour Bearer Candi-date in the belief that he will never become a Colour Bearer or a Helper either.

There is not much to remark in the curriculum at Gordonstoun. It has not departed greatly from a conventional grammar school range although a modified Dalton plan has been operated. At the same time the school has not aspired to intensive high-level work for university scholarships. This was Hahn's preference and is maintained by the school now:

> The conditions imposed by the present examination system must be accepted but it is often harmful and unwise to force a boy to reach certain academic standards at the cost of his natural mental develop-ment. An early scholastic success brought about through undue pressure is often followed by a sad anti-climax because mental re-sources have been tapped at the wrong moment and in the wrong way. . . . It is the design at Gordonstoun to stimulate by variety of interests minds that are endowed with the reserves of energy which spring from willing and well-conditioned bodies.[6]

Here the part played by the other features of Gordonstoun life is vital. There is a range of individual projects, the *grandes passions* which have already been commented upon, on which some hours are spent each week and these can be an extension of some physical pursuit or music, acting, painting, sculpture, craft, or a piece of 'research'. In short, it is one or a series of projects such as we have seen in a number of the other radical schools, and with older boys these have sometimes

[6] Op. cit., p. 10.

been submitted for consideration in the competition for Trevelyan scholarships. Bryanston, Abbotsholme, Bedales, and other schools have followed the same course, but Hahn in his 1938 address gave a special moral colouring to these enterprises :

> ... the building instinct can perhaps protect the biggest proportion of boys ; exploration and adventure come next in the wideness of their appeal ; music, painting, will protect not many, but those very much worth protecting. ... Each of these non-poisonous passions may grow to be powerful enough to prevent the sexual impulses that well up during adolescence from absorbing the available emotional energy.[7]

Another part of the Gordonstoun life is physical work with all the moral significance that it generates in Hahn's scheme of things. All boys undertake training in practical seamanship and the school keeps boats of varying sizes in Hopeman harbour, a mile or two away. There are special courses and more applied training for boys who intend to have careers in the Royal Navy or the Merchant Navy. When Hahn was in Salem, the Bodensee close at hand gave the contact with sailing. The Moray Firth is different, with fishing villages along the rugged coast and a naval base not far away at Lossiemouth.

A second physical activity greatly valued at Gordonstoun is mountaineering, which developed when the school was evacuated to Wales and when, after the war, a branch of the school was housed sixteen miles from Gordonstoun and at a distance from the sea at Altyre. During the war the Sea School at Aberdovey in Merioneth in Wales had strengthened the rather limited appeal of the Moray Badge scheme in which Hahn had placed a good deal of faith in 1936 and 1937. In the 1930s seamanship, and in the late 1940s, climbing were added to the athletics for which Salem boys had been noted between 1933 and 1938.

Like many innovating schools Gordonstoun has required estate work of its boys from the beginning, partly from financial necessity, partly on educational principle. There is in addition 'the services' which Hahn felt offered deep satisfaction to boys and in which he saw the element of training transformed into pride in responsibility. In 1935 a school Coastguard Service was formed and when there is a likelihood of rough weather a Watchers' Corps, trained to handle life-saving apparatus, mans the school lookout point on the rocky coast. In 1940 a school Fire Service was formed and was incorporated into the war-

[7] Op. cit., p. 5.

time Fire Service. It continues now to serve the school as an efficient unit with mobile pumps and tenders which can be called on in an emergency in the area. Gordonstoun boys have also been trained in mountain rescue and more recently a surf rescue unit and a ski patrol have been formed. All of these organizations illustrate the concern for life-preservation, for rescue, which Hahn and his successors feel to be affirmative and outward-looking, the antidote to the selfishness and apathy which too often assails adolescents in general, and boarding schools in particular.

In 1961 Gordonstoun formed a Combined Cadet Force and boys may choose to do their advanced training in the naval or army sections of the Force or in one of the rescue services or may train throughout in the Scout Troop. The C.C.F. is an organization providing the kind of training that most of the other progressive schools rejected in the inter-war period and, in this day of small peace-time forces of professionals and appallingly technical warfare, they have felt no urge to revise this decision.

Gordonstoun speaks of hardening while sparing, of responsibility to and for the community, of maintaining the spiritual strength of child-hood unbroken and undiluted through 'the loutish years', of love of enterprise, love of aloneness, love of skill. The purpose of fitness is, to quote the title of a recent book, the unfolding of character.[8] Hahn attributes much of the proper growth of persons to 'a healthy pasture' and the discipline of increasing responsibility. Greek athletics is a guide to the running, jumping, and throwing that Gordonstoun boys know well. The morning run and the details of the Training Plan have much in common with Reddie's exact regime for Abbotsholmians. The hierarchy leading through an *élite* to the Guardian raises echoes of the Attic *ephebia* and the philosopher-king or guardian of Plato. Gordonstoun has a Headmaster, a Warden, and a Director of Studies in its government, a model reminiscent of Eton and Winchester and of the checks and balances of *The Republic*. The Director of Studies is expected to see that the academic programmes of each boy are suitably planned and if necessary he has to defend the claims of schoolwork against a head who may take boys out of class for sudden assemblies

---

[8] A. Arnold-Brown, *Unfolding of Character: the Impact of Gordonstoun* (London, 1962). Mr. Arnold-Brown was a boy at both Abbotsholme and Gordonstoun. Some of his facts on Abbotsholme (pp. 4–5) are inaccurate but he shows how Gordonstoun has affected one old boy.

or for a few days in the hills. The Warden represents a wise counsellor who is not caught up in the day-to-day administration, 'the philosopher in the watch tower', who can advise in any way that seems appropriate and whose problems relate more to policy and guidance than to precise decision-making.

Hahn spoke often of a responsibility to the community which led him to forge, or seek to forge, links with the neighbourhood. The Moray Badge became the County Badge scheme, the Sea School led to Outward Bound, the Outward Bound scheme leads on to the Duke of Edinburgh Awards and all of these are linked with the name of Kurt Hahn. Gordonstoun has always welcomed a number of overseas pupils, but this has been usual in many schools. In addition attempts have been made to offer some of the school's facilities, notably the athletics track, for the use of the young people of the neighbourhood, but neither Arnold-Brown nor other sympathetic commentators on Gordonstoun have thought that over the years this has really counted for much. The special nautical course at Gordonstoun from 1941 until 1965 gave a shortened programme for boys going into the Merchant Navy and a group of fifteen or so were members of the school for this two-year period, all of them unlikely to receive a public school education otherwise.

Hahn began, and the school continues, a graded scheme of fees. An average fee is worked out which must be maintained for each boy and a minimum fee (usually about half) is fixed which must be paid. The rest is an assessed fee and from a list of assessed fees, which range from about two thirds above the average to one third below, parents are asked to assess their own ability to contribute on the general assumption that anyone making a claim on the Gordonstoun Society's fund must, as far as possible, be balanced by someone else offering a correspondingly larger sum. A recent estimate stated that about one quarter of the boys are supported by the Gordonstoun Society. In the school's thinking the need for such remissions of fees is as follows:

The law of deterioration cannot be broken unless children born to wealth or position are placed in an environment that frees them from an enervating sense of privilege. This environment can be assured by a sufficient admixture of boys drawn from homes where the conditions of life are not only simple but somewhat hard. Upon such a basis alone can a vital and vigorous school society be maintained.[9]

[9] *Prospectus*, p. 19.

As the fixed fee is in itself about £300 the number of children from 'simple' or 'hard homes' cannot be high even though one quarter of the families are getting some financial help.

Hahn does not write of child development in psychological terms. His way of thinking is impressionistic and his descriptions have rather vague, theological content and a literary romantic, moral, unscientific, dogmatic quality. There can be no doubt that as a headmaster he made a very strong impression on many boys and that as a promoter he had convinced a great number of shrewd people that his kind of compassionate integrity deserves support. To illustrate these points we can turn to his writings on Gordonstoun which are listed by Arnold-Brown and lodged in the library of Cambridge University; understandably these are not substantial and are mostly talks to conferences, broadcast talks, annual reports to governors, letters to *The Times* and so on. He is a practitioner and promoter whose theories are more felt and practised than explicated. One of the most developed of his presentations appears in an essay he wrote in 1957 in which he reflects upon the results of Salem and Gordonstoun as a prelude to the Outward Bound developments.[10] He considers that Salem had established beyond doubt two principles which were as much matters of health as of education. The first was that purposeful athletic training helps to build vital health and that this has psychological concomitants enabling boys and girls to defeat their own defeatism. The second principle 'deserves the name of a discovery: that the so-called deformity of puberty should not be regarded as a decree of fate.'[11] There is a treasure of childhood in joy of movement, compassion, curiosity, innocence, a spiritual strength, as Hahn saw it, and these things can be preserved through the period of the deformity of puberty, the loutish years, because each child has 'a guardian angel' capable of protecting the dangerous period of sexual change. Words like these sum up development from childhood into adolescence almost as a morality play, which Hahn, usually a brilliant, fastidious, and dramatic phrase spinner in English, occasionally takes close to melodrama.

It is not difficult to draw fairly precise Platonic parallels with much of Hahn's theory. Socrates in *The Republic* traces reason, emotion, and basic appetites as the elements of man's responses and what is found

10 K. Hahn, 'Outward Bound', in *Year Book of Education* (London, 1957), pp. 436–62.   11 Ibid., p. 436.

in the individual may also be found in the state. Plato even goes so far as to equate the Guardian with reason, the Auxiliaries (the executive classes) with the emotions, and the Producers with the appetites. Virtue is a kind of health and good habit of the soul, vice a disease, deformity, and sickness[12] and when emotion can be diverted as energy on the side of reason, virtue can grow as a habit of the soul. The civic qualities which follow are temperance and justice, and elsewhere Plato indicates that 'children, women, servants and the vulgar mass' are the readiest victims for wayward and uncontrolled behaviour. The simple and moderate desires which are guided by reason are to be found in men of the best endowment and education whose influence is acknowledged and accepted by the rest.[13] In the Gordonstoun community everyone was either a silver or a golden citizen, and to be fair to Hahn he does not accept Plato's tendency to write off the masses.

To Hahn a boy's soul at puberty is in special danger of being led away by the passions of the body and this dualism is at the root of all Hahn's ideas and he speaks out against current psychological views: 'We feel a certain missionary obligation to unmask the psychologist's dogma as the fallacy which it is. . . . What they consider a normal development during adolescence is in fact a grave and avoidable malady.'[14] The psychoanalysts are wrong, in Hahn's view, and the ground for his opposition is really a combination of his practical experience with adolescents, his Christian conviction, his Platonic interpretations and his moral fervour. He would not claim much first-hand knowledge of young children, nor would it appear that he has read widely in the psychological literature. He would not claim that he was a classroom teacher of great experience in the sense that Reddie or Badley or Curry or Coade was, for Hahn has been more the director of a school and an inspirational figure to staff and boys. He is not a countryman or a noted climber or a sailor but he speaks of a love of the high hills and of the sea and these have merged into the ideals of physical striving, self-knowledge, service, rescue, and reverence for life which are part of the Gordonstoun mystique.

Hahn was baptized into the Anglican Church in 1945. He had become a believing Christian long before, but had felt that he should

---

12 *The Republic*, book iv, sec. 444.
13 Ibid., sec. 431.
14 *Year Book* (1957), p. 437.

continue to ally himself with other Jews in their appalling sufferings after Hitler came to power and during the war. Hahn's opposition to Hitler was from the start on general liberal principle and not particularly because of Nazi anti-Semitism, and this example illustrates two fundamental beliefs which Gordonstoun exists to express. First, that when all philosophical refinements have been permitted, there is discernible right and wrong, sometimes incontestably clear as in the Potempa incident or the mistaken Allied demand for unconditional surrender, sometimes difficult to detect as in the need to be truthful about the errors and deficiencies of others as well as one's own. The second fundamental precept is that only persons affirm right and wrong, but they need training for the job. These propositions may be disputed by philosophers on logical grounds, but Hahn is a moralist, interested more in ethics and a kind of metaphysics and believing that a school takes less from logic than from the behaviour and conviction of its founder and his colleagues.

Gordonstoun has its critics and one of them sums up Hahn's plan as an attempt to keep boys out on the beautiful mountains and on the majestic sea so that they might develop beautiful souls. This, he says, 'is a muddled rehash of the pathetic fallacy and belief in *mens sana in corpore sano* and is typical of Hahn's so-called idealism'.[15] Wilkinson attacks Hahn for making extravagant claims for the value of drill routine and physical training in the Gordonstoun services. Physical fitness, says Wilkinson, will not necessarily restore the soul, nor will rescue routines normally enable boys to discover God's purpose in their inner life. He says that so much character training through willing bodies has led to a neglect of exacting intellectual pursuits and points to a percentage of university entrants well below what might be expected. The Director of Studies in the *Gordonstoun Record* has lent colour to this view, although he comments in 1961 that there is an improvement in the academic quality of the entrants which should be reflected in the next few years. Expressing university entrants as a proportion can be misleading but from figures available it would appear that in the 1950s, of every hundred entrants to Gordonstoun about twelve to fifteen went on to universities in Great Britain or overseas, although this proportion is now rising somewhat and in a survey

---

[15] E. Wilkinson: 'Poisonous Passions' in *Granta*, 1 Dec. 1962, pp. 14–17. Mr. Wilkinson was Guardian at Gordonstoun in 1959 and wrote the article when an undergraduate at Cambridge.

of four hundred and sixteen leavers between 1960 and 1966, 34 per cent went to universities and 19 per cent to other places of higher education.[16] The figures do not compare favourably with those of Bryanston or Bedales. Wilkinson makes the point, however, that Gordonstoun is, to quote the Director of Studies, 'weighted on the less gifted side'. Where character building has been stressed, learning and intellectual rigour together with artistic achievement have not been made desirable goals for boys who could have been challenged by them. Wilkinson also doubts very much that the routine honesty of the Training Plan and the other features of the trust system lead to lasting moral qualities because boys are not faced with real moral problems in the school, where the spirit and method offer support in dealing with the relatively simple school situations. A rude shock awaits the Gordonstoun boy who thinks he is well provided for morally when he leaves school and is on his own. Finally, Wilkinson claims that in sexual matters the school is not as balanced and 'healthy' as it claims to be, and this partly because of Hahn's conviction that poisonous passions are released if sexual powers are not diverted to good purposes. To finish the denunciation Wilkinson sums up Hahn's idealized Atlantic Community as jingoistic froth. As Hahn retired from Gordonstoun in 1953 when Wilkinson was twelve or thirteen years old, this attack is in one sense an admission of the lasting influence of the founder's ideas and at the same time sharp but for the most part fair if overstated criticism of some of Hahn's more romantic formulations which are far out of touch with the modern mood. But the structure of the Gordonstoun System stands and can absorb criticism and modify itself without serious surrender.

Criticisms of a different kind came from a man who, in his fifties, spent nearly two years at Gordonstoun as an adviser on many matters for which he had the title of Research Officer.[17] Heckstall-Smith had been a master in a public school, the head of two country grammar schools, had joined the Society of Friends before the Second World War, having been an officer in the first. He had been a successful farmer on resigning a headship in 1939 a few months before the outbreak of war and Hahn invited this many-sided man to take a general, constructively critical place at Gordonstoun. In Heckstall-Smith's account there appears a courteous incompatibility with the school's

[16] See *Gordonstoun: Some Facts*, produced by the school in Mar. 1967.
[17] H. Heckstall-Smith, *Doubtful Schoolmaster* (London, 1962).

ideas. For him Hahn had immense personal charm and uncomprehendingly patrician ways : 'The Platonic theory of the absolute supremacy of the golden citizen allowed Dr. Hahn to interrupt anything whenever he happened to feel like it . . . no teaching arrangement was safe.'[18]

Heckstall-Smith said the trust system generated latent tension which, with 'rather emotional talks to the whole school in assembly' and what he calls a snakes-and-ladders system of promotion and demotion produced an atmosphere amongst the boys of mutual sympathy such as might be found in villagers living on the slopes of an active volcano.

Elsewhere Heckstall-Smith speaks of Hahn's wish to have girls as well as boys at Gordonstoun, with a considerable majority in favour of the boys. This never came to anything but it leads Heckstall-Smith to say : 'I got the impression that Dr. Hahn regarded the girls as a gymnastic apparatus for improving the character of the boys (the ones who really mattered) by giving them regular practice in chivalry.'[19] Heckstall-Smith believes that constantly present in Hahn's mind was the idea of dramatic rescue — not just rescue, but dramatic rescue and the fire service, the coastguards, the mountain rescue, and the whole Outward Bound concept spring from this root principle. Certainly Hahn's view of adolescence has this same theme of rescue in it ; the non-poisonous passions acting as guardian angels to protect the vitality of boyhood.

Heckstall-Smith left Gordonstoun in 1949 to go to Dartington and his comment on the change was that it was for him like a dressing on a burn. In his book he does not really try to place Hahn in a proper life-context, treating him more as a charming and wrong-headed despot, forgetting the comments that he had made about himself when he was head of a country grammar school : 'Instead of being the expert critic on the side I was now the Establishment.'[20]

Does Gordonstoun deserve to be considered as an innovating school ? Academically, probably not, except that it has not yielded to the lure of examination success. In the amount of physical work done in the school day it is unusual and deliberately so, and in the devotion to the sea, the mountains, and the rescue services it has a different emphasis from other schools. In its explicit concern for moral integrity and the emphasis placed on the physical basis for much of this, Gordonstoun is different

[18] Ibid., p. 130.   [19] Ibid., p. 121.   [20] Ibid., p. 57.

again. The need for quietness, for aloneness is part of the discipline of self-knowledge.

Hahn's rejection of psychoanalysis placed him far away from Neill or Curry or Badley or the Russells, and Gordonstoun is conservative on the interpretation of puberty. The conventional criticism of the public school of the 1920s and 30s was that sexual problems were dealt with by cold baths and team games. Hahn had an answer which was also based on baths and exercise, but with hobbies, idealism, a trust system, the idea of service, and a certain disseminated responsibility to add to the total effect.

Hahn retired in 1953 and the school has now modified itself in many ways, but not in any that are significantly different. There are about ten schools in this country and overseas following on the Gordonstoun pattern, mostly with headmasters who taught or were pupils at the parent school. These schools are all in the public school mould, but with a difference, and there has never been a metropolitan Gordonstoun. Perhaps the closest resemblance to the school itself is to be found in the Outward Bound movement through which Kurt Hahn saw the ideas and practices suitable for a right-wing radical progressive school made available in some measure to working-class, city-bred boys.

III

In the 1957 *Year Book* Hahn wrote the essay on Outward Bound enterprises already mentioned[21] and he refers to his own conviction in the mid-1930s that he had failed to spread the health-giving attitudes of Gordonstoun beyond the limited circle of boarders and day-boys in the school. At the end of 1936 Gordonstoun and a large day school, Elgin Academy, combined to start the tests for the Moray Badge: certain standards were required in athletics, life-saving, and cross-country expeditions and no smoking or drinking was permitted during the training period. The local response was poor in 1937 and the national reaction was negligible to a letter Hahn wrote to *The Times* appealing for help and an extension of the plan. However, by the time of the outbreak of the War in September 1939 the response of schools in Morayshire was greatly improved and during the early part of the War men like Dawson of Penn, Boyd-Orr, Admiral Richmond, and William Temple advocated a wide extension of the Moray Badge training plan.

[21] *Year Book*, pp. 436–62.

Early in 1940 a County Badge Experimental Committee was formed under the chairmanship of the then Master of Balliol, Lord Lindsay, with a membership including the Headmasters of Eton and Winchester, the chairman of the University Grants Committee, Julian Huxley, Members of Parliament, and other notables. The County Badge scheme was the Moray Badge programme with improvements and amendments and this was based upon what has been the Salem and Gordonstoun regime of athletics, swimming, testing expeditions, and projects of skill, art, or study. The necessary stages in the scheme were to be covered in part-time courses run under the auspices of certain existing voluntary associations, or else in intensive, residential courses of about a month conducted at Gordonstoun's Welsh war-time base where many of the visiting boys were found to be healthy but not fit. From the model of this kind of course the War Office set up in Glenfeshie the Highland Field-craft Centre for young soldiers lacking the skills, confidence, and experience which the Experimental Committee were trying to produce at their intensive courses and which were necessary for officers.[22] The Centre remained in being from March 1943 till November 1944, the Normandy invasions having begun in June of that year.

The Experimental Committee did not get the financial support it had hoped for from the Board of Education, the voluntary bodies were not providing much help for the programme, and the first move came from private sources. In 1941 Lawrence Holt of the Blue Funnel Line was able to offer the financial backing necessary to open the 'Outward Bound' Sea School at Aberdovey: 'The training . . . must be less a training for the sea than a training through the sea, and benefit all walks of life.' The requirements in athletics and land expeditions were maintained and to these were added, but not emphasized, the sea-going enterprises together with rescue training — fire-fighting, resuscitation, and sea rescue. Short courses of four weeks for boys sent by local authorities or by industry were offered at Aberdovey and boys from Gordonstoun, then about forty miles away at Llandinam, were able to join regularly in this work. The Sea School is still in existence and something like twenty thousand boys have passed through in groups of about eighty in each month's course.

In 1946 the Outward Bound Trust was founded and the financial

---

[22] An account of this Centre and the work done there is to be found in Arnold-Brown, *Unfolding of Character*, pp. 72–110.

burden on Lawrence Holt was shared, enabling the work to extend. By the end of the 1950s the Trust controlled four schools in Britain, two sea-schools, one at Aberdovey and a second at Burghead not far from Gordonstoun in Morayshire, and two mountain schools, Eskdale, opened in 1950, and Ullswater in 1955. Courses for girls were started in this country in 1955 and Outward Bound centres for boys have been established in Nigeria, Kenya, Malaya, Australia, Germany, Austria, and elsewhere.

Hahn has been the moving spirit in the start of all this. The inaugural meeting of the Outward Bound Trust was held early in 1946 at Trinity College, Cambridge, with G. M. Trevelyan as host and Geoffrey Winthrop Young in the chair and Admiral Richmond as a member, all founder-governors of Gordonstoun. Many of those connected with the Moray Badge scheme, with the Experimental Committee, and with the Aberdovey Sea School came in to support the new Trust. Arnold-Brown was the first Warden of Eskdale in 1950 which, as he says, was not to be a climbing school but a character-training school based on mountaineering.

The objects of the Trust have been set forth in many places and with some minor variations can be summarized as follows: short-term residential schools, normally of twenty-six days' duration, aim to open to boys and girls, usually aged fourteen and a half to nineteen and a half, a fuller life both for themselves and for the community they live in. The young people in these schools are supposed to come from all levels of society, from a wide range of schools, and from industry, from a variety of religious backgrounds and, if possible, from many nationalities — this has been of particular importance in multi-racial or tribal societies such as Kenya, Nigeria, and Malaya. The main appeal of the course is to adventure and endurance on the sea or in the mountains and to seek from these experiences new areas of confidence and competence in oneself. Those who know what service and dependability are, are thought to be more likely to show initiative, to undertake leadership with Christian humility.

All these principles are of the Gordonstoun stamp and the courses are compressed versions of those to be found at the school. Outward Bound was one of Hahn's means to spread more widely through society an important part of what the Gordonstoun boys receive, although, of course, many others besides him were engaged in its beginnings. The more recent development of the Duke of Edinburgh's Award is another extension of Hahn's work, because this is in direct line with the Moray Badge, the part-time parallel to the full-time arrangements of Outward Bound and Gordonstoun.

IV

Another extension of Hahn's influence and interest can be seen in the Atlantic College at St. Donat's in Glamorgan which began its teaching in 1962. This College is intended to be the first of a number of residential international schools for boys between sixteen and nineteen usually aiming at university entrance. The first boys at St. Donat's came from the countries of the western community, including the U.S.A. Later the boys are to come from a wide variety of countries, always provided that a national group will be large enough to have an identity and will give variety and tang to the community life. The policy was at first to have 25 per cent of the boys from Great Britain and then to build up seven national groupings each of about 10 per cent of the total number which is likely to be four hundred and fifty. Desmond Hoare, the headmaster, is a retired Rear-Admiral who has not only guided the school since 1962 but, by 1967, has persuaded the board of governors to make the school co-educational.

The long-term aim is concerned with social integration, at first in the context of the European and the American peoples and later in the context of countries behind the iron curtain. The short-term aim is to provide an international school for boys (and now girls) who are likely later to be in positions of importance. Such a school will provide courses for entrance to the universities of the country in which it is set and by arrangement these qualifications are expected to admit each boy or girl to university in his native country if he or she so wishes. Thus German boys educated at St. Donat's will qualify for admission to German universities by taking Advanced level courses in English together with any necessary additions. The teaching of languages is an important feature in this whole enterprise both as a tool for necessary communication and as a means of deeper understanding of national characteristics and cultural assumptions. These emphases are, of course, acceptable to Hahn, but not specially individual to him. More familiar and characteristic ideas and phrases appear, as exposition of the aims continues:

The advancing material prosperity of the western world has brought evils in its train. Among these are a decline in the physical fitness of young men, insufficient satisfaction of the youthful interest for adventure and that decline of compassion which is reflected in the plain business of individual unhelpfulness one to another.

Services exist for beach rescue, cliff rescue, canoe lifeguards, and while the College is right on the sea coast it is also a short distance from Welsh mountains and so all the practices of Gordonstoun in physical endurance, initiative, team work, and individualism can be repeated. During his time at the College each boy, like boys at Gordonstoun, works on a project which is based on the requirements of the Trevelyan Scholarship. The courses at the College aim to take each boy to three A levels and to insist on a breadth of study which includes a common course on philosophy and, for non-scientists, some study of science, and the results in the last three years have been markedly better than the English national average. To ensure contact beyond the walls of the castle, youth groups, schools, conferences, are invited to St. Donat's and for British entrants a proportion rather over one half is aimed at from maintained schools and about one fifth from private schools, the remainder of the entry being transfers from industry and commerce. In fact in 1966 only about 10 per cent were 'private' pupils, the rest being supported mostly by government grants from the variety of countries represented.

Familiar names appear among the Council from whom the Governing Body was chosen. Air Marshall Sir Lawrence Darvall, formerly of the NATO Defence College in Paris, was a governor of Gordonstoun and the chairman of the council of the Atlantic College, Mme. Besse was on the board at Gordonstoun and her husband on the council of St. Donat's, H. L. Brereton the Warden of Gordonstoun was on both, as was Hahn himself. Whatever may be thought of Hahn's educational specifications they are always recognizable whether seen at Gordonstoun, Outward Bound, or at St. Donat's and it is his achievement that he has left a group of institutions with a similar stamp upon them and in each case his flair for attracting the money and the interest of influential people has marked him out as an educational promoter who has convinced men and women of the desirability of the Gordonstoun product. He is the one educationalist who has helped to found since the 1930s not one, but a series of schools, the Outward Bound movement, the Duke of Edinburgh Awards scheme, and the Atlantic College. Hahn says his ideas are derivative and he is sincere in thinking so, but his own interpretation and presentation are peculiar to him, not permissive, not Freudian, physically rather than psychologically based, favouring single-sex education rather than co-education (except at Salem and the Atlantic College), morally emphatic and not indulgent, both continental and British in theory and practice, Platonic, romantic, Christian, claiming collective and individualistic response. This is the most pervasive and successful of the new school models in the last thirty years.

Chapter Eleven

THE SECOND WORLD WAR

Wennington

THIS book does not pretend to name every radical school in England. No mention has been made of the Hall School founded at Weybridge by Miss Gilpin and now at Wincanton, or Dauntsey's which G. W. Olive transformed, or St. Mary's Town and Country School founded in Hampstead in 1937 with a second location in the country, or Monkton Wyld founded in 1940 in Charmouth in Dorset, or the remarkable communities for young delinquents described by David Wills in *The Barns Experiment* and *The Hawkspur Experiment*, or Finchden Manor founded by George Lyward, or Red Hill School founded by Otto Shaw, or many others.

Wennington School, which in 1945 moved from its first home in north Lancashire to its present accommodation in Yorkshire, near Wetherby, may serve as an example of several radical community schools which were formed in the stress of the Second World War as a gesture both of survival and idealism. These schools are not a further wave of new foundations corresponding to the first surge of the 1890s and the second of the 1920s. Evacuation and the shock of total mobilization and the whole deployment of world war produced improvizations and a flexibility enforced by events. The war years yielded the last innovating group we shall consider.

Kenneth and Frances Barnes are both Quakers and between 1930 and 1940 Barnes, after some years of teaching in grammar schools, was head of the science department at Bedales. He and his wife felt the need to try to affirm in a school human and religious values at a time when a flood of destruction was pouring over the world. In 1940 bombing had started in London, in Bristol, and on Merseyside and the vast human problems of evacuation of children cried out for help.

A large guest house, Wennington Hall in North Lancashire, furnished and at nominal rent, was offered as a school, and Kenneth and Frances Barnes gathered round them a few like-minded colleagues and families prepared to set up a community for children as a pacifist counter-statement to destruction. The children came from all over the country and the numbers of boys and girls grew slowly. There was no endowment for this school and Barnes says that they had the bare necessities for living, no educational equipment, and about £200. For some time there was not sufficient money to pay the staff and during the first term they and their families had to pay for their keep. As the numbers of children increased the teachers were able to draw an equal rate of pay, with additional family allowances, these financial arrangements being arrived at by common consent. The parents of the children paid what they could afford and the school was, for quite a time, close to financial ruin. Only the devotion of the staff and the frugality of life tided the school over to more prosperous times.

By 1948 the number of pupils and the resources were such that the Ministry of Education inspected and recognized the school as efficient which brought in its train the condition that the Burnham scale be used in salaries and so financial communal egalitarianism disappeared. A trust had been formed in 1942 and a group of governors, with strong professional and academic interests represented, took some of the planning off the shoulders of Mr. and Mrs. Barnes.

It had not been the Barnes's intention that Wennington should be a war-time undertaking only, but, like others who have founded schools then which have continued to the present, they found the comprehensive realities of war-time conditions gave a firm and unique quality to the life of the school:

> Personal responsibility, full co-operation in the life of a community, the sharing of every kind of work, domestic, agricultural, constructional, these were not merely ideals but rooted in necessity. Experience of the tradition of 'outdoor work' established by Abbotsholme and Bedales was specially valuable at this point. The one thing we had to spend money on to begin with was equipment for a workshop — for we had to make all the rest of our equipment.[1]

In a lecture given by Eleanor Urban on Monkton Wyld a similar point was made. This school was founded near Lyme Regis in Dorset

[1] K. C. Barnes, 'Wennington', in *The Independent Progressive School*, ed. H. A. T. Child, p. 157.

in 1940 by a group of friends with Carl and Eleanor Urban as leading spirits :

> We had in common several things : a lack of interest in money making as the main motive for work, a dislike of dictatorship, power politics and militarism. . . . We wanted to provide something of a microcosm with basic human activities such as farming and building going on. . . . The origin of the school certainly had something to do with war and peace . . . destructive forces in European politics had stimulated us to an attempt to be constructive.[2]

At Wennington, constructional and renovating work is still done, some of it, under expert direction, quite advanced and ambitious like the laying of hard tennis courts and the concrete constructions for an extended sewage plant. This is a part of the thinking on which the school was founded, although in 1940, without money or equipment, the sheer necessity of economics and physical survival made the work essential in a sense different from the contemporary situation. It has been characteristic of Wennington that boys, girls, and staff have taken part in such work. A good deal of classroom furniture has been built in the workshop, and this has been true of a number of the schools considered so far — Reddie made this a feature of Abbotsholme, Hahn tried to build up working relationships between the boys and girls of Salem and the local workmen and craftsmen, Dewey maintained that work done which was meaningful in terms of the community's needs was significant in a special sense. The arts and crafts, including pottery and music, have always been encouraged at Wennington, as at the other innovating schools, because it is believed that they give to a person a means of creating and experiencing which intellectual exercises do not offer.

Experiments in teaching have been tried over the years — the Dalton system was used for some time, but was discontinued when the staff thought that the weaker pupils were finding the record-keeping and the self-direction of their time and assignments too complex. The productive relics of the full system can be seen today in time given to 'private' study in which individual work based on the course has to be done and periodically scrutinized. Such flexibility permits boys and girls to fit in music lessons and extra time on individual projects or corporate activities. While Wennington accepts the need to prepare

---

[2] From a manuscript sent to the author by Mrs. Urban.

students for higher education by training on examination courses, it remains critical of specialist sixth formers and is ready to encourage children with the appropriate ability to keep their intellectual frontiers open, to study arts, sciences, and social sciences for their personal enrichment.

At most times the majority of the staff and Governing Body at Wennington have been members of the Society of Friends. The teaching on religious matters aims to provide as sound a knowledge as possible of the development of religion in the western world so that if commitment to belief follows it should be well informed : 'What we seek is that religion should be regarded as a matter for serious and discriminating discussion, from whatever point of view, and as a significant force in history.'[3]

In 1944 Barnes wrote a review of the first four years in which he said that from the outset one of the chief enemies of the school's progress was idealism, because progressive education was too much influenced by the traditions of Rousseau and too many schools achieved an unreal freedom by an illusory repudiation of the society outside their gates. At Wennington there had been talk about equality between adults and children and this had given rise in practice to mistrust and carping criticism. There was mention of 'a free school' and some members of staff interpreted this as synonymous with independent choice for individuals ; it took time to establish that a group the size of a school demanded some structure of authority and some sentiment of loyalty to decisions. Mistakes were made in school government and, writing in 1944, Barnes concludes that it was an error to start off with a School Council on formal lines because the children were then too young, too inexperienced and the school too immature for the idea of self govern-ment to be appropriate in any real sense.[4] He and his colleagues looked forward to the time when a School Council could take on real responsi-bility. Writing nearly twenty years later he gave an account of the transitions to the present arrangement of counsellors, a Wennington variant on prefects, and an elected Senate representative of members of the staff and the various forms in the school. This body was arrived at after there had been for a while a full school meeting when numbers were small enough to make this profitable but this time passed within

---

[3] K. C. Barnes, 'Wennington', *Th eIndependent Progressive School,* p. 161.

[4] K. C. Barnes, *The First Four Years* (1944), 16 pages. These ideas on the period are taken from the pamphlet *passim.*

a few years of the foundation of the school. The Senate now has sub-committees and an established procedure and is an advisory body of weight; however, no attempt is made to evade the fact that final authority for decisions rests with the heads and the staff.[5]

On a number of occasions Barnes has written of the dangers of permissiveness, the snares of too little, rather than too much efficiency in progressive schools. He sees education as being concerned with leading children towards 'the abundant life' which offers opportunity for intensity of effort and feeling and a wide range of knowledge and aspiration :

> The abundant life to the person who lives it is not necessarily happy; it is certainly not continuously happy. . . . Education is not like taking a child on a journey from town A to town B, deciding on your objective and making sure that you get him there. It is, on the contrary, an adventure [which] . . . may alter profoundly your ideas on where you want to go.[6]

One fixed point for Barnes is co-education and he writes that when he went to Bedales in 1930 after some years of grammar school teaching he was prepared for shocks :

> What I found seemed to me remarkably wholesome and normal in the best sense of the word. I found an astonishingly high standard of physical vigour and health. When I looked at the girls and remembered the statement of a certain headmistress that 'co-education took the bloom off the girls', I wondered that anyone could have been so ill-informed and so far from the truth. Equally false seemed the idea that it made boys soft.[7]

Barnes believes that every boy and girl is the better for contact both with men and women and he considers that anyone who regards Plato's *Republic* as a reliable text book on education should try discussing it with the sixth form of a co-educational boarding school. Elsewhere Barnes has said that Gordonstoun looks to a training of character rather than to academic achievement and that it undertakes this training through certain definite procedures associated with physical fitness and resourcefulness. He both accepts and rejects these principles. He rejects the maleness, he accepts the notion of challenge,

5 *The Independent Progressive School*, p. 162.
6 Ibid., pp. 164–7.
7 K. C. Barnes, *The Co-educational Boarding Schools* (1953), p. 2.

and envies Gordonstoun the proximity of mountains and sea. But for him the essentials are to be achieved between persons:

> There are no tricks in education; we cannot use physical endeavour, intellectual effort, gamesmanship, musical or artistic experience, nor the outward patterns of religion to 'do things' for us. They cannot take the place of the essential experience — the encounter of person with person.... This encounter must be direct, not mediated by mutual submission to a pattern of thought or a system. It must not be in terms of 'loyalty to the school' or a desirable *type* of character.[8]

Later in the same article he says that he considers, with Suttie in *The Origins of Love and Hate*, that in our patriarchal society thriving on possessions and ownership there is a taboo on tenderness and we are driven by the desire for power and not the impulse to love. Barnes wants Wennington to nourish persons who will be sensitive and will love and who have the steadiness of understanding to detect and to overcome unscrupulousness in all its forms. In 1962 in company with some other members of the Society of Friends, Barnes wrote a pamphlet *Towards a Quaker View of Sex* in which, amongst other things, he drew attention to the fundamental importance of the inner quality of any relationship, which was tender, responsible, and enduring. This is more significant to him than codes of behaviour dutifully observed and Barnes believes that co-education, especially in a boarding school, gives a special opportunity to seek for and find the fundamental criteria of moral conduct.

As a Quaker, Kenneth Barnes sees 'that of God in every man', and the co-education at Wennington and his existential awareness suggest that he is somewhat similar to A. S. Neill. However, Barnes maintains the need for authority and community power, he has beliefs about what, when, and how children should be taught. He is not as permissive, as truly anarchic as Neill. They both feel keenly the paradox of their exclusive position as heads of independent schools and try to offer the facilities of their two schools to as wide a range of child and parent as possible.

The problem of weaving principle into practice confronts all schools perennially, but most have recognizably a method, a routine, a structure of authority, a formality which is expected and which they exert. In Wennington these things exist but in a form which makes them different in so large a degree as almost to be different in kind and

---

[8] The school magazine, *Wennington School 1961–62*, p. 4.

the heart of the matter is in the quality and structure of community life. Teachers at Wennington may be known to children by their Christian names, as might members of any company of friends. While a school is for learning and teaching, the best of this kind is thought to be a by-product of a way of living in which function and responsibility can be seen to come from a mutual respect. The adults decide what is to be offered in teaching, they take the lead in guiding the way of living of the school, but the children are expected to understand what is being offered, to have views on everything, and to come to see what way of living is being required and why. Barnes and his colleagues expect the children to agree with the regime for the most part, because the psychological distance between adults and pupils ought to be small and the common nature of the enterprise in learning ought to be easy to grasp. These generalized ideas are worked out in day-to-day living with children who are expected to comment, to criticize, and not necessarily to submit.

We have already seen that no school can live on its history, and those that began, like Wennington, in the stress of war, have an affluent, egalitarian, disenchanted present to contend with. Wennington in 1967 is still led by its founder, who is now to be succeeded by his senior colleague, Brian Hill, who has served the school for many years. The transition to its second generation of leadership is critical for Wennington's institutional steadiness. At present it can reasonably be placed to the right of Summerhill and rather less to the right of Dartington and probably to the left of nearly all the other schools we have considered.

Chapter Twelve

THE INTERNATIONAL MOVEMENT
IN PROGRESSIVE EDUCATION

I

WHILE most of the schools and personalities so far considered have been British because the main focus of this book is upon England, schools in Germany, France, Holland, Switzerland, and the United States of America have been mentioned and men and women from many nationalities have rightly come into the foreground at different points. Because educational innovators have been such individualists and because they have been engaged in creating schools by teaching and living with children, they have not had the time, the energy, or the desire to create strong and powerful national and international movements. They have been small minorities in national educational systems and they have been permissive in their organization. The New Education Fellowship is the most representative example of the progressive movement in education over a period of nearly fifty years.

We saw in an earlier chapter how the loose organization of the Fellowship came into being, developing out of the Conference of New Ideals in Education which had its first meeting in 1914. Within this Conference the Theosophical Fraternity in Education grew large enough to acquire identity and by 1920 from a meeting at Letchworth of this Fraternity the New Education Fellowship began to take form.[1]

The Fraternity wished to bring together the efforts of pioneers in

---

[1] Much of the material in this chapter is based upon the manuscripts of the late Dr. William Boyd entitled *The New Education of the Twentieth Century*. When Dr. Boyd died in 1962 the manuscripts were edited by Wyatt Rawson and published under joint authorship in 1965 with the title *The Story of the New Education*. This book has been called upon *passim* as well as in the passages indicated.

education working both in state and independent schools and to emphasize the part to be played by education in winning the peace. Mrs. Beatrice Ensor had started in January 1920 a magazine entitled *Education for the New Era, An International Quarterly Journal for the Promotion of Reconstruction in Education* and this was intended to support the outlook and work for peace of the newly formed League of Nations which developed political, economic, and social functions but no educational organization. The *Journal* was international and set out to record the growth of experimental education and it envisaged the establishment of an international fellowship of teachers, with an annual conference. The first conference was arranged for Calais in 1921, one of its purposes being to give shape and organization to the proposed society. As the origin of the whole undertaking was the Theosophical Fraternity it was agreed that to avoid narrowing the appeal of the conference, care should be taken to keep theosophy in the background and so the invitations were sent out in the name of Mrs. Ensor's journal, which by that time had changed its title from *Education for the New Era* to *The New Era in Home and School*, the conception of the new education having by this time widened out beyond schools and teachers. Interested parents, social workers, psychologists, doctors, and administrators were also invited to Calais to the first New Era International Conference on Education held at the Collège Sophie-Berthelot from 30 July to 12 August 1921 on the theme 'The Creative Self-Expression of the Child'.

Over one hundred members from fourteen different countries attended. Germans were not admitted to a conference in France at that time and French Catholics were suspicious of the spiritual assumptions of the organizers, but pioneers who had not previously met or who had been separated by war were able for the first time to talk and to exchange information. Reports of the conference show that there were at least three main divergences of view in the opinions on self-expression in children. Robert Nussbaum, a Swiss, called into question the whole idea of creative self-expression on the grounds that children were imitators who drew upon ideas derived from their family and society and that their work should be looked on in this sense. Followers of Dr. Montessori distrusted the whole notion of imaginative activity in children because the learning situations that Madame Montessori advocated were so structured that free-ranging activities were at a minimum and, as we have seen, an environment provided in which necessary learning (necessary for the ends Dr. Montessori had in mind, that is to say) was willingly undertaken by the children. In different ways Nussbaum and the Montessorians were presenting similar objections. A. S. Neill, on the other hand, wanted even more freedom for self-expression not so much to achieve new, creditable, and spontaneous learning by children, but to break the shackles of the moralists. His interpretation of freedom in 1921, as in the present day, appeared to many as dangerous doctrine.

While this conference was interesting in itself there was the question of the construction of a society. As *The New Era* had officially issued the invitations, it was thought valuable to base any more definite organization upon it, both because this gave a sufficiently general foundation to permit national and individual variety and because the theosophical backing to the whole enterprise was thus not publicized :

> It was due to Theosophists that the Fraternity came into being and for the first few years the Fraternity, *The New Era* and the Fellowship were financed by the generosity of two wealthy Theosophists. It was never an aim however to spread the tenets of Theosophy. . . . The greatest care was taken not to theosophize the schools or the Fellowship.[2]

An international committee proposed the following scheme which was accepted. Two other publications were to be established comparable to *The New Era*, one in French to be edited by Adolf Ferrière, a Swiss, who as we have seen had started the International Bureau of New Schools as far back as 1899, one in German to be edited by Dr. Elizabeth Rotten who was born in Germany of Swiss parents but who had worked from England as a Quaker dealing with prisoners of war. These journals gave communication in the three major languages of the western world and all subscribers to any of the three were by that fact to be members of the international organization which as to the English Section kept the conference designation, The New Education Fellowship, the French version of which became *La Ligue Internationale pour L'Éducation Nouvelle* and the German at first *Internationaler Arbeitskreis für Erneuerung der Erziehung* and later *Der Weltbund für Erneuerung der Erziehung*.

The principles of the Fellowship, which will be mentioned later, were published in all editions of the three journals and this was con-

---

[2] From notes contributed by Mrs. Ensor to Dr. Boyd's manuscripts.

sidered sufficient to give the Fellowship identity without recourse to a constitution or rules for the international body. Countries were expected to make their own arrangements for national branches of the movement but it was agreed that the autonomy of the journals, language groups, and countries would be supplemented by the common recognition that *The New Era* would provide the international links. The editors of the three journals, *The New Era, Pour L'Ère Nouvelle,* and *Das Werdende Zeitalter* were given the task of calling a conference every two years and, with additional advice as they required, to decide on the programme.

Early in 1922 the three journals appeared with substantially similar statements of the principles of the New Education Fellowship which had been generally agreed at Calais and which appeared in each issue until 1932. We have to state them in detail so that we can see where later disagreement arose :

1. The essential aim of all education is to prepare the child to seek and realize in his own life the supremacy of the spirit. Whatever other view the educator may take, education should aim at maintaining and increasing spiritual energy in the child.
2. Education should respect the child's individuality. This individuality can only be developed by means of a discipline which sets free the spiritual powers within him.
3. The studies, and indeed the whole training for life, should give free play to the child's innate interests — interests which awaken spontaneously in him and find their expression in various manual, intellectual, aesthetic, social and other activities.
4. Each age has its own special character. For this reason individual and corporate disciplines need to be organized by the children themselves in collaboration with their teachers. These disciplines should make for a deeper sense of individual and social responsibility.
5. Selfish competition must disappear from education and be replaced by the co-operation which teaches the child to put himself at the service of his community.
6. Co-education — instruction and education in common — does not mean the identical treatment of the two sexes, but a collaboration which allows each sex to exercise a salutary influence on the other.
7. The New Education fits the child to become not only a citizen capable of doing his duties to his neighbours, his nation and

humanity at large, but a human being conscious of his personal dignity.[3]

A few moments' scrutiny of these articles will show how vague they are. They are not a creed either in philosophy or methodology but could be made the sketch for one. Followers of Dewey would probably not agree that all education should prepare the child to seek and realize the supremacy of the spirit, because pragmatists often doubt the validity of the spirit. However, the second half of the first article tones down any sharp clash between, say, theosophists and naturalists. Many of the articles emphasize the uniqueness of a child's individuality and the readiness of children to initiate learning, although this takes different forms at different ages. In the fifth article 'selfish competition' must disappear from education, but this does not exclude the possibility of unselfish competition while it also stresses co-operation. In article six co-education is not actually commended as the right educational organization, but an unexceptionable moral is drawn on the salutary influence of the sexes on one another. Thus Catholic members and single-sex educators in England and elsewhere are not excluded. These seven articles are sufficiently definite by implication to indicate what the New Education is about and sufficiently permissive to avoid offending too much those who have an orthodoxy of their own, whether liberal-Catholic like M. Georges Bertier's of *l'École des Roches* or anarchic like A. S. Neill's.

The three editors were virtually directors of the international undertakings of the Fellowship and two-yearly conferences followed at Montreux (1923), Heidelberg (1925), Locarno (1927), Elsinore (1929), Nice (1932), and after a break of four years at Cheltenham (1936).

In August 1939 a European conference was to take place at the Sorbonne, but in the light of events it was postponed *sine die*. The international activities of the Fellowship after the end of the War, with UNESCO in existence, can be mentioned later. Meanwhile the national movements came into existence with varying strength between the wars in Switzerland, France, Holland, Italy, Spain, Belgium, Germany, Austria, Denmark, Sweden, Finland, Russia, Poland, Estonia, Czechoslovakia, Hungary, Bulgaria, Jugoslavia, Egypt, Japan, China, United States. Later India, Pakistan, Ceylon, South Africa, Australia, and New Zealand provided numbers of delegates to the international conferences and a national membership which was, for

[3] Quoted from Boyd and Rawson, *The Story of the New Education*, pp. 73–74.

example, in Australia very strong. The movements in England, Wales, Northern Ireland, and Scotland which had independent existence from 1928 as the English New Education Fellowship gave steady support to the international movement, and some branches of the N.E.F. were established in Latin America.

After the 1927 conference at Locarno the international organization was made more definite. As many national Sections began to produce Fellowship magazines of their own, subscription to one or other of the original three journals was not considered sufficient as a credential for international membership. National Sections had to be formally affiliated to the international movement and represented on an International Council which in turn came to have an Executive Board which was at first called a Consultative Committee. The days of the scale of organization which could be managed by three largely voluntary editors acting as joint directors from England, Switzerland, and Germany were over.

The time for financial reappraisal was at hand. Voluntary service or work for token payment had enabled the Fellowship to start and to grow, but the size of the enterprise and the conditions of slump in the early 1930s made it necessary to try to provide a more stable financial base for this loose federation of movements. Trusts, foundations, educational research organizations, and private individuals had for more than ten years financed the Fellowship but as the national Sections and branches grew in number and in size they wanted more money for their own undertakings and had less to spare for international costs. A subscription for international work was added to the national subvention and the liaison and administration was carried out from a London Centre, but by 1937 the deficit was mounting dangerously and any development of large-scale international work faded. However, the international conferences of the 1920s and 1930s were the only world-wide exchange of ideas on educational innovation by an organization with such coverage. This aspect of the work of the New Education Fellowship continues at the present time in a very different style, and the pre-eminence of these conferences ended with the beginning of the War.

When the first conference took place in Calais in 1921 there were about one hundred participants from fourteen countries and many of them were theosophists, socialists, or pacifists, according to the recollections of some of the delegates. At Montreux in 1923 over three hundred and seventy attended from at least twenty-two countries and noticeably a few Germans were present. More remarkable still, the 1925 conference was held in Heidelberg, in Germany itself, and four hundred and fifty people from twenty-nine countries attended, including government representatives from several of them. At Locarno in 1927 over eleven hundred attended, with about 25 per cent from Germany and about 15 per cent from Great Britain and slightly fewer from the United States. At Elsinore in 1929 there were about eighteen hundred present with large numbers coming from the Scandinavian countries but still with much the same coverage of countries as at Locarno. In 1932 at Nice there were again about eighteen hundred participants and so great was the demand on organizers that it was 1936 before what was really the last of these gatherings was arranged in Cheltenham and here the numbers were noticeably smaller, about one thousand in all. The Russian bloc, the Germans, and the Italians together provided only about 5 per cent of the numbers — the restrictions of totalitarianism had tightened dramatically despite special attempts to invite Communist, Nazi, and Fascist countries to participate. We have already seen that the 1939 conference in Paris was cancelled before it began.

The national movements during the eighteen years before 1939 developed each its own programme of activity and in many cases they were influential in discussions leading to educational legislation and change. Boyd and Rawson in their book report some of the developments in many countries during this period and a more detailed statement is provided in the successive issues of the three journals in French, German, and English to which were added, especially in the 1930s, other national publications in new languages — in Scandinavian languages in Sweden and Finland, in Spanish, in Dutch, in Bengali, in Japanese, in Hungarian, in Italian. Many of these publications were reports of conferences within nationalities or with a common language.

To get some feeling of the themes which engaged the attention of the N.E.F. before 1939 we can look at the reports of conferences and the symposia which appeared from time to time in *The New Era*, *Pour L'Ère Nouvelle*, or *Das Werdende Zeitalter*. At Calais in 1921 the general theme of the lectures and discussions was 'The Creative Self-Expression of the Child' and at Montreux two years later it was an education for creative service — this word 'creative' has been from the start one of the hall-marks and danger signals for the N.E.F. At Heidelberg in

1925 the schools of the New Education movement were passed under review, schools like those considered in earlier chapters of this book. In 1927 at Locarno the theme was the meaning of freedom in education, in 1929 at Elsinore it was the relevance of the new psychology of Freud, Adler, Jung, Piaget, of behaviourism and mental measurement, to the curriculum.

These themes were all related to educational and individual salvation by some kind of personal dynamic, they were nearly all critical of the rational in education and were psychological in the sense that they were devoted to personal development through freedom. We have seen earlier that the new psychology achieved at least a European surgence in education in the 1920s and the N.E.F. was one of the instruments for this. While Montessori's psychology was more restricted in scope and focussed more sharply on education than Freud's or Jung's or even Adler's it is really the thinking of the three dynamic psychologists with its awareness of unconscious factors which had most repercussions in the N.E.F.

The Fellowship had declared itself non-political and uncommitted in religious matters in the 1920s, concerned only with the freedom required for personal development. The slump forced national economic realities into educational discussions. Mussolini, Hitler, and Stalin made it increasingly difficult for liberals to survive, and discussing the personal dynamic in education by itself was seen not to be enough. The conference at Nice in 1932 showed the change of viewpoint and context, for here the delegates discussed education and changing society. In 1921 the N.E.F. wanted to concentrate into education some of the intense desire for peace and, like many other liberals, to think that boundless disgust with the waste, terror, and degradation of war was enough to stir compassion and steel resolve. The achievements on a fingernail budget over ten years were an encouragement to hope that new men and women were growing for a new world. By 1932 the members knew they had seriously and urgently to think on how education could help in preserving peace in the world, or, more brutally, in preventing war. The theme was 'Education and Changing Society', and when one reads the report itself the bitter anxieties and premonitions of the early 1930s arise strongly again through one's awareness of the nobility, the sincerity, the irrelevance, and the importance of so much that was talked about. Mrs. Ensor said that human relations needed changing so that we could assent to and accept what living in a world society meant. Dr. Rotten wanted educators to be aware of their own aggressiveness and purge themselves from it, recognizing that it would take decades rather than years to achieve. Van der Leeuw of Holland saw in art a way to equilibrium and Dr. Montessori wanted to disperse all hostility between adults and children which could best be done under her system. These may all be called psychological contributions. There were others which may be called, for the present, sociological. Dr. Becker, the Prussian Minister of Education, asked the N.E.F. to face the fact that there were views on behaviour and education other than those of the Fellowship and that it was a sign of maturity to understand the interpretations of morality and the ways of behaving of nations different from one's own. The French wanted all countries and delegates to extend their knowledge of other cultures and to agree on the basis of a secular humanism which would indicate the values that were supported and commended by believers and secularists alike. Dr. Harold Rugg of the United States put before the delegates the view that educationalists needed to be committed to a reconstruction of society as a whole, with education as one feature in the whole complex structure.

At Cheltenham in 1936 the theme was the educational foundations of freedom in a free community and in the circumstances it is not surprising that few delegates from Russia or Germany or Italy were present. There was some straight political and social analysis — R. H. Tawney spoke of hardship, deprivation, and privilege in England and repeated some of the powerful arguments he had presented a few years earlier in his Halley-Stewart lectures on equality. Charles Freinet, a French Communist, spoke in the same critical vein on human injustice and hypocrisy. There were contributions designed to clarify the meaning of the term 'freedom' from participants like Sir S. Radakrishnan, Professor Henri Wallon, and Dr. G. P. Gooch. Dr. J. H. Hadfield spoke as a psychiatrist and Dr. Carlton Washburne as a theorist and practitioner in education and each touched on the theme of indoctrination, teaching, and the encouragement of choice and value-judgement. At Cheltenham many of the discussions were sociopolitical and controversial and for the first time the content and significance of religion in the free community came up for open consideration as a restricting or as a liberating force.

At Nice in 1932 a new statement of principles had been worked out which replaced the 1921 version and was more precise in its awareness of the threat to free peoples everywhere.

In twenty years education might transform the social order and establish a spirit of co-operation capable of finding solutions for the problems of our time. . . .

It is only an education which realizes a change of attitude to children . . . that can inaugurate an era free from the ruinous rivalries, the prejudices, anxieties and distress characteristic of our present chaotic, insecure civilization. . . .

1. Education should enable the child to comprehend the complexities of the social and economic life of our times.
2. It should be so planned as to meet the diverse intellectual and emotional needs of children of different temperaments. . . .
3. It should help children to adapt themselves with goodwill to the demand of social life by . . . a developed sense of personal initiative and responsibility.
4. It should promote co-operation . . . by bringing teachers and children to realize the importance of diversity of character and independent thinking.
5. It should lead children to appreciate their national heritage and to welcome gladly the special contribution made to human culture by every other nation.[4]

The 1921 statement spoke of the supremacy of the spirit, setting free spiritual powers, giving free play to a child's innate interests, the abolition of selfish competition. The 1932 statement is more definite, but in 1921 there was explicit mention of co-education. In 1932 there was none.

In 1937 the English Section produced a fairly clear programme based on the two principles of co-operation rather than competition and discipline by consent rather than coercion. The authors stated that they wanted to raise the school leaving age to sixteen with adequate maintenance grants, to adjust education to individual abilities as gauged by modern psychological methods, to give equal status to all kinds of school, to re-examine the selection and training of teachers and reconsider the purpose and effectiveness of examinations, to reduce the size of classes, and increase the number of nursery schools. Here again is an example of a greater readiness in the 1930s to make principles match to more definite objectives, which in a permissive organization is by no means easy to achieve.

[4] Translated from the French version.

The American Progressive Education Association was, according to Cremin, rather wary of coming into full association with the N.E.F. Although the P.E.A. had been in existence since April 1919 they sent two representatives to an N.E.F. conference only in 1925 'probably fearing the taint of pedagogical and political radicalism that attached to the N.E.F.'[5] Some two hundred American delegates attended the Elsinore conference in 1929 and in 1932 the P.E.A. became the American branch of the N.E.F. Although the P.E.A., which changed its name to the American Education Fellowship in 1944 and back to the P.E.A. in 1953, came to a petering end finally in 1955 because, according to Cremin, 'it simply failed to comprehend the fundamental forces that move American education',[6] it produced in 1938 an indictment of Nazi brutality under the title 'For the Understanding and Defense of Democracy'. This declaration inspired the English Section to state its position in 1939 saying that it regarded with abhorrence the deliberate encouragement in the young of racial prejudice, of totalitarian and militaristic views, the suppression of information and the distortions of propaganda as well as the distortions of art and science to political ends. They deplored the use of fear, distrust, cruelty as instruments of policy, and the persecution of persons and racial minorities. They detested the glorification of war and militarism and the readiness to repudiate international co-operation.

The totalitarian regimes had forced the authors of this statement to confront the belief that 'the fate of Democracy is a first and immediate concern of educationalists'. This kind of political commitment represents a radical change of outlook from the earlier belief of the Fellowship in the efficacy of the emancipated school community to transform life. Which is perhaps another way of saying that three years after the First World War in history is a more likely time for faith in human magnanimity than one year before the second.

The Fellowship over nearly twenty years in the inter-war period set up many commissions and published many reports and symposia on subjects which are commonly thought of as characteristic of the progressive movement. *The New Era* had symposia on self-government, free time tables, new methods of art teaching, drama in education, psycho-analysis and its derivatives, youth movements, new schools in

[5] L. A. Cremin, *The Transformation of the School*, p. 248.
[6] Ibid., p. 273. For the most recent and authoritative statement on the Progressive Education Association, see Patricia A. Graham, *Progressive Education: From Arcady to Academe* (New York, 1967).

England and other countries, on sex education, intelligence and intelligence testing, on examinations, on international understanding, on the Dalton Plan and other special educational systems, on the training of teachers. National and international commissions drew up reports on psychology and education, on reform in the curriculum, on examinations, on education for leisure, on the schools and the state, on co-education. Noticeably less was done in the sciences and mathematics, although, of course, these did appear in places throughout the period.

Probably enough has been said in passing to indicate the distinction and quality of participants in the conferences of the N.E.F. Men and women of the highest repute across the world were invited and this is some indication of the position the Fellowship had established for itself, and of course the standing of the people who accepted the invitations made the reputation of the Fellowship more secure. Men like Baudouin, Coué, Jung, Dalcroze, Michael Sadler, Ballard, Burt, Percy Nunn, Tawney, Buber, Adler, Pierre Bovet, Paul Langevin, Harold Rugg, Carson Ryan, Fred Clarke, Piaget, Robert Ulich, A. D. Lindsay, Radakrishnan, Gooch were all participants, some of them regularly. Women like Beatrice Ensor, Maria Montessori, Susan Isaacs, Helen Parkhurst added their support. The International Council of the movement consisted of representatives elected by national Sections and this Council elected by invitation the Executive Board, consisting of persons distinguished in education and not necessarily directly connected with the N.E.F. Many of the names mentioned above have from time to time been members of the Board. But the burden of the Fellowship's work has been borne until well after the end of the war in 1945 by a number of devoted officers all of whom have lived long to serve the N.E.F. Beatrice Ensor was the main originator of the Fellowship and served it fully until she went to live in South Africa in the later 1930s, although she continued to work for the N.E.F. Elizabeth Rotten also continued to give similar service and Clare Soper came to London in the early years to help to administer the international work from which she retired in 1951. J. B. Annand who combined the international work and the English Section secretaryship after Miss Soper retired himself went into retirement in 1962. Dr. Peggy Volkov until her retirement in 1962 served as the editor of *The New Era* for nearly thirty years, having taken it over from Mrs. Ensor.

The devotion and energy of this group of persons, each of whom devoted a long life to the movement, and of many others in England

and all over the world in the inter-war years, during the war and after gave a remarkable coherence and continuity to an organization which places no great store by its institutional mechanisms. The emphasis on people rather than on precept, we are told in many places in the Fellowship's publications, has been the notable feature of the N.E.F. organization and activity ever since its beginnings. During the inter-war years the Fellowship's activities were at their peak and it might now be valuable to turn to the wartime and post-war developments.

II

From 1939 to 1945 the national movements in U.S.A. and in England were able to keep a surprising amount of activity going. Many refugees had fled to both countries in the years before the war, the allies had their forces in both, and there were exiled allied governments in London. Obviously the official international work of the N.E.F. was finished for the duration, but in India, in Australia, New Zealand, and South Africa there was much N.E.F. activity, the Middle East countries held two regional conferences in Cairo during the war and in Sweden and Switzerland N.E.F. members worked mainly through child relief organizations to undertake as much welfare and educational activity as possible. Many of the N.E.F. members in German-occupied countries were already marked men as known liberals. In Norway and Denmark, and especially in Norway, teachers, with support from parents and children, tried to resist imposition of educational pro-grammes by the Nazis and any interference with the teaching in schools. N.E.F. members were, of course, only part of this heroic resistance, but for many people reprisals followed in forced labour, imprisonment, and deaths. In France there was a methodical take-over attempt in Alsace and Lorraine and a consistent Nazi pressure throughout to con-trol schools, training colleges, and universities. N.E.F. leaders like Pro-fessor Langevin (the Minister of Education after the war who effected such striking innovations in the French educational system), Professor Wallon, Professor Marcault, and Professor Pieron either escaped to Switzerland or England or hid or fought with Resistance forces.

The American Progressive Education Association took up the responsibility of maintaining some international work after the out-break of the European War in September 1939 and in July 1941 at the University of Michigan they staged what was called the Eighth

International Conference (the abortive Paris Conference of 1939 would have been the eighth) on the theme 'Educational Reconstruction'. Mrs. Eleanor Roosevelt was the Chairman with John Dewey as the President and he spoke on democracy and civilization. Visitors from abroad who took part at that period of depression for the Allies were Thomas Mann, in self-imposed exile, Laurin Zilliacus from Finland, and Professor Fred Clarke from England. After Pearl Harbor in December 1941 international work for educational innovation ceased for the U.S.A. as it had done for Britain in 1939.

In 1941 there were three N.E.F. conferences in Oxford in eight months at each of which Karl Mannheim took an important part. Mannheim, a Hungarian by birth and a Jew, had built an international reputation for himself in Heidelberg and Frankfurt in the 1920s and early 1930s by his writings. He was listed as an enemy of Nazism because his criticisms of totalitarianism in *Ideology and Utopia* in 1926 and later in *Man and Society* showed the strength and ruthlessness of both Fascism and Nazism on the one hand and Communism on the other. He fled from Hitler in 1933 first to Holland and then to England, where he began to teach at the London School of Economics. He was deeply aware that Germany was inviting another world war and that it might lead to the eclipse of democracy, for democratic countries, as he thought, had not the ruthlessness to organize the affairs of men and the state so as to provide really effective resistance to militant dictators. The Weimar Republic had been so permissive that there was no dynamic purpose or organization of control out of which democratic change could grow. At the beginning of the English version of *Man and Society* published in London in 1940 he wrote that the German version was written in the early 1930s in the conviction that the democratic system had run its course because the Weimar Republic had revealed the helplessness of the old *laissez-faire* order to deal with modern mass society, either politically or culturally, but that when he had lived for a while in England he had found a much more deeply rooted liberal democracy which tempted him, as he said, to an optimism that hid the profound crisis :

> To the Western countries the collapse of liberalism and democracy and the adoption of a totalitarian system seem to be passing symptoms of a crisis which is confined to a few nations, while those who live within the danger zone experience this transition as a change in the very structure of modern society.

The need for priorities in wartime quickly made the theme of 'planning for freedom' urgent and relevant. Mannheim was not specific about the changes likely or necessary in society in the way that Marx was. Instead, he indicated key points at which diagnosis was needed if social change was to take place cumulatively over society as a whole. He wrote and spoke of economics and economic organization, of property, law, individual and group values, the nature and influence of élites, the meaning of freedom. Inevitably he spoke much of education. In 1940–1 Professor Fred Clarke, Sir Percy Nunn's successor as Director of the University of London Institute of Education, invited Mannheim to become a part-time lecturer in the sociology of education and he gave courses there until he was appointed to a Chair of Education at the Institute in 1946, when he left his general concern with sociology at the London School of Economics to concentrate his energies on educational sociology, a study virtually unknown in England. He had this post for one year only and Mrs. Floud says of him :

> . . . the attraction of his mind and personality had us all in his power. As a Professor of Education his success was astonishing and his death in 1947, at the age of 54 . . . deprived London of a formidable teacher at the height of his powers.[7]

Mannheim took part in all three conferences arranged by the N.E.F. in Oxford in 1941 and the themes show the marks of his interests — *The Future of Society*, *A New Deal for Youth*, *Towards Education in a Planned Democracy*. Besides his interest in the social context in which schools and colleges grow and take forms of organization which affect the pupils, he considered the relationship between the school and the other institutions of society. While the first of these emphases was related to the N.E.F. interests in child development,[8] the second was new.

In 1942 the N.E.F. held a conference on the educational and social problems of adolescence and later held another on the social aims of post-war European education. One of the participants was Dr. Drzewieskí, who had been secretary before the war of the Polish Section

[7] Mrs. Jean Floud in an essay on Mannheim in *The Function of Teaching*, ed. A. V. Judges (London, 1959), p. 66. See also K. Mannheim and W. A. C. Stewart, *An Introduction to the Sociology of Education* (London, 1962), pp. 187 and xvii.

[8] For further elaboration of this aspect of Mannheim's thinking which came later in his life, see Mannheim and Stewart, *Introduction to the Sociology of Education*, particularly chapter x.

of the N.E.F. and who later became head of the Reconstruction Department of UNESCO. In 1942 in relation to this second conference six commissions were set up to study the kinds of reform needed in English education, and some of this thinking was valuable in the planning which led to the 1944 Act. The commission or working party was a long-established activity of the N.E.F., as shown by its work on examinations begun in 1927, and on teacher training, nursery schools, and curriculum reform begun in 1929. Also in 1942 a so-called 'children's charter' was drawn up. The N.E.F. took advantage of the presence of Allied Governments and other representatives in Britain to call together a conference in which nineteen countries were represented (and this at a time before the war had really turned in the Allies' favour). The President of the Board of Education, Mr. R. A. Butler, gave the opening address and the charter, with an explication, was issued as an act of faith:

> The Inter-Allied Conference convened by the New Education Fellowship and meeting in London on April 11 and 12 1942, humbly requested the Governments of the Allied Nations to approve and adopt the following Charter for Children as a statement of the basic and minimum rights of children to be secured and guarded, above and beyond all considerations of sex, race, nationality, creed, or social position.
>
> 1. The personality of the child is sacred; and the needs of the child must be the foundation of any good educational system.
> 2. The right of every child to proper food, clothing and shelter shall be accepted as a first charge on the resources of the nation.
> 3. For every child there shall always be available medical attention and treatment.
> 4. All children shall have equal opportunity of access to the nation's stores of knowledge and wisdom.
> 5. There shall be full-time schooling for every child.
> 6. Religious training should be available for all children.

The committee which drafted the charter went on to urge that an International Office of Education should be set up in London or Washington or Moscow charged with responsibilities for reconstruction after the war — feeding and caring for children of all nations, ex-enemy and Allied alike; rebuilding schools, re-equipping libraries and laboratories; encouraging international life by exchanging teachers and children; attending to the problem of an international auxiliary language. These aims bear the hallmark of N.E.F. concerns and this proposal for an International office of Education reminds one that in 1920 Mrs. Ensor and her colleagues had pointed out that with all the bright promise of the League of Nations and its subsidiary associations, no international bureau of education had been set up and this was a most serious deficiency.

As early as 1942 the Council of Allied Ministers of Education began work on preparing a draft constitution for a new educational and cultural organization and at the joint invitation of the French and the British, delegates from forty-four countries, with a chair reserved for Russia as a forty-fifth, were called together.

In London in November 1945 the Allied Ministers of Education together with representatives of the U.S. State Department met to form the preliminary commission from which the United Nations Educational, Scientific and Cultural Organization (UNESCO) was officially set up in Paris in 1946. It would be foolish to ascribe to the N.E.F. the major initiative for this tremendous venture, but enough has been said in earlier pages of this chapter to show how close to the international aspirations of the Fellowship this enterprise was. Indeed, Professor Lauwerys, the then Deputy Chairman of the International Fellowship, was chairman of the commission of the Conference of Allied Ministers charged with making recommendations on the psychological and political re-education of children in Occupied Europe, part of which involved the revision and writing of textbooks. W. B. Curry of Dartington, an active worker for the N.E.F., was specially concerned about the proper teaching of history and this reappeared in a later UNESCO project on the writing and presentation of a cultural history of mankind.

A further advantage of the Allied presence was the opportunity in 1943 to arrange conferences to enable each country to understand the educational system and problems of the others. The tide of war was beginning clearly to turn for the Allies and understanding of the problems of occupied Norway, France, Poland, and Czechoslovakia and of China and Russia and the U.S.A. was compounded with hope and expectation that before long the theoretical grasp was going to be directed on to the practical tasks of actual reconstruction in liberated countries.

Boyd and Rawson say that for two or three years the international issues overshadowed British interests for the English New Education

Fellowship and that it was mainly the efforts of the small central group in this country rather than of the rank and file which kept the N.E.F. with a clear consciousness of the great issues of the time. This is probably true most of the while in national and international organizations, but was certainly true in wartime for the N.E.F.

However, educational reform was also being discussed in and for Britain and the Executive Committee of the E.N.E.F. submitted a report to the so-called Fleming Committee which in 1942–3 met to make recommendations to the Government on the future of the public schools. The suggestions of the E.N.E.F. reports make its position clear and indicate some developments within the movement which we have already noticed as an accompaniment of increased political sensitivity. In their analysis predominantly sociological rather than psychological judgements were given — the report says, for instance, that too much importance was being attached to 'the public school question', in which a small proportion of children were being given special attention. The E.N.E.F. report recommended that these schools should be taken over into the general provision of national education and made 'to serve a useful purpose', for at that time their favoured position and provision gave them a standing which was not any longer suitable for a democratic society. In addition, the report went on, the methods and ethics of the schools were still out of touch with more recent educational thinking and hierarchical, authoritarian, and single-sex structures of this kind were not appropriate any longer. There was still, of course, the difficult problem of the other independent schools like the progressive group, which had many of the educational virtues which the E.N.E.F. were looking for but which could only admit those who could afford the fees.

In 1943 the E.N.E.F. spent a summer conference in discussing the Government White Paper mapping the territory of the 1944 Act, and again the egalitarian, sociological temper was evident. They wanted all fees abolished in maintained schools; equal educational opportunity regardless of income; the extension of maintained nursery school provision; the reorganization of secondary education on what would now be called the comprehensive principle or something like it; some residential schooling for all and non-sectarian religious teaching for all; day-release education, county colleges, educational settlements and adult education, free meals and milk where needed, wider opportunities for higher education. In the atmosphere of reform, the 1944 Act was for the E.N.E.F., as for many people, as much a proposal about the social and economic order as it was about education. The E.N.E.F. had strength from the maintained schools in its membership in 1943, and the independent progressive schools, although they continued to advertise in and give a special flavour to *The New Era*, were less dominant in the Fellowship's discussions.

After the end of the war international conferences were quickly resumed, national Sections revived, and a great number of monographs and booklets produced, ranging from summaries of new plans in a variety of countries to guidance on children's communities, fatherless children, psychological services, play, and mental health. Before the war there had been ten or twelve journals in various languages and of these *The New Era* and the American *Progressive Education* continued, but *Pour L'Ère Nouvelle* which had lapsed was not revived. It is not possible here to speak in detail of the growth of Sections picking up threads again often in great political confusion and conflict, as for example in France, in Germany, in Belgium, and in the U.S.A. In most countries where the Fellowship movement was largely supported from private schools or by private money, the financial future was bleak. Political factors were sharper, secular-religious cleavages were deeper, individualist-collectivist dichotomies harsher, with time and opinion more on the egalitarian and collectivist side of the argument. And so it has tended to remain.

By 1955 it had become clear that the pre-war pattern of what might be called the main-theme conference addressed by celebrities accompanied by sessions or sectional specialisms was no longer appropriate. An innovation tried at Chichester in 1951 provided each delegate with time to be spent in one or another of the arts, learning together and in a personal way. It proved successful and exciting and came to be a common feature of many succeeding N.E.F. conferences, adopting with adults what had been since the start in 1921 an article of faith in the Fellowship concerning the education of children — that the arts contribute uniquely to the personality and its development.[9] At Askov in Denmark in 1953 about two hundred and seventy participants from twenty-three different countries addressed themselves to 'The Teacher and his Work' with learning and work groups getting to grips with painting or pottery or mime and drama, movement, music, poetry-making, or mathematics or astronomy. By working in such

[9] See Boyd and Rawson, *The Story of the New Education*, chapter x, pp. 166–76.

areas as these the teacher became a learner again with others in a context of encouragement and discovery with the indirect psychological benefits that this gives.

Once or twice conferences have been arranged since the Utrecht conference of 1956 calling upon the techniques of group dynamics, with lectures on educational topics followed by permissive and wide-ranging small group seminars guided by well-briefed and non-directive chairmen. Such innovations reiterate the Fellowship's concern for psychological and personal factors and the advantages in self-realization which these are expected to bring to persons both in their own life and in their professional skill and sensitivity. As an indication of this the 1966 conference in Chichester looked at psychological, social, moral, and economic problems of the future, basing the meeting on working papers and intensive group work, with comparatively few lectures.

It might be thought that UNESCO would displace and ultimately destroy the N.E.F., but this has not so far happened, and for some good reasons. Although the N.E.F. has a very loose organization, what there is rests on two complementary principles. Nationally members of the Fellowship provide a body of opinion and a pressure group dealing first with home problems. Internationally there is a small permanent secretariat and a larger board of consultants who deal with broad policy throughout the world. Support is dispersed through one broad international network and through a series of much more coherent national groupings. Because money is always tight, the expectation of financial backing is small and the voluntary participation has to be high. This makes the organization much more varied, more durable if more liable to breakdown in places. UNESCO can provide money for experts to identify problems and try to deal with them. The national Sections and the N.E.F. itself are able to provide valuable information and sometimes the organization through which inquiries may be conducted. Besides, the N.E.F. is a voluntary body with the *esprit de corps* that can go with it and UNESCO is the mammoth which has to learn to work with those who have lived in the forest for a long time. Correspondingly, the N.E.F. can find the official existence of an enlightened purpose reassuring:

> The purpose of the Organization is to contribute to peace and security by promoting collaboration among the nations through education, science and culture, in order to further universal respect for justice, for the rule of law and for the human rights and funda-

mental freedoms which are affirmed for the peoples of the world . . . by the Charter of the United Nations.[10]

Since 1947 the N.E.F. has taken part, in some way or another, in many UNESCO projects, too many to list in detail, but important enough to illustrate by example. First of all factual inquiries like surveying textbooks, collecting data with bodies like the World Health Organization, the International Labour Office, the Food and Agriculture Organization on national health statistics, diet, physical education, bringing together facts for a yearbook in education. Besides the factual inquiries there were early projects on fundamental education, on methods of teaching international understanding. Later the N.E.F. took part in what was called the Tensions Project which sought to discover deeper causes of human conflict, the nature of prejudice and stereotyped thinking. The full scale of this very difficult inquiry brought in universities and other bodies, but the N.E.F. tried to understand especially the problems and techniques of attitude change and about this time began to employ the methods of group dynamics at its conferences, at first with limited success. Other examples of N.E.F. enterprises which were linked to UNESCO were the inquiry into methods of teaching the background to human rights in different countries; or preparing the working papers for a conference on education and the mental health of children in Europe; or the unusual and valuable conference on the role of the inspector in a variety of school systems; or the pilot project in the early 1960s on the relationships between adults and adolescents.

The N.E.F. has had the advantage of some financial support from UNESCO for these and other projects, and it must be admitted that a few of the reports can scarcely be considered as highly successful. However, the Fellowship's undeviating attention to international understanding, to the role of the school and the teacher and the pupil in building a positive world outlook and teaching a balanced conception of history, has developed alongside a concern for the psychological factors in aggression and fear. Boyd made this point in a manuscript read by the present author:

The child-centred education of 1921 has been supplemented by the culture-centred education of 1955: the basic idea of freedom was still to the fore but with a greater stress on self-control. The

[10] From the *UNESCO Declaration*.

over-emphasis on conscious mentality had been modified by the discoveries of the analytic psychologies and corrected in practice through free creative expression.

Harold Rugg, a leading American participant, said in Germany in 1955 at a conference of the pioneers of the N.E.F. that a much sounder theory of education was now available than in the early days of the movement. This was based on a clearer understanding of the kind of civilization to be striven for; a more comprehensive theory of behaviour based on biology, psychology, and sociology; a grasp of aesthetics as it is related to self-expression; an acceptance of the nature and importance of religious experience. He might also have added a new realism about politics and economics. A more recent example of the contemporary emphasis is in *Look Out* written in 1965 and subtitled 'a contribution to World Studies', by Dr. J. L. Henderson, one of the Honorary Advisors to the N.E.F.

III

The progressive schools of the first quarter of this century provided many persons who gave the N.E.F. its start. Its early history is very like that of many of the schools we have considered earlier. Some Theosophists took the initiative with known supporters in this and other countries after the First World War. They were innovators with liberal principles, often religious, sometimes agnostic or atheist. They were convinced internationalists working for peace and understanding through education and they had faith in persons, especially children as persons. Some of the leaders were pacifists — Kees Boeke of Holland, for instance, Paul Geheeb and Elizabeth Rotten of Germany and Switzerland; others were socialists or communists. As we have seen many times in these pages, in the 1920s faith in persons meant very often an emphasis on free expressiveness for children both in their school activities and in their social behaviour. Besides the educators who advocated this view, there were psychologists who provided the theoretical argument and clinical evidence to support it and the interpretations of Freud, Jung, Adler, and Rank were well known to members of the N.E.F.

The periodicals and the conferences were concerned with teaching method and the whole texture of life in a school community. It would probably be fair to say that the progressive schools in England and other countries made the sharpest impact in N.E.F. affairs in the 1920s and the emphasis on the child and his development was accompanied by the belief that he would develop best in a specially prepared community, often co-educational and often residential and usually small. As Boyd put it : 'On this conception of education, the essential thing was not the subjects nor the methods of learning, but right relations between parent and child, and between teacher and pupil.'[11]

All the problems and programmes of curricular and community organization were discussed and written about, from the Dalton Plan, through Montessori's learning material to Neill's freedom, from Cizek's methods of teaching art, through science by discovery and the direct method in modern languages to courses in sex education. The German reformers were concerned with what they called integrated instruction and the English and Americans invited the initiative of the pupils by projects and centres of interest. Learning was to come from the performance of meaningful tasks rather than obedience to instructions. For the first ten years the N.E.F. was child-centred and the password was freedom and that carried the gloss of neutrality in religion and politics.

For the next decade until the outbreak of war there was a growing tension in the movement between those who continued to want free school communities as an example which might influence more and more people and those who wanted the schools of the innovators to become deliberately aware of conflict and to educate for social reconstruction. From 1933 it became increasingly obvious that Germany was using schools as part of a vaster strategy, as Italy and Russia were also doing. Mannheim, Clarke, and others in England made the N.E.F. see how close was the weave in the fabric of society, and schools were part of it. This affected the movement in two main ways. It began to bring the independent progressive schools more into the public eye as examples not only of freakish behaviour and ideas, but as schools which were trying to think about the part education should play in a world approaching, and later at, war. Secondly, it brought the maintained schools as much into this problem as the independent schools. If most maintained secondary schools in 1939 were not very free in their organization, evacuation and the difficulties of war made it imperative that new and less strictly controlled practices had to be adopted

[11] W. Boyd, 'The Basic Faith of the New Education Fellowship', in *Yearbook of Education* (1957), pp. 198–9.

and this brought many of them unwillingly, without great experience, and often in conditions of real difficulty into more permissive ways.

After the War what has often been called democratic planning and the trend to egalitarianism and collectivism have affected the New Education Fellowship as much as any other society. The old days of the spearhead of advance in education being in the progressive school have gone. Post-1944 the state became increasingly confident in its assumption that 'privilege' would die and maintained schools would be able to challenge quality wherever it was found, whether in the public schools or in the progressive schools. Time would be on the side of local and national government and if the N.E.F. wished to make a continuing impact in education, it had to talk most of the time about maintained schools and less about the minority of private ventures which had virtually carried the Fellowship through the 1920s.

For nearly thirty years N.E.F. principles have influenced the training colleges and through them a good deal of primary schooling. Now these ideas are beginning to affect the secondary schools, and the influences in this direction come from national and local agencies, through professional associations, and through reports of influential working parties. In England the strongest initiative in curriculum reform is going to come from the Schools Council, the original sponsors of which in 1965 were the Department of Education and Science and the Local Education Authorities and on which all the leading educational interests are represented.

The N.E.F. as one of these interests has been active and resilient for nearly fifty years and remains committed to freer ways than yet exist at any rate in England's schools. As a movement it brings together those in the maintained and the private sectors and has persisted despite chronic financial difficulties and with a minimum of organization. It represents a remarkable achievement of voluntary effort based on principles that cannot be too precisely stated if schisms are not to appear. With new mobilizations of power and influence in education much more starkly related to politics and economics in one direction and to research in another, the future of this permissive organization may be even more difficult, but its vitality and importance to the history of educational innovation in England and in the world cannot be doubted, and its confidence can be seen in the fact that in 1966 the New Education Fellowship changed its title to the World Education Fellowship, and in 1967 it continues to seek to initiate research.

Part Two

Three Headmasters

Chapter Thirteen

CECIL REDDIE AND ABBOTSHOLME

ABBOTSHOLME opened its doors in October 1889 and it has continued in unbroken occupation of the same estate ever since, not even being displaced through two World Wars. This estate is just within the south west border of Derbyshire, the River Dove running through it and joining the Churnet not far away. If any one man should be named as the originator of the twentieth-century innovation in English education it is Cecil Reddie, the founder of Abbotsholme, but for reasons which will appear he has seldom been given this recognition in England.

II

Cecil Reddie was born on 10 October 1858 in London at Fulham as the sixth child in a family of ten. James Reddie, his father, the son of a Fifeshire landowner, was a Scot who was born near Dunfermline and studied for the Scots bar at Edinburgh University. He came to England and became a Civil Servant and later as Deputy Comptroller of Navy Pay he had a position of middle-class security. He was a man of Christian pretension, founding the Victoria Institute 'to defend the Christian faith against the advance of science'. Reddie's mother was English, the daughter of a considerable landowner in Norfolk. She died in 1867 after her tenth child had been born three months before Cecil's ninth birthday. Four years later James Reddie died and the family was scattered into the care of relations. So from the age of twelve and a half Cecil Reddie had no family roots and throughout the rest of his life we read only of one unmarried sister with any regularity, Miss Florence Reddie, and she was at Abbotsholme for many years as a combination of housekeeper and hostess for her brother in a post entitled 'Lady Superintendent'.

Cecil had been for four years at Godolphin School, Hammersmith, a London day grammar school and for one year at Birkenhead School before he went to an uncle in Scotland and was sent as a Foundation Scholar to Fettes College in Edinburgh, a boarding school formed on the English public school pattern in the Scottish academic tradition. He did well there, particularly in classics, mathematics, and science with creditable performances in German, but he was consistently weak in French. He played rugby for the school First XV in his final year and in the opinion of Professor J. J. Findlay, who first met Reddie in 1890 and who was for many years the Chairman of the School Council at Abbotsholme, '[Reddie] was shaped for life by his closing years at Fettes. . . . As a Senior Prefect his affections became deeply engaged on behalf of younger boys.'[1]

He seemed to want to give them the encouragement and security which he as an orphan at their age had lacked and Findlay considers that this was at least part of his motivation in a lifework devoted to helping boys of his own class to develop happily and safely through adolescence to young manhood.

Reddie has given an account of his schooling in a paper he read at the Authors' Club in London in 1909[2] which we can compare with Badley's account of his schooling at Rugby. All three of Reddie's schools, Godolphin, Birkenhead, and Fettes, were concerned mainly with the classics and he learned Latin and Greek on the basis of a different scheme of pronunciation in each school. In two of the three he was taught some English, history, and geography but in none was he taught to speak or write his own language properly. He learned some French and German, some mathematics and natural science, but 'our chief intellectual disciplines were Latin and Greek grammar and composition, with fragments of Greek and Roman history'.[3] They had an hour a week of drawing 'during which a battle of bread crusts nearly cost me an eye' and two hours a week of singing which together comprised their aesthetic education. In summer there were twenty-

[1] B. M. Ward, *Reddie of Abbotsholme* (London, 1934), 'Introduction' by Professor J. J. Findlay, p. 15.

[2] *How Should We Educate Our Directing Classes?* A paper read at the Authors' Club, 5 July 1909. In the records of the Authors' Club and more fully reported in *The Abbotsholmian*, iii, 3, 1909, pp. 7-26. This is the school magazine.

[3] *Abbotsholmian*, iii, 3, p. 14.

four hours a week of cricket which for Reddie, with undiscovered astigmatism in both eyes, was as he called it, purgatory. In winter there were four hours a week of football, cross-country runs and throughout much of the year, swimming. Nevertheless, at the age of fifty he sums it all up : 'This education was of the best then available. If the program was imperfect, we had plenty of leisure in which to do what we listed and educate ourselves. Best of all, we had lovely scenery, bracing air, magnificent buildings and genial masters.'[4]

He left Fettes when he was nearly twenty, an unusually late age as he admits. From the age of eight he had had this predominantly classical training and his headmaster says of him :

He distinguished himself in the classical and mathematical studies of the school and left high in the sixth form. He bore an admirable character in all respects, and though entering fully into the life of the school, was marked by a greater thoughtfulness and spirit of inquiry than is usual with boys at school.[5]

Reddie says he knew nothing about geography or politics or about his own body and mind and lived in a state of massive confusion because of his own inability to co-ordinate what he was being taught in the classroom, the chapel, and the playing fields : 'Education should aim at unity. If it leaves the mind chaotic, it can hardly be commended.'[6] Yet despite this, he said, most boys left their public school full of devotion to their *alma mater*, and in this Reddie included himself, perhaps not surprisingly, for, in the Introduction to the volume *Abbotsholme* he speaks of the difference between an orphan's view of school and that of boys who could look on it from

the fixed and secure vantage ground of home : to them school was, at most a second interest. To me, on the contrary, school was home [where I had to] try and find some new object with which to allay the hunger of the heart, increased as it was by a not unnatural idealisation of the scenes and persons which had vanished. [I] had, indeed, as early as I can recall, a bias towards idealising not only the absent but the present . . . an olympus of heroes . . . objects of reverence and worship.[7]

Reddie admits to periods of bitter disillusion about the age of

4 Ibid., p. 14.
5 A testimonial written on 7 Mar. 1888, ten years after Reddie left Fettes where he had returned to teach 1886–7.
6 *Abbotsholmian*, iii, 3, p. 15. 7 Reddie, *Abbotsholme*, p. 5.

seventeen with people, and a chaos of principles, ideas and ideals. A woman relative 'somewhat our senior' discerned his problems and with patience and quick intelligence helped to prevent the growth of a hard scepticism. By now he was among the most senior boys at Fettes and he found a new enthusiasm for work in 'a friendship with a youngster' whom he wanted to educate. In these disenchanted days this stirs a leaden echo and leads often to interpretations of unconscious motivations, post-Freud, post-Robert Graves, post-Wolfenden. All we wish to say at this point is that at Abbotsholme, from the start, Reddie spoke of a fearless frankness and cordial trust between boys and masters and a sense of responsibility and manly affection in the older boys for the younger. The reverberations from Homer, Pericles, and Plato and Victorian sex-reform are not difficult to hear. Nor are the signs hard to read of emotional hunger and intensity in an orphan of high intelligence and principle in a conventional Edinburgh boys' boarding school where he remained for six years. '... We got little satisfaction from "classics", "mathematics" or "modern languages". We, none the less, recall with gratitude the general life of the place, as well as our personal intercourse with the masters.'[8]

II

In 1878, at the age of twenty, Reddie entered the University of Edinburgh, his father's University, as an Exhibitioner to undertake the study of medicine which he had chosen because he hoped it would connect science and human life — at Fettes he had used his free time to do a good deal of experimental work on his own in the laboratories, especially in his last two years. But he reports that he found the aim of the whole training was to cure people when they were ill rather than to keep them healthy and after a year of satisfactory work as far as his examinations were concerned, Reddie moved from medicine to chemistry. Medicine was 'too material and mechanical to satisfy a nature which was travelling fast towards poetry and metaphysics' and he did not expect a great deal more from the study of natural sciences. He was devouring books in an attempt to gain some understanding of contemporary life, and the university curriculum was incidental: 'Nothing learnt at school seemed to give a clue to the actual life of the city and the big world.'[9]

[8] Reddie, *Abbotsholme*, p. 19.   [9] Ibid., p. 11.

It was in 1880–1 that his first contact with early socialist-utopian ideas was made. He was interested in the notions of H. M. Hyndman who in 1881 had founded the Democratic Federation which became the Social Democratic Federation in 1884, probably the first important Socialist body in England. I cannot here follow through in detail the complex developments of Socialist politics in the 1880s which led to the formation of the Independent Labour Party in 1893 and to the Labour Party (first known as the Labour Representation Committee) in 1900. In any case it would not be relevant to Cecil Reddie's life after the foundation of Abbotsholme in 1889.

In 1882, when he was nearly twenty-four, Reddie graduated as a Bachelor of Science mainly in Chemistry but with supporting Physics and Mathematics. He had become Hope Prize Scholar by competitive examination and a little later in 1882 he was elected by the Senatus after another competitive examination the Vans Dunlop Scholar in Chemistry and Chemical Pharmacy and given the opportunity to study chemistry for three years in a European university. He chose Göttingen and at the end of his course there in 1884 presented his thesis in German and was awarded the Ph.D. degree *magna cum laude*, the highest degree usually conferred on a foreigner. Undoubtedly a good academic future would have been available to Reddie had he chosen it.

He came to the conclusion very rapidly that the intellectual life and the social order in Germany were incomparably stronger than they were in Britain, that the quality of the teaching and the level of work done in Göttingen were higher than in Edinburgh, which was better in these things than most universities in Great Britain. 'Every day in Germany one felt the mind expanding and the fog melting away.'[10] In one place Reddie says that, besides his study of science, best of all for him was the chance to study Germany, its people and its language. This was the resurgent, confident Germany of the 1880s and Reddie's love-affair with its idealized *Zeitgeist*, although shockingly darkened in 1914, lasted through his life.

An interesting side-effect of his Göttingen days was that he was thrown together with many American students who, in the second half of the nineteenth century and up to 1914, chose German rather than British universities for their graduate studies in Europe. Reddie says that from the Americans he met he learned independence of thought

[10] Ibid., p. 13.

and mutual helpfulness. Another side-effect was the opportunity to attend some university lectures on Socialism where, according to Reddie, the facts quoted were largely drawn from British Blue Books; these lectures must have been based on work done by Marx, Engels, and their associates and followed on Reddie's respect for Hyndman who became the best known interpreter of political Marxism in England.[11] The period 1880–8 was the time during which Reddie was, in Findlay's words, 'a red-hot Socialist'. But it was not Hyndman's Marxism that came to appeal to Reddie when he returned to England in 1884.

III

There were three men who played an important part in Reddie's life about this time and whom he met in Edinburgh. The first was J. Archibald Campbell of Barbreck in Argyllshire; the second was Patrick Geddes, at first a biochemist who later became important in the development of sociology in Great Britain; the third was J. Edward Carpenter.

Archibald Campbell aroused Reddie's artistic sensibilities when he was an undergraduate, for Campbell was interested in the visual arts and poetry. He knew Ruskin and was in general accord with Ruskin's social thought as this also developed and it was probably through Campbell that Reddie first came across Ruskin's and Carlyle's writing even before he went to Germany. Campbell was also deeply interested in mysticism and seems to have possessed, as some Argyllshire Highlanders are reported to do, psychic powers — it was Campbell who about 1901, in a trance after one of Reddie's 'great rows' with some of his colleagues, told him what the dismissed masters were like and roughly where they then were. Reddie refers in some of his Abbotsholme leaflets to Campbell's poetry[12] and undoubtedly it was Campbell who started Reddie the scientist on the trail that led to Jacob Böhme, William Blake, Edward Maitland, and Anna Kingsford, the spiritualist

[11] See *Historical Bases of Socialism* (1883), *Commercial Crises of the Nineteenth Century* (1892), *Economics of Socialism* (1896).

[12] As only one example, in a broadsheet entitled 'What are the Educative Influences of Haymaking?': 'When we think of the unfortunates cooped up in the modern town, who have never worked in the Hay, and never perhaps even seen a Hay Field, we immediately recall the beautiful lines:
"Can He be born, where no little one
    Touches Earth, or Water, or Air, or Sun?"'
Ode on the Nativity by J. A. Campbell of Barbreck.'

borderland, the theosophical country, and the Eastern religions. The *Abbotsholme Liturgy* which Reddie compiled over the years for use in the school bears plenty of evidence of this eclectic approach to religious orthodoxy. Mysticism, occultism, and spiritualism offered on the one hand a fine counterpoise for an intensely emotional man who showed an obsessional attention to detail, and on the other rare scope for a highly idiosyncratic escape from the reality of men, women and boys. However this may be, Campbell gave the young Edinburgh undergraduate the flavour of art and poetry, of mysteries both human and transcendental, of radical social thinking in England and Europe. These things started in 1880, before Reddie went to Germany in 1882; they were renewed on his return to Edinburgh in 1885 and Reddie shows from his writing at Abbotsholme and from the further meetings with Campbell that the friendship remained.[13] Campbell's name appears in the list of the Advisory Council for Abbotsholme until after the First World War.

Patrick Geddes was the second man who was particularly important at this phase of Reddie's development. Campbell of Barbreck was of the family of Inverary Castle and a relative of the Duke of Argyll and Geddes was the son of a Gaelic-speaking warrant officer from the Deeside in Aberdeenshire. The boy had ambitions to be an artist after his schooling at Perth Academy, but they did not mature. He never attended a university as an undergraduate and he was never awarded a degree, but he lived much of his active life in, or connected with, universities. He served T. H. Huxley in London as an apprentice and demonstrator and then was recommended by him to work in Paris and study zoology. Geddes saw Paris in the early 1870s when the reconstruction of France was going on after the shock of defeat. When Geddes returned in 1877 at the age of twenty-three to be Senior Demonstrator in the zoology department at University College London, he was already concerned about life-habits, whether of insects or of humans. Frédéric Le Play's methods of examining the life of communities were familiar to Geddes and he translated the formula *Lieu, Travail, Famille* into the English form which offered a model for investigation to generations of geographers and sociologists — Place,

---

[13] See *Abbotsholme*, pp. 11 and 13, references in Broadsheets, an early prospectus, confidential documents in the Abbotsholme archives written by Reddie on 'the great rows' and correspondence of the present author with Dr. G. Lissant Cox who was a boy at Abbotsholme from 1892 and who, although he did not meet Campbell 'heard much about him' from Reddie. Dr. Cox died in 1967.

Work, Folk.[14] In 1880 he became Senior Demonstrator at the University of Edinburgh.

Geddes had become interested in the life and lot of students and began to concern himself with self-governing and self-supporting lodgings for them and by 1892 after his marriage he started 'the world's first Sociological Laboratory' in the Outlook Tower in Castlehill. Geddes was also interested in the work of the Fellowship of the New Life, a socialist-utopian society whose importance for the beginnings of Abbotsholme we shall consider later. Many Ruskinians belonged to the Fellowship and the idea of a wholesome community which emerged in Geddes's building co-operatives and his later work in town and country planning in Great Britain, Cyprus, and India was the expression of the principles of the Fellowship.[15] Reddie says of Geddes: '[His] object appeared to [me] nothing less than the creation of a Synthesis of universal Thought and Action . . . [He] aimed mainly at a reorganisation of Knowledge which would enable the human unit to reconstruct society.'[16]

Reddie's re-entry to Scottish society brought him directly under Geddes in whose laboratory he demonstrated in biological chemistry in 1884-5. Geddes reinforced Reddie's growing understanding of the linkages between the physical and biological sciences, geography, sociology, economics, and politics and his increasing dissatisfaction with what was taught in schools. It was probably as a result of Geddes's influence that Reddie during that year lived in a poor village in the valley of Leith Water below Dean Bridge 'so as to learn how the workers actually existed'.[17] The young Socialist was putting theory to practice.

After a year in Geddes's laboratory Reddie was appointed as a Lecturer in Chemistry at Fettes, his old school, where he stayed for

[14] Geddes widened Le Play's formula from 'family' to 'folk' which enabled him to view towns and cities as living organisms and not only as collections of family units. See S. H. Beaver, 'The Le Play Society and Field Work', in *Geography*, July 1962, p. 230.

[15] Lewis Mumford is probably Geddes's best known disciple. Geddes collaborated with Victor Branford in and after 1902 and when they helped to found the Institute of Sociology in London and to start its periodical *The Sociological Review*. Both Geddes and Branford appear on the list of members of the Advisory Council in Abbotsholme prospectuses for twenty five-years. Geddes accepted a knighthood from a Labour Government in 1931.

[16] *Abbotsholme*, p. 14.

[17] From an obituary notice of Edward Carpenter by Reddie in *Everyman*, 11 July 1929.

two years, and during that time he delivered a University Extension course of lectures in chemistry. He spent part of the summer of 1886 visiting schools in Germany and Switzerland, interesting himself in their methods of teaching science and their books on educational theory and practice, for as he said when he began to teach on his return to Edinburgh in 1884, '[I] entered the scholastic profession without having had an hour's training in it.'

Reddie met Edward Carpenter in Edinburgh in February 1886 when Carpenter lectured on one of his favourite themes 'private property' and Reddie was captivated by him. Edward Carpenter was born in 1844 at Brighton into a family of established naval connection. He graduated at Cambridge in 1868, took orders a year later and became a Fellow of Trinity Hall and was for a short while one of J. F. D. Maurice's curates at the University Church before Maurice's death in 1872. By 1874 Carpenter's religious position was so unorthodox that he resigned both his curacy and his fellowship and until 1881 he lectured in the newly formed University Extension programme in Cambridge, as Reddie did in Edinburgh a few years later. In 1877 Carpenter visited the United States and came to know Walt Whitman, whose writing he greatly admired as much for its content as its new style of unfettered dithyrambs which Carpenter adopted himself for his book *Towards Democracy*. This first appeared in 1883 and he gave an inscribed copy to Reddie at their Edinburgh meeting in February 1886.

In 1881 Carpenter had begun the simple way of living, like Whitman's, which he pursued for the rest of his life:

The two words Freedom and Equality came for the time being to control all my thought and expression. The necessity for space and time to work this out grew so strong in April of this year 1881 I threw up my lecturing employment. Moreover, another necessity had come upon me which demanded the latter step — the necessity, namely, for an open-air life and manual work. I could not finally argue with this any more than with the other. I had to give in and obey.[18]

In 1883 he bought a seven-acre small holding at Millthorpe in Derbyshire, built a house on it and worked with his labourers to make the holding into a paying proposition as a market garden. He became

[18] From a personal note concluding the 1902 edition of *Towards Democracy*.

accustomed to the care of horses and cattle, the carting of stones and manure, the use of the hoe, the spade, the scythe, the pick, and the shovel. Such work became integral to Abbotsholme six years later. Carpenter became the champion of a simple-life Socialism, did much street-corner speaking in northern industrial towns and interested himself in the self-supporting Ruskinian communities at Totley near Sheffield and Norton near Nottingham. He wrote on 1 September 1914 in reply to an address of congratulation for his seventieth birthday as follows:

> I have sometimes been accused of taking to a rather plain and Bohemian kind of life, of associating with manual workers, of speaking at street corners, of growing fruit, making sandals, writing verses, or what not, as at great cost to my own comfort and with some ulterior or artificial purpose — as of reforming the world. . . . I have done the thing primarily and simply because of the joy I had in doing it, and to please myself. If the world or any part of it should in consequence insist on being reformed, that is not my fault.

This was the man whom Reddie first met in Edinburgh in February 1886. In August of the same year he spent some days with him at Millthorpe, Carpenter's Derbyshire house. Reddie left Fettes in the winter of 1886 to take up work as a science master at Clifton, his first and only contact as a master with an English public school, and before he left Scotland, Dr. Potts, the Fettes headmaster, wrote to tell Reddie that he would find 'a well-developed Red element in Bristol'. After a year of successful teaching during which he lived not in a poor man's house but in College Gate with six other bachelor masters, Reddie asked Carpenter for advice on his future. Carpenter, who had visited Reddie at Clifton, advised him to leave the school, saying that Reddie had got all he ever would from it and he took Carpenter's advice, the more particularly as Carpenter invited him to Millthorpe to spend time thinking over what to do next. Reddie had just applied unsuccessfully for the headship of a new London day school, St. Dunstan's College, on the suggestion of the Clifton headmaster, the Reverend James Wilson, who wrote in his letter of support:

> He has an unusual degree of originality in educational views, and has to some extent tested them here and elsewhere.
> It is by my advice that he is seeking some post where he may have

greater freedom for developing his methods than he can have here, where he is not senior in any department and has to work on fixed lines. . . . [He] would require considerable freedom in the management of detail.[19]

This support from Wilson first put the thought into Reddie's head, so he writes,[20] that he might at twenty-nine, with three years of school teaching experience, launch out on founding a school of his own to express the educational and social ideas which he discussed with Carpenter so eagerly during the summer of 1888. During the winter of 1888 Reddie lectured for the Scottish Universities Extension Scheme and returned in April 1889 to Millthorpe to work out precise proposals, the details of which we shall see later. For the moment we can say that Edward Carpenter was the man who helped Reddie to discover what his life's work was to be and to begin to make it actual, Carpenter the aristocratic simple-life Socialist, who farmed and made sandals, the writer and poet, the admirer of Whitman and the mystical religions of the East, the reformer of sexual attitudes, the advocate of dress reform, manly love, and comradeship.

Carpenter's name appeared together with Reddie's and two others as one of the founders in the preliminary announcement in the early summer of 1889 of the commencement of Abbotsholme, but he withdrew before the beginning of the school term in October. Although Carpenter is named in 1889 as one of several 'Fellows of Abbotsholme', he is not named as a member of the Advisory Council in 1910 although J. A. Campbell and Patrick Geddes are. In his obituary of Carpenter, Reddie mentions occasional visits to Abbotsholme up to 1908 but dwells mostly on the period 1888–9 which undoubtedly was the time when Carpenter and Reddie made their deepest impressions on one another:

It is those six months when I lived close to him that I recall most vividly. I was 29 and he 43. In that quiet valley there was a wonderful peace. Our meals were simple, but marvellously satisfying. . . . We would go to the little brook at the bottom of his garden for a bathe; but we stripped rather for the sun and air bath. . . . Edward Carpenter was slightly built, but wiry and very masculine. He believed that mere nudity in sun and air and water was a blessed physician for body, soul and spirit. He was opposed to excessive intellectuality. . . . He preferred on the whole to be with

[19] *Abbotsholme*, p. 631.　　　[20] Ibid., p. 20.

hand-workers because . . . he found talking with them rested his own sensitive brain . . . I sometimes, perhaps often, troubled him because of my rather quick brain.

As I look back over all these years, I feel that he was one of the greatest teachers of his time, all the more because he worked quietly and personally with no self-consciousness or desire for publicity and fame.

When Reddie returned to Edinburgh from Germany in 1884 he came into contact with the Fellowship of the New Life, to which Geddes and Carpenter were attached and probably Campbell too. In 1900 Reddie wrote of Carpenter:

[He] had developed original but very sane and wholesome views on social questions. If they were tinged, perhaps, with some elements of democratic enthusiasm, they were quite free from anything approaching public theft or violent prescriptions of any kind. They owed their origin, doubtless, to a preformed knowledge of our social chaos, and a powerful sympathy arising from strong affections.[21]

Badley's estimate of Carpenter was almost precisely similar without the implicit disapproval of democratic enthusiasm. The Fellowship of the New Life was an association for people of such views. Thomas Davidson, the prime mover in founding the Fellowship, was a Scot a few years older than Carpenter. After graduating at Aberdeen University and teaching in England and Scotland, he went out to Canada and the United States in 1865 whence he returned to Europe during many summers, spending time in travelling on the Continent, but particularly visiting and revisiting the Rosminian community at Domodossola a few miles from the Swiss border of Italy. In the meanwhile he lectured on and translated Rosmini's writings. The idea of what could be achieved in and by the life of a community devoted to spiritual values and the workaday needs of living dominated Davidson's thinking. He came to England in 1883 and tried to interest people in setting up a community where everyone could cultivate 'a perfect character'. By the end of 1883 the Fellowship of the New Life was constituted and the implications were considered of trying to reform society by creating communities which subordinated material to spiritual things. These communities would live simply by the sweat of their brows, would share a liberally conceived religious conviction,

[21] *Abbotsholme*, p. 14.

and would be committed from the start to providing responsible education.

Some of those who took part in these discussions were very dubious first about the stability of communities of this kind and second about their cathartic effect on mass society in any case. While Frank Podmore, E. R. Pease, and H. H. Champion agreed to the inevitability of gradualism on which the Fellowship was relying, their particular gradualism was the steady exposure of factual, logical, political, economic, and social inadequacies in the government's programmes. They wanted to form an intellectual pressure group, as Armytage says, rather than a communitarian experiment. So the Fabian Society formed itself and broke away from the Fellowship of the New Life. Bernard Shaw, who joined the Fabian Society in May 1884 soon after it was formed, characterized the communitarian gradualists as 'sitting among the dandelions' and the intellectual gradualists as 'organizing the docks'.[22]

Reddie had an understanding of both groups but temperamentally he was with Davidson. He wanted 'to help to create a higher type of human being'.[23] When Davidson returned to the United States later in 1884 he said that he had not been in sympathy with the socialist ideology of many members of the English group as he believed it was only by individual reformation that social and political changes could really be brought about. Such beliefs were shared by Carpenter, Reddie, and Badley. Carpenter's answer was a spiritually based anarchism. Reddie's and Badley's answer was to found schools which were called 'New Schools' and which had an emphasis on community. Before Abbotsholme opened in 1889, *The Sower*, which was the journal of the Fellowship (the title was later changed to *Seed Time*), announced that while the Fellowship itself had not yet had the means to sponsor and open a school based on the principles it had enunciated in 1886,[24] friends and associates were going to establish such a school aiming 'to develop all the faculties of the boy'[25] and to provide a 'new transmissable consecration'[26] which might redeem the ethical and economic confusion of society.

[22] W. H. G. Armytage, *Heavens Below* (London, 1961), p. 332.
[23] *Abbotsholme*, p. 16.   [24] *The Sower*, July 1889.
[25] See below, p. 256.   [26] *Seed Time*, Apr. 1890.

IV

In the second half of 1888 Reddie published a series of articles in a periodical called *Today* under the general title of 'Modern Mis-Education' and in these, while making some approving remarks about the public schools, he developed a fierce critique of their principles and practice. When they speak of industry, he says, all they mean is incitement to compete for academic or athletic success; they have no notion of the virtues of co-operation either for the school or for society which so desperately needs to learn how to develop corporate responsibility. When the public school teaches lessons of restraint it does so by developing a code to which boys conform and not by enabling them to see both the necessity and the satisfaction of social duty and self-control. When the public schools speak of modesty, says Reddie, it is narrowed to false modesty on the one hand and prudishness on the other; they ignore the lusts for money, power, and comfort which can corrupt and they ignore modesty as the consequence of genuine humility. Finally, Reddie claimed that when the public schools spoke of purity it became a niggling and debased evasion of their responsibilities for the sexual and moral education of their boys. He wanted schools to help boys on the one hand to see the debilitations of materialist England and on the other to develop a positive morality and an understanding of social responsibility.

This series of articles has in it many of the main themes for Reddie's invective which appear and reappear through his professional life — the lusts for power and wealth, selfishness, prudishness, sexual ignorance, intellectual torpor, contempt for manual work. These state *per contra* what he hoped to find in a school and each of these themes has less to do with schoolroom practice than with social analysis, with faults outside school which need to be recognized and against which attitudes must be prepared in school. The themes are more in the nature of moral affirmations which could offer a basis for political proposals. They seemed to be in keeping with the radical position of the Fellowship of the New Life. In a memorandum of the Fellowship drawn up in 1886[27] it had been stated:

> The Members of the Fellowship of the New Life desire to submit to those interested in education the following proposals for the establishment of a school.... Such an education would be the

[27] 13 Aug. 1886.

nurturing and disciplining of the young child so that it might come to live the life of true freedom ; to be a law unto itself and a beneficial power in the world.

At that time nothing came of the proposal but in 1888 it looked as though the author of 'Mis-Education' was the man to open the New School for the Fellowship. During the time when he was writing the articles he was also planning the school with Edward Carpenter at his house at Millthorpe. Through Carpenter's good offices two others were drawn into the scheme and in 1889 Abbotsholme house and estate were found. Reddie had £88 to put into the venture ; R. F. Muirhead, an ex-army tutor who was to teach mathematics and be treasurer, put in rather more, and William Cassels, who was a disciple of Ruskin and who was to run the farm, was prepared to put up £2,000. As we have already said Edward Carpenter, who signed the early statements of purpose and practice, withdrew from active participation before the school opened, but lent money free of interest until the estate was bought outright by Reddie in 1894. Undoubtedly Carpenter saw that Reddie's political and social intentions were becoming very different from his own and those of the Fellowship of the New Life and this Muirhead and Cassels quickly discovered also. Nevertheless Carpenter supported and approved of many of Reddie's educational practices.

Reddie was to be the headmaster of the school and it was he who drew up the details of the Prospectus and of the academic planning. Carpenter, Muirhead, and Cassels had hoped that the emphasis on the land and the dignity of labour and Reddie's castigation of the foundation of the public schools would make the New School into an agricultural community for practical Socialism, where schoolwork would be related to understanding the economics of living and the equality and brotherhood of man. Instead they found the Prospectus stating that Abbotsholme was 'a school for the sons of the Directing Classes' and Reddie thinking in aristocratic terms. He set these down most clearly in a series of lectures which he gave nearly ten years later and which he published in 1901 having delayed the appearance of the book until the South African War was over :

Our task then is to lay aside the ideas and system which perhaps suited our national childhood and set to work to devise an educational engine suited to our Imperial future. . . . In particular we need to create a Directing Class. We can create it through sane and wholesome education. We must, however, create also a class trained to obey. And for this I know no better agent than compulsory military service. . . . It would cure at one stroke our two chief national vices, lack of honourable subordination and lack of unselfish patriotism.[28]

In *John Bull* and other writings Reddie builds up a highly idiosyncratic interpretation of the historical and geographical factors by which Great Britain obtained control of one fifth of the dry globe during her ascendancy, which she was certainly losing, and which according to Reddie she deserved to lose. Anglo-Celtic civilization was decaying through emigration to the New World, through the exploitation of men and markets after the Industrial Revolution by a new governing class, and through the readiness of our land-owning classes to idle and surrender their leadership. The masses, says Reddie, are prepared to do as little as they can and as badly as possible without actually falling into unemployment.

One of the ways in which Reddie differs from Carpenter, Hyndman, Cassels, and others of the early Socialists is in his readiness to blame not only the exploiters, but also the feckless, self-regarding masses. Carpenter and Cassels wanted to build up communities from the bottom and so dissolve class distinction by examples of enriched and unselfish living in self-supporting groups in agricultural surroundings, and Reddie wanted to begin at the top, accepting a hierarchy, and assuming that if the masses had more power they would not know what to do with it. We have to get rid of our 'idiotic idea of democracy' realizing that equality of opportunity is only a half-truth. Democracy needs an aristocracy and without it would perish. By the time Abbotsholme began, Reddie's 'red-hot Socialism' had cooled into something else and we recall his deep respect of Carlyle. In 1894 Reddie, now the sole owner of Abbotsholme estate, wrote: 'If Oxford did her duty, artizans would not want "labour members", nor to substitute for "cultured selfishness" the still worse selfishness of the ignorant.'[29] Badley and Reddie had similar political sympathies in the 1880s, with Reddie much the more committed of the two. Badley remained sympathetic to the Left in politics, but Reddie, with characteristic emphasis, did not.

[28] *John Bull: His Origin and Character* (London, 1901), pp. 49 and 53.

[29] *Abbotsholme,* p. 126. From an article comparing conferences at the Universities of Oxford and Edinburgh.

VII

Reddie was a striking looking man of immense vitality, just under six feet tall, upright, and military in bearing. Writing of 1900 an Abbotsholmian said:

> During haymaking Dr. Reddie moved with a brisker step, his dark eyes more piercing, his black hair more lustrous, his vivacity more overwhelming, his laughter more compelling, and his whole personality more vivid and dynamic than during the rest of the year. . . . He was a little terrifying to a small boy and the retreating back was a not unwelcome sight. The retreating back was clothed in a light-grey Norfolk jacket and the muscular legs by which it was borne along in white shorts and neatly fitting grey stockings. The shoes were strong, terribly expensive and beautifully polished.

R. F. Muirhead and William Cassels as Reddie's partners when Abbotsholme opened in 1889 were prepared to be active workers in the school with Reddie as headmaster. In a few weeks Muirhead and Cassels proposed majority decisions of the triumvirate for school practice and policy and Reddie refused this. He proposed to resign and start up elsewhere, taking the twelve boys whom he had brought to Abbotsholme of the first sixteen who were then there. Muirhead and Cassels decided to resign instead and leave Reddie as sole owner provided he repaid to them their invested capital, which he did in a few years.[30] For thirty-seven years he owned Abbotsholme and it is reported that when he bought the estate 'through the generous assistance of a friend' in 1894, he went out and rolled on the grass for joy. The young Socialist of the 1880s had become the Tory landlord of the 1890s.

In 1892 J. H. Badley, who came to the school when it opened, left to marry and to start Bedales. Reddie regarded this as an act of betrayal and in October 1894 he drew up an agreement which each

[30] 'We beg to inform you that the partnership between us as proprietors of the New School, Abbotsholme, Rocester, Stafford, was determined (that is, terminated) on 31 December 1889 and that since that date Dr. Reddie the Head Master has been the sole Proprietor of the School.

We are,
Yours faithfully,
Cecil Reddie
R. F. Muirhead (Engineering & Maths)
W. Cassels (Agriculture)'

The letter ending the partnership.

master was requested to sign on appointment. By this Reddie placed his own experience and skill at the disposal of his staff, expecting that they would not use this opportunity and the experimental results which the school was building up for their own private advancement.

> No individual has any legal or moral right to make these results or the methods of obtaining [them] known to outsiders ... nor to allow outsiders, whether visiting the school or not, to get to know these results except as sanctioned expressly by the Head Master in writing.[31]

If a master preferred not to agree to be bound in this way, he was to be regarded as only temporary and would not be permitted to take a full part in the 'advantages which the agreement renders possible'. Reddie wanted to form 'colonies' of Abbotsholme to spread over the whole land the principles and practices peculiar to the school and to provide legitimate promotion-chances for capable Abbotsholme-trained masters. He did not want pirate imitators and looked to a federation of like-minded schools resolved to avoid competition and to encourage co-operation.

Bedales was hailed in the *Pall Mall Gazette*[32] as 'an offshoot of Abbotsholme' and Badley was called 'Dr. Reddie's lieutenant' in a later issue.[33] In the course of this interview Badley spoke of the importance of the influence of women in a boys' school and said that he thought the school of the future was probably a mixed day school. Reddie was angry with Badley for starting Bedales anyway for boys of nine to fifteen and not eleven to eighteen as at Abbotsholme, and he was ferociously opposed to co-education during adolescence. Thus, although Reddie said he looked for a federation of like-minded schools, the only one which was a brother school was rejected from the start. Many years later, after three or four Abbotsholme masters had left or been dismissed as a consequence of some of 'the great rows' and had gone to Bedales, Reddie wrote an article in *The Abbotsholmian*[34] entitled 'The Relation of Abbotsholme to Bedales' in which the following signally anti-federal sentiments appear:

> Have they not exploited to the full the fact that they originally sprang from Abbotsholme and hoisted our banner ... whenever the connection seemed likely to benefit them?[35]

[31] *Abbotsholme*, p. 218.   [32] 22 Aug. 1892.
[33] 5 Oct. 1892.   [34] Vol. ii, July 1908, pp. 13–16.   [35] Ibid., p. 14.

We have never been intimate with Bedales. Our respective points of view appear to us to be, and to have always been, radically different. It is quite certain we have never adopted anything from Bedales.

We have never been there, never troubled our heads about it, and no-one from there has been invited to visit us. . . .

We wish Mr. Badley a prosperous voyage on his own peculiar course and only beg him to leave us alone and not mislead the public by pretending that he knows anything about our life.[36]

Relationships were much less strained between Reddie and his Continental followers in Germany, Switzerland, France, and elsewhere. But they were farther away, were not Abbotsholme's competitors and he visited them rarely.

Abbotsholme in the 1890s was an exceedingly stimulating place and many visitors and birds of passage on the staff took away ideas which they did not acknowledge as generously as Badley did. In December 1896, for instance, a book which was well reviewed appeared under the title of *The Foundations of Success: A Plea for a Rational Education*. The author was Stanley de Brath who was a member of Abbotsholme staff 1894–95 and in his book, after outlining a number of theoretical approaches to education, he sketched in principles and practices which very closely resembled what Reddie had written and created. But de Brath made no acknowledgement of his indebtedness. Reddie had shattering quarrels with his colleagues in 1900, 1904, and 1906 and he felt that a number of them were vilifying him and Abbotsholme while capitalizing on his ideas in the schools they started, which in no case lasted any length of time.

When all justifiable allowance is made for his feeling that educational plagiarism was being practised all round there remains Reddie's erratic psychology. Manic-depressive cycles can be detected, recurring paranoia, obsessional attention to detail combined with an empyrean of mysticism and symbolism. His violence of temper was known and feared and was matched by his violence of language. Writing in December 1908 he says:

It seems to us quite clear that the chief impediments to reformed Education are: the stupidity of Parents . . . and the treachery of ambitious persons who attach themselves to new movements, like

[36] Ibid., p. 16.

Judas to Jesus . . . and who after picking the brains of their Master as well as his pocket, betray him to the Philistines.[37]

There were two 'great rows' in 1900 and 1904 and Reddie prepared a fifty-page 'true story of the 1900 episode' which is in the confidential archives at Abbotsholme and which reads at times like something from Strindberg and Chekhov with overtones of Kafka and Mauriac and occasional glimpses of Victorian farce-melodrama. Dr. Van Eyk, a Dutchman, came to Abbotsholme to teach in 1898 but by 1900 he considered Reddie was 'trying to be like Napoleon and have all your subordinates mere tools'. As a result of the quarrel between Reddie and five of his subordinates, all five were dismissed or left. Van Eyk was dismissed summarily, and characteristically left owing a large sum to the school tailor. In 1901 he set up a new boarding school on borrowed money within twenty miles of Abbotsholme[38] employing a number of the dismissed staff, but he went bankrupt within a year and fled to France where he met and married a woman with £300 a year. While Van Eyk is something of a picaresque figure, the 1900 quarrels had a seismic effect on Abbotsholme and on Reddie himself. Breakdowns occur and recur for the rest of his active life. In 1906 when he went to the United States partly for reasons of health, two of his colleagues wrote to parents alleging that Reddie was 'morally unsuited to be Head'. Some parents came together to examine the charges and Reddie was exonerated from the homosexual innuendoes and we are told that the two men recanted but it was nineteen months before he was permitted to return to Abbotsholme. Reddie had his greatest decade in the 1890s and by the turn of the century the school began the decline which only really ended when Reddie retired.

During the First World War the numbers dropped disastrously. This was partly due to the withdrawal of boys who were foreign nationals, partly to the difficulties of staffing in wartime, and partly to Reddie himself. One of his pupils at this time, who became a friend later in Reddie's life, and was with him when he died in 1932, wrote a disturbing account of this war period.

The war shattered Abbotsholme. . . . The numbers dropped from 39 in the summer term 1914 to 22 the following term. . . . The

[37] From an article, 'Attempts to Wreck Some of the New Schools', in *Abbotsholmian*, vol. 3, no. 1, Dec. 1908, p. 24. I make no comment on the significance of the simile.

[38] Imperial School, Hatherton Hall, Cannock, Staffs.

strain of the situation rapidly affected C.R.... He personally supervised every detail of administration [and] ... he now trusted no-one ... his authority became absolute and unquestioned. Always a complex of devil and saint, the devil now took command. His temper was ungovernable. He shouted, stormed and raged. He seldom came into class without a cane. Teaching, what there was of it, was thrown completely to the winds, and instead we suffered tirades against the English, against women and against public schools. Only Germany was extolled, although at that very time German bullets were tearing Old Abbotsholmians to death. His classes became reigns of terror and lay like a dead weight upon the happiness of the boys.... The freedom and gaiety of the school completely disappeared. Instead there was a feeling of oppression and failure.... Each term more boys left. With the school melting away before his eyes, and being powerless to stop it, C.R. was a picture of tragic impotence.... By February 1917 there were only 13 boys.[39]

The same author goes on to say that he had gone to Abbotsholme at the age of ten intending to stay until he was ready to go to Oxford, but in the wartime conditions at the school such a plan was impossible, so he was removed and sent to Repton at the age of fifteen having to, have special coaching to gain entrance, so little had he been taught at Abbotsholme in his last year or two.

I am not likely to forget my last night at Abbotsholme. C.R. talked to me in his study until two in the morning. He gave me a horribly distorted picture of public-school life and life in general. He finished by describing me as a rat leaving the sinking ship, and for many years after that we were not on speaking terms.[40]

The man whom Reddie had singled out as his likely successor, Roderick Bemrose, died nearly at the end of the War, and Reddie never really sought for another. There was a temporary resurgence of Abbotsholme's fortunes in the early 1920s as far as numbers went, but looking back, a pupil of that time says that staff problems were constant. He recalls two main types of master, one which wanted to rebuild education on freedom of expression and one which wanted to drown war memories in drink. 'C.R. quarrelled violently with the former and sacked the latter.'[41]

[39] G. H. Dixon, 'During The War', in *Fifty Years of Abbotsholme 1889–1939*, pp. 37–38. [40] Ibid., p. 38.
[41] Geoffrey Peach, 'Post-War Days', in *Fifty Years of Abbotsholme*, p. 40.

When Reddie was prevailed upon to retire in 1927 at the age of sixty-eight the school had two boys in it. Attempts had been made since 1919 by old boys and friends of the school to bring about the change, but although Reddie was theoretically willing, there was always an insuperable difficulty — not least, of course, that few men were prepared to take on a school at such a low ebb. These old boys were resolved to save the school despite the impossible old man, whose best insights these men perceived and represented, and their patience and tenacity are a profound tribute to the strength and secret potency of Reddie's magnetism. After negotiating the mine-field of Reddie's resistances, in 1927 they persuaded him to permit Colin Sharp, then Reader in English at St. Stephen's College, Delhi, to visit Abbotsholme to study Reddie's methods and ideas with a view to succeeding him. The school then consisted of Reddie as the only member of the teaching staff, his secretary Miss Gifford, four domestic staff, a gardener, a farm bailiff, and two lads working for them. There were two pupils 'one at first away with a cold'. For ten weeks Colin Sharp lived with Cecil Reddie and listened:

> Dr. Reddie, ill, broken-hearted, but full of pluck, most charming in his speech, but bitter towards the world that had not recognized and accepted his message, impressed me as an outstanding and delightful man. Nightly he never stopped talking from 6 p.m. to 2 a.m., but when not riding his particular hobbies of . . . sex, the inferiority of women and the 'putrid' English character, he talked with humour, decisiveness and a delicacy of sympathy and artistry which provoked a quick and deep affection. . . . Most of the rooms in the School were locked. . . . It was a cold January with snow and fog for six weeks, but the only fires in the house were in his study, Miss Gifford's office, the kitchen and the boiler. . . . The study . . . had two arm-chairs, one with broken springs . . . the seat of honour for the listener in his nightly talks.[42]

Reddie proposed Sharp as his successor in March 1927 and the limited company which took over the school and estate from Reddie was incorporated as Abbotsholme School Ltd. on 20 July 1927 with Reddie as Emeritus Warden, the only school owned by a company of former pupils. The late Professor Findlay was the first Chairman of its Council, and he wrote:

I know few stories in the history of schools more romantic than the

[42] C. H. C. Sharp, 'The Change Over', in *Fifty Years at Abbotsholme*, p. 44.

way in which the second founder, Colin Sharp, amid every sign of discouragement, took the helm with a cheerful resolution that heartened the whole crew. . . . [He] rescued Abbotsholme because he saw that . . . the loss to secondary education would be poignant if this flickering flame were suffered to expire.[43]

In 1927 there were two boys. In 1937 there were one hundred and five and in 1967 and three headmasters after Colin Sharp who retired in 1949, and who died in 1966, there are over two hundred, in accommodation which is now expanded to take about two hundred and thirty.

VIII

When Reddie retired on an annuity in 1927 to Welwyn Garden City he seemed to slough off his past as an educational pioneer and although Emeritus Warden he revisited Abbotsholme only twice, for the last time in November 1929.[44] He turned to many of the minority interests which he had not fully pursued at Abbotsholme, some of them characteristically idiosyncratic. He read much on the theme of the historicity of Jesus, he played Gregorian melodies on his organ, he joined the Shakespeare Fellowship which was concerned with establishing the authentic authorship of the works of William Shakespeare. In his years at Abbotsholme he had worked out a new version of writing down musical notation and supported the simplification of spelling and the development of phonetics. He did not use a pen but a kind of quill or reed and this was linked with an interest in print calligraphy and the abolition of capital letters. At Abbotsholme he had also perfected a form of the perpetual calendar and supported the double summer-time reform, and these causes he continued to champion. He joined the British Society for the Study of Sex Psychology. He said again and again he was going to write his memoirs but he never managed to start them.

[43] J. J. Findlay, 'Later Years with Colin Sharp', in *Fifty Years at Abbotsholme*, pp. 46 and 47.

[44] Sir Stanley Unwin, an Old Abbotsholmian and a member of the first Abbotsholme School Council in 1927, in his autobiography *Truth About a Publisher* (1960), p. 55, says that a group of old boys persuaded C.R. to sell the school and estate and to accept an annuity 'on the condition that he did not come near the place again'. A contemporary at Abbotsholme and friend of Sir Stanley, Dr. G. L. Cox, corrects this error in a review of his book in *The Abbotsholmian*, no. 76, Spring 1961, pp. 5–9.

Reddie prided himself on his Scottish or Celtic connection and used language of extravagant ferocity when speaking of England, 'that cesspit and madhouse'. His school in Derbyshire he called a state and said that it was 'half a mile from England'. Germany offered him the pattern of submissive hard work and training and he asserted day in day out that in Germany there was thoroughness, industry, social purpose and intellectual quality altogether lacking in England. Not only was he a Doctor of Philosophy of Göttingen, he visited Professor Rein of Jena in 1893 and learned about pedagogy from him, claiming that there was nothing of this kind in England and sending his staff to Jena as well. Reddie's maps and diagrams, his furniture design, his Herbartian principles (without, interestingly enough, any trace of Freud or psychoanalysis in his psychological interests) his authoritarianism, his compulsive love of detail were Germanic. His desire to serve as well as dominate his boys and his general temperament were not at all Germanic.

Reddie had not the deep respect for Oxbridge that Badley had by reason of his Rugby and Cambridge background. It was an alien tradition which, with one foot in Edinburgh and the other in Jena, Reddie perpetually trounced. But Abbotsholme could not reasonably expect to survive in England after 1918 on the strength of an idealized German *Zeitgeist*. Reddie's individual conflicts were so great and his range of ideas so intensely personal that he could not take, and certainly did not want to take, realistic sociological stock in England. His assessment was always in terms of moral degeneration and moral renaissance. It was Colin Sharp who with generous patience and insight saw to the heart of Reddie's message and reinterpreted it in such a way that Abbotsholme could survive and prosper in England :

> [Reddie] bristled with inconsistencies. A believer in love, friendship and co-operation as the mainsprings of life, yet impatient, intolerant, even ruthless toward those who opposed him. The creator of the school war memorial 'The Radiant Lover', radiating love from every inch of his body, yet the man who at one period ordered boys to be publicly flogged. Convinced of the importance of individuality and independence of thought, but an imperious autocrat who sought to crush all resistance to his will both inside and outside the school. A realist who dabbled in the occult and stressed the value of the symbol. Unsentimental to the point of indifference, yet capable of deep and lasting affection for boys, to whom he devoted his life,

and also for a few specially favoured women. An ascetic who loved flowers, the colour of wine in a wine glass and was never without an abominable cigar. . . . But whatever his mood he was always the supreme personality of the place. He created it and it seemed empty without him.[45]

This is perceptive, true, and deeply felt and here we have the inward-looking Reddie, the king of his castle, unable to give to, and receive full adult affection from, either men or women, proud, orphaned, and didactic. This is not Reddie the Socialist who lived in the miner's cottage or who planned for the revolution that would end the injustices of private property. Reddie the opponent of the conventional public school was not greatly sympathetic to or interested in popular education and the emerging structure of the Local Education Authorities and the Board of Education in 1902 or the growth of the civic universities. To be sure he had ideas about these things, or some of them, as his evidence to the Bryce Commission clearly shows.[46] But he gave no thought to Abbotsholme in its national educational context. He rejected any federal associations with Bedales or with Clayesmore, founded in 1896.

This man was the progenitor of modern progressive education in this country, the Tory radical, the Platonist who believed in the dignity of labour, the progressive who abhorred co-education for adolescents despite some latter-day qualifications, who slandered England and her public schools from 'an educational laboratory' in south-west Derbyshire which during his headship of thirty-eight years only once had more than sixty boys on the roll at the beginning of a term.

[45] G. H. Dixon, 'Cecil Reddie', in *Fifty Years of Abbotsholme*, p. 9.
[46] See *Abbotsholme*, pp. 151–92.

Chapter Fourteen

J. H. BADLEY AND BEDALES

I

JOHN HADEN BADLEY was born in Dudley, near Birmingham, in 1865, the youngest in a family of four. His father was a well-respected and comfortably successful doctor who had inherited a prosperous practice from his father.[1] Still earlier generations had been doctors but more remote ancestors had been Staffordshire farmers and small land-owners. Badley remembers his father as a man who spent little time with his children, and whose reserve was somewhat forbidding. At meal times and very occasionally at Christmas or some such season they saw him and talked with him — on the occasion that Badley reports his father as going on holiday with the family, he stayed for only two days and 'it was something of a relief when the visit was over'. Recollecting in tranquillity, Badley speaks with affection and respect of the unpretentious goodness of his father in his care of poor patients and his forbearance with his son who showed no wish to study medicine. Had Badley senior had his own choice of career he would have become a lawyer, but he acceded to his father's wish that he should come in as an assistant in the medical practice. He made no such request of his own son and being also a good business man who invested in land and property he was able to offer John Haden the opportunities of life at Rugby and Cambridge. When Badley senior died he divided his possessions equally between his four children and

[1] Biographical material is based mainly on J. H. Badley, *Memories and Reflections*, and on written records provided by Mr. R. A. Wake, H.M.I., who was Senior History Master at Bedales during the 1950s. In addition I had a number of conversations with Mr. Badley at Bedales in Nov. 1962 and later. At ninety-seven years of age then, his memory was astonishingly accurate as subsequent checking has revealed.

J. H. Badley writing long afterwards said: 'It was his business ability and the value of the property he left that eventually made possible the building of Bedales.'[2]

Mrs. Badley was a woman of sincere, evangelical Christian convictions who, in the first ten years in particular of her son's life gave him and his sisters a secure and reasonable upbringing. The migraines which affected her earlier in life made her into a semi-invalid later, but Badley recalls the contrast between her lively temperament and his father's restraint. She introduced the children to painting and sketching, to literature, and to music. Like many families, they acted in charades and made up their own dramatic entertainments, although the theatre for Mrs. Badley was forbidden territory. However, there were family readings of Longfellow, Tennyson, Bunyan, Shakespeare, Dickens, and Scott. All the children were 'great readers' and their father usually gave them well chosen books as birthday and Christmas presents. They also painted a great deal and the children wrote many vivid stories which they read in secret to one another.

On Sundays Mrs. Badley took them to church, but Dr. Badley did not accompany them although he conducted daily family prayers. Writing nearly seventy years later, Badley concluded that his father probably believed in the ethic of Christianity but not in its theology: 'We should now find ourselves much in sympathy.'[3] The children learned by heart passages from the Bible and collects and on Sundays they were expected to spend much of the day in the drawing room in the company of improving books.

There were few visitors of any kind to the Badleys' comfortable home, and fewer still who were contemporaries of the children. At Christmas there was a day-long party and in the summer Mrs. Badley took her son and his two elder sisters on holiday to a house not far away on the edge of the industrial Midlands, given to the family much earlier by a grateful patient. Here John Haden met two boy cousins with whom he climbed, swam, learned to shoot (though he refused to hunt and wound animals) and to ride a penny-farthing, and with whom later he rowed in three days from Oxford to London Bridge.

As his mother became more of an invalid, nurses and governesses took over the care of the children. John Haden did not go to school

[2] J. H. Badley, *Memories and Reflections* (London, 1955), p. 19.
[3] Ibid., p. 22.

until 1878, when he was thirteen years of age. Until that time he was taught the basic skills at home and built up a considerable love for history, literature, and the visual arts, together with the necessary knowledge and accuracy in arithmetic. Rather unexpectedly Dr. Badley and his wife gave their children a sound basis in human and animal physiology, illustrated by the doctor's dissections and instruction from the skeleton. When a cat gave birth to kittens on a cushion on John Haden's knees, to his undisguised astonishment, Mrs. Badley gave the children a clear and simple account of conception and parturition: 'From this memory grew, in due course the resolve that such knowledge should be given in a straightforward manner ... to those, boys and girls alike, under my charge.'[4] In addition Dr. Badley gave instruction in general science and in astronomy, often choosing his gifts of books in relation to these.

II

After this sheltered childhood young Badley went at the age of thirteen to a preparatory boarding school where he had two years which 'were the only period in my life that gives me little or no pleasure to look back upon'. At the age of fifteen he went straight into the Upper School at Rugby and he was Head of his House for three years. There were more periods of Greek and Latin in the curriculum than of all the other subjects added together, there was no spoken French, modern history was taught perfunctorily as compared with ancient history, and science was optional. Art, craft, and music were just beginning as free time pursuits. Much that Badley experienced at Rugby constricted his interests and he doubted the wisdom then and later of subjecting average or poor students to the classical routines.

Nevertheless Badley was a good student who did outstandingly well at Rugby. He gained the top leaving exhibition in classics and in 1884 went as a scholar to Trinity College, Cambridge, although the school advised that he go to Oxford. His credentials as a 'swot' at Rugby were therefore unimpeachable, but in addition he gained a football cap as a member of the school Rugby XV and so he was also a 'swell'. 'For the self-reliant, whether scholarly or athletic, and most of all for

---

[4] *Memories and Reflections*, p. 25.

those happy few who combined all these qualities, it was a good school, if a hard one.'⁵

During his vacations Badley had learned to climb and swim and row and sail. Encouraged by the wise freedom offered by his parents he travelled round England and the Continent with a tutor and later with his sisters. The Cambridge undergraduate had all the advantages that considerate Victorian parents could make possible from their position of quiet affluence.

At Cambridge, Badley read classics for his Tripos and gained a First. He formed the interests in music, the theatre, literature, religion, politics, and travel which were common to an intelligent, enlightened, and comfortably off undergraduate at that time. One of his closest friends was Edmund Garrett, a President of the Union, who interested Badley in politics and social questions generally and whose sister Badley later married. He came to know Roger Fry, Lowes Dickinson, and the writings of Edward Carpenter whom he afterwards met. In literature Shelley, Tennyson, Browning, Swinburne, Rossetti, Hugo, and Walt Whitman all appealed to his developed love of poetry. He once heard Ruskin lecturing at Oxford towards the end of his career there and although he struck Badley as ranting somewhat, his prose writings on art and social questions greatly impressed the young man. For a while William Morris's poetry engaged Badley's interest, but later it was displaced by his prose writings on socialism and the rediscovery of art and community.

When Badley got his First after three years he was attracted by the prospect of taking a fourth year at Cambridge in order to gain a Fellowship. But he now felt the specialism of the classics to be a heavy yoke and decided to spend the fourth year reading in subjects of his own choosing. He read some modern history, some social and political theory, philosophy, English and German literature, and turned his back on the Fellowship. He had ideas of becoming a classical master in a public school, probably eventually at Rugby, but a short period of temporary teaching in Bedford finally confirmed his dissatisfaction with this career. Badley left Cambridge in the summer of 1888 bearing the imprint of many experiences the significance of which resonates through his later life.

Of his classical training Badley said : 'It was a great experience for its

⁵ Ibid., p. 48. A full account of his life at Rugby can also be found in his book *A Schoolmaster's Testament* (Oxford, 1937), pp. 12–25.

own sake and for the lasting gains that it left . . . an experience for which I have always been profoundly thankful in spite of the cost . . . exacted by the classical education of those days.'[6] It is no surprise, therefore, to find in the first Bedales prospectus :

> We had better give up the idea that Latin is studied at school for the sake of the literature. Not one boy in ten ever reached at school the point at which it becomes literature to him, or goes on to it afterwards. . . . For the other nine the main value of Latin is in the process of language-study, and the literary value must be brought to them in readings, stories, translations, plays. This admitted, Latin will hold a much smaller place in school-work [at Bedales] for most boys than hitherto. But it should have a place for all.[7]

Cambridge had greatly changed his outlook upon religion, for instead of the evangelical beliefs of his childhood or the formal Anglicanism of his years at Rugby, 'Henceforward, what I felt to be real and all-important in religion was . . . not to be found in the doctrinal framework of the Church.'[8]

The 1892 Bedales prospectus says :

> . . . Of religious teaching, if religious teaching means Jewish history, collect-learning, the critical study of a Greek text, or insistence upon certain 'religious' forms, there will be little. If it means all such teaching as may make us understand better and wish and strive more earnestly for what we daily pray for, 'Thy Kingdom come, Thy will be done', there will (it is hoped) be little else.[9]

III

An undergraduate who had a fine academic record at Rugby and Cambridge and who rejected the opportunity to be considered for a Fellowship ; who could not conscientiously go on to teach classics at a public school both because he no longer thought classics a suitable study for other than a small minority of boys, and because he could no longer accept much of what the public schools stood for ; who rejected traditional Christianity but whose spiritual conviction revealed him as more than an ethical humanist — such a man represents a cast of mind that was not uncommon in the eighties of the last century. Although

[6] *Memories and Reflections,* p. 88.   [7] Cambridge, 1892, p. 11.
[8] *Memories and Reflections,* p. 99.   [9] p. 16.

the writings of Carlyle, Ruskin, Morris, and Edward Carpenter influenced Badley greatly, he did not join the Fellowship of the New Life or the Fabian Society or later the Independent Labour Party or the Labour Party. Instead he attended meetings, read books and pamphlets, talked with many of the leaders and attracted the interest of others. For instance, after Badley met Edward Carpenter at Abbotsholme, Carpenter was almost a termly visitor to Bedales for a time, finding what Badley was doing more acceptable than what Reddie was doing; Ramsay MacDonald sent two of his children to Bedales after the First World War. Badley met the Webbs, Shaw, Wells and has recorded that, although not a member of the party, he was in full sympathy with the Labour movement.

A careful reading of Badley's memoirs and further discussion with him of his political position show the changes in his alignments over a long life. In his early days and through much of his time at Cambridge like many a Rugbeian he thought of himself as a Liberal Imperialist of the Rosebery school belonging to a nation which had conquered an Empire which it now had the privilege and the duty to rule and lead. At home his liberalism led him to seek to improve the lot of the poor by educational and social action, to reduce class distinctions, to extend the franchise. By the end of his time at Cambridge in 1888 he had become the kind of vague socialist which, essentially, he has remained:

> Edward Carpenter was at heart an anarchist in the exact meaning of that term, with no connotation of violence. Through him ... I learnt to distrust any system involving more than a minimum of State control to ensure ... freedom, equality of opportunity and treatment and methods of production in which the common benefit should not be subordinated to private profit.[10]

He says that, although he consistently voted Labour, he did not join a party 'whose aims in its earlier days seemed limited to furthering a particular class-interest'.[11]

Amy Garrett, whom he married in the autumn of 1892, was a champion of women's rights who was later prepared to join the activist wing of the suffragette movement, but her poor health made this impossible. Badley supported his wife in her concern for women's rights, although he did not approve of her becoming a militant. After

[10] Ibid., p. 306.   [11] Ibid., p. 307.

K

1893, when he opened Bedales, he had a public reputation to consider as well as a personal and somewhat generalized political loyalty, and he maintained that a headmaster aiming at encouraging children to think for themselves should not have a particular political or religious label. Carpenter's community anarchism probably attracted him more as a moral affirmation than as an expression of a well grounded political and economic theory. Badley decided to make his moral affirmation in terms of a school and so to show what life between persons should or could be like : 'Every school is, consciously or not, an embodiment of social aims, and it was by making Bedales a working model of what a community should be that I thought I could do most to realize mine.'[12]

IV

However, to return to Badley going down from Cambridge in 1888 knowing only that he did not want to be a classics don or a public-school master, feeling intensely moved at leaving the University which had meant so much to him, and without a clear idea of what to do with his life. He says of this period : 'Of all that has been of greatest value in my life — friendships, marriage, an absorbing lifework and the powers and aims that shaped it — there is little that had not its roots in those four years at Cambridge.'[13]

But in July 1888, having missed his final summer term at Trinity by teaching as a replacement for a sick master at Bedford, he had only the friendships, the hope of marriage, and no settled career to go on. He spent the winter and spring in Germany developing his knowledge of the language, the literature, and the social and political thought of that country. In the early summer of 1889 his old Cambridge friend Lowes Dickinson wrote to him of a new venture, a school in which he might be interested. Dickinson mentioned that Edward Carpenter was working with others in planning this new venture and that in itself was an attraction. Badley read the preliminary statements about the school and he came hurrying back to consult the new head, and was appointed to teach mainly history and French and later, of course, classics. He was to be given board and lodging and paid 'a living wage', for this was an educational venture supported by impecunious Socialists to do unorthodox things. But Badley had his private income and the low pay did not bother him. He spent the summer in

[12] *Memories and Reflections*, p. 307.   [13] Ibid., p. 320.

France improving his spoken French; and in October 1889 he began
to teach in the New School in Derbyshire which at last gave him
unwavering assurance of where his career was to be found. Cecil
Reddie and Abbotsholme needed a man like Badley to bring boundless
energy, academic excellence, and a fresh, critical mind to bear on
educational theory and practice. He needed Badley for the pedigree
of Rugby, Cambridge, classical scholarship, and for his quiet moderation: 'I have an innate distrust of extremes both in ideas and expression of them, which inclines me always to take a middle course.'[14]

Equally, Badley needed Reddie and Abbotsholme to launch him on
the career that led to his life's work at Bedales: 'Abbotsholme was the
most momentous turning point in my life. . . . But for my marriage I
should not have wished to leave the surroundings in which I had first
found myself.'[15]

Badley considered Reddie a man of great gifts and originality to
whom he owed much, both as a master-craftsman in the classroom and
as a daring thinker. Undoubtedly Reddie was the first to give form and
expression to a new radicalism in education, and Badley was for two
and a half years his disciple, helper, and critic. In the first Bedales
prospectus he acknowledges this:

> The present scheme seeks to embody ideas on which most exponents
> of the modern scientific view of education are agreed, and to embody
> these ideas in practical methods suggested by the writer's experience
> of the New School, Abbotsholme, at which he has been an Assistant
> Master from its foundation to the present year, and to which he
> wishes to acknowledge his deep obligation.[16]

Badley had asked Reddie if he could bring back his wife, whom he
proposed to marry in the summer of 1892, to live with him in Abbotsholme, and this Reddie did not want. He had no suitable accommodation and he preferred bachelor masters who could give unstinted
service to the school, as he did himself, without the demands made on a
man by his wife or by his children. It is probable that by 1892 Badley
had gained sufficient confidence and experience to wish to be independent of a despot like Reddie, whom he remembered as the most
striking example of a teacher whose personality so completely domi-
nates and moulds his pupils (and his staff) that they are apt to lose
their individuality. Badley always maintained that Reddie was right
in his educational aims and much of his practice, but wrong in his

[14] *Memories and Reflections*, p. 318.   [15] Ibid., pp. 320–1.   [16] Ibid., p. 1.

understanding of the community. For Badley, autocracy in a school, as in a state, stood condemned by its long-term if not also by its short-term results, and he claimed that he had learned from Reddie how to think about and conduct a school and, hardly less, how *not* to.

V

The contrast of temperaments and experience between these two major figures in modern educational innovation when summed up are striking. Reddie, the sixth of ten children, had lost his mother when he was eight years old and his father when he was twelve, after which the large family had been scattered to relations. He had grown up in a Scottish public school and had a distinguished academic record as a scientist at a Scottish and a German university. After some fumbling he had settled on his career, had been attracted by the same kind of Socialism as Badley, had taught briefly in two public schools, and then saw his course clear before him. By dominant energy he brought Abbotsholme into being when he was thirty-one years of age, having very little money of his own, but possessing and publicizing a massive and sometimes comically precise rationale of the theory and practice of education. He remained the owner and head of Abbotsholme, didactic, autocratic, the captain with subordinates. He had a commanding presence and a strong and attractive personality, apparently confident in all company. He was a bachelor who was courteous to women, but who seldom understood them and later developed some crankish antipathies to them.

Badley was the only son with three elder sisters ; and his parents, his sisters, and his wife gave him secure affection throughout, although his mother was a semi-invalid through his late childhood and his father's was not an outgoing temperament. Badley says of himself that he has been plagued by diffidence and shyness and that he inherited his father's intensely reserved nature. We have already commented upon Badley's preference for control and moderation and one of his earliest pupils gives us a glimpse of this. 'For Mr. Badley I have awe and reverence. To most of the subjects he taught he gave an interest, which, for me, was a kind of suspended excitement; his presence always made me nervous, but often pleasurably so.'[17]

[17] E. L. Grant Watson, 'Pioneers', in *The Old School*, ed. Graham Greene (London, 1934), p. 219.

Where Reddie had a fine academic record as a scientist, Badley's distinction was as a classic. Badley remained in politics sympathetic to the Left. Reddie, after a decade in contact with the Fellowship of the New Life and the early Fabians, rejected their egalitarian ideas, and concentrated on the sons of the directing classes although he rejected equally the plutocracy. Professor Findlay in his obituary of Reddie said '. . . for Labour or Liberal politics . . . he had no use'.[18]

Badley was comfortably off, although he spent his own money (and more than once was supported by the generosity of his sisters) freely on Bedales. Reddie also spent a great deal of his own money on Abbotsholme but he had no private income to devote to the cause. Each of them was the legal owner of his school, Reddie for thirty-seven years and Badley, later in conjunction with his wife and two sisters, for forty years. Only when Abbotsholme was threatened with extinction in 1927 and Reddie at the age of sixty-eight was the only teacher left, with two pupils, did he consent to make the school over to a committee of old boys who found a new headmaster, formed a limited company, and saved the school. Badley had resolved to retire in 1935 at the age of seventy; and to prepare for it a limited company, largely made up of Old Bedalians, was formed in 1933 when the school was thriving and had one hundred and fifty pupils.

Badley often asserted that his ideas on the development of Bedales came from the principle of free growth. The first school prospectus suggests, however, that Badley had many clear ideas on what he wanted :

> The first lesson a child must learn is absolute obedience to authority. Then, by calling reason and affection into play, obedience becomes rational and willing, and the learner becomes in some degree a teacher, and can be trusted with a measure of direction. The day must be full of occupation . . . but there must also be times without a fixed occupation for individual tastes to assert themselves and for self-development.[19]

Colin Sharp, Reddie's successor, said of him,

> His way was not to state problems and leave them open for the boys' solution, but directly or indirectly to lead the boy to the solution which he himself held and not to tolerate any other. . . . Opposition made him all the stronger in compelling boys and staff and even parents to conform to the framework of his organization.[20]

[18] *Manchester Guardian*, 9 Feb. 1932. [19] Prospectus, 14.
[20] B. M. Ward, *Reddie of Abbotsholme* (London, 1934), pp. 309–10.

This seems to be the universal opinion together with a general agreement on the magnetism of the man. Badley, in a recorded conversation in 1962, said he thought Reddie was something of a Prussian, and that Abbotsholme was a one-man school in a way that Bedales was not. Abbotsholme found itself associated with an authoritarian and hierarchical political and social ideal, but Bedales aimed at an increasing freedom and equality under Badley; and Alex Devine the headmaster of Clayesmore, a flamboyant personality, bore this out when he wrote in 1903:

> The attitude of [Abbotsholme] has always been that of 'the new education'. Its headmaster ... takes his stand on the platform of 'There is but one Education, the new Education, and Reddie is its prophet' ... Badley has a much broader mind than Reddie can claim, and he has far too sane and comprehensive an outlook to do extravagant things. ... I know no school in England so absolutely interesting [as Bedales].[21]

A final point of comparison and contrast between the two men is in their approach to religion. Each was unorthodox in that neither belonged to any branch of the Church, though each was Christian in sympathy. Whereas Reddie was interested in symbolism and mysticism, as his appreciation of Blake, Maitland, and the writings of the Eastern religions shows, Badley said, in connection with the Blake studies of his colleague, Joseph Wicksteed, that symbolism, in Blake or elsewhere, had little magic for him.

Yet, when all is said it was Reddie who focussed Badley's ideas, it was Reddie who sparked off the potential in Badley which led to Bedales. It was Badley's more stable temperament and restraint, as well as his originality and determination, that gave Bedales the steady understanding it needed and it was Reddie's penetrating but imperious cast of mind that created and nearly ruined Abbotsholme.

Reddie regarded the foundation of Bedales in 1893 as an act of betrayal, despite Badley's acknowledgements to him and to Abbotsholme. The two men met only once after that, about thirty years later, at a conference at which they were both speaking, and Badley says that Reddie was then mellow, kind, and courteous. On the occasion of Abbotsholme's fiftieth anniversary in 1939, Badley returned to Abbotsholme and wrote in the Jubilee volume:

[21] In a letter dated Jan. 1903 to Dr. Edward Lyttleton then head of Haileybury.

... I can look back as one of those who knew its first beginnings and shared the glad feeling of creative activity under ideal conditions that was to spread so far and open a new era in education. .... It was [Reddie's] vision, worked out by one who had something of real genius ... that has made Abbotsholme a model from which so many 'New Schools' of different types have derived their general pattern and their inspiration.[22]

VI

Although John Haden Badley claimed with justification that throughout his time at Bedales he aimed at continuously increasing the areas of freedom and equality for pupils and staff and that he was not an autocrat, it is not without significance that his unofficial title was 'the Chief'. In its practices Bedales contrives to be decentralized, but the fact has to be admitted that Badley founded the school and controlled and ran it for forty-three years of its entire seventy-six years of existence.

Bedales can point to an extraordinary longevity and stability in a proportion of the teaching staff in the first fifty years. Badley served for over forty years and his second master Oswald Powell went to the school only a few months after Badley and left in 1933. Basil Gimson taught mathematics and many other things for thirty-three years, Geoffrey Crump taught English for twenty-six years, and T. J. Garstang taught mathematics for twenty-five years, Miss Thorp was matron for thirty years, and Mrs. Fish head of Bedales Junior House at Dunhurst for twenty-two years.

However, when a man is the first to promote a really lasting co-educational boarding school in England, when he is regarded from time to time in common gossip as a progenitor of socialism, atheism, unlimited freedom for children, sexual precocity, and the subversion of patriotism, when he is also the owner of the school — when such a man appoints and holds a staff which builds the reputation of the school high in public regard, institutional factors are not enough to account for it all. In 1958 a pupil at Bedales visited Badley when he was ninety-three and her words are fitting conclusion of this brief sketch of the founder of the school:

It is hard to realize that this frail but still incredibly active old man ... is entirely responsible for the origin of Bedales. Bedales is not something inevitable in the history of education ... [it] is no

[22] *Fifty Years of Abbotsholme 1889–1939*, pp. 56–57.

longer very revolutionary (because the outside world has caught up with it) but it is still unique.

He is an old man, so old that he seems once more to be young. . . . The Chief is wearing old, grey flannel trousers, an open-necked and comfortably crumpled shirt, a tweed jacket and white gym-shoes; by his side is a dark liquorice-brown walking stick which his thin hand grasps firmly. His skin is brown in patches and freckled; his white hair is fine and wispy; a sparse beard decorates with the moth-like touch of an impressionist's brush his mouth and chin. A pair of delicate gold-rimmed spectacles bridges his prominent nose. Super-flous flesh has disappeared from his face, leaving the handsome bone-structure visible.[23]

John Haden Badley enabled others to join in building Bedales with him, while no one could stay at Abbotsholme with Cecil Reddie for more than a few years.

VII

When Badley retired in 1935 after forty-three years as headmaster Frederic Alfred Meier was appointed as his successor and remained headmaster until 1946 when he retired at the age of fifty-nine to go to the University of London Institute of Education as a Senior Lecturer in Physical Sciences concerned with training teachers of physics. Meier was trained as an engineer who, besides graduating with high distinction at the University of London, served his apprenticeship in 1906–07 in a shipbuilding yard. In 1907 he went on to Cambridge to take Mathematics in Part I of his Tripos and Natural Sciences in Part II, again graduating with distinction. It was in 1910 that his teaching career began and he served at Glenalmond and Marlborough before going to Badley's old school Rugby in 1914. He went to Bedales in 1935 after a career at Rugby as head of the Science Department which made his name widely known as an outstanding teacher of physics.

Badley said that it might appear to be strange to choose a man as headmaster who had no previous experience of a progressive school and even more odd to choose a public school master who had no personal knowledge of co-education. However, an Old Bedalian had been head of the Science Department at Rugby before Meier, with whom he worked for some years as a colleague. It was felt by the Bedales Governors that the appeal should be spread as widely as

[23] *Bedales Chronicle*, vol. 42, no. 8, June 1958, pp. 1–2.

possible and that when a good candidate who had no experience of progressive education offered himself he should be asked why he wished to run the possible risk of moving away from the kind of school with which he was familiar and in which he might be expected to rise to the top. In this way the choice was as extended as it could be and it was seen that Meier well understood what was involved, and he and Mrs. Meier served the school well for eleven years.

The same pattern reappeared when Hector Beaumont Jacks was appointed in 1946. Mr. Jacks was an Oxford classic with experience at Wellington College and other public schools and at the Junior School of Cheltenham College and another preparatory school. He had no previous direct contact with a progressive or a co-educational school. Again the Governors looked for the best candidate, satisfying themselves that he understood what he was undertaking and letting Bedales teach him the rest. Mr. Jacks retired in 1962 and his successor, Mr. Timothy Slack, is a Wykehamist who read Modern Greats at Oxford and taught at Repton; but unorthodoxy appears in a period of service at Salem, the German school on which Gordonstoun is modelled, and in another period of work in Burma.

Badley enjoyed his retirement without coming back into school affairs. Where Reddie had to be persuaded against his will to give up when ruin stared Abbotsholme in the face, Badley made arrangements to retire at seventy and kept to them. The confidence and gratitude were such that a few years ago, after the death of Mrs. Badley, the Bedales Governors provided a flat for Mr. Badley attached to the school sanatorium where he lived until his death aged one hundred and two early in March 1967, a revered and almost legendary figure whose vast span of experience gave a sense of depth and stability to the first seventy-five years of the school's existence.

Chapter Fifteen

A. S. NEILL AND SUMMERHILL

I

BOTH Reddie and Badley had been educated at a public school, one in
Scotland and one in England. Despite being orphaned from an early
age, Reddie grew up as Badley did in a middle-class surrounding and
each had a highly successful university career straight from school.
A. S. Neill had a different start in life and has remained a different kind
of influence in progressive education from his first entry. Both the
older men had established their reputations as educational radicals by
the end of the century and Neill did not start his life work, for reasons
which will appear, until after the end of the First World War. He was
twenty-five years younger than Reddie, he started Summerhill thirty-
five years after Abbotsholme, about three years before Reddie's
retirement. This third educational innovator comes from a different
generation and he has remained for more than forty years true to a set
of educational ideas not only much more extreme than Reddie's or
Badley's, but more radical than those of any other educator in England
at any time.[1]

II

Neill was born near Forfar in the east of Scotland in 1883 in a
family of eight surviving children. His father was a village schoolmaster in Kingsmuir on a salary of about £120 a year and life was very
simple and pleasures few — an annual school picnic in farm carts and a
winter social. Neill says that the children had no pocket money and on
market days they tried to pick up a copper or two by holding farmers'

---

[1] The account of Neill's life which follows is based on his account 'My Scholastic
Life' in the Summerhill periodical *Id*, nos. 2–7, Sept. 1960–Oct. 1961. I have also
drawn on a recorded conversation which I had with Neill (he prefers the plain
surname) in Oct. 1962 and on other sources which are acknowledged in the text.

horses. Neill was at this time a poor scholar who could not really bring his mind to bear on classroom tasks, although he enjoyed practical work and mechanical problems. His father cuffed him often because he could not or would not learn and as the schoolmaster's salary was paid on the basis of 'payment by results', his impatience with the only member of his family who did not pass on to Forfar Academy was understandable.

At fourteen years of age Neill started as a clerk in a gas meter factory in Edinburgh 70 miles from his home, in lodgings and lonely, miserable and homesick. After pleadings and promise of diligence he returned home to study for the junior grades of the civil service, but he could not keep to his resolve and was sent to work in a Forfar draper's from 8 a.m. to 8 p.m. on week-days and till 10 p.m. on Saturdays. After a period at this job the boy was clearly overtaxed and his father and mother decided that they had better try to make him a teacher. 'It's about the only thing he's fit for', was his father's comment according to Neill. He started as a pupil teacher in his father's school and he served the usual period of four years before taking the competitive examination for entry to what was then a Normal School and would now be called a College of Education. Neill tells us that there were one hundred and four entrants and he came one hundred and third and returned to the ranks of ex-pupil teachers as those who failed to enter the Normal School were called.

The only way to adequate qualification, as his full-time training at the Normal School had been refused, was to study part-time for the Acting Teacher's Certificate while working during the day in school. He says that he had three years in a school in Fife which were, to him, misery, for he did not like his headmaster or his draconian discipline. The village minister taught him Greek and lent him books by the classic authors and poets and for a variety of reasons Neill developed a burning desire to improve his own education. He had passed the Acting Teacher's Certificate in the third class and found his intellectual ambitions leading him towards the university. By further part-time study he passed the university entrance examination, thereby becoming a fully certificated teacher. After two much happier years in another school, he entered Edinburgh University, starting by studying chemistry and natural philosophy, but changing his course to the honours school of English, working under George Saintsbury and editing the university magazine, though Neill would characteristically reverse the order. He got a second class degree in 1912 and declares that he was a conventional young Tory with no convictions about education and no desire to re-enter teaching but rather to become an author. He got a job with an Edinburgh publishing firm and worked as a sub-editor on a one-volume encyclopaedia and later transferred to London to write sections on English language and literature and mathematics in another of the firm's publications, *Jack's Self Educator*. In 1913 he was engaged as art editor to a new publication, *The Piccadilly Magazine*, where he enjoyed the whole creative business of producing a new journal. But war broke out, the journal never appeared and the staff was dismissed. At the age of thirty-one Neill returned to Scotland and applied for a post at a school in Gretna Green where he had served as a pupil teacher. This time he was appointed headmaster and began seriously to think about education.

The boys and girls he was teaching in the village school were mostly destined for farmwork or domestic service and the formal curriculum seemed to Neill irrelevant. So began his interest in the kind of thing children ought to be asked to do in school. In a rural setting of the Lowlands, where country conservatism was blended with the Scottish veneration for knowledge and schooling, Neill began to experiment with play methods and he says his discipline began to become slack. He sums up the hostility of a number of the parents in the words of one of them: 'I send my laddie to the school to learn, no' to mak' snowmen.'[2]

Neill was and remains a skilled journalist and all the way through his educational life he has written of his experiences in one form or another. He wrote two near-novels about his Scottish experience, the first *A Dominie's Log* and later *A Dominie Dismissed*. The first book is an imagined account of a young graduate teaching in an unorthodox way in a village school and in *A Dominie Dismissed* the teacher is forced out of his job by dissatisfied parents, seeks to enlist in the army, is found to be unfit and ordered to live an open-air life. The dominie returns as a cattleman to the village where formerly he had been the schoolmaster, witnesses the discomfiture of his successor, a conventional disciplinarian, and finds the friendship and support of the children freely given to him. Finally, he marries Margaret Thomson, a simple, uneducated girl, who attended the dominie's evening classes and who is the daughter of the farmer he works for. His fictional account of the

[2] *Id*, 2 Sept. 1960, p. 4.

Gretna Green freedom is summed up in various parts of the two books, in each of which visitors or natives are tools for the dominie's spate of wisdom and humane speculation and in which the children are natural, shrewd moving, and impish when given their freedom by the dominie and lumpish, cowed and dull when they are with his successor, the well-meaning, efficient disciplinarian Macdonald. The pawky Scots sentimentalism makes these books a plain man's *Émile* and the didactic destruction of culture, discipline, convention and timidity make them a *Candide* without style :

> I don't suppose any of you understand why I am going away, but I'll try to tell you. I have been dismissed by your fathers and mothers. I haven't been a good teacher, they say ; I have allowed you too much freedom. I have taken you out sketching and fishing and playing ; I have let you read what you liked, let you do what you liked. I haven't taught you enough. . . . Bairns, I don't want to leave you at all ; you are mine, you know, and the school is ours. You and I made the gardens and rockeries ; we dug the pond and we caught the trout and minnows and planted the water-plants. We built the pigeon-loft and the rabbit-hutch. We fed our pets together.[3]

After the war Neill produced *A Dominie Abroad* about his school at Hellerau in Austria and in 1920 *A Dominie in Doubt* appeared, dedicated to Homer Lane 'whose first lecture convinced me I knew nothing about education'. In the customary expository, humorous, conversational style of the books, the dominie says in *A Dominie in Doubt* :

> As a work on education the *Log* isn't worth a damn. . . . I say that because when I wrote it I knew nothing about the most important factor in education — the psychology of children . . . I was looking at children from a grown-up point of view. I thought of them as they affected me, instead of as they affected themselves. . . . If your aim is to make boys joiners and girls cooks . . . cookery and woodwork ought to be chucked out of schools. . . . Creation and self-expression are the only things that matter in education. I don't care what a child is doing in the way of creation whether he is making tables, or porridge, or sketches or snowballs. . . . There is more education in making a snowball than in listening to an hour's lecture on grammar. . . . Making snowballs is nearer to true education than the spoon-feeding we call education to-day.[4]

[3] A. S. Neill, *A Dominie Dismissed*, p. 10.
[4] A. S. Neill, *A Dominie in Doubt* (London, 1920), pp. 12–15.

To return from this digression on the *Dominie* books to the main biographical line. Even though Neill was not dismissed from Gretna Green some of the parents were undoubtedly hostile to his methods and outlook and in 1915 Neill says that he began to feel guilty about not volunteering for war service and he applied to join the army. Some years before he had been treated for phlebitis and he now found himself rejected on medical grounds. However, a few months later when manpower needs were far more severe and conscription was introduced Neill found himself classed as A1, and was called up. As a second-lieutenant in the artillery he was posted to Trowbridge, where he instructed gunners in mathematics and did not serve abroad. We mentioned earlier the lady in Hampstead who, according to Neill, wrote him a fan-letter after reading his two *Dominie* books, enclosing a copy of one of Homer Lane's lectures. From Trowbridge, Neill arranged to travel to Cerne Abbas to see the Little Commonwealth at work and so began a friendship which Neill acknowledges as one of the most important in his life. Not only did he see a free community at work, he was introduced to psychology by Lane and discovered Freud, and this marks the change between the tone of the first two *Dominie* books and *A Dominie Abroad* and *A Dominie in Doubt*, the two post-war publications.

Before he was demobilised the Little Commonwealth had been closed and Neill's hope of returning to teach there was dashed. By now he was clear that he wanted to devote his energies to educational innovation and he did not want to return to the restrictions of maintained education or the censoriousness of unsympathetic parents in a village. The lady from Hampstead who wrote the fan-letter enabled Neill to take up a post at King Alfred School, his first experience of a private, progressive school. We have already noted his criticisms of John Russell, the headmaster who was just reaching the end of his career, 'a kindly, humane soul one could not help loving'. After experience of Homer Lane, Neill found Russell and King Alfred's with its governing committee too constricting and resigned in 1920 to join Beatrice Ensor as co-editor of *The New Era* at the time of the foundation of the New Education Fellowship:

> I was always critical of this body; to me it seemed too much to sit on the fence, but it had a very difficult task. Its members were of different races and religions and it had to study their feelings, and also it strove, rightly, to make the new education part of the State

system. I thought that it gradually became conservative and timid. I attended its international conference at Calais in 1921 and from there went to lecture in Salzburg and thence to stay with friends in Hellerau near Dresden in South-East Germany.[5]

In the aftermath of the War Neill helped Mrs. Ensor to bring refugee children across to Holland and at Hellerau decided to set up an international school in a building which had been built for a Dalcroze establishment. Neill found one section of the building being used as a school for local children, a second as a centre for eurhythmics, and it was the third that the international section was to use. He recalls that he had £400 saved and that this was riches at a time when the value of the mark was desperately low. It was characteristic of the internationalism of the N.E.F. that they should be active in relief work with children in Germany itself and of Neill's compassion that he was prepared not only to work, but to live in Germany and Austria for four years, two years after the end of the War. There were many nationalities in the school and Neill began to put into practice the theories of freedom which he had advocated for so long.

When his international school joined with the German division the theoretical and practical differences produced immediate friction. Neill's version is that the Germans took their moral duties seriously and did not drink or smoke or go to cinemas so as not to be a cause of stumbling to their pupils. Neill calls this character moulding and it is a term of abuse which appears in his writings frequently. In the evenings the children in his section at Hellerau would dance to gramophone records but the children under the German staff would be listening to Goethe or Nietzsche (or so Neill reports). While he thought this pitiful, he became very much aware of good music, art and philosophy which his cultivated German colleagues took for granted but which had been very little in evidence in Neill's world up to that time. But we shall have more to say later about his attitude to what is loosely called culture.

The political and economic tensions of the early 1920s increased when the French occupied the Ruhr in an attempt to enforce reparations payments, and the United States and Great Britain dissociated themselves from the French policy. In 1923 there was the abortive *Putsch* of the National Socialist German Workers party in Munich and

---

[5] *Id*, 3 Oct. 1960, p. 4. For an account of his thinking at the time of the existence of Hellerau see Neill's *A Dominie Abroad*.

in 1925 shots were fired in the streets of Dresden. In the alarm and
chaos which followed, Neill took his small international division to
Austria where they lived in an old monastery up the Sonntagberg
mountain in the Tirol and experienced fierce opposition from the
traditional Catholic peasantry, who found the relaxed habits, behaviour
and dress of these youngsters very shocking: 'The Roman Catholic
peasants around were the most hateful people I had met; grown up
men and women threw broken bottles into the pond we bathed in.
To them we were pagan and unwelcome foreigners.'[6]

The Austrian education authorities said that every school had to
teach religion and this Neill was determined not to do. The law was
difficult also in a number of other ways and so after seven months in
Sonntagberg Neill and his wife (he had married an Australian in
Dresden) decided to return to England and to continue their freedom
school there. Reflecting on his experience in Germany and Austria
Neill finds that he learned little from their educational theory
and practice, which in the five years after the War is not surprising.
However, his interest in psychology and particularly psychoanalysis
sharpened and he undertook analysis with Wilhelm Stekel. Neill
became very clearly aware of the direction his educational ideas had to
take and his German experience helped him to sharpen the edges of his
own position. In general, he concludes, Germans were thinking in terms
of conscious abilities of children and teaching them in terms of adult
knowledge of what children ought to know and how they ought to
behave. Neill says that he wanted to think of the unconscious, the Id,
and while this position has changed a little over the years, substantially
he maintains that viewpoint. Besides the music and the art he had
learned about and enjoyed in Germany and Austria, he recollects that
most importantly of all he returned to England a convinced internationalist for ever. 'One cannot run an international school and have
any trace of racialism and insularity.'[7] In 1924 the dominie whose
first venture out of Britain these four years in Europe had been,
returned to Lyme Regis where at short notice he was able to find a
house in which he could start with five pupils brought from Austria,
three of them on reduced fees and two of them on none. The Neills let
the house as holiday accommodation in the height of the season, and
were able to make ends meet and when their three-year lease was up
they had twenty-seven children on the roll. There was nothing

---

[6] *Id*, 3, p. 5.   [7] Ibid., p. 5.

especially memorable about the Lyme days except perhaps that 'Summerhill' was the name given to the house after Mrs. Neill's family house in Australia, and this name was taken to Leiston in Suffolk in 1927 when the present house was bought and the most widely known school of the extreme progressive group came to the location with which it has been associated for forty years.

Before we turn to more detailed consideration of Summerhill and its principles and practice it is well to recall in summary that Neill came from a poor Scottish family, did badly at school, experienced a harsh introduction to child labour at the age of fourteen and completed nearly ten years of pupil teaching before his university career. With the incidence of war his chance to settle to his life's work was delayed for another six or seven years and only at the age of thirty-five, deeply influenced by psychoanalysis, did he start at King Alfred's on the path of independent innovation in school and it was not until he was forty-one that he launched Summerhill.

III

Perhaps the easiest way to make entry to the ideas that lie behind Neill's Summerhill is to start with a brief summary of a typical day. This form has changed little in all the life of the school and certainly not in any underlying principle. Breakfast is from 8.15 to 9 a.m., lunch from 1 p.m., tea at 4 p.m. and supper early in the evening. Children and staff have a self-service arrangement, sitting down in the dining room where they wish to and Ena Neill, Neill's second wife, is in charge of the domestic arrangements. Beds are supposed to be made by 9.30, when lessons begin for those who want them. At the beginning of each term a time table is posted with class divisions according to the level of work being attempted. Younger children of about seven to nine years have a class teacher but are able to use the science room and the art room at various times. Nobody is compelled or expected to attend lessons and the afternoons are free for everyone. Neill says what they all do in the afternoon he does not know — playing games, tinkering with bicycles, listening to records, painting, walking, cycling, reading.

After 5 p.m. what might be called hobby activities in some other schools are undertaken — pottery, woodwork, photography, painting, story-telling to young children, further schoolwork for those who want it. On one night of the week, or often more, children go to the cinema ; on another there is a dance — Summerhillians claim that they are good, informal dancers ; on a third Neill or someone else may give a talk for staff and senior children ; on a fourth there may be a rehearsal for a play. Saturday is the night of the General School Meeting and Sunday usually a drama evening. The facilities for handiwork are always open and available. Bedtime is usually intended for 10 p.m. or earlier according to age.

There are as few restrictions as possible on freedom of choice at Summerhill :

> Before the war we had certain out-of-bounds rules made by the staff. Pupils were forbidden to use the front stairs and the staff lavatory ; the round lawn at the front door was out of bounds. The staff room was free from invasion. Gradually these . . . have disappeared. Gradually the staff-room furniture goes the dilapidated way of the pupils' sitting-room furniture.[8]

As Summerhill has always been badly off, the buildings and equipment have not been lavish and the treatment they get is evidence of the irresponsibility and destructiveness of children for whom Neill thinks freedom is more important than orderliness or submission.

There are other more lasting safety-prohibitions — children are not permitted to bathe unless there is a life-saver present for every six others : children under eleven are only allowed to cycle in the street if accompanied by an older person : no airguns are allowed and no climbing on roofs. Alcohol is forbidden and smoking is actively discouraged.

Moral judgements on children's behaviour are not passed and discipline is in the hands of the General School Meeting. No religious instruction is given, bad language is not encouraged but is permitted as normal, particularly in newcomers to Summerhill. Children in this co-educational school are expected to accept sexuality as a normal, liberating experience and to anticipate that in the conventional day-to-day world this open-mindedness will not necessarily be shared or understood.

Children have been known to attend no classes for terms, occasionally for years, and no one urges them to do so for they are not ready to respond, or so Neill's interpretation would run. His faith is based on the child's capability for self-direction and on the school as a com-

[8] *Id*, 7 Oct. 1961, p. 2.

munity in which the tolerance and confidence are available to make this possible. If freedom of this kind, which allows a child to be primitive without censure for as long as he feels he needs to be, is offered it makes possible an education of the feelings which is more fundamental to Neill than an education of the intellect, which can follow. This conception of education as therapy by freedom is profoundly different from most other interpretations we have so far met, though closer to what is done at Dartington than to what is done at Gordonstoun. Erich Fromm in an Introduction to the latest symposium from Neill's writings summarizes Neill's educational principles roughly as follows :[9]

1. Neill maintains a faith in 'the goodness of the child' with full potentialities to love life and be interested in it.
2. The aim of education, as of life, is to work joyfully and to find happiness.
3. Intellectual education is not enough and emotions and feelings are in educational territory.[10]
4. Education should be attuned to the psychic needs and capacities of children and this means accepting their aggression and self-centredness and not expecting maturity and altruism too early. Only so will children build up sincere values and attitudes and avoid hypocrisy.
5. Fear creates hostility, and discipline and punishment create fear. The adult exercising authority and enforcing discipline will distance himself from children.
6. Any respect between teacher and child must be mutual. If a teacher does not use force against a child, the child must learn that he has no right to do violence to the teacher and intrude upon the adult and expect to be attended to just because he is a child. Compassion and sympathy are all very well in Neill's psychological world, but they have to be realistic and two-way and this is his interpretation of the cliché that freedom does not mean licence.
7. If these qualities are sought for in the pupils they have no less to be part of the teacher. Neill says that in 40 years he has never lied to a child, and even if one re-phrases this to say that Neill never steps back from telling the truth as he sees it, the claim demands searchingly steady integrity.

[9] A. S. Neill, *Summerhill: A Radical Approach to Education* (London, 1962), pp. xii–xv.

[10] While this theme recurs through Neill's writings *passim*, it has a book to itself, *Hearts not Heads in the School* (London, 1945).

8. This sort of education assumes that persons have ultimately to accept their aloneness, their independence and their personal responsibility. To do this the primary ties with father and mother or later social substitutes must eventually be cut. One finds security in accepting the world intellectually, emotionally and artistically to the realistic limit of one's abilities.

9. If this is the ultimate assumption, feelings of guilt are an impediment, for the primary function of guilt is to bind children to some form of authority. Fromm claims that in our society guilt is not usually a response to the voice of conscience but far more often an awareness of disobedience to authority and fear of reprisal, whether that reprisal is physical punishment, withdrawal of love or social ostracism.

10. Summerhill is concerned with basic humanistic values and Neill has made his opposition quite clear to the Christianity of the churches as he paraphrases it in terms of sin, guilt, repression and hypocrisy.

Summerhill is intended to be, in the true sense of the terms, an anarchic community in which children may grow up. In that we depend upon one another for survival, Summerhill is part of Leiston, whose tradesmen supply it; of a cash-based society in that it is kept going by fees from parents who earn a living; of a nation with a school system in that Neill and others ceaselessly attack conventional practice by comparing it with what goes on at Summerhill. In most other senses Summerhill opposes the society in which it is set and the values on which it is based and calls itself a freedom school:

> If I tried to reform society *by action* society would kill me as a public danger. If, for example, I tried to form a society in which adolescents would be free to have their own natural love life, I should be ruined if not imprisoned as an immoral seducer of youth. Hating compromise as I do, I have to compromise here, realising that *my primary job is not the reformation of society, but the bringing of happiness to some few children.*[11]

This school is a form of utopist-community similar to the ideal communities which have appeared from time to time in our history, particularly in the nineteenth century.[12] It has a life and purposes of its own but it has the intention to point the way to society on how to

---

[11] *Summerhill*, p. 36. Italics in the last lines mine.
[12] See Armytage, *Heavens Below*.

rear its children and on the values in human relationships on which the life and organization of that society should be based. Summerhill has few sociological pretensions, no sense of the co-existence of institutions, it makes no concessions to history, and has no strategy of continuity nor does it know how to effect change. It grounds its case on persons and abhors organization insofar as that requires control, foresight, regulation, absence of freedom. Some consequences and by-products of this are that Neill regards the use of force and war as atavism, the power-struggles of politics as dirty and evil, the control by the patriarchal society as the castration of the young. When he claims that he refuses to mould character he means that he tries to give the maximum opportunity to his pupils to grow up in a children's society where adults are available but not setting the standards. Summerhillians are bound to be influenced by the presence and ideas of Neill and his colleagues and by the behaviour of the other children and the inevitable dilapidation of the amenities and equipment.

The emphasis on happiness, on the psychoanalytic interpretation of personality development and the freedom principle, leads Fromm to admit to two reservations. The first is that Neill 'underestimates the importance, the pleasure and the authenticity of an intellectual in favour of an artistic and emotional grasp of the world'.[13] The second is that Neill 'overestimates the significance of sex as Freudians tend to do'. Each of these reservations indicates the distance between Summerhill and the intellectual and moral traditions in education. All the progressive schools speak of a concern for the whole personality and an unwillingness to force the intellectual pace, while increasingly coming to terms with examination requirements that lead on to further and higher education or qualify for a career. Summerhill gives no undertaking to prepare anyone for an examination and does not regard this route as a specially commendable one:

[Some parents say], 'If my son cannot read at twelve, what chance has he of success in life? If he cannot pass college entrance exams. at eighteen, what is there for him but an unskilled job?' But . . . I never doubt that in the end, if not molested or damaged, he will succeed in life.

Of course, the philistine can say, 'Humph, so you call a lorry driver a success in life!' My own criterion of success is the ability to work joyfully and to live positively.[14]

[13] Summerhill, p. xv.   [14] Ibid., p. 29.

For Neill what a pupil learns should be what he wants to learn and Neill has no prescription to offer on basic general education. Besides anything else, he does not present a case logically with arguments, but didactically with anecdotes from which the reader is expected to make generalizations and this matter of basic education is a case in point :

It is an absurd curriculum that makes a prospective dressmaker study quadratic equations or Boyle's Law. . . .

Indifferent scholars who, under discipline, scrape through college or university and become unimaginative teachers, mediocre doctors and incompetent lawyers would possibly be good mechanics or excellent bricklayers or first-rate policemen. . . .

Creators learn what they want to learn in order to have the tools that their originality and genius demand. We do not know how much creation is killed in the classroom with its emphasis on learning. . . .

It is taken for granted that every child should learn mathematics, history, geography, some science, a little art, and certainly literature. . . . The average young child is not much interested in any of these subjects. . . .

I ask what earthly good can come out of discussions about French or ancient history or what not when these subjects don't matter a jot compared to the larger question of life's natural fulfilment — of man's inner happiness. . . .

Parents are slow in realising how unimportant the learning side of school is. Children, like adults, learn what they want to learn. . . . Only pedants claim that learning from books is education.[15]

Neill claims that he is not decrying learning but wanting it to follow play. If a child, however, chooses all play and no work, Neill is not prepared to say that this makes him a dull boy. This is what the child wants to do and until his spontaneous motivation changes this is what he should do. Summerhill does not consider knowledge in terms of content, coherence, range or scholarship. It does not consider learning in terms of habit formation or stimulus-response or association, only in terms of feeling-readiness or of acceptance-rejection. The quality, type, or range of what is accepted or rejected and how it is presented do not often enter into Neill's discussions. He says that this is the part of the child that is above the neck, not the emotional, vital part. It also brings up the old question of criteria and evaluation, and this Neill

[15] Summerhill, pp. 24–27.

does not fully answer saying instead 'Let the child be himself. Don't force him to do anything.' He cannot be himself except in living with others in some kind of culture, influenced by it, forming habits and making choices.

Neill sees this and says that where children are allowed to play for as long as they want or need to, there should ideally be workshops, gymnasia, libraries, playing fields, good teaching to balance the endless repetition of jazz records. He goes on to say wistfully that his library has always been poor, consisting mainly of parents' cast offs, his playing fields bad, his teachers underpaid and often wrong for the job, working out their own problems and constantly changing. Had he been rich enough he might have had two schools, one with a full range of fine and beautiful things and the other, some distance away, for those who had much hate and antagonism to work out. Most of the time Neill writes as if the fine and beautiful things are not the vital things, because if you give freedom it leads to destruction and they will be spoiled and broken and all will come to dilapidation. Here is a dilemma.

Neill writes out of practical experience, not out of theory. Summerhill started with what Neill calls the problem era when he could not get enough ordinary pupils to make the place pay and took in all kinds of problem children — 'destructive, thieving, hateful brats'. At this time he thought psychology could work miracles and he took in cases of birth injury, the mentally ill, the educationally subnormal, and the strain on the total community was too great. The more normal suffered although for a time it broadened their tolerance. From time to time as conditions have made it necessary, Neill has had to accept more abnormal children than he wanted to. Hence, writing of Summerhill he has never been able to say how his principles would work with a school of predominantly average children, mentally and socially. His conclusion is, however, that if freedom can succeed to the extent it has with the range of problem children he has had, how much more will it succeed with those who are quicker to benefit and less deeply disturbed.

Neill may be prepared to admit that high culture has created fine things through dedicated effort of head, hand, and heart, but he is Calvinist enough to say that man is born into social evil, although he has through freedom, Freud and Reich the chance of salvation. This is not far from Rousseau, though Neill says he does not know enough about Rousseau to be a disciple. Children need to grow in their own way, at their own speed, he says, so that they can enjoy the products of high culture with sincerity if they want to, and will not be looked down on if they do not.

IV

Neill's lifework has lain in lonely territory. Summerhill is not 'recognised as efficient' by the Department of Education and Science and reports of Her Majesty's Inspectors in 1949 (quoted in full, with Neill's comments, in *Summerhill*) and 1959 indicate that on the whole, standards of building and equipment, staffing, teaching success, continuity, and learning achievement did not reach a level satisfactory to the visitors. The life of the school is inevitably wearing upon the head, his wife, and the staff, and Neill for reasons of finance has had to take too many pupils who came in at fourteen or older, when it was really too late for them genuinely to appreciate the ethos and method of a freedom school. These in a community of about forty to fifty pupils of all ages, rising occasionally to seventy, make a disproportionate disturbance in the life of the whole group. Besides anything else, it affects the weekly General School Meeting and the degree of sophistication which these children can display can pollute the genuine atmosphere of freedom.

The School Meeting arises out of Summerhill life and is different from the Moot at Dartington or School Councils in other schools as we have met them in earlier pages. First of all the school and staff are small enough for everyone to attend it if they wish and it deals by vote with all social matters. Neill says that the vote of a six year old carries as much weight as his own and he gives instances of occasions when he strongly advocated a case which was defeated — forbidding smoking to those under sixteen, suggesting penalties for those who stayed out of bed late, banning indoor football played in a room near to Neill's own which disturbed him when he was working. Some basic matters of school policy and arrangements are not discussed by the School Meeting — bedroom arrangements, payment of school bills, appointment and dismissal of teachers. But the regulation of bullying, of cases of stealing, of inconsiderate behaviour, and so on, come under the care of the School Meeting.

Each meeting has a new chairman nominated by the previous chairman, and a voluntary secretary, but the records of meetings are completely inadequate and precedent is referred to little, because any plea can be brought up again and again. 'Laws' are few and kept until changed, 'regulations' are too many to be remembered by all, especially as there are no records of them, *ad hoc* decisions are most frequent and most open to perpetual reconsideration. At a recent School Meeting there were several grievances about aggressiveness — hitting, interfering with food, calling names and provoking. Cases are made by the plaintiff and the proceedings are informal so that interruptions are frequent and the defendant need not wait until his turn, though much depends on the skill and finesse of the pupil in the chair. The staff can speak, as anyone can, and sometimes they offer extenuating comments for a defendant. The chairman has to get to a decision if possible on each item and this is supposed to be recorded. Sometimes a reprimand, usually from pupils to the offenders, is thought to be enough, occasionally fines are levied, sometimes the chairman rules ('You're not to be allowed to have matches in bed, so stop it').

Meetings can get disorganized and noisy, and it is not easy to keep to the point. At one meeting a bag of nuts became a source of difficulty and it was ruled that the meeting should have one minute of nut-throwing after which it returned to the agenda. There is monotonously frequent discussion of behaviour at bed-time and keeping of bed-times, of bad behaviour in the dining room, of taking and interfering with private property, of damage to possessions. The School Meeting is a weekly reminder that the cost paid if there is not even a loose structure of precedent is perpetual repetition, but this, says Neill, is not repetition for the children involved. Talking shows what the community really wants and the children do not want to be against the sense of the meeting — but clearly there are times when the decisions are by no means clearcut and even if they are some children are not prepared to accept them, and here the resources of reasonable persuasion in the community are sorely taxed.

The position of the adults at Summerhill provides a difficulty for commentators and often for members of the staff, both those who succeed and those who fail. Accommodation is in keeping with the comment in one report 'living conditions both in the house and in the huts have an austerity usually associated with extreme asceticism . . . the main impression is drab, Spartan and comfortless'. Salary to all staff has been for a while at the rate of £20 a month, net income, for the school pays any income tax and national insurance and provides free accommodation throughout the year, vacations included. However, £240 a year with an extra dividend declared in favourable times, in these days of the Burnham scale with a variety of allowances and increments, is so low that only the rich, the devoted, the bird of passage, or the desperate would accept it, and Neill has had them all as colleagues at different times. At Summerhill it is not possible to limit teaching to the areas in which the staff are professionally qualified. A graduate who combines sciences and arts in his degree has taught at different times biology, history, geography (which he had not previously studied), mathematics, general science and a little Latin. Leaving aside Neill's convictions that schools should be concerned with hearts not heads (significantly, not hearts *and* heads) it is impossible that teachers faced with this variety of demand upon them, as well as the wide age and ability range, could offer the quality of teaching that would attract children consistently. When the children can take it or leave it, it is not surprising that the intellectual achievements are low. Summerhill cannot really offer teaching beyond O level, and Neill says: 'Books are the least important apparatus in a school. All that any child needs is the three R's; the rest should be tools and clay and sports and theatre and freedom.'[16]

This has led some teachers to say that while they got used to becoming subservient to the children and to being out of touch with adult things, they thought that children were being deprived of challenges and intellectual pleasures and were the victims of a misguided philosophy. Readers of *Id* will note that almost every article is about the Summerhill freedom in one form or another. There is nothing about national problems of education, no continuing assessment of how Summerhill methods may or may not have permeated to primary schools, no real discussion of teaching methods, no recognition that there is a crisis in the national supply of teachers. Usually the theme is the creative, courageous minority, the radical right-minded few, and this view, of course, needs to be defended and reaffirmed. However, convincing evidence is difficult to come by because records have not been kept, neither records of individual pupils nor the customary statistics. The memories of Neill, his wife and his senior colleagues represent the school archives, and it is virtually impossible to provide a cumulative record of, for instance, the number of children of foreign nationality at Summerhill over the last five years or the number of

[16] *Summerhill*, p. 25.

O level passes since 1960, or the occupational background of the parents of all children since the end of the War. The records are not there because there is no money to pay for a regular school secretary and in any case Neill does not think this kind of record is of any real use. While this may be a rationalization, it is also part of his belief that these data are trivial compared with the chronic, profound, important aspects of a person. While there has been a move recently to keep reports on children, in Neill's mind no worthwhile report can be kept, or else it ought to be a considered statement with perspective and therefore so lengthy as to be impracticable. Yet proper research comparing Summerhill performances with those of other schools in a whole range of activities cannot be undertaken until reliable data are available. At present only anecdotes can be obtained, or biased samples where it is difficult to get total figures for the whole group, or statements about the life of the school such as some of those mentioned in this chapter, for and against.

It would be exceptionally difficult to get evidence on which to try to assess the effect and effectiveness of a Summerhill education, and even more difficult to compare it meaningfully with what is achieved in other kinds of schools. As an example, Neill claims, with instances, that a fair proportion of Summerhillians achieve intellectual or professional distinction and that this in large part is due to the chance to play, to be free, without intellectual compulsion in their Summerhill days. For this to be more than a hunch it would be necessary to examine the length of time spent at Summerhill, the age of entry to more ordinary competitive life in school, college, or university, the proportion of effect of the more orthodox training on the ultimate performance. Equally, comparisons would have to be made with performers of comparable distinction who did not go to Summerhill at any stage. Obviously, social-class background comes into this and the whole undertaking is very complex indeed. But it is now beginning to become possible, as techniques of measurement, assessment, comparison are more sensitive than even a few years ago. Only in this way can Neill's hunches and claims be substantiated in the disinterested fashion of research. Although he does not think research tools could do justice to the truth of assumptions about freedom and self-regulation, the strategy of trying to show how far his ideas are right will have to lie in this direction.

Neill has said from time to time that he resents and regrets that for the most part only well-to-do parents can send their children to Summerhill. He would like to take boys and girls from homes lying across the class structure and by cutting costs to the bone and accepting a few children supported by local authorities he has some variety in parental background. For the most part, however, it is the liberal intelligentsia who send their children to Summerhill, both from this country and abroad. A group of children recently at the school had fathers and mothers who were between them a psychiatrist, a fabric designer, an engineer, an actress, a drama-therapist, an architect, a surgeon, a university lecturer, a jewellery designer, a business man, a journalist, a publisher. Fundamentally Neill's school is so different that he has always had difficulty in keeping going. The Department of Education and Science will not recognize Summerhill as efficient, but they do not try to close the school. Local authorities take up a few places, but very few. Neill's royalties help to keep Summerhill afloat and the recent appearance of *Summerhill* in America led to an influx of American children and visits from prospectors who planned the American equivalent of the English school. Scandinavia has recognized Neill, so has Japan, and his ideas are known widely in the world. Yet his school is not widely copied, his lists of applicants are not solid or reassuring, certainly not with working-class applicants.

V

Neill was a late developer. He discovered what he wanted to study when he was twenty-five after more than one false start, and he had plenty of experience of family pressure and school failure until he was over twenty. He combines the strong feeling, directness and dogmatism that characterize many Scots, with the moral determination and devotion to purpose that owe more to Calvin than to Freud. He has no party political affiliations and never has had, the nearest being a long membership of the Progressive League, of which he is a former President. The League is a politically independent organization which holds that political and economic problems must be viewed in relation to cultural, sociological and psychological factors. Its aims include the initiative of action on particular issues and the promotion of co-operation between progressive organizations. He is the most radical of the educational innovators because he is the most radical critic of our society. It is difficult to draw up an ordered statement of the kind of world Neill wants to see or of the steps by which we move from where we are to the transformed social life of the future. Like any religious man, he believes that men need to renew a right spirit within them. But that spirit is to be an affirmation of love which, to use one of his favourite phrases, says yes to life. His notion of love has most of St. Paul's magnificent catalogue of qualities, but with the addition of a special tribute to the pleasures and the rightness of sex. Happiness is a word Neill often uses and this appears to be difficult to attain in terms of respect for the law, restraint, the clarification of right and wrong, self-denial. Realization of the self is not discussed by Neill in these aspects, though Neill's life and work bear witness to the fact that he understands them and the necessity for them.

Children are, he claims, innately wise and realistic. Elsewhere he admits that in some cases their primitivism can make them hateful brats and he has met some with whom even he could do nothing, and these have been known to disturb the wisdom and realism of the rest. Neill's assertions about the innate qualities of children are acts of faith in a 'good' force in children and a 'good' force in a certain kind of free society which will enable the 'good' psychological force to express itself in social life and institutions. If the intellect can look after itself, as Neill has said, when men have been thus 'saved', so too can the kind of society good and wise people with a freedom school background will make. This again is a religious kind of statement: 'except ye be born again ye cannot enter into the Kingdom of heaven.' Neill is under no illusions of the roughness of the road — how could he be after forty-five years of the stresses and anxieties of Summerhill and his place crying at the edge of the wilderness?

When children have been made happier, when their aggressions have been transformed and their fears dispelled, what kind of action will they take? Neill's prescriptions are as full of denunciatory yearnings as those of other radicals, religious or secular, and often as vague. They will denounce force, they will champion honesty and sincerity, they will oppose fear with love, they will have the integrity of self-knowledge, they will not need to delude themselves with religion or symbols of status or cant, they will suffer aggression from others with forbearance, they will challenge shams in hypocritical appearances and in grossly materialist public life. All of these unexceptionable aspirations have been taken from Neill's writings and as many others could have been chosen.

What of the future ? Neill is well into his eighties and there is no-one else in Britain quite like him, though some approximate to him or have done so — Aitkenhead of Kilquhanity, East of Burgess Hill, which closed in 1962; Curry of Dartington, who died in 1962; Michael Duane formerly of Risinghill, a London comprehensive school; and on the Continent the late Kees Boeke of Holland and Paul Geheeb of Germany and Switzerland, though neither was a Freudian. Neill has written of the future of Summerhill, and it is best to end with his own words and opinions :

I have not spent the last forty years writing down *theories* about children. Most of what I have written has been based on observing children, living with them. True, I have derived inspiration from Freud, Homer Lane and others ; but gradually I have tended to drop theories when the rest of reality proved them invalid. . . . In the day-to-day working of the school, my wife and the teachers are just as important as I am. *It is the idea of non-interference with the growth of the child and non-pressure on the child that has made the school what it is* . . . I do not think the world will use the Summerhill method of education for a very long time — if it ever uses it. . . . Politics will not save humanity. It never has done so. . . . Too many are socialistic because they hate the rich instead of loving the poor. . . . I cannot look upon education as a matter of exams and classes and learning. The school evades the basic issue . . . [which is] to make the home more loving, the child free from inhibitions, the parent free of neurosis.

The future of Summerhill itself may be of little import. But the future of the Summerhill idea is of the greatest importance to humanity. . . . The bestowal of freedom is the bestowal of love. And only love can save the world.[17]

[17] *Summerhill*, pp. 89, 91, 92.

Part Three

Some Facts, Figures and Interpretations

WHEN these unorthodox schools were founded they did not want or expect to have the seal of the central authority's approval. As the years have passed nearly all have come to be 'recognized as efficient' and included in the lists issued from time to time. First, to recall the relationship between the central authority and schools in this country.

It has been possible for independent secondary schools to be inspected by Her Majesty's Inspectors on behalf of the central authority since soon after the formation of the Board of Education in 1902, and many have been recognized as efficient for more than half a century. The option to seek recognition was in the hands of the schools, and as time passed more and more independent schools of all kinds thought the approval desirable. Leighton Park was among those accepted in the early groups in 1906, Bedales followed in 1911, and Badminton in 1919 while public schools also took up the recognition, Harrow in 1910, Rugby in 1913, Winchester in 1919, but Eton did not consider it necessary until 1936. While all of this relates to secondary schools, there are of course large numbers of independent schools in the nursery, primary, and preparatory sectors and these had a similar option open to them from about 1927. Schools recognized as efficient were inspected at fairly regular intervals and if standards were not maintained recognition could be suspended or withdrawn.

However, it was not compulsory to seek recognition or to invite inspection. There were attempts to introduce powers of inspection by either the Board of Education or the local authority in the Education Act of 1921, but while these were available they were never seriously enforced and by 1944 had become a dead letter. Part III of the 1944 Act provided for the registration of all independent schools, and these are defined briefly as establishments which are not maintained by local authorities or in receipt of grant, in which full-time education is provided for five or more pupils of compulsory school age.[1] Such was the congestion of other educational business following on the passage of the Act that this registration was not enforced until thirteen years later in 1957. In the meantime, however, another clause of the Act was brought into effect which was able to prepare the way for registration. The Minister was empowered in Part IV of the Act[2] to require inspection by H.M Inspectors of all educational establishments and so to make compulsory what had been largely ignored after the 1921 Act. The Inspectorate was able to take up this work from 1949 and by the time registration was brought into effect on 30 September 1957 much was already known about the independent sector. Six months grace was offered to schools which had to register and provide the required information and since 31 March 1958 it has been an offence to conduct an independent school which has not been registered. All the schools which had already been recognized as efficient were accepted on the register and we can note that nearly all of the innovating schools considered in earlier pages which were founded before the outbreak of war were already recognized by 1944. Exceptions were Dartington Hall, Summerhill and the Rudolf Steiner schools.[3]

What are the conditions which a school has to satisfy for this approval? These are listed in Rule 16 and quoted at the beginning of the document now known as *List 70* and may be summarized as follows :

1. the school must be discharging its declared purpose efficiently and in essentials it has to reach a comparable level of efficiency with a similar grant-aided school.
2. the teaching must be satisfactory in standard and wide enough in scope for the age-range.
3. the school has to be large enough for reasonably economical running. In fact no school of less than thirty is considered.
4. teachers are expected to be adequately qualified and acceptable on

---

[1] *Education Act 1944*, Section 114. [2] Section 77(2).

[3] Dartington was provisionally recognized in 1959 and this acceptance was later confirmed. Michael Hall was recognized in 1950 and Wynstones in 1952. Summerhill has not yet been accepted, although, of course, it has been inspected more than once.

medical, professional and moral grounds to the Secretary of State.

5. the accommodation and equipment must reach an acceptable standard and the living conditions for staff and children in boarding schools have to be approved.

6. registers and records must be kept in good order.

The Burnham scale is a guide to the standard of salary expected and recognition offers a school the opportunity to join the teachers' superannuation scheme and so to widen the field of staff recruitment. According to the Department of Education and Science, in January 1965 there were in England and Wales 3,560 independent schools of which 1,539 were recognized although the number of pupils in the recognized schools was more than twice the number in the unrecognized schools, 306,638 as against 151,569. To put it another way, about 58 per cent of the registered independent schools were not in 1965 approved as efficient by the above criteria. Just over 90 per cent of the radical schools considered in this book were so recognized.[4] To mention a few in addition to those already noted — Abbotsholme was accepted in 1933, Clayesmore in 1925, Bootham in 1907, Saffron Walden in 1920, St. Christopher in 1929, Frensham Heights in 1935, Bryanston in 1933 and Wennington in 1948. In other words, during the pre-war period of optional recognition only a very small number of these schools declared themselves so much at odds with national standards that they opposed this kind of scrutiny. We have seen that Curry of Dartington held out against what he regarded as inevitable incomprehension of his aims and a drift to standardization, until in the end he had to accept inspection after the War. It was only after he left that recognition was sought for the school. The Rudolf Steiner schools are very different from most others and have only come into the reckoning for official acceptance since the end of the War, and not all of them are yet approved. Neill, like Curry, has accepted inspection since the end of the War without much confidence that H.M. Inspectors will see what he is trying to do as deserving their support. However, extreme as they have found Summerhill, the Inspectorate have recommended its continued existence, whereas several schools have been closed. In 1965, for instance, recognition was withdrawn from four schools, 217 were removed from the register because of change of status (that is they moved out of the independent sector into some form of grant-aided position), or because they were closed either

4 *Statistics of Education*, 1965, part i, table 10(5), H.M.S.O., p. 29.

voluntarily by the proprietors or by an order of the Secretary of State after failure of the proprietors to comply with the conditions laid down earlier by the Department of Education and Science.

Therefore, despite any unorthodoxy, these innovating schools are competent enough for official approval:

> Ministry recognition of independent schools means something more than the arbitrary application of standard. It means that a school has been sifted and tested by experienced men who are genuinely concerned for education. . . . As a result of visiting a number of unrecognized schools . . . I had no difficulty (even in the case of a 'Borderline' school) of seeing why recognition had been refused. Moreover the gap between the best unrecognized school visited and the worst recognized was considerable. . . . I came to see the Inspector's job as doing with a great deal more skill and experience exactly what the careful parent would do if he had the opportunity to inspect a school himself.[5]

II

Exactly comparable figures for the number of pupils who have attended the progressive schools over the years are not obtainable. The publication *List of Independent Schools* which early in its history was known as *List 60* and is now *List 70*, presents its data in different styles in different years. For instance in 1938–9 *List 60* gives one sub-total for boys and girls over eleven and under sixteen and another for those over sixteen. It then lists the grand total for the school, from which by subtraction it is possible to find if there is a junior section which is not listed separately. In 1950 the distinctions of ages are no longer drawn and boys and girls are not listed separately and again in 1965 only totals for the school as a whole are found, with boys and girls grouped together when it applies. In some schools the age-range is from four to eighteen (in one case three to eighteen), in others eleven to eighteen, and in others thirteen to eighteen. Numbers of boarders are given where this applies. From these data, reliable as they are, it is not possible to compare the numbers in schools from thirteen to eighteen, or the proportion staying at school after sixteen, or the proportion of boarders in the secondary age-range. In addition not all the

[5] P. Wood, 'What is Ministry Recognition Worth?', in *Where?* 14, Autumn 1963, pp. 5–6. Published for Advisory Centre for Education.

progressive schools are registered as efficient and so included in *List 70*, or where they have been they have been accepted at different times, so the record stretches back unevenly. For instance the Quaker school at Sidcot in Somerset was recognized in 1905, Frensham Heights in 1935, and Michael Hall in 1950.

The schools have tried to provide me with figures when they have been asked for them, but complete records are not always kept and so it has not been possible to fill in the gaps reliably. However, the numbers are so comparatively small that allowing for the degrees of error only general kinds of categorization are really possible.

If we total the number of pupils at the following schools in 1965, whether from three or four to eighteen or eleven to eighteen or thirteen to eighteen we shall have a rough aggregate of pupils at the kind of schools we have been considering in the earlier pages. The schools are : Abbotsholme, Ackworth,* Ayton,* Badminton, Bedales, Bembridge, Bootham,* Bryanston, Claesmore, Dartington, Frensham Heights, Gordonstoun, King Alfred's, Leighton Park,* Michael Hall, Monkton Wyld, The Mount,* Rendcomb, St. Christopher, Saffron Walden,* Sibford,* Sidcot,* Summerhill, Wennington, Wigton.* The total in 1965 was almost exactly 7,000 in all the age groups with the large preponderance in the secondary group aged eleven to eighteen, although 8 of the 25 schools take children aged below eleven, mostly in small numbers. If this aggregate is compared with the total of children of secondary age-range at maintained schools some idea of the proportion of children in progressive schools can be obtained. In 1965 there were 2,819,054 in this group and if the numbers in other secondary schools are added (special schools, direct grant schools, other independent schools) the total comes very close to 3,500,000 in secondary schools. As a percentage of 3,500,000 the total of 7,000 at the innovating schools comes out at 0·2 per cent.[6]

If we make some comparison with the public schools these small numbers in the progressive schools may be seen in a different perspective. Kalton has estimated that there were about 86,000 boys from age eleven onwards in the public and direct grant schools of England and Wales at the beginning of 1964.[7] This represents about 2½ per cent of

---

* These nine schools are run by the Society of Friends.

6 Figures for maintained schools may be seen in *Statistics of Education*, 1965, part i, table 10(5), H.M.S.O., pp. 28–29.

7 G. Kalton, *The Public Schools* (London, 1966), p. 14.

the secondary school aggregate and is more than twelve times the number of pupils in the progressive schools, though it must be admitted that some of those in the progressive group are also counted in Kalton's public school sample — for example, Bootham, Leighton Park, Bryanston, Clayesmore. The difference would be much larger if girls' public schools were added.

This tiny minority of pupils in progressive schools is part of the independent sector and will come into the reckoning of Sir John Newsom's Public School Commission which was set up in December 1965 to 'advise on the best way of integrating the public schools with the State system of education'. For the immediate purpose of the Commission, public schools are defined as those independent schools now in membership of the Headmasters' Conference, Governing Bodies Association, or Governing Bodies of Girls' Schools Association. Abbotsholme has now joined the four schools mentioned in the last paragraph on the Headmasters' Conference, and they will come under that rubric, but elsewhere the terms of reference state:

(e) To recommend whether any action is needed in respect of other independent schools, whether secondary or primary.

Educationally, Abbotsholme, Bedales, Rendcomb, St. Christopher, and the rest were established either as correctives to the public schools or else to develop a religious or social principle into practice in a school which bore little educational resemblance to a public school. There is none of the presumed advantage of 'the old boy network' in progressive schools which are too liberal-anarchic, too small, and too new to have any organizational power and whose ideas are *ex hypothesi* supposed to run counter to any notions of an establishment. The irony is now that their educational ideas may count for little when integration is in the wind. Their independence makes them bedfellows with the public schools where a decade or two ago neither had any desire to breathe the same educational air as the other.

By looking at the size of individual schools at different times we can get an impression of stability or change. The following comparison of twelve schools at periods before and after the War is based on figures provided in *List 60* and *List 70*. Where there are boarders they are given as a total in brackets, and the age-range of the schools has not been given because the comparison is made in order to detect growth within schools as distinct from comparison of size between schools.

Number of boys and girls at schools named on dates shown

Name of School	1933	1938	1950	1957	1965	Increase 1933–65 as a percentage
Abbotsholme	78 B (78)	81 B (81)	108 B (108)	145 B (145)	193 B (193)	140
Bedales	201 B+G (161)	174 B+G (c. 130)	202 B+G (194)	261 B+G (c. 200)	389 B+G (295)	94
Claysmore	70 B (70)	211 B (207)	199 B (199)	210 B (209)	216 B (216)	205
Saffron Walden	157 B+G (132)	187 B+G (171)	272 B+G (c. 200)	334 B+G (228)	365 B+G (238)	140
Leighton Park	129 B (114)	156 B (121)	267 B (c. 150)	278 B (c. 168)	292 B (273)	124
Badminton	150 G (97)	119 G (c. 75)	187 G (c. 110)	225 G (132)	342 G (229)	112
St. Christopher	183 B+G (54)	155 B+G (c. 70)	206 B+G (c. 120)	260 B+G (c. 160)	380 B+G (221)	110
Michael Hall*	—	—	—	270 B+G (c. 90)	393 B+G (101)	44
Frensham Heights	—	100 B+G (c. 70)	182 B+G (c. 145)	197 B+G (c. 150)	222 B+G (161)	122
Bryanston	198 B (198)	291 B (291)	326 B (325)	424 B (424)	445 B (445)	120
Dartington Hall*	—	—	—	—	256 B+G (150)	—
Wennington*	—	—	87 B+G (85)	86 B+G (c. 80)	119 B+G (111)	38

* Entry on the Table is shown after the school was first recognized as efficient.

In this matter of increase in numbers much depends, obviously, on the kind of buildings and area of ground available for new building, and on financial backing, whether in endowment or income.

During the same period Gordonstoun grew from about fifty at its beginning in 1934 to over four hundred pupils. The increase in all the schools has been fairly steady in the thirty years which straddle the Second World War. The days of the eccentric, when Reddie and Devine nearly ruined their schools financially, were over. Curry ran risks at Dartington but he was backed by sound finance in other Elmhirst enterprises. Barnes had to build from a war-time start and Neill, who is not on this chart, wavered between having forty and sixty pupils during most of this time.

All schools, except one, which have a return for 1938 show an increase by 1950 and a steep upward gradient in the 1950s and 60s and this corresponds to a period of growth and prosperity in independent schools after the end of the War. Clayesmore is the exception partly because of extraordinary expansion between 1933 and 1938 when the school increased by 200 per cent and gave the kind of numbers at which it has held since. The other schools showed this proportionally sharp increase in the ten years after 1945 when the effect of the 1944 Act was being felt in radical reforms of the maintained schools. The school leaving age was raised; school fees in maintained schools were abolished; the early warnings of dissatisfaction with secondary school selection and the beginnings of comprehensive reorganization could be detected; building and rebuilding to deal with the ravages of war and the vast increases in numbers occupied the foreground. The Fleming Report, *The Public Schools and the General Educational System*, appeared in 1944 with its suggestions of a 25 per cent intake of pupils to boarding schools on bursaries related to a means test. But the many other huge enterprises in education through the 1940s and 50s left very little time or attention for the independent schools. Two indications of this were, first, the repeated attempts at the annual Labour Party Conference to propose drastic resolutions on the reform and often the abolition of the public schools together with the regular postponement of definite action by the platform: the second indication has already been mentioned — the Ministry of Education was not in a position to enforce registration of independent schools until 1957, thirteen years after the requirement was put on the statute book. Reports by all three political parties in the 1950s and 60s indicated that they had in mind to do something, but only in December 1965 was Sir John Newsom's Public Schools Commission set up.

The matter of priorities in the period 1944–66 is probably the main single reason for the postponed attention to the independent schools. In addition there are two difficult problems which have led to most L.E.A.s and most Ministers of Education turning a blind eye or a deaf ear to the Fleming Scheme B recommendations to take up to 25 per cent public school places for L.E.A. pupils. The first of these is the question of selection — who should be chosen for these places, as they mean a higher expenditure of L.E.A. money on each pupil, and in any case it is hard to reach agreement on criteria for choice.[8] The second difficulty arises from the age of transfer, which in most independent schools is thirteen plus through Common Entrance and preparatory school channels, and in the maintained system through primary schools at eleven plus by means of objective testing or more recently through non-selective procedures to a comprehensive secondary range. Ways around this have been found, but the number is not large.

These remarks arise primarily from the situation created by the Fleming Report in the public schools. Linked to this is the clause in the 1944 Act itself (Section 8(2)(d)) encouraging local authorities to give thought to the need for boarding places. The progressive schools are predominantly boarding establishments, so these recommendations can apply to them. Equally, the fluctuations of numbers which affected the public schools to a much larger extent appear to have been reflected in similar variations in the radical schools. As we have seen from the earlier table, the increase in numbers in the twelve schools mentioned was in nearly every case markedly large since the end of the Second World War, and if the readings are taken from 1933 the average increase is 133 per cent for the eight schools of the twelve listed which were then in existence. Even now, however, only five of the twelve are within striking range of four hundred, and of these five, three have an age-range down to junior and infant years. The proportional and aggregate increases are large, but not one of the establishments is large, or even average, by contemporary secondary school sizes. They rank among the smallest secondary schools in the country and this

---

[8] In so far as these are candidates for boarding education there have been several reports offering guidance, the last of which is *Report of the Working Party on Assistance with the Cost of Boarding Education*, 1960. This is sometimes known as the Martin Report. For general discussion of this question see R. Lambert, *The State and Boarding Education* (London, 1966), chapter 1.

reflects the principle of the extended family from which they began and to which most of them still hold. It also exposes them to criticism on grounds of inequality and the need for social justice.

In the post-war atmosphere of planning, with education considered nationally as a social investment both in terms of money and manpower and the sequence of input, throughput and output, many of the educational principles and practices of progressive, as of other schools, are being seen in the framework of viable educational units, of minimum economic size, of cost-creep and Burnham salary reviews. Of course, these features were there at all times and no school can run without realistic financial control and hard-headed accounting. But between the wars the institution and its legitimate demands were subordinated to the care of the child and his personal growth and development. This led to consideration of individual objectives and the school had to be relatively small to encompass these purposes. While the head and the governing body and the bursar saw to the solvency of the institution, the pressure of state rationalization at that time was not great and schools relied upon the *laissez-faire* market competition to enable them to produce a minority educational product. Now, the institutional and organizational pressures are much tighter on each of the schools and on all of them as a body, and at this point we can look at their financial situation.

III

It is impossible to give precise financial statements that are useful as a basis for discussion about the innovating schools. The difficulty is the familiar one about the scales within which comparisons are being made. If again we make use of *List 60* and *List 70*, as being reliable statements of the basic scales over the years, we find a number of schools which quote a range of fees, for example, Badminton where in 1950 the fees ranged between £144 and £189; or St. Christopher where in 1965 the range was £417 to £519. These fees, and the others to be quoted, include boarding charges, and the fees for day scholars would obviously be much lower. Many other independent schools quote a single figure and it is not always clear whether this is a fee which everyone pays or if it is an average which the school quotes.

The range of difference is usually related to the length of time a pupil is at the school. For instance, a boy who starts at the age of eight or eleven often pays an annual fee that is less than for a boy starting at thirteen, who may in turn pay rather less than one who comes in only at sixth form level. This is based on the assumption of a longer period of subscribing years in the case of the younger boys and so a larger financial guarantee for the school. While this kind of transaction can be easily read from the information given, the figures do not indicate how many there have been of each category at any particular time and so it is not possible to work out a reliable average fee.

The charges quoted below in Table III 2 have been obtained from *List 60* and *List 70* for the same years as for the numbers of pupils at the range of schools shown in Table II 1. At the same time figures were obtained for a matching number of public schools and these were chosen for the most part from the same county area as the progressive school. In a very approximate way some comparisons between the two groups of schools can be made. The recent work by Kalton gives a much more comprehensive range of data on the public schools.[9] Where there is a range of fees quoted for any one year, calculations which have been done for what follows have been based on the mid-point between the two figures given.

For this group of progressive schools the average fee charged in 1933 was £153, although the fluctuations were wide — Saffron Walden cost parents 55 per cent of the charges at Bedales which were the highest. By 1965 the Saffron Walden fees were only about 5 per cent less than those at Bedales, and as the column shows, the discrepancies between fees in different schools narrowed dramatically over the thirty-three years between. The highest fee in 1965 was charged by Bryanston (£540) and the lowest by Michael Hall (an average of £405) and Saffron Walden (£417). This puts Michael Hall at exactly 75 per cent of the Bryanston charge and Saffron Walden at about 80 per cent, a very different position from 1933 when the Essex school, as was said above, was charging 55 per cent of the Bedales fee. In 1965 the average for this whole group of schools was £456, almost exactly three times the 1933 average of £153.

Three general comments can be made from these figures. First, and obviously, the narrower margins in 1965 indicate an evening up of charges which is likely to be due to a more comparable range of facilities, for it is improbable that schools which have a poorer staff–student ratio, a narrower curriculum, inferior equipment and

[9] G. Kalton, *The Public Schools.*

TABLE III 2

Fees of Progressive and Public Schools in £s

Name of School	1933	1938	1950	1957	1965	Increase 1933–65 as a percentage
Abbotsholme	144/180	144/180	198/252	302	474/513	205
Denstone	120	120	180	270/300	472	290
Bedales	180	155/170	231	225/360	390/490	145
Rugby	201	201	270	411	537	168
Clayesmore	157–10	157–10	192	279	420	173
Canford	157–10	170	225	345	462	134
Saffron Walden	99	99	174	267	417	315
Felsted	95/123	140/150	210	324	435/498	325
Leighton Park	157–10/189	157–10/189	171/255	231/315	459	185
Radley	185	185	240	330	552	198
Badminton	126/157–10	121/157–10	144/189	204/300	390/480	207
Cheltenham Ladies' College	126/157–10	150/162	210	300	459	226
St. Christopher	150	150	185/200	240/326	417/519	212
Aldenham	90/115	90/115	165	351	522	410
Michael Hall				218/312	366/444	54
Eastbourne				252/325	510	73
Frensham Heights		151	180	264/330	510	240
Cranleigh		130/150	195/216	273/318	543	290
Bryanston	168	180	210	360	540	220
Sherborne	165	165	225	336	474	187
Dartington					405/504	—
Kelly College, Tavistock					441	—
Wennington			189	200	417/435	126

accommodation, could compete on equal financial terms with schools which offered a notably better standard for the money, or with well-equipped maintained schools. The second comment is that the period during which the gap was closed between the most expensive and the cheapest schools is in the post-war years. The differences were as wide in 1938 as they were in 1933, but by 1950 they were shrinking. The post-war boom in independent education gave the poorer schools a chance to face the reality of competition with others and the means to strengthen their own offerings.

The third comment relates to the changing value of money. It is notoriously difficult for economists to make valid comparisons between the pre-war and post-war periods because the data on which calculations have been made have differed. In official tables of retail prices between 1914 and 1947 the spending pattern of poor people on necessities in 1914 was taken for the weightings arrived at in the periodical statements. Although a revision was introduced for the period 1938–47 because spending patterns had changed so greatly, this was clearly not a sufficient modification and between 1947 and 1956 a new interim index was constructed. This index was based on a review of budget studies made in 1953–4 and this review was used for the weightings given for the index of retail prices between 1956 and 1962. Since 1962, three-yearly averages have been drawn up on which annual weightings in the index have been based. Economists are therefore understandably not willing to lean heavily on detailed retrospective comparisons of the retail price index. However, 1958 is taken as a year when the value of the index is set down as 100.[10] In this rating 1964 is returned as 115·4; 1957 as 97·1; 1950 as 68; 1938 as 37; 1933 as 33. These are the years on which we have already made the financial readings indicated in the above table.

If we work in averages for this group of schools we find that the average fee of 1950 at £197 is only 3 per cent below the 1958 figure of £293, if one makes appropriate allowances for the value of money and assumes that fees in 1958 did not change from those quoted for 1957. The average fee for the pre-war years of £153 is proportionately a much higher charge. The 1933 equivalent of £293 in 1958 is rather under the £99 which as we have seen was the lowest fee in this group, charged by Saffron Walden. However, if we move on to 1964 when the average fee was £455 and the retail price index was just over 115,

[10] *British Economy : Key Statistics 1900–1964.*

the fee which would have matched the 1958 charge would have been about £350.

These comparisons show that the radical schools were charging comparatively high fees before the War by 1958 standards and that the level climbed steeply again between 1958 and 1964 and this trend has continued till now. Small schools which maintain a staff–pupil ratio of 1:11 or so are likely to be expensive, especially at a time when teachers' salaries and allowances have been increased. Equally, the cost of secondary education in particular has mounted sharply as a range of new equipment and materials and developed facilities in many subjects from craft to science have come into use. Nearly all the innovating schools have been involved in large building programmes since the end of the War. The cost per place in any secondary school, maintained or independent, is much higher now, even allowing for the changing value of money, than it was only ten years ago, and there is no sign of the end of this climbing graph.

If we turn to the public schools whose fees were listed in the earlier table, we find that the average fee in 1933 which in the innovating schools was £153, was in the public schools £169, or about 11 per cent higher, the lowest fee and the highest being about that distance above the corresponding fees in the progressive schools. In 1965 the differences have been halved and the progressive school average is £456 while the public school figure is £483, or about 6 per cent higher. The differences between the averages of both groups in 1950 is about 7½ per cent and in 1965 about 8 per cent, the public schools still the higher in each case. Kalton's more comprehensive data place the public school average fee a bit higher, but not significantly so.

Whatever educational differences there may be between these two groups of independent schools the income level to which they must direct themselves is similar. One of the named objectives of Sir John Newsom's Commission is to ensure that increasingly the public schools should be open to boys and girls irrespective of the income of their parents. At this stage all that need be said is that parents sending their children to progressive schools have to make inroads into their incomes very similar to those made by parents of public school boys and girls.

The salaries paid to masters and mistresses in all the recognized progressive schools are at least as good as the Burnham scale and in most cases better. In boarding schools, masters and mistresses take on many additional duties and the supervision and general care in out-of-school hours inevitably go further in claiming time. Some consequence of this is seen in the apparently more generous staffing ratios, where, as has been mentioned, 1 : 11 or 12 is not uncommon. The 1965 returns state the ratio in Direct Grant schools as 1 : 16·8; in independent schools as 1 : 12·8; and in maintained secondary schools as 1 : 18·7.[11] A ratio weighted for sixth form and residential duties makes the proportions look much less uneven.

A further consequence of the demands of boarding schools is often seen in the salary scale. The days of pecuniary sacrifice by devoted teachers in pioneer schools are finished in the recognized progressive schools — they cannot gain recognition until the salary and superannuation structure compares with the national scales and provisions. In a number of the progressive schools the scale starts at a point or so above the comparable Burnham scale and keeps this position : generous responsibility allowances, living accommodation on favourable terms, occasionally children's allowances, reduced fees for children attending the school — these and other inducements are available. It would not be fair to suggest that all of these are found together or can be gathered by all masters as a matter of course. After a scrutiny of the salaries and emoluments available to the staff of these schools, it can be said that they are on average more favourable than the Burnham scale, but not more than might be expected as a return for boarding duties and the consequences of a residential community life.

This favourable position has been reached in the majority of the schools only in the last twenty years. In the 1930s and the 1920s, equal subsistence salaries were not uncommon, the adherence to Burnham scales where they were applied was strictly interpreted and allowances were few and competitive. This was true of the country as a whole, of course, but in most cases the unorthodox schools had no solid financial backing to sustain a generous allowance policy. Since the end of the War the schools have recognized the stronger bargaining position of teachers and have had the confidence to raise the fees to meet the mounting costs.[12]

[11] *Statistics of Education,* 1965, part i, H.M.S.O., pp. 61 and 50.
[12] These conclusions are based on salary statements provided by the schools to the author for the years mentioned in the table of fees used earlier in this chapter

IV

It would be useful if some statements could be made about the career patterns of former pupils from progressive schools and with this in mind an inquiry was conducted to collect necessary data. As in most investigations of this kind, a deceptively simple account can be given of the purpose, the strategy, and the procedure. The practical problems that arose in this case are very familiar to all social investigators, and I must underline that the comments from this part of our whole inquiry are presented as impressions rather than as authenticated conclusions.[13]

In earlier pages of this book at least twenty-five schools have received substantial mention and sixteen of them were visited in 1963–4 in order to compile lists of names and addresses of all pupils who left the schools in the years 1933, 1938, 1943, 1948, 1953, and 1958 — the choice of years was related to the extraordinary war-time conditions between 1939 and 1945. Old pupils who were known to have died in the intervening years were excluded from the lists and additional information on the remaining persons was obtained — the length of time they were at school, the age at which they left, further education and choice of career, if these were known, and so on.[14] The schools chosen were co-educational and single-sex day and boarding and covered the spectrum of unorthodoxy which we have already noted. Five of them were conducted by the Society of Friends and the remaining eleven were unattached schools like Abbotsholme or Bedales or King Alfred's. A questionnaire with a covering letter was sent by post to every person whose name and address had been obtained, with appropriate follow-up to those who did not at first respond. There were in all 1,535 persons on our lists.

The questionnaire asked for factual data — period spent at the progressive school with dates; examinations taken with results; further and higher education, if any, with relevant qualifications or experience; marital status (particularly important in relation to

[13] I have been helped in this part of the study first by Miss Margaret Thomas and later by Mr. Colin Creighton. A more detailed account of the work on which this section of this chapter is based will be published elsewhere.

[14] I should like here to express gratitude to the heads of these sixteen schools for their readiness to make records available and to offer time and help to enable these lists to be made up.

women's careers); military service or its equivalent; career and experience, with dates; a statement of present salary within broad markers in eight categories ranging from 'under £500' to 'over £5,000', together with any fringe benefits. Another question was aimed to discover whether respondents who had children would consider or had already arranged for attendance at a progressive school for their sons and daughters. The occupations of fathers and guardians when the respondents were at school were asked for and this enabled us to establish a rough social class position for the school leavers by classifying these occupations according to the 1951 categories of the Registrar-General which fall into five groups ranging from professional and higher administrative grades in Group I through lower grade non-manual workers and skilled manual workers in Group III to unskilled workers in Group V.

Of the 1,535 people to whom questionnaires were sent 798 responded, or about 54 per cent. This is not a high proportion, but represents a very respectable sample of the total. The records at the sixteen schools varied considerably in completeness and comprehensiveness.

TABLE IV 3

Numerical distribution of replies through sample years

1933	1938	1943	1948	1953	1958	Total
74	89	124	146	164	201	798

The numbers in the aggregates of replies increase as the years advance because, as we have seen, the numbers in the sixteen schools increased greatly over this span of twenty-five years and so more leavers were approached in each of the groups indicated, and in any case the information and addresses were more reliable later. The total response of 798 was not evenly or proportionately divided either between the years or, in aggregate over the six years, between the sixteen schools, or between Quaker schools and the rest, the Friends' school responses being just under twice as numerous. Two of the sixteen schools were eliminated from our final analysis because the response rate in each was under 33 per cent — and one of these was in the rare category of day school. When these two were eliminated the proportion of response rose to 56 per cent. The five Friends' schools yielded at 62 per cent, a rate well above the average, and one of these schools exceeded a 70 per cent response. The other schools averaged 48 per cent response. Approximately 52 per cent of the respondents were female and 48 per cent male. In the statements which follow based on the 798 replies we have tried to make such allowance as we can for these differences and we often analyse the results by treating the Quaker schools and the 'unattached' schools as two separate groups.

If we look first at the social class background of fathers of the respondents using the Registrar-General's 1951 categories the results come out as follows over the whole sample:

TABLE IV 4

Social Class background of fathers of respondents as a percentage

R-G's Group	I	II	III	IV	V	Retired, don't know, etc.
	38	43	11	0·3	—	7·7

If we break this formulation down into the response for Friends' schools and for those we have called 'unattached' because they are separate institutions the results are as follows:

TABLE IV 5

Social Class background by School Grouping

R-G's Group	I	II	III	IV	V	Retired, don't know, etc.
Friends' Schools	34	45	12·5	—	—	8·5
Unattached Schools	45	38	7·5	0·7	—	8·5

If we break these results down further as between boys and girls in each school grouping the results are again slightly different.

TABLE IV 6

Social Class background by School Grouping separated into boys and girls

R-G's Group		I	II	III	IV	V	Retired, don't know, etc.
Friends'	Boys	33	42	16	—	—	9
Schools	Girls	35	49	9	—	—	7
Unattached	Boys	38	43	11	0·7	—	7
Schools	Girls	53	33	4	0·7	—	7

The fathers of 81 per cent of the children at these progressive schools fall into social classes I and II as compared with 19 per cent of 'the economically active and retired males in England and Wales, 1961'.[15] Whereas 11 per cent of the fathers in our sample fall in Group III (lower grade non-manual workers and skilled occupations), 51 per cent of the male population comes into this category. Only 0·7 per cent of our sample comes into Groups IV and V combined, whereas the national figure is 30 per cent.

If we compare these figures with those provided by Kalton for the public schools[16] we find that 84 per cent of fathers in these schools fall into Groups I and II as compared with 81 per cent in our sample. The larger proportion of Quaker boys in Group III of our sample is probably accounted for by the fairly generous provision of scholarships and bursaries at Friends' schools either from the Friends' Education Council or other Quaker sources or through special arrangements with Local Education Authorities. Inevitably, however, there is a large predominance from upper income and social groupings and this in its turn is likely to influence the career patterns of the children.

We examined the age at which our sample left school and 70 per cent of them stayed until they were at least coming up to seventeen.

TABLE IV 7

Percentage of 798 respondents leaving progressive schools at different ages

Age	14–15	15–16	16–17	17–18	18–19	19+
	1·9	6·0	22·2	42·5	25·9	1·4

[15] *Census 1961, England and Wales, Occupation Tables,* H.M.S.O., 1966.
[16] G. Kalton, *The Public Schools,* pp. 35–36.

It will be useful to compare these figures with the proportions in other types of school. Kalton collected these for public schools, Direct Grant schools, and maintained grammar schools. He also provides data on the percentage of boy leavers at all maintained secondary schools in the country. Figures are set down in Table IV 8 below so that rough comparisons may be made. The figures in Table IV 7 above are for both boys and girls and Kalton's figures are for boys only. The figures have been conflated here to give one reading in each cell, where Kalton gives separate readings for day pupils only, day and boarding pupils mixed, and boarding pupils only.[17]

TABLE IV 8

Percentage of leavers from different kinds of secondary school by ages

Type of School	14–15/15–16	16–17	17–18	18–19	19+
Progressive	7·9	22·2	42·5	25·9	1·4
Independent	2	12	28	50	8
Direct Grant	3	14·3	26·3	45·3	11
Maintained Grammar	7	36	18	29	9
All Secondary	67	20	5	6	2

The Kalton figures are based on 1962–3 returns and the progressive sample is based on returns for school leavers over the twenty-five years from 1933 to 1958. The proportion of leavers between fourteen and sixteen from the grammar schools is not very different from the figure for the unorthodox schools. It is known from our data that about 53 per cent of the 7·9 per cent who left their progressive school under the age of sixteen went on to another school and do not represent a loss to full-time education. This is much less true of the grammar-school sector. Parents of some children at the radical schools clearly thought that their sons and daughters stood a better chance in examinations and careers if they moved at this stage to more conventional schools. The percentage loss at this point from the independent or direct grant school is between one half and one quarter of that from the other schools.

A second matter of note is the loss after Ordinary level at sixteen and seventeen from the grammar school and the progressive school. If eighteen is taken as the usual age at which Advanced level examinations in the General Certificate of Education are taken, something like 61

[17] Kalton, *The Public Schools*, p. 81.

per cent of grammar school pupils have left at or by that stage and the figure for the progressive schools is over 72 per cent. Only 42 per cent from the public schools leave by or at the age of eighteen and about 44 per cent from the direct grant schools. However, it should be remembered that our sample for the progressive schools covers a period in the 1930s when the statutory minimum leaving age was fourteen and when the school-leaving pattern in the country as a whole was not as it was in 1962–3 when Kalton's figures were obtained.

The proportion of eighteen- and nineteen-plus students together is very similar at about 58 per cent in independent and direct grant schools with grammar school pupils next at 38 per cent and progressive schools at about 27 per cent. Again the picture in all these innovating schools in the 1960s is different.

We broke down this school leaving in progressive schools by social class and between Friends' schools and unattached schools. The most striking thing here was that there was no sign of early leaving across the five class groupings, or to put it another way, roughly the same percentage in all classes stayed up to sixteen–seventeen years of age, up to seventeen–eighteen, and up to eighteen–plus. Children whose parents were dead or retired, or not in an active, earning job, often stayed on until eighteen plus — the figure was just above 42 per cent of this rather special group. There is a high percentage of late leaving in Friends' schools among those who were not getting much financial support from the family. Perhaps the generous scholarship and bursary position in Friends' schools helped this situation, as has already been noted.

Of the 798 there were 509 who were married — about 64 per cent, and 427, or about 84 per cent, of this group had children. Of these parents as a group about 79 per cent said they would arrange or had arranged a progressive school education for their children and just under 20 per cent said they would not send their children to a progressive school. Many of these rejected the proposal because they thought they could not afford it, and some thought a day school more important than anything else but would have liked to find one run on unorthodox lines although they usually could not. The parents often claimed that the family upbringing would be permissive and in line with progressive school practice even if they could not afford to send their children to such an establishment — they had come to value it for what it had done for them.

We examined the record of those who went on from unorthodox schools to get further qualifications whether by full-time or part-time study. Some of these qualifications required study at a university, others at a college of education or a technical college, others through professional associations, and so on. Of the 798 respondents at least 84 per cent gained one additional qualification by further study and a sizeable proportion took still higher qualifications in addition. About 36 per cent of these qualifications were degrees or diplomas in technology and this is almost exactly the same as the proportion for boys quoted by Kalton as going from the public schools to the universities in 1962–3.[18] About 19 per cent of maintained grammar school boys at that time went from school to university or College of Advanced Technology. About 16 per cent of the progressive group qualified as doctors or dentists. These figures should be read against the relatively high proportions leaving their progressive school by or at the age of eighteen.

About 14 per cent of the progressive school sample gained teachers' certificates in education, about 9 per cent through Colleges of Education or Training Colleges as they used to be called, the remaining 5 per cent as graduates in university Departments of Education. About 2 per cent of the boys in the independent and Direct Grant schools went to Colleges of Education in 1962–3 and from the grammar schools about 4 per cent. The interest in teaching of former pupils of progressive schools is noticeably high and will be detailed later.

Perhaps it should be mentioned here that in our sample something over 5 per cent from Friends' schools had to take additional entry qualifications after leaving school, like the former Higher Schools Certificate or Advanced level subjects in the present General Certificate of Education or the Ordinary National Certificate or Diploma. The comparable figure from the unattached progressive schools was above 11 per cent. There is a moral here, perhaps, which may be traced out later. For the moment it is enough to say that these pupils for the most part got what they tried for after leaving their progressive school, and adds a dimension to the conclusion already arrived at, that there were quite a number leaving progressive schools at or before the age of eighteen.

Many of these schools have junior sections, or eleven plus as well as thirteen plus entries, and it is not uncommon for pupils to enter at the

[18] Kalton, *The Public Schools*, p. 95.

sixth form level. Of those who left by the age of sixteen, 35 per cent had been at the school for five years or longer, while of those who left at eighteen or over, some 25 per cent had been at school for less than five years. The table looks like this:

TABLE IV 9

Length of time spent at progressive school by percentage of age-group

Age at leaving school	Under 5 years	5 years and over	Don't know
14–16	65·1	34·9	—
16–17	47·5	52·5	—
17–18	35·7	63·7	0·6
18+	24·8	75·2	—

This distribution indicates the difficulty of relating career choice to the influence of the progressive school, for many pupils in the sample will have spent at least as long at other schools. But some differences there clearly are.

First of all it may not be unexpected, when 81 per cent of the fathers of the sample are in Groups I and II of the distribution of occupations, to find that much the same percentage of the respondents themselves were in these groups — about 80 per cent. The breakdown within this large proportion yields some interesting variations and these might be set out in tabular form, following the model given first in 1951 by Roe.[19] She distinguished eight categories of occupation and plotted against these five levels of responsibility and class positions. This work was done in America but it has provided a useful structure on which, with few modifications, we can establish a sketch of the distribution of occupations reported by our sample.

The largest proportion of occupations is to be found in the 'service' group (number 1) where, of 24·9 per cent of the total, 18·5 per cent were teachers which is a notable proportion by any standards, especially when one remembers again that this sample stretches over twenty-five years from 1933 to 1958. Teachers who are graduates are not yet required to take a teaching qualification, hence the difference from the 14 per cent who did so quoted above. When we differentiate between

[19] Anne Roe, *The Psychology of Occupations* (New York, 1956).

TABLE IV 10

Percentages of the sample by Groups of Occupations with examples

Registrar-General's Group	1 Service	2 Business Contact	3 Organization	4 Technology	5 Outdoor	6 Science	7 General Culture	8 Art and Entertainment	Total
I	0·1 (Clergyman, psychiatrist)	—	3·3 (Director, company secretary, chief accountant, higher civil servant, actuary)	4·9 (Engineer, surveyor)	—	8·0 (Doctor, dentist, research scientist, statistician)	3·9 (Lawyer, journalist, economist)	3·3 (Architect, writer, producer)	23·5
II	21·9 (Teacher, social worker, inspector, educational therapist)	0·3 (Auctioneer, public relations officer)	9·4 (Manager, administrator, local government official,	4·4 (Technical manager, draughtsman, ship's officer)	4·3 (Farmer, smallholder, agricultural development officer)	9·0 (Nurse, optician, veterinary surgeon, physiotherapist)	3·6 (Lecturer, translator, publisher, bookseller)	3·9 (Lecturer, artist, T.V. or film director, teacher of the arts)	56·8

	nurse, chef, hair-dresser, home help	repre-sentative, market research inter-viewer	clerk, shop assistant	manual worker, technical assistant	technical worker	tory tech-nician, chiropodist, auxiliary nurse		musician, model, photo-grapher	
IV & V	0·9 (Recep-tionist, domestic servant)	—	—	0·7 (Semi-skilled and unskilled worker)	0·7 (Labourer)	—	—	—	2·12
TOTAL	24·9	1·1	21·7	11·6	5·3	19·7	7·5	8·3	100·1

the group from Friends' schools and those from unattached progressive schools we find the Quaker group are about 28 per cent higher as compared with the unattached group in the proportion of the sample under this heading of service. Neill claims in a number of places that scarcely any Summerhillians are teachers — they are too free for positions involving authority.

The second largest group (21·7 per cent) has to do with organization (number 3), and it is mainly business, industry, trading, or administration that is involved. Even if the business contact group is added, the proportion (22·8 per cent) is still smaller than the service group, and there is no real difference between the Quaker and unattached samples under this heading.

The science category (number 6) provides us with nearly 20 per cent of the sample and here again those from Friends' schools are about 28 per cent more numerous than the unattached respondents. What this seems to suggest is not very surprising — pupils from Friends' schools find themselves drawn to careers of service and to careers in science, by far the largest proportion of which are in medicine as doctors or nurses and this might, in a different cross-classification, be allied to the service category. But it should not be thought that the response from the unattached schools under this heading is negligible — it is not.

In technology (number 4) the Quaker respondents are over 25 per cent fewer than the unattached respondents, which may appear surprising. In the art and entertainment (number 8) the unattached return is about 60 per cent higher than that from the Friends' schools, which with the rather more conservative Quaker tradition is not unexpected, but anyone knowing the Friends' schools today would not think that the gap is now as wide as all that. A rather smaller discrepancy, but still a significant one is to be found in the higher number of respondents from the unattached schools under the heading of general culture (number 7).

When we look at these results in relation to men and to women from the Friends' schools and the unattached schools, there are one or two surprises. We have already seen that the Quaker group are considerably more numerous in the service category (number 1), but the women are in similar proportions from each type of school. The Quaker men, however, are more than three times as numerous as the unattached men. Although there is not much difference in the combined returns under the heading of organization (number 3) the Quaker men are over 35 per cent higher in proportion. However, the women from the unattached schools are nearly 25 per cent more numerous than the women from the Friends' schools.

In the science category (number 6) there is no real difference between the proportions of the men's responses but there were, first of all, about 30 per cent more responses from women as a group, and of these the Quaker women were over 35 per cent more numerous than the women from the unattached schools.

We have already noted that the returns from the unattached schools under the heading of technology (number 4) are over 25 per cent higher than the returns from the Friends' schools. This is almost entirely due to the readings for the men, because the women in the two groups of schools combined return only about 2 per cent of the total registered in this category.

In the art and entertainment (number 8) the wide gap in favour of the unattached schools is shared by both the men and the women with a slightly higher proportion of men.

Without trying to lean too heavily on these figures we can see a broad distribution of careers with teaching and service highest of all, organization and science close behind, and Quaker patterns of service revealing themselves predictably. Again the arts have a higher place than is usual, especially for the unattached schools.

Two professions do not appear, except marginally, and these might also be predictable. The first is the Church, and as Friends have no order of priesthood this is likely, although about half of the pupils attending Friends' schools do not come from Quaker families. We have noticed elsewhere that in the unattached schools the approach to religious teaching is usually not aligned to any ecclesiastical position and of course the women in the sample cannot follow this profession to all intents and purposes. The second low-scoring profession is a career in the armed forces, and this again might be expected for both groups of schools. Friends are committed as a body to pacifism and the unattached group of schools have no sympathy for military organizations. At least 6 per cent of public school leavers in Kalton's sample joined the forces and this relates to the proportion of parents who are in the forces.[20] There is, however, a proportion of public school leavers going into farming which compares well with the 5·3 per cent in the progressive group (number 5).

[20] Kalton, *The Public Schools*, pp. 96–97.

We classified the occupations of the parents of the respondents on the Roe model as above — they gave this information on the questionnaire.

TABLE IV 11

Percentage of parents by Occupational Group

1	2	3	4	5	6	7	8
13	1	41	15	6	11	9	4

The dominance of the organizational group (number 3) is surprisingly heavy, followed by technology (number 4) a long way behind, with the service category (number 1) lying a very close third, and a scientific career (number 6) coming next, when most of the sample are doctors.

As we now know the occupational distribution for the children of the sample mentioned above we can compare this with the distribution for their fathers and it would be best to compare only the returns for the males of our sample for obvious reasons. Taking the whole male sample we find that only half as many of the sons went into organizational jobs compared with the fathers and this means that the distribution to categories other than organizational does not drop as steeply as with the fathers. The shortest and clearest way to make the comparison is to state it in tabular form (see p. 333).

Some influence in the changes between fathers and sons must be ascribed to the changes in national opportunity. For instance, the number of openings in science and technology has greatly increased. The highest proportion here is in the unattached sons, and this has something to do with the school. However, the percentages of fathers and sons in the unattached group concerned with art and entertainment (number 8) are comparable and significantly high as compared with the Quaker return and here both school and parental influence have been almost equally at work as a further breakdown of parent-child occupation shows. The highest percentage in the service grouping (number 1), is to be found in the Quaker sons, where 15·6 per cent of the sample are. In general, the move away from the high preponderance of organizational jobs in the fathers to service, technology, science, and general cultural work for the sons, together with a relatively high return from the unattached fathers and sons in art and entertainment, indicate the interest in individualistic and socially useful

TABLE IV 12

Percentage distribution of occupations of fathers and sons in the total male sample

	1 Service	2 Business Contact	3 Organization	4 Technology	5 Outdoor	6 Science	7 General Culture	8 Art and Entertainment
Fathers	10·5	1·7	42·0	16·0	4·7	8·7	10·2	6·1
Sons	12·8	1·6	21·5	22	6·8	13·6	14·1	7·6
	1	2	3	4	5	6	7	8
Quaker Sample								
Fathers	10·5	2·7	45·2	16·4	5·5	7·8	9·6	2·3
Sons	15·6	1·7	24·9	19·8	6·3	13·9	12·7	5·1
	1	2	3	4	5	6	7	8
Unattached Sample								
Fathers	10·5	—	36·3	15·3	3·2	10·6	11·3	12·9
Sons	7·6	1·5	15·3	26	7·6	13	16·8	12·2

work that characterizes the progressive group as a whole through the schools. If anything, the unattached group shows up somewhat more often in the individualistic categories and the Quaker group under the socially useful headings — and this we might expect.

Although scarcely any men and women in the sample had entered upon a career in the armed forces, 58 per cent of the men and 9 per cent of the women had undergone national service. Sixty-four per cent of the Quaker men and 48 per cent of the unattached had served, together with 10 per cent of the Quaker women and 9 per cent of the unattached women. We have included under this heading, mostly an adult war-time and early post-war generation, those who were conscientious objectors who usually had some form of alternative service to perform.

TABLE IV 13

Percentage and form of military service

	All men	Quaker men	Unattached men
Army	35·1	26·8	55·4
Navy	11·7	10·2	15·4
R.A.F.	23	24·8	18·5
Merchant Navy	1·4	1·9	—
Conscientious objectors	28·8	36·3	10·8

The proportion of conscientious objectors is high, predictably so in the products of Friends' schools, but also much above the average in unattached schools. When asked if they could name benefits they thought the various forms of service might have offered for their career, nearly 70 per cent of the Quaker sample and over 50 per cent of the unattached said that they had gained in self-assurance or experience in authority. About 12 per cent claimed the practical experience was of value for their career and almost none said they had learned habits of discipline. Forty-nine per cent of all those who had undergone service said it had no value at all.

Of the 798 respondents, 531 were in employment at the receipt of the questionnaire. Of the 267 not in employment about 65 per cent were housewives and another 18 per cent were in full-time study and about 12 per cent were doing unpaid work, a few were unemployed or sick, a similar tiny fraction had either retired or had never worked because they did not need to. Those in employment were asked about their present gross salary, and 94 per cent answered the questions.

TABLE IV 14

Percentage earning salaries at various levels in £'s

Below 500	501– 750	751– 1,000	1,001– 1,500	1,501– 2,000	2,001– 3,000	3,001– 5,000	over 5,000
8·7	16·5	19·0	23·6	10·5	11·7	7·1	3·0

The median income falls in the £1,001–1,500 category, but there is a fairly wide dispersal over the whole range. On the whole, the earnings of the Quaker sample are higher than those of the unattached — 65 per cent of the Quaker earnings fall below £1,500 and 35 per cent above: the figures for the unattached are 74 and 26 per cent. If we take the total numbers of men and women and analyse them in the same way we find that 45 per cent of the men earn over £1,500 and only 7 per cent of the women. About 21 per cent of the women earn less than £500, though some of these are in part-time jobs. It would appear, however, that the women from the unattached schools have a higher average income than the Quaker women — it is the Quaker men who earn more than their counterparts.

Naturally the average income is higher the older the age group, and this can be shown in tabular form:

TABLE IV 15

Average income by percentage and year of sample

Year of leaving	£1,500 and under	over £1,500
1933	19·2	80·8
1938	23·8	76·2
1943	26·7	73·3
1948	51·5	48·5
1953	76·5	23·5
1958	95·4	4·6

A fuller version of this table shows more clearly the kind of development that has taken place.

TABLE IV 16

Percentage of men in salary groupings by year of sample in £'s

Year of leaving	750 and under	751– 1,500	1,501– 3,000	3,000 and above
1933	—	19·2	30·8	*50·0*
1938	4·8	19·0	*50·0*	26·2
1943	6·7	20·0	*50·0*	23·3
1948	3·0	*48·5*	33·3	15·2
1953	4·4	*72·1*	20·6	2·9
1958	*50·8*	44·1	4·6	—

The italic figures show where the large groups in each year's sample are to be found and the table represents a flight of steps so that more than half of those who left in 1958 were earning less than £750 and half of those who left in 1933 were earning over £3,000 with correspondingly ascending steps in the intervening years. The figures were obtained in 1963-4 so that the large proportion of the 1958 sample who went on to a university or some other form of higher education had just started on their careers. If we recall that 84 per cent of the 798 respondents gained at least one further qualification after leaving school, that over 38 per cent took a university degree or the equivalent, and that most courses take three years, the picture of more than half the 1958 sample earning less than £750 is to be expected. Obviously the progressive schools would not consider earnings by themselves as a measure of educational success. However, the figures in this table show that, while children in progressive schools come from families where over 80 per cent of the fathers are in occupational Groups I and II, the education given by the schools has not been so unworldly that it has hampered pupils in their careers. Nevertheless, because a large proportion of our sample have entered teaching or other social welfare professions, the average income is lower than, say, a comparable sample of boys from public schools, both because the latter have gone into the better paid professions, the armed forces, the higher civil service, industry, and because there are women in the progressive sample, which in itself brings a lower average.[21] Without taking time

---

[21] See I. Weinberg, 'The Occupational Aspirations of British Public Schoolboys', in *The School Review* (University of Chicago), vol. 74, no. 3, 1966, pp. 265–82. Also chap. 6 in I. Weinberg, *The English Public Schools* (New York, 1967).

on detail, 79 per cent of the men and women teachers were earning under £1,500 and if this was limited to men teachers only, 58 per cent of those were under £1,500. On the other hand the same proportion of lawyers (58 per cent) were earning over £1,500 and the majority of this group were above the £3,000 mark; much the same pertained for the group of architects and all those in television, film, or radio work earned over £1,500.

The age at which the respondents first took up permanent paid employment is a useful index of their social and educational standing:

TABLE IV 17

Age on commencement of permanent paid employment as percentages

Age	Percentage
15 or 16	6
17 or 18	24
19 or 20	21
21 or over	49

If the parents of these children were predominantly members of the liberal middle class, the children themselves follow in their fathers' footsteps with a wider spread of professions and occupations to show for it.

We were not able to make a comparison between this pattern of results with readings across twenty-five years, and a similar maintained school sample, for the data do not exist. The best we could do was to make a comparison between the 1958 returns for the progressive schools and the national survey of twenty-one year olds carried out in that year. We chose those educated at maintained grammar schools whose parents were placed in social classes I and II as more than 80 per cent of those children in the progressive schools had parents in these groupings, as we have seen. The grammar school leavers and the progressive school leavers were compared on the Roe classification (see Table IV 10 above). There were certain occupational groups in which there was no significant difference in the frequency distribution between the two samples — for instance in the readings for the business contact occupations. There were some headings under which there were significant differences, and as the statistical analysis is too detailed

M

for verbal description, those categories are set down in tabular form. Sub-divisions for the two social classes have been made and for the two groups of progressive schools :

TABLE IV 18

Comparison of progressive leavers and grammar school leavers in 1958 according to Roe categories *

Roe classification	1	2	3	4	5	6	7	8
Registrar-General's Group I								
Friends' Schools	+		−	−				
Unattached			−				+	+
Registrar-General's Group II								
Friends' schools				−			+	
Unattached	−		−				−	+	+

* A higher proportion is shown (+) and a lower is shown (−).

The Quaker service category in Group I is significantly larger than the grammar school return, and a large part of this can be ascribed to the proportion of those in what might be called the medical helping professions. In no other category in Group I do the Quaker schools by themselves produce a higher proportion than the grammar schools, and in organizational jobs and careers in technology they produce a lower proportion and in the rest break fairly even. The unattached schools have a much higher proportion than the grammar schools in the general cultural and the art and entertainment categories and a lower proportion in the organizational and scientific categories. In the Registrar-General's Group II the Friends' schools score high in the general cultural category, as do the unattached schools once again, and again the Quaker leavers score low in technology, with all the rest breaking fairly even. It is surprising that the proportion of teachers does not bring the Quaker schools higher in the service category. In Group II the unattached schools score high in general culture and in art and entertainment and are once again lower in science and organization, with another low rating in the service category. Group II teachers in grammar schools and Friends' schools are relatively of the same high proportion and both significantly higher than in the un-attached schools.

These are rough assessments, and if the progressive schools are bulked as a single return, they score higher than the maintained schools in the service category, in the outdoor category, and in the science, general culture, and art and entertainment groupings. In other words out of the eight categories in the Roe table, there is a detectable difference in five of them in the proportion of alumni from progressive schools as compared with those from maintained schools. In business contacts the score is even and the high score moves to the maintained schools under the heading of organization and to a lesser degree in technology. Substantially, the picture that has already been sketched continues in the comparison with the maintained schools — service, culture, the arts, science, outdoor pursuits, are leading categories of employment for the progressive schools. As compared with main-tained schools, they score lower in business contacts and technology, and to some extent in organization.

V

In this chapter on facts and figures an attempt has been made to review the growth of the radical schools from four points of view. Recognition by the Board or Ministry of Education is a sign of standards of provision, of facilities and staffing, of educational achievement and nearly all of the schools have aimed for this and obtained it. Those which have not are now under scrutiny and pressure will be upon them. The progressive schools cannot now be as defiant as they used to be, or to put it another way, the Department of Education and Science has now more experience of permissive education on which to base its recommendations.

The second topic was numbers, growth, expansion. Numbers show a relatively slow growth and a strong attachment to a small school community, the upper limits at Bryanston and Gordonstoun, the biggest schools, still being under five hundred. Here, in the dawn of the comprehensive school, is a sharp difference from the current thought in the maintained sector.

Third, there is the theme of cost, of fees, salaries, economic survival. Fourth is the sketch of the career pattern of former pupils to see what effect the education provided by these schools has produced and to chart any preferences that have appeared over the years.

The story of the development of the schools, the ideas of the founders and the educational principles of a loosely connected movement have been set down in earlier chapters. The facts, figures and suggested interpretations in this chapter have sought to add data and perspective to the record.

Part Four

Conclusion

I

THE progressive schools have, since the foundation of Abbotsholme in 1889, started from a position of protest made against other types of school, against certain procedures in schools, against condescension to children in any society, against academic emphases in the curriculum, against formality and lack of spontaneity in personal relationships, and against authoritarianism in all its forms. The affirmations corresponding to these protests can be detected scattered through the earlier pages of this book and ought now to be brought together.

While only Abbotsholme claimed in 1890 to be providing an education for the sons of the directing classes who might ordinarily go to public schools, the other schools had the same clientele in mind — daughters as well as sons at Bedales and King Alfred's. These schools in the 1890s provided between them a curriculum such as we find in many schools today — English, modern languages, mathematics, sciences including geology, physics, chemistry, biology, history, geography, some economics, and social studies. Physical education included walking, climbing, swimming, cycling, canoeing, and, to a limited degree, gymnastics and the usual school games. Work on the land and in the daily routine of the home was related to physical fitness, and was intended to lead to an understanding of basic crafts and skills and a deeply woven awareness of the interdependence of a human community. Boys and girls painted, sculpted, worked in wood, and made music as a part of normal life. None of this kind of thinking was found to any notable degree in the public or maintained schools at the time.

Reddie and Badley were concerned for mental health and wanted to be explicit about this rather than to accept the unspoken attitudes and disapprobations implicit in public school good form. Frankness, a reasonable enthusiasm for the good name and good behaviour of the school, were encouraged among the pupils at Abbotsholme and Bedales. At the public schools, sex, religion, and politics were not discussed as part of the open exchange of ideas between masters and boys. At Abbotsholme, Bedales, King Alfred's, and Clayesmore, particularly at the first three, education was concerned with such matters. King Alfred's was even so unusual as to base its case on humanism, and this rationalism appeared all the more extreme and objectionable to public school religion.

The new schools were opposed, root and branch, to the hierarchy of the public school. Fagging and the privileged élite were replaced by the ideal of the school family, although even in these radical schools caning was retained; but the relationships of teachers and pupils were informal — distressingly casual as some critics said. Even though Reddie was an autocrat and Badley remained sufficiently aloof to be called the Chief throughout his time at Bedales, their involvement in the life of the boys was far more comprehensive than the formalities of the public schools in the 1890s allowed to their heads. Reddie and Badley went cycling and camping and walking and climbing with their boys and at Bedales after 1898 girls joined the parties. The assistant masters and mistresses also entered into this spirit in the schools, but it was rare in other schools of the time.

Reddie, Badley, and Devine sought to reform all sides of school life. The boys' clothes at Abbotsholme and Bedales were far more comfortable and practical than at Eton, Harrow, Winchester, and Westminster. The heads and their assistants at Abbotsholme and Bedales were informal in their Norfolk jackets as compared with the respectable dark suits and ritual gown and square of Rugby or St. Paul's. Chapel services at the radical schools had no historic liturgy or established form of service. Worship gathered together prayers, invocations, and hymns from the Bible, from sacred literature in many lands, from poetry and prose. Music both sacred and secular was part of the worship and of the daily life in a way unique to schools of the time, but much more frequent in the last twenty years.

The heads of these new schools were at one time allied to the radical Left, but later they addressed themselves directly to the middle classes. From the start of Abbotsholme and Bedales there was only a nominal connection with the Fellowship of the New Life and this not in any political or egalitarian sense. The schools were communities set in the country and many of their ideas are to be found in the same family of thought as those of Ruskin or Edward Carpenter. Whereas earlier in the century Robert Owen had ventured into industrial and urban renewal, as the Fabians and the Independent Labour Party did at the turn of this century, the radical schools of the 1890s, indeed progressive schools generally from that time, have not made an impact on education in the city. The school set in the country and therefore usually a boarding establishment, makes it appeal to the intellectuals of the Left and the liberal intelligentsia. It is highly significant that none of the four protest schools of the 1890s made common cause with new state schools. The Balfour Act of 1902 called out little answering approach from these four. There was simply no mutual recognition because maintained schools were not aiming at the same things as the progressive schools. At the beginning the progressive schools did not see the emergence of the central authority and the local authority as anything which might later threaten the autonomy of all independent schools.

These radical schools were (and are) numerically small centres of protest aiming at reforms in educational practice in model school communities. Their founders were not social revolutionaries, prepared to desert at an early stage the schools they were bending all energies to establish in order to start a political organization. We have emphasized more than once that no corporate movement was shaped in radical education, and we have said that the strength of this group of schools has been their individual identity, their family life and the assumption that parents of the real families of the pupils would be prepared to join the school family in a shared enterprise. This liberal individualism was thought to be so extreme before 1914 that the public schools attempted to neuter it by implacable condescension. The new state grammar schools were too preoccupied with their own identity to be much concerned about anyone else's, and they inevitably found respectability more enticing than revolt. But until the beginning of the Second World War, and especially until 1930, the progressive schools were crusading to reform secondary education and pupils were expected to be critical of the educational and social establishment.

Reddie and Badley and Devine laid out their educational beliefs and practices and waited for takers. As they provided boarding schools their pupils could come from anywhere rather than only from the

M 2

locality and as substantial fees had to be paid there was no guaranteed clientele. Since the heads had declared their unorthodox position they expected to attract parents and staff colleagues tolerant of these views because the exceptional beliefs and practices were in the open and could be voluntarily accepted or at least taken on trust by all concerned. Abbotsholme, Bedales, and Clayesmore were personal enterprises, despite all the expertise and support offered by the governing bodies. Parents were choosing and buying what Reddie, Badley, and Devine had to offer and in the first forty years what they provided was risky. Unlike the local authority foundations these schools could never have a guaranteed supply of pupils, and if the ideas were too extreme, the cost too high, or the organization faulty the venture would end in bankruptcy and there have been times when all three schools have been perilously near it.

The Quaker schools took the hint and moved in the same direction as these three, rather more moderately and rather less far, as might be expected. They were not individual enterprises and they moved at the pace of the shared view of a Friends' meeting. Because their centre of gravity was not one man and his conviction and energy, but a committee of a dispersed national religious movement, their stability has been in some ways the greater.

The progressive schools of the 1890s were aiming to reform education and hindsight takes over if we blame them for not having the foresight to see what it would all look like seventy years on, in the fundamentally different world of the later 60s of the twentieth century. Reddie, Badley, and Devine had, each in his way, an ideal of the liberal-Christian gentleman who had the moral qualities of Arnold's Rugby, together with a wide range of intellectual, artistic, and practical skills and a developed understanding of sexual, social, moral, and religious problems. Their programmes and their schools were very much out of the ordinary at their time of origin, and in practice and in community values Abbotsholme, Bedales, and Clayesmore still are.

After the First World War the target for criticism was still the public schools. But England was a different place in the 1920s. The internationalism of these pioneer schools and of the New Education Fellowship grew in the years following the establishment of the League of Nations. Rendcomb, Dartington, Summerhill, the Malting House, Beacon Hill were all founded in a fresh, post-war conviction that much needed changing and the public schools were exposed to new and savage attacks in books like Alec Waugh's *The Loom of Youth*, Robert Graves's *Good-bye to All That*, and Lytton Strachey's onslaught on Thomas Arnold in *Eminent Victorians*. This mood of disenchantment and intellectual and moral emancipation was right for the new schools.

The new feature was Freud and psychoanalysis and his insistence on the primacy of infantile experience, with the attendant dangers of misdirection by parents of their children's libidinal energy and free growth. Co-education was at a premium, children's freedom and self-regulation were preached with new conviction, the radical schools ran more defiantly counter to the public schools and the state secondary schools than ever before or since. The parents were commonly of the intellectual Left and there was a middle-class interest in Labour and Liberal politics and a corresponding desire to spread progressive ideas from the radical schools to state schools and public schools and also to training colleges. These sympathies led to active political participation by a number of former pupils of progressive schools in the late 1920s and 30s. Schools like Eton and Haileybury and Berkhamsted and Rugby and Winchester produced Orwell and John Strachey and Connolly and Attlee and Graham Greene and William Plomer and Hugh Gaitskell, but these were the known rebels and *francs-tireurs*. Former pupils of the progressive schools were expected to be radicals, and if one of them was a political or cultural conservative he was looked upon as a rare specimen.

Educational theory in the radical schools was taken very seriously indeed in the 1920s and 30s and the three points of emphasis were the importance of freedom rather than restraint in infancy; the importance of spontaneity and expressiveness with the consequence that play and exploration and the child's initiative, especially in the arts, were stressed; the importance of positive attitudes and the primacy of emotions rather than intellect in education. Freud and sex, Adler and the will to power, McDougall and the instincts, Jung and individuation all had a major place in progressive educational theory and practice of the time. Perhaps most important of all was the pervading acceptance in these circles of the unconscious mind and its educational significance. For the bulk of people education was pre-eminently concerned with intellectual, moral, and spiritual training, with premeditated and selected goals and practices, with curricula, subjects, and explicit methods, with teachers teaching and pupils learning, with lessons understood and examinations passed. Neill, the Russells, Susan Isaacs, Curry were, as we have seen, committed to something very different. So too were the followers of Rudolf Steiner, whose beliefs were different again.

Bryanston and Gordonstoun were nearer the centre of a spectrum which had Summerhill at one end and Winchester at the other. The two progressive boys' schools had affinities to the public schools as well as to Abbotsholme and Clayesmore, and this has been commented upon in earlier chapters. In the later 1920s and early 1930s, when Bryanston and Gordonstoun were founded, politics and economics had broken the social vacuum that surrounded psychoanalysis and its derivatives. The depression around 1930 brought the misery and poverty of millions before the public eye and conscience, and however balanced your psyche was, an empty stomach and unemployment were going to disturb psychological equilibrium just as surely as infantile frustration or inhibition. The growing political burden of Communism and Nazism, and more particularly the second, became heavier and its consequence in the flood of refugees pressed heavily on the internationally-minded progressive schools. Psychoanalysis and free discipline appeared to be socially and politically misdirected to many men and women whose relatives and friends had died in gas-chambers or who had left possessions and position to escape alive with their children from Germany. But the liberals in the progressive schools extended a welcome as far as they could and they were obvious enemies of Fascism and Nazism, many of them meeting the totalitarian threat as convinced pacifists. Monkton Wyld and Wennington were founded in 1940 to reassert these values to refugees and evacuated children even in war-time.

There have been no new progressive schools of this kind founded since 1945 except the Atlantic College and a few other schools of the Gordonstoun stamp.

II

The preceding section was an historical retrospect. Now we turn to a number of conceptual points arising from the progressive tradition. Any school may be considered as a certain place, a special community with a unique life because of the people who make it up. The same school may be thought of as an institution with a particular kind of organization, a responsibility to instruct and train, a generally stated theory of education. The school is also only one institution among many others, and like them, susceptible to change because of the effect o political, economic, social, and cultural factors on the fabric of society.

The radical schools have been much concerned with the unique life of the school community. Insofar as a school can be said to have a purpose which the teachers and the pupils together realize, the progressives have been fairly explicit in stating their general intentions and shaping the means. Perry has made a valuable analysis of what he calls 'the child-centred model' from which some of the following points are taken.[1] Using such a model the knowledge-dimension in school is reduced and the role of the teacher as intellectual authority is diminished. The fact is neglected that curricula abridge and compress knowledge for coherence and mastery — pupils are expected to look after the knowledge aspect for themselves far more than in the traditional school situation. In the personality aspect the child-centred teacher is not expected to instruct the pupil in what to believe, but to lead him by discussion and by example to accept worthy, but not very well-defined objectives, and discussion is seen as a good instrument in itself. Essentially the teacher is a guide, a therapist, a psychologist more than an instructor and the assumption is that the pupil will come to see this and co-operate in the whole process. If the response of the pupil in the knowledge-dimension or in the personality-dimension is not co-operative, the child-centred teacher sees this in terms of breakdown in personal relationships, whereas the traditional teacher sees it as laziness or incomprehension or moral weakness. A major part of the responsibility for conducting pupil-teacher relationships in the child-centred mode of thinking is placed on the child, in the expectation that he will exhibit a maturity beyond his years, although in another area of the theory it is assumed that there is a developmental sequence whereby children's problems lead into and become adult problems. Here is a dilemma in child-centred thinking — the encouragement of spontaneity, and the expectation of maturity beyond a child's years.

Traditionalists emphasize the secondary school age range and are less sure of what to do with young children; the child-centred supporters stress the development of younger children, and their interest-based principles of self-regulation are more difficult to maintain with the standard of knowledge required for older adolescents.

[1] L. R. Perry, 'What is an Educational Situation?', in *Philosophical Analysis and Education*, ed. R. D. Archambault (London, 1965), pp. 59–86.

These broad categories form a sketched recapitulation of many beliefs and practices instanced in the schools we have considered through these pages. I now turn to some rather different conceptual points.

Education may be seen as a deliberate attempt to induct younger members of a society into ideas, skills, and attitudes which arise from the past or are intended to be of use in dealing with the present and the future. It would be possible to trace this argument through a very broad social context, but for the moment I wish to keep it within the school. In general terms school education has to do with teachers, pupils, knowledge, and the institutions within which the transaction of education takes place. The teachers and the pupils can be grouped together as persons, but this would be to overlook the relationship between them that the existence of a school presupposes. The school is in business to teach and to enable children to learn, whether by traditional or child-centred methods. Ross Finney put the matter like this: 'The [primary] purpose of school is to pass on cognitive capital. Only secondarily is it for getting young people together.'[2]

Of course, because they *are* together the young people and their elders do in fact strike up human relationships of all kinds and the progressive schools regard this as a prime necessity, but the classroom and the school present a pattern of relationships in which a leader is needed whose institutional function to instruct has already been decided. The teacher is not the 'natural' leader of the group — only children in the group, spontaneously chosen either by election or by acceptance of their superiority, can be that. Personal or natural leadership arises when somebody leads spontaneously, being readier to act, more unexpected and complex, maybe more ruthless, than the led. An 'institutional' leader may not do this because he has an expected pattern of behaviour to follow and a conventional framework in which to operate — as one writer has it, his personal influence must be strained through the sieve of formality.

The teacher is, in the first place, an institutional leader. Prestige attaches to the office and authority rests, at the beginning, in the laws and traditions of the office and only later on the teacher as a person. Willard Waller in *The Sociology of Teaching* puts this point trenchantly:

[2] R. L. Finney, *A Sociological Philosophy of Education* (New York, 1928). For a recent contribution to the discussion of this whole issue see Elizabeth Richardson, *The Environment of Learning* (London, 1967).

'Until the teacher's definition of the situation has been accepted he cannot relax. Friendly attitudes must spring up only in a situation defined in terms of teacher domination.'[3] So bald a statement may perturb many people and it appears to be the antithesis of the principles of Homer Lane, Neill, and Curry, but Waller is only stating what happens in most schools. In any case the statement offers wide variations of interpretation and indicates simply that the teacher has the training and the responsibility for planning how to communicate knowledge to a group of children who may not wish to learn what he presents. If this is so, some kind of final authority and incentive has to be available within the structure of the group and, according to Waller, it is vested in the teacher. This dominance-submission aspect is a basic condition of the relationship between the teacher and his pupils, whether it is arrived at by the traditionalist's method or by Neill's method of waiting for inner development in the child. The final recognition by the child is that this adult has something to give for which his pupils must accept conditions which will allow him to teach them.

In this area of leadership, authority, dominance, and submission, one is constantly moving between psychological and sociological interpretations. The psychological interpretation is concerned with the content of, the changes and motives in, human experience. Sociology is concerned far more with the structure of the groupings in which the content, changes, and motives express themselves. The territory of institutional and personal relationships between teachers and pupils is a borderland because from one point of view we are concerned with the content of human attitudes and experience and from another we are interested in the kind of grouping and organization which gives direction to these psychological processes. The progressive schools are committed to a psychological emphasis in the relationship between teacher and pupil and seek to accept only the necessary minimum of dominance-submission structure, a sociological emphasis, to make this possible. The traditional model would reverse the order and this is a very important distinction in trying to understand the difference of ethos between a grammar or public school and a progressive school. This may be illustrated from Friends' schools in the early 1950s:

One teacher wrote soon after starting his work, having come from a grammar school:

[3] W. Waller, *The Sociology of Teaching* (New York, 1932), p. 297.

'We find no imposed control and no self-control. I do not want the former, but I do seek after the latter.'

Another new teacher commented in rueful summary after his first term:

'Every community is built on a slave class. Here it is the staff.'

A third teacher said, after a year in a Friends' school:

'Children further up the school give me increasing friendliness. I suppose the hallowing effect of time is becoming apparent. But, my God, the initial stages are uncomfortable.'[4]

It was said earlier that school education has to do with teachers, pupils, knowledge, and the institutions within which the transaction of education takes place. Enough has just been said on teachers and pupils to show the importance progressive schools attach to the personal part of the teacher's relationship. Earlier still in this chapter, calling on Perry's work, some attempt was made to show the tendency in these schools to diminish the importance of the factual side of knowledge. In the past the evidence for this is seen in the readiness to wait until a child wants to learn; in giving initiative to the pupil in the project method; in avoiding a stereotyped examination objective; in new methods of teaching such as those advocated by Montessori, Dalcroze, Cizek, Caldwell Cook, Dewey, and seen in Helen Parkhurst's Dalton Plan, Gordonstoun's Training Plan and Rescue Services, and the three phases of growth in Steiner's methodology. However, since the end of the Second World War new initiatives in educational methods have come from sources outside the progressive movement, notably in curriculum reorganization — the New Mathematics, Nuffield Science, French in primary schools, programmed instruction, the Schools Council's School Leaving Age Project and its many other undertakings now being developed. These are the new experts who are experimental and test out ideas and methods. Professor Peters makes the point about the changed state of affairs today in this way:

A novel feature of the 1960's is the extent to which education has become a subject for public debate and theoretical speculation. Previously it had been something that was prized or taken for granted by those few who had it, but not widely discussed. Of course there were plenty of schoolday reminiscences [rather than] a passionate interest in education. All this is now changed.[5]

4 W. A. C. Stewart, *Quakers & Education* (London, 1953), p. 265.

5 R. Peters, 'Education as Initiation', in *Philosophical Analysis and Education*, ed. R. D. Archambault, p. 87. Also as a published Inaugural Lecture, pp. 8–9.

So far in this consideration of conceptual points arising from school education we have looked at teachers, pupils, and knowledge. Now we must turn to the institutions within which the transaction of education takes place, and at this point the argument must move back into the mainstream of historical and social analysis.

III

A school cannot maintain existence for long without stable financial backing: it needs pupils, teachers, and equipment and in England, as we have seen, it has to be recognized as efficient by the central authority. If the school is part of the national provision its building and upkeep are, within broad limits, the responsibility of the local education authority and the Department of Education and Science. Many schools were originally, and still are, religious foundations, supported as to a small part from church funds and as to a much larger part from local authority and central sources. Education has become a social service which has to compete for its share of the gross national product with the other services, like health, housing, foreign commitments, and defence, and there is a tendency for the interests of the local areas and regions, which have administered education since 1902, to detect and combat increasing control from the centre. The Royal Commission on Local Government currently at work is expected to redraw the present map of over one hundred and forty authorities to form a much smaller number of regions, with the obvious redistribution between local and national taxation.

With an expanding education service like ours a vast amount of central financial planning is necessary. The planning has to include forecasting the number of school places needed for children of different ages and a long-range provision of the facilities for the training of teachers in corresponding numbers. A consequence of this decentralized organization with ultimate responsibility at the centre in the hands of the Secretary of State for Education and Science is that he can insist upon equality of standard throughout the country. The spurs that prick him to maintain this could be as much political expediency as humane concern and the professional conscience of his permanent civil servants and Her Majesty's Inspectorate.

Political policy and calculation appear in many government decisions on educational matters, as for instance in the voting of money, where an increase for education usually means a decrease elsewhere. While these are economic decisions, they are obviously made on political grounds too. But recently political policy is even more obvious. A Labour Government has decided that in one form or another secondary education shall be comprehensive in form. Where in 1962 about a dozen local authorities operated comprehensive schools, in 1967 the application by all one hundred and forty-six authorities of the comprehensive principle is being worked out following upon the central requirement in Circular 10/65 to draw up plans. This represents a strong blow to the so-called tripartite system of grammar, technical high school, and secondary modern schools and it has as one of its aims to break intellectual separation and in so doing to make selection in secondary education more fluid and, as the inelegant phrase has it, to improve the social mix. There are, of course, strictly educational arguments for comprehensive education, but there are many political ones too, and many of them have to do with making life-chances more equal, with reducing middle- and upper-class privilege.

Another line of argument is economic. Secondary education is expensive and the country has a right to expect efficiency and value for money. Implicit in this is a concern for as fair a distribution of manpower and equipment as possible, and so there is talk of a proper use of plant, rationalization of teacher supply, the minimum size for an economic unit in secondary education, the use of mechanical aids of all kinds, the problems of man-management in large-scale organization. In 1950 there were only two chairs of sociology in British universities and there was no proper management studies until after 1960. The crest of the wave of the social sciences in British educational thinking curled spectacularly in the fifteen years from 1945 to break with great power in the 1960s.

Richard Peters speaks of some of these features as extrinsic to education :

> Some politicians whose noses quiver at the scent of any sort of under-privilege have found in education a quarry that they think they may more safely run to earth than the ferocious old foxes of private ownership and disparity of income. Others, with nervous eyes on the technical achievements of the U.S.A. and U.S.S.R., gladly listen to economists who assure them that education is a commodity in which it is profitable for a community to invest. Sociologists tell teachers that they have a role of acting as a socializ-

ing agency in the community. . . . In all the hubbub about plant, supply of teachers, shortage of provision, streaming and selection too little attention is paid to what it is that so many are deemed to be without.[6]

The grammar secondary schools of 1902 were for a minority who showed intellectual ability, the 'scholarship-winners'. The older foundations, such as the livery company schools which accepted a percentage of 'scholarship-winners', kept a proportion of fee-paying places. Only in 1947 was fee-paying abolished in these older foundations so that they became part of the grammar school provision of the local authority, leaving the fully private schools and the centrally supported Direct Grant schools to form the independent section, though even here the Direct Grant schools accepted up to 50 per cent of their pupils from local authority selection tests and these pupils were paid for from local authority funds.

In the meantime the 1944 Act had stated that secondary education in its totality, for the whole range of pupils, would be available according to age, ability, and aptitude, and no longer on the basis of ability to pay. The first step in organization was the so-called tripartite plan in which 'parity of esteem' was looked for as between grammar, technical high, and secondary modern schools, and the latest step in this progression is the policy of comprehensive schools. But schools persisted which admitted children whose parents could pay and the teachers continued to say that they wanted to provide education of this kind for these pupils. We have seen earlier how these schools have come under the professional eye of the central authority and have to be recognized as efficient, and few of those we have dealt with in this book are not regarded as being well run educational establishments. The three principal criticisms are that these schools provide teaching conditions which demand a larger proportion of trained staff than the maintained schools ; that the schools take in a sector of the child population which comes from affluent homes and so acts as a socially divisive group ; that, in the case of the public schools, former pupils are at a position of advantage in entry particularly to the older universities and in careers by reason of their school education — what is often called 'the old boy network'.

The maintained, tripartite, secondary system now appears in 1967

[6] Peters, 'Education as Initiation', pp. 9 and 11.

to be considered by the government as an historic blunder in social administration. We are participating in a very clear way in reshaping educational organization as part of political strategy. Sociologists, economists, and social theorists have perspectives for society as a whole in which education is seen as an instrument for self-preservation or prosperity, for conservation or change. They are not primarily concerned with a person being educated, still less with the liberal or the progressive tradition, and here lies the cause of a good deal of recrimination between the teacher, the administrator, the economist, and the politician. Each adopts a different viewpoint or emphasis on education with variable attempts at cross-comprehension.

The progressive schools have been founded by teachers who had ideas of what should be taught and how it should be taught. Each school was to be a place in its own right, sufficient for the children and parents who supported it, and the foundation owed nothing to local or national administration, it was not thought of as an economic or political agency in any direct sense, and history has not given these unorthodox schools any disproportionate influence in entry to higher education or to certain careers.

The National Union of Teachers, in numbers and influence by far the greatest of the teachers' associations, recently gave evidence to the Newsom committee on the independent schools demanding the complete integration into the maintained system not only of the public schools but of all other independent education, largely on the principle that fee-paying education is inconsistent with an egalitarian democracy and a maintained school range of high quality. A number of other bodies have submitted evidence of a similar kind, and writing on this Kenneth Barnes, the head of Wennington, said:

> Can anyone be so complacent about mass-organized education as to believe that it needs no more shocks from independent innovators? Is it certain that in large-scale organization the odd-man-out on the school staff, the chap with the queer ideas, will some day be given a headship to show whether he is a creator or only mad?... Because my school is independent I can say frankly to parents that I put personal development before academic success, that I value maturity, originality, resourcefulness, love and generosity before examination results.... There are many State-school teachers, especially in the primary schools, whose convictions are similar, but my independence makes it possible to stand out firmly and to get all-round support for

a thorough-going project.... Does the N.U.T. wish to deny the right of Wennington School to exist, to take away its independence with that of Summerhill and Eton ?[7]

Barnes goes on to ask what kind of legislation would be necessary to take away the independence that already exists and to prevent the future establishment of schools, and concludes that legislation no less venomous than that of the Conventicle Act of 1662, which forbade the religious meetings of dissenters under mounting penalties, would be required. He does not believe that any British government would be so stupid or so totalitarian as to try.

The progressive school communities claim to have been and to be unique and they wish to preserve their way of educating. The case that can be made to support that claim is outlined in the earlier chapters of this book. The challenge to them is that they take children from too narrow a social background.

In fact, Barnes says that now he has established a successful school the local authorities shower their applications upon him — nearly one third of the children at Wennington are supported in this way. This is the dilemma we have come back to again and again and shows the institutional aspect of education in social, political, and historical context.

IV

Dr. Pedley, writing of comprehensive schools, has said:

It would seem more difficult for the head of a school with over 1,000 pupils effectively to carry out a radically progressive policy. Such a policy depends for success upon the faith of the teachers that it is right: preferably the faith of all the teachers and certainly the great majority. A head can only work through his staff. He can inspire them, encourage them, set them his own example — but he cannot expect always to convert them.... Is it likely that fifty teachers could be found to staff one local school who believed, for example, in more self-government for the pupils; who were prepared to abjure the convenience of routine control of young children by prefects, prepared to share in these chores themselves and to share out the sense of power which comes from taking decisions that really matter; who were prepared to renounce the aids of orthodox rewards and punishments ? And even if it were likely,

[7] K. Barnes, 'Do they know what they want?', in *The Guardian*, 29 Mar. 1967.

would not such a large team of individualists tend always to diverge? It is significant that all our really progressive schools are small schools.[8]

It is undoubtedly hard for a maintained day secondary school to be noticeably unorthodox because of parental misgivings in the area which it serves and the pull of the norm of the other schools of a particular local authority. Yet there have been exceptions. Two which are often quoted are Prestolee Elementary School near Farnworth in Lancashire whose headmaster was Edward O'Neill, and St. George-in-the-East in London's East End with Alexander Bloom as head. O'Neill went to Prestolee in 1918 after service in two or three schools of legendary ferocity elsewhere. He had himself come through a harsh childhood in a Salford slum, where he lived with his mother and sister in an off-licence, his father being a drunkard. O'Neill's scholastic career was not good, and after service as a pupil teacher, he went to Crewe Training College from which he qualified in 1913. At Prestolee, between Bolton and Manchester, for a long time he encountered hostility from teachers, managers, and parents as he revolutionized the curriculum and the conduct of the school. There were the usual letters in local papers about children doing what they liked, without a timetable. We have seen this kind of thing in the independent progressive schools. O'Neill and the pupils made furniture, set up aquaria, produced self-written books, built gardens, mounted exhibitions, decorated the school. Many of the children when he first went were half-timers in the mills and he fought the mill-owners, some of the parents and managers, and children themselves to do away with part-time earning.

O'Neill addressed the Conference of New Ideals in Education and was known to all the leaders of the progressive movement during his headship of over thirty years at Prestolee. During that time he won substantial support from parents, the Lancashire authority, and in the area at large. As teachers came to know of the kind of school Prestolee was, most of those who joined the staff were prepared to sympathize with the aims and methods.[9] But when O'Neill retired continuity of his ideas and methods was not expected of the L.E.A. or the governors.

[8] See R. Pedley, *The Comprehensive School* (London, 1963). Quoted here from 'Comprehensive Schools', in *Anarchy*, Aug. 1962, p. 231.

[9] For details see G. Holmes, *The Idiot Teacher* (London, 1952).

Alexander Bloom was appointed to the derelict St. George-in-the-East in Cable Street, Stepney, at the end of the Second World War and before his death ten years later he had conducted a school on free lines. When he began there was no careful selection of colleagues by the head and no consultation between parents and the school. Bloom was given two hundred and sixty boys and girls from local primary schools and ten teachers, mostly strangers to one another and to him. He had close knowledge of war-time and post-war Stepney with its babel of tongues and desert of bomb ruins. He started a community rather than a school and the style was alien to Stepney. As with O'Neill, his ideas drove away many of his teachers and led to public criticism of him and his work in the local juvenile court. A. S. Neill and others praised Bloom's work and the L.C.C. later on sent especially difficult children to him from outside the vicinity of his school, recognizing worth in his unorthodoxy. But again, after his death there was no educational policy that guaranteed continuity of his ideas and methods.

Mention has already been made of Mr. Duane, the former head of Risinghill, an L.C.C. comprehensive school in Finsbury. Duane went there in 1960 and adopted a permissive discipline in an area which was described as having 'some of the worst slums, brothels and clubs in North London and being opposite a market from which a constant stream of rubbish is blown into the school grounds'.[10] As with St. George-in-the-East children were collected from four other schools to start it off, with the obvious results at the beginning of gang-conflict, destructiveness, and obscenities. About one hundred pupils were on probation and in three years children from Risinghill appeared in the juvenile court over two hundred and forty times. Mr. Duane would not use corporal punishment and claimed that after a few years the pupils on probation were less than one tenth of what they had been, that many of the juvenile court cases were not due to delinquency by the children but to gross neglect by the parents so that the children were appearing before the magistrates as in need of care and protection. The comprehensive nature of the school presupposed a proportionate spread of intellectual ability from high to low. At Risinghill at first the lower end of the ability range was very heavily weighted — many parents and teachers of children of ability did not choose the school for their boys and girls. There were many immigrants in Islington, especially Cypriots and West Indians, and Mr. Duane had members of staff who spoke

[10] From an article by M. Hamlyn in *The Sunday Times*, 10 Jan. 1965.

Greek and Turkish as well as other languages to help with this kind of assimilation. He declared himself a humanist and antagonized many people thereby. Gossip, press reports, some bad behaviour by pupils tended to obscure the increasing academic and social success the school appeared to be having.

In January 1965 the L.C.C. produced a statement stating that acute accommodation pressure in other nearby schools made it necessary to rearrange premises. Risinghill in 1960 and soon after had over fourteen hundred pupils on the roll and the new intake at eleven plus had nearly all put the new school as their first choice. In 1965 there were two hundred and forty first year places but only one hundred and fifty-two boys and girls actually started at the school and of those only a half had made the school their first choice and only one fifth made it their second choice. In 1964 the numbers at the school had fallen from over fourteen hundred four years before to about eight hundred and fifty, and the L.C.C. report says:

> There is substantial evidence of increasing parental preference for single-sex schools in the area. The Council must take these considerations into account if its arrangements for secondary education are to be based on the best interests of the pupils and parental wishes, as they must be.

The claims of other schools for greater space were real enough and in 1965 Risinghill was closed, amid loud protests from the progressives, to make way for another secondary school. Mr. Duane believed that Risinghill had just reached its turning point. He considered that parents and local primary schools were seeing that the pupils were by no means only wild and in a short while the school would have got its proper, first-choice share of children of good ability. However, the school was closed and Mr. Duane was displaced but to him 'the Council's long-established practice of safeguarding such head teachers' salaries, and so far as possible, their status, will apply'.

Very many articles and news reports were written on the subject. One of these expressed the hope that if the recommendation in *Half Our Future* to found an experimental school were carried out, it might be Risinghill:

> If the L.C.C. doesn't appreciate Risinghill there are plenty of people who do. It has received petitions from the staff, from the Islington probation offices, from the parents and from several groups of

children. As *Freedom* puts it . . . 'When kids march through the streets demanding that their headmaster should not be sacked, that headmaster has made a breakthrough in education.'[11]

It would appear that the points made by Pedley have been borne out at Risinghill. Comparing the school with some of those considered in earlier chapters of this book, of course the community advantages are with Ackworth with nearly five hundred pupils and Bedales with fewer than three hundred as compared with Risinghill's fourteen hundred. Of course the two progressive schools have boys and girls from homes whose parents have selected these schools because they want their children to live in that kind of educational atmosphere. Of course the physical surroundings in Yorkshire and Hampshire are startlingly different from those in Finsbury. Of course the staff are hand-picked and have voluntarily become a part of the educational enterprise at Ackworth and Bedales. Of course even if all local education authorities were as good as the best, they must safeguard public money and see that justice is done as between schools and as between parents. Clearly if a particular approach to schooling is so unorthodox as to unsettle many parents in a neighbourhood and lead to falling numbers, the local education authority cannot be required to sustain the experiment within the framework of zoning and compulsory schooling for the years necessary for the idea to be tested and accepted. Perhaps, however, it will now be possible for at least some local education authorities to take the risks involved, and to invest in a Reddie or a Neill or a Barnes or a Bloom, and try to assess the results. The recommendations of Dr. Lambert on the foundation of local authority boarding schools, of which there are at present only a few, may help in this direction.

V

In curricular matters there are many growing points in schools of all kinds and these have come through original teachers like Cizek or Caldwell Cook or Armstrong or in our own day Gerd Sommerhoff: or through psychological thinking as in Piaget or Skinner or Bruner: or through sociological thinking as with Willard Waller, Bernstein, or Mannheim: or by academic revaluations as with Dienes in mathematics or I. A. Richards or F. R. Leavis in English or Namier in history: or in group rethinking of which good examples are the Nuffield science

[11] J. Ellerby, 'Mr. Duane of Risinghill', in *Anarchy*, Feb. 1965, p. 56.

curricula, the American ventures in physics, chemistry, and biology, and the Schools Council enterprises in the social sciences and the humanities just beginning in this country. The progressive schools cannot any longer claim that they are in any special sense educational laboratories. They have no particular likelihood of being uniquely original now that many others are actively engaged in giving their best efforts to academic and curricular reconstruction on the basis of what expert knowledge in subject matter, sociological context, and learning theory can provide.

Sevenoaks, a fifteenth-century grammar school, became a public school about twenty years ago, and its work in art, mathematics, technical activities, and English is original by any standard, as is the social outlook in its voluntary service unit and the international centre. The head has taught at Dartington as well as Repton and the combination of the ancient and modern may account in part for the quality and vitality of the whole curriculum there.[12] Other examples could be quoted to show that in the field of curriculum the progressive schools are not likely to be the lone pioneers any more. In art, drama, mathematics, modern languages, music, science, good and original teaching can be found in many maintained and in many public schools as well as in the radical schools we have considered.

VI

Progressive schools have a belief that education is made for man and not man for education. Uniformly they have a fundamentally religious, if not always a Christian, view of the worth of persons; knowledge and competition are subordinate to the ideal of relationship; intellectual achievement is ultimately part of your way of living with yourself and others, and even if you cannot grasp this until much later, your school should so balance your learning and living that you are on the way to seeing that this is a real issue. This demands a proper respect for a range of experience — intellectual, aesthetic, religious, moral, social, physical, emotional, and expressive. It also requires a comprehensive view of what the curriculum provides and what the rest of school life is directed towards.

The progressive schools see the economic framework in which schools are set, they see the sociological, political, and administrative

[12] Various authors, *Experiments in Education at Sevenoaks* (London, 1965).

structure, but for them all real life is meeting. A secular society concerned with parity of esteem, an equitable system of school provision, and a rationalized distribution of facilities in the context of planning and social engineering will settle a number of economic and structural questions and will probably provide a social service to which society is entitled in terms of efficiency. But what then? Progressive educationalists have been teachers with a conviction that what they taught was a symbol, an excuse, for something more profound and personal — a relationship of the kind indicated in earlier pages. They have set up independent schools to bring together others of like mind to help in this, however imperfectly. Where secular maintained schools provide the places and the amenities as a social service and where research has improved and refined the instruments of teaching, a school can be a humane, intellectually lively, well-organized, and efficient organization. While it may have, it need not have a declared set of principles and values which teachers and parents voluntarily select for themselves and their children.

Perhaps at the end we may now have to say that what has been called progressive in relation to a world between 1890 and 1967 no longer signifies. To meet a new challenge of size, mechanization, rationalized manpower, and the transformation of work and leisure, a different kind of progressive school must arise to correct the social and economic inequalities which history has provided and to take opportunity by the forelock. Here large, comprehensive schools are the norm and mechanical aids the necessary supplement to teachers. The simulations of mental processes which have been applied in programmed instruction and the computer provide a new dimension and may enforce a revaluation of the school as a social community. Here the notion of the extended family is not only not progressive any more, it may be an anachronism. This is a field of comparison rich in research possibilities which this book as a study of a movement has not explored. Such an investigation would be very complex indeed, but more sensitive techniques of inquiry now make it almost feasible.

VII

In this final chapter we have recapitulated the historic position of protest of the progressive schools and in so doing have sketched once again the main recognizable features of this outlook over the years.

We have also considered conceptual points about education and schools in general and this kind in particular. The traditionalist emphasizes formal structure in syllabus, teaching, the relationship with pupils, the life of the community. The progressive is more informal, less dominant, more credulous. We have looked at some of the political, economic, and institutional features of the maintained and the independent schools and I have suggested that it has been far more difficult to run a progressive school within the maintained system than it has been as an independent establishment. If O'Neill and Duane managed it for a while, there is no assurance that the school under their successors need bear any recognizable relationship to their unorthodoxy.

In most cases progressive schools over the years have shown a gradual regression in educational practice towards an imaginary average, but even now they are still recognizably unique as communities, as Caroline Nicholson found when she visited them in 1963 and thought them freer, more receptive, more informal, more permissive than other secondary schools and as Edward Blishen corroborated in 1966 : 'There seemed to me to be a dignity [at Dartington] that arose from the agreeableness and frankness of the relationships.'[13] These schools have been and are important in maintaining options in education which extend the range available. It may be that in future maintained schools will offer what Bedales or Summerhill offers, and will remain committed to these kinds of principles and practice for long enough to earn an identity and reputation such as the two progressive schools possess. So far I have not found evidence that such local authority schools exist, though the gap is narrow at some points and young people as a whole now appear more ready for this kind of educational ethos.

If the progressive schools have been mainly the preserve of the liberal intelligentsia it is because they have represented a minority product in which such groups are interested. The implied assumptions are that the child should be an initiator who accepts only necessary, minimal submission to his adult teacher so that, as a consequence, he is not overawed by adult life when he attains to it. His habits of relationship to adults and his self-concept are expected to lead to an open-minded confidence and readiness to question. Alongside this scepticism, however, he is supposed to realize the need for mutual understanding

[13] E. Blishen, 'Experiments in Education', in the *Daily Telegraph*, 22 Apr. 1966, p. 19.

and the acceptance of responsibility. This is part of a kind of adult life-view which has usually been found in the past in certain parts of the upper middle reaches of the class structure; detachment, insight, and confidence in the ability to influence or change the situation are all necessary for it. If this is so the political criticism of progressive education, that it is an example of privilege, is shallow. Admittedly, the schools charge higher fees and have the advantages of smaller classes, but if the kind of education offered by Bedales and Summerhill were open to all, would many parents find it easy to share the educational and cultural assumptions of these schools and others like them? What they offer is, by definition, in the extended form we have seen outlined in earlier chapters, in minority demand. Only a minority of parents is likely to want it at present. Will the L.E.A. take the risk and provide it? If so it will have to be as an unusual commodity, and not as the ordinary school provision. And if they will not provide it at all, will they then say that future Badleys and Neills will not be allowed to start such schools privately and take their chance of public support? This is what Barnes is talking about when he speaks in terms of a new Conventicle Act.

Richard Peters makes two points which can bring the long recapitulation of this final chapter and the rediscovery of all that has preceded it to a point of rest:

> Education, then, can have no ends beyond itself. . . . To be educated is not to have arrived at a destination; it is to travel with a different view. . . . 'There is a quality of life which lies always beyond the mere fact of life' [as Whitehead said]. The great teacher is he who can convey this sense of quality to another, so that it haunts his every endeavour and makes him sweat and yearn to fix what he thinks and feels in a fitting form. . . . It is education that provides that touch of eternity, under the aspect of which endurance can pass into dignified, wry acceptance and animal enjoyment into a quality of living.[14]

Many teachers as persons have this in mind and so do schools of many kinds. Those who have made and worked in independent progressive schools have in addition tried to build a place and a community which they thought was nearer to this heart's desire.

[14] R. Peters, 'Education as Initiation', pp. 47–48.

Bibliography

BOOKS

Archambault, R. D. (ed.), *Philosophical Analysis and Education*, London, 1965.

Armytage, W. H. G., *Heavens Below*, London, 1961.

Arnold-Brown, A., *Unfolding of Character : the impact of Gordonstoun*, London, 1962.

Badley, J. H., *Memories and Reflections*, London, 1955.

  Bedales : a pioneer School, London, 1923.

  A Schoolmaster's Testament, Oxford, 1937.

Bazeley, E. T., *Homer Lane and the Little Commonwealth*, London, 1928 and 1948.

Besant, Annie, *Gospel of Atheism*, 1877.

Blavatsky, Helena, *The Secret Doctrine*, London, 1931.

Blewitt, T. (ed.), *The Modern Schools Handbook*, London, 1934.

Bonham-Carter, V., *Dartington Hall*, London, 1958.

History of Bootham School, 1823–1923, London, 1926.

Boyd, W., and Rawson, W., *The Story of the New Education*, London, 1965.

Brath, S. de, *The Foundations of Success : a Plea for a Rational Education*, 1896.

British Economy : Key Statistics 1900–1964, Cambridge.

Carpenter, E., *Towards Democracy*, 1883 and 1902.

Child, H. A. T. (ed.), *The Independent Progressive School*, London, 1962.

Cook, E. T., and Wedderburn, A., *The Works of John Ruskin*, London, 1905.

Cremin, L. A., *Transformation of the School*, New York, 1961.

Cresswell, D., *Margaret McMillan : a Memoir*, London, 1948.

Culverwell, E. P., *Montessori Principles and Practice*, London, 1913.

Curry, W. B., *The School*, London, 1934.

  Education for Sanity, London, 1947.

Demolins, E., *Anglo-Saxon Superiority : to what is it due?*, London, 1898.

  L'Éducation nouvelle, Librairie de Paris, 1901.

Dewey, Evelyn, *The Dalton Laboratory Plan*, London, 1924.

Dewey, J., *The School and Society*, New York, 1899.

  My Pedagogic Creed, New York, 1897.

  The Child and the Curriculum, New York, 1902.

  Moral Principles in Education, New York, 1909.

  How We Think, New York, 1910.

Dewey, J., *Interest and Effort in Education*, New York, 1913.
  Democracy and Education, New York, 1916.
Edmunds, L. F., *Rudolf Steiner Education*, London, 1962.
Elmhirst, L., *Rabindranath Tagore, Pioneer in Education*, London, 1961.
Farrar, F. W. (ed.), *Essays on a Liberal Education*, London, 1867.
Fichte, J. G., *Wissenschaftslehre*, 1795.
Finney, R. L., *A Sociological Philosophy of Education*, New York, 1928.
Flexner, A., *A Modern College and a Modern School*, New York, 1923.
Freud, S., *The Interpretation of Dreams*, London, 1900.
  The Psycho-Pathology of Everyday Life, London, 1904.
  Three Essays on the Theory of Sexuality, London, 1905.
  Totem and Taboo, London, 1912.
  Introductory Lectures on Psycho-Analysis, London, 1915–1917.
George, W. R., *Citizens Made and Remade*, New York, 1913.
  The Junior Republic, its History and Ideals, New York, 1910.
Graham, Patricia A., *Progressive Education : From Arcady to Academe*,
  New York, 1967.
Graves, R., *Good-bye to All That*, London, 1929.
Greene, G. (ed.), *The Old School*, London, 1934.
Hart, B., *Psychology of Insanity*, Cambridge, 1912.
Harwood, A. C. (ed.), *The Faithful Thinker*, London, 1961.
Heckstall-Smith, H. *Doubtful Schoolmaster*, London, 1962.
Henderson, J. L., *Look Out*, 1965.
Holmes, E., *What Is and What Might Be*, London, 1911.
  In Quest of an Ideal, R. Cobden-Sanderson, 1920.
Holmes, G., *The Idiot Teacher*, London, 1952.
Hyndman, H. M., *Historical Bases of Socialism*, 1883.
  Commercial Crises of the Nineteenth Century, 1892.
  Economics of Socialism, 1896.
Isaacs, Susan, *Intellectual Growth in Young Children*, London, 1930.
  Social Development in Young Children, London, 1933.
Itard, J. E. M. G., *An Historical Account of the Discovery and Education
  of a Savage Man*, trans. 1802.
Jones, E., *The Life and Work of Sigmund Freud*, 3 vols., London, 1953,
  1955, 1957.
Judges, A. V. (ed.), *The Function of Teaching*, London, 1959.
Jusmani, A. A., 'The Attitude to the Child in Progressive Educational
  Theory and Practice in England since 1890'; unpublished M.Ed.
  thesis, University of Leicester, 1961.
Kalton, G., *The Public Schools*, London, 1966.
Kant, I., *Critique of Pure Reason*.
Laborde, E. D. (ed.), *Education of To-day*, Cambridge, 1935.
Lambert, R., *The State and Boarding Education*, London, 1966.

Lampe, D., *Pyke the Unknown Genius*, London, 1959.

Loukes, H., *Friends and their Children*, London, 1958.

Lowndes, G. A. N., *The Silent Social Revolution*, Oxford, 1937.

(ed.), *Margaret McMillan*, Nursery Schools Association, London, 1960.

Lynch, A. J., *Individual Work and the Dalton Plan*, London, 1924.

McCallister, W. J., *The Growth of Freedom in Education*, London, 1931.

Mack, E. C., *Public Schools and British Opinion since 1860*, New York, 1941.

McMillan, M., *Early Childhood*, 1900.

Education through the Imagination, 1904.

Labour and Childhood, 1907.

MacMunn, N., *A Path to Freedom in the School*, London, 1914.

Differential Partnership Method of French Conversation, London (n.d.).

The MacMunn Differentialism : A New Method of Class Self-Teaching, London (n.d.).

The Child's Path to Freedom, 1926.

Mallinson, V. (ed.), *Adolescent at School*, London, 1949.

Mannheim, K., *Ideology and Utopia*, London, 1926.

Man and Society, London, 1940.

and Stewart, W. A. C., *An Introduction to the Sociology of Education*, London, 1962.

Mayhew, K. C., and Edwards, A. C., *The Dewey School*, New York, 1936.

Montessori, Maria, *The Discovery of the Child*, 3rd ed., Adyar, Madras.

The Secret of Childhood, Calcutta, 1936.

Neill, A. S., *Summerhill : A Radical Approach to Education*, London, 1962.

A Dominie's Log (n.d.).

A Dominie Dismissed (n.d.).

A Dominie in Doubt, London, 1920.

A Dominie Abroad (n.d.).

Hearts and not Heads in the School, London, 1945.

Talking of Summerhill, London, 1967.

Nunn, T. P., *Education : Its Data and First Principles*, London, 1920.

Parkhurst, H., *Education on the Dalton Plan*, London, 1923.

Parkin, G. R., *Edward Thring*, London, 1900.

Pedley, R., *The Comprehensive School*, London, 1963.

Plato, *The Republic*, book iv.

The Public and Preparatory Schools Yearbook, London, 1937.

Reddie, C., *Abbotsholme*, London, 1900.

John Bull : His Origin and Character, London, 1901.

Richardson, Elizabeth, *The Environment of Learning*, London, 1967.

Roe, Anne, *The Psychology of Occupations*, New York, 1956.

N

Rousseau, Jean-Jacques, *Émile*, 1762.

Russell, B., *Principles of Social Reconstruction*, London, 1916.
   Autobiography, 1872–1914, London, 1967.
   On Education, London, 1926.
   The Practice and Theory of Bolshevism, London, 1920.

Russell, Dora (ed.), *Thinking in Front of Yourself*, London, 1934.

Séguin, E., *Idiocy and its Treatment by the Physiological Method*, 1866,
   Traitement Moral, Hygiène, et Éducation des Idiots, 1846.
   New Facts and Remarks on Idiocy, 1870.
   Report on Education, 1876.

Simpson, J. H., *Schoolmaster's Harvest*, London, 1954.
   Howson of Holt, London, 1925.
   An Adventure in Education, London, 1917.
   The Future of the Public Schools, Rugby, 1943.
   Sane Schooling, London, 1936.

Steiner, R., *The Philosophy of Spiritual Activity*, 1916.
   Mysticism (n.d.).
   The Story of My Life, London, 1928.
   The Education of the Child in the Light of Anthropology, 1922.
   The Spiritual Ground of Education, 1947.
   Education and Modern Spiritual Life, 1954.

Stewart, W. A. C., *Quakers and Education*, London, 1953.
   and McCann, W. P., *The Educational Innovators 1750–1880*, London, 1967.

Strachey, L., *Eminent Victorians*, London, 1918.

Sturge, H. W., and Clark, T., *The Mount School, York, 1785–1814, 1831–1931*. London, 1931.

Suttie, I., *Origins of Love and Hate*, London, 1935.

Taylor, C., and Matern, J., *Institutiones Pietatis*, 1676.

Taylor, L. C., *et al.*, *Experiments in Education at Sevenoaks*, London, 1965.

Unwin, S., *Truth about a Publisher*, London, 1961.

Waller, W., *The Sociology of Teaching*, New York, 1932.

Ward, B. M., *Reddie of Abbotsholme*, London, 1934.

Waugh, A., *The Loom of Youth*, London, 1917.

Weinberg, I., *The English Public Schools*, New York, 1967.

Whale, J. S., *Christian Doctrine*, London, 1942.

Whitbourn, F., *Lex : Alexander Divine Founder of Clayesmore School*, London, 1937.

Whitehouse, J. H., *Creative Education at an English School*, Cambridge, 1928.
   America and Our Schools, Oxford, 1938.
   Ideals and Methods in Education : a Boy's Symposium, London, 1932.
   The School Base, Oxford, 1943.

Wills, W. D., *Homer Lane*, London, 1964.

The Barns Experiment, London, 1945.

The Hawkspur Experiment, London, 1941.

Wood, A., and Russell, Bertrand, *The Passionate Sceptic*, London, 1957.

Yearbook of Education, London, 1935. H. R. Hamley, 'The Testing of Intelligence'.

Yearbook of Education, London, 1957 — W. Boyd, 'The Basic Faith of the New Educational Fellowship'.

Yearbook of Education, London, 1957 — K. Hahn, 'Outward Bound'.

ARTICLES, PERIODICALS, PAMPHLETS

A New School, published April 1889 to introduce Abbotsholme School.

Fifty Years of Abbotsholme, 1889–1939.

The *Abbotsholmian*, magazine of Abbotsholme School.

The *Abbotsholmian*, iii. 3, 1909. Report of paper 'How shall we educate our Directing Classes?', read by C. Reddie at the Authors' Club, 5 July 1909.

Academy, 24 September 1898.

Anarchy, January 1967. D. Russell, 'What Beacon Hill Stood For'.

Anarchy, February 1965. J. Ellerby, 'Mr. Duane of Risinghill'.

Badminton School 1858–1958, published by the School.

Barnes, K. C., 'The First Four Years', 1944.

'The Co-Educational Boarding Schools', 1953.

et al., Towards a Quaker View of Sex, 1962.

Bedales (Haywards Heath, Sussex). *A School for Boys : Outline of its Aims and System*, 1892.

Bedales Chronicle : vol. 42, no. 8, June 1958.

vol. 44, no. 2, Spring 1960.

vol. 45, no. 1, 1960.

Bedales School Roll, 1952, ed. B. Gimson.

BOARD OF EDUCATION REPORTS

Inspection of Friends' Boarding Schools by the Board of Education, 1905.

Report by H.M. Inspectors on Bryanston School, Blandford, 1933.

Ministry of Education — Education Act, 1944.

Ministry of Education — Statistics of Education, part i, table (10)5, 1965.

Ministry of Education — Report of the Working Party on Assistance with the cost of Boarding Education, 1960. (Martin Report.)

Ministry of Education — List of Independent Schools : list 60 or List 70.

BOARD OF EDUCATION REPORTS (*contd.*)

Ministry of Education — *The Public Schools and the General Educational System*, 1944. (Fleming Report.)

Ministry of Education — *Half our Future*, 1963. (Newsom Report.)

Brain, 1911. B. Hart, 'Freud's Conception of Hysteria in a Symposium on Hysteria'.

British Journal of Educational Studies, vol. xiv, no. 1, November 1965. C. Duke, 'Robert Lowe — A Reappraisal'.

Child and Man, Summer 1964. (Periodical of the Anthroposophical Society.)

Child Study Society, London : *Journal of Proceedings*, vol. vi, 1926. Margaret McMillan, 'The Nursery School'.

The Christian Socialist, 1889.

The Clarion.

The Book of Clayesmore School (n.d.).

Cornhill Magazine : May 1860, December 1860, March 1861 : Letters from Matthew James Higgins.

The Daily Telegraph, 22 April 1966. Edward Blishen, 'The Lessons are now Compulsory'.

The Daily Telegraph, 22 April 1966. Edward Blishen, 'Experiments in Education'.

The English Review, June 1924.

Everyman, 11 July 1929.

Forum of Education, vol. v.

Friends' Quarterly Examiner, vol. 70, 1936. E. B. Castle, 'The Position of Friends' Schools'.

National Froebel Foundation *Bulletin*, February 1949.

Geography : Beaver, S. H., The 'Play Society and Field Work', July 1962.

The Gordonstoun Record, 1961.

Gordonstoun : Some Facts — produced by the School, March 1967.

Granta, 1 December 1962. E. Wilkinson, 'Poisonous Passions'.

The Guardian, 29 March 1967. K. Barnes, 'Do they know what they want?'

Hahn, K., *Education for Leisure*.

Id. Journal of the Summerhill Society, nos. 2–7. Neill, A. S., 'My Scholastic Life'. September 1960–October 1961.

Lane, H., *Four Lectures on Childhood*, 'The Age of Loyalty', ed. Rev. H. H. Symonds.

The Listener, 28 November 1934.

Report of the Committee on the closing of the Little Commonwealth, July 1918.

The London Echo.

McMillan, Margaret, 'Citizens of Tomorrow', 1906.

'The Child and the State', 1907.

'London Children : how to feed them and how not to feed them', 1907.

'Schools of Tomorrow', 1908.

Manchester Guardian, 11 May 1897.

Report of the First Summer Conference of the New Educational Fellowship in Calais, 1921.   H. Baillie-Weaver, 'La Co-éducation'.

The New Era, 1920s.

Education for the New Era — an International Quarterly Journal for the Promotion of Reconstruction in Education, January 1920. Title changed to *The New Era in Home and School*.

Pour l'Ère Nouvelle, 1920s.

Das Werdende Zeitalter.

The Discipline of Freedom.   Conference of New Ideals in Education, 1923 : 'Introduction'.

New Ideals Quarterly.

The New Statesman.

Pall Mall Gazette, 22 August 1892.

Pendle Hill Pamphlet, no. 9, 1940. H. H. Brinton, 'Quaker Education in Theory and Practice'.

Mason, Charlotte, 'A Short Synopsis of the Educational Philosophy Advanced by the Founder of the Parents' National Educational Union' (n.d.).

Progressive Education, U.S.A.

Progress To-day, vol. xvii, no. 1.   L. B. Pekin, 'The Way of Life at St. Christopher School, Letchworth'.

Prospectus for Dartington Hall, 1954.

Prospectus for Bryanston School, 1962.

Review of Reviews, 1893.

Saga, Bryanston School magazine.

Anniversary Saga, 1928–1948 (symposium).

Grant, C., 'St. George's School : A Retrospect'.   Address to St. George's Parents' Association, 5 July 1941.

The School Review, University of Chicago, vol. 74, no. 3, 1966. I. Weinberg, 'The Occupational Aspirations of British Public Schoolboys'.

Freeman, A., *Who was Rudolf Steiner ?* (published privately by Sheffield Educational Settlement, 1944).

Report of the Educational Conference of the Society of Friends, 1879.

Proceedings of a Conference called by the Committee on Education of New York Yearly Meeting, 1881.   Wood, J., 'Education among Friends in England'.

The Sower, later *Seed Time*. Journal of the Fellowship of the New Life.

Spectator, 18 September 1897.

The Sunday Times, 10 January 1965. Article by M. Hamlyn.

The Times, 30 September 1955.

The Times Educational Supplement, 2 August 1963. 'The Dalton Plan'.

To-day, 1888. Series of articles by C. Reddie entitled 'Modern Mis-education'.

The Toynbee Record, 1908 : magazine of Toynbee Hall.

Wennington School, 1961-2.

The Westminster Gazette, November 1897 ; 30 September 1898.

Where ?, Autumn 1963 (A.C.E.). P. Wood, 'What is Ministry Recognition Worth?'

Wigram, D. R., *The System of Work at Bryanston School*, 1947.

Index

The page references in italic types indicate the main treatment of the subjects.